PARIS REVISITED

▪ ▪ ▪ The Guide for the Return Traveler ▪ ▪ ▪

Gary Lee Kraut

▪ ▪ ▪

Words Travel International Press
www.parisrevisited.com

PARIS REVISITED
The Guide for the Return Traveler
Published by Words Travel International Press.

Library of Congress Control Number 2002112602

ISBN 0-9723985-1-1

Cover design, book layout & design, maps:
Barton Design, Inc. • www.bartondesigninc.com
Illustrations: Laura Barton • www.laurabarton.com

Front cover image, "Paris Dream,"
by Janet Davis. • www.janetdavis.com

Notification to readers Although every effort has been made to provide accurate, up-to-date information in this guide along with commentary and advice offered in good faith, neither the author nor the publisher can assume responsibility for any errors, omissions or misleading information in this guide, nor for any loss, damage, injury or inconvenience sustained by any person using any of the information or advice in this guide. We cannot assume responsibility for the goods or services of the individuals and businesses mentioned in this guide. Pricing, opening times and other details may change after press time. As with all travel writing, you are advised to always confirm information when necessary for the enjoyment of your travels.

Notification to businesses mentioned in this book If an establishment or business believes that details have been misrepresented concerning that establishment or business, it should contact the author to rectify or better understand the alleged misrepresentation, keeping in mind that this book presents subjective commentary and selections and is intended as a service to travelers rather than advertisement for the establishments and businesses mentioned herein. Write to reviews@parisrevisited.com.

Inquiries may be addressed to:
Words Travel International, Inc.
740 River Road
Trenton, New Jersey 08628, U.S.A.
publisher@parisrevisited.com

Printed in the United States of America

In memory of my grandparents,
Sam and Ida Rosenthal,
who went to Niagara Falls
for their honeymoon.

Acknowledgement

Getting Parisians—or at least my friends in Paris—to test restaurants outside of their neighborhood is more difficult then you'd imagine. So I wish to thank the various friends who joined me on the restaurant adventures that led to the selections in this book for making the job of a restaurant critic so much fun. Special thanks to L. for being the ideal companion for a restaurant romance, may it long continue.

I thank the many travelers on my tours who shared with me their travel impressions and experiences, with added appreciation to those who allowed me to use them as guinea pigs in hotels.

Finally, I am deeply grateful to Laura Barton for approaching this project with so much enthusiasm as she created the design and illustrations to give breath to my text.

About the Author

Award-winning travel writer Gary Lee Kraut is the author of four previous guides to France and Paris, as well articles and essays on travel, culture and the expatriate experience. He is the recipient of FrancePress's 1995 *Prix d'Excellence* for his work on France.

In further recognition of his expertise, he has been interviewed by *U.S.A. Today* about Normandy, invited by the Western Loire Tourist Board to speak to the region's annual assembly of travel industry partners, and commissioned by the Burgundy Tourist Board to write about that region.

He has translated into English Louis Vuitton's *Paris City Guide* as well as numerous writings on subjects as diverse as cardiovascular surgery and intellectual property law.

Gary's work goes beyond the written word. He has personally guided hundreds of travelers on customized tours in Paris and elsewhere in France and offered personalized advice to many other business and leisure travelers.

Gary brings the right accent to American travel writing, one informed by years of experience exploring the many facets of life and travel in Europe. Originally from Trenton, New Jersey, he has lived in Paris since 1988, while returning frequently to New Jersey and other great states—because travel isn't just about where you're going, it's also about where you come from.

TABLE OF CONTENTS

The Louvre, the Orsay and Other Museums 151

The Gardens of Paris 175

DEATH IN PARIS 203

CHÂTEAUX OF THE PARIS REGION 219

Shop 'n' Stroll 261 (with food and drink along the way)

Hotels 279

Wine, Wine Bars & Wine Restaurants 323

The Paris Restaurant Adventure 337

Practical Information to Refresh Your Memory 425

WELCOME BACK!

Sooner or later everyone discovers that the true pleasure of Paris is the café between sights, the seat in the park after the museum, the pastry chosen after intense deliberation, the little shop discovered by chance, the prolonged aperitif, the full range of restaurant adventures, the walk home. That's when romance is in the air. That's when insights come. That's when you're one step closer to feeling at home in Paris.

For some travelers that happens on the first trip. But first-timers typically approach Paris with a list of must-sees, sights that reveal the monumental beauty of the French capital. Further, fuller discoveries await on the return. That's when the pressure of having to see it all is off, and you have your own to-do list, not, dare I say, some guidebook's. And so return travelers—and curious first-timers—set out on a deeper, wider, more insightful and more personal exploration.

You don't need to be a snob to return to Paris, though sometimes it helps. But curiosity helps even more: cultural curiosity, culinary curiosity, human curiosity, linguistic curiosity, historical curiosity, romantic curiosity, political and religious curiosity, and plain old wonder-what's-down-that-street curiosity.

At the risk of sounding like a snob myself, I refuse the idiot approach to travel writing, the top-40-radio of the road. I also don't care for the trendy-means-quality or the newer-is-better approach to travel. And I'll neither tell you how to travel as cheaply as possible nor try to flatter your portfolio.

Instead, I assume that you can afford to have a sense of value overseas. Therefore, the most important thing an insider can tell you is the options, as I have here. I also assume that you are curious enough about foreign culture, foreign history and foreign people to wonder what makes this old city tick and to delve deeper into its pleasures and treasures.

▪▪▪

This book covers the monumental, the lesser-known and the intimate sides of Paris and its surrounding region. But don't try to see it all on a single trip. Remember the mantra of the return traveler: I'll be back.

Personally, I favor the unhurried approach to foreign travel, which is why this book devotes many pages to the fine art of dawdling in Paris: cafés, tearooms, gardens, parks, cemeteries, settings for the aperitif, restaurants, riverside walks. I like traveling at my own pace. I like knowing which *boulangerie* in my area has the best bread and which café is best for which time of day. I like contemplating a poster for an exhibit, even if I'll probably never go. I like venturing into an unknown quarter to try a new restaurant one night then returning to my local favorite the next. I like recognizing people on the street, having crossed paths with them several times already. I like getting to know the French on their turf. I like getting to know a place in different seasons. I like when someone asks me for directions—and I know how to get them there. I like the return, and I like the way it makes me make feel at home in a foreign place, until one day I might actually live there—rather, here, in Paris.

I live in Paris, and I also spend several months each year in my home state of New Jersey and in other great states. That makes me a frequently returning traveler on both sides of the Atlantic, with the added luxury of having an apartment, work, friends, an ex, a cat, in a word, a life in Paris.

In writing this book I returned everywhere. I actually went up the Eiffel Tower for the umpteenth time, even though I could see it plain as day from the end of my street—and after you've read the chapter on it here you'll find that the Iron

Lady stands taller than on your last visit. I revisited the Mona Lisa because something was missing when I sat down to write about it from a photograph; what was missing was the real McCoy and all that surrounds it. I reconsidered ways of presenting history in light of the questions of American travelers met on private tours. When I retested restaurants that I'd enjoyed in the past, I sometimes discovered that I didn't care for them any more (the return trip always carries the risk of disappointment), but sometimes I liked them even more (the way acquaintances that become friends). And I've gotten acquainted with (or befriended) many new, and sometimes very old, restaurants along the way.

▪▪▪

This book is intended to satisfy the full range of your curiosities about Paris, while raising others. It offers insights into the familiar and the unfamiliar and into the ways of the French and the ways of the traveler.

Use this book to lead you back for a fresh look at a famous sight and then to visit a museum that you never knew existed until reading about it here. Use it to guide you to an out-of-the-way château in the morning and on an enchanting shop 'n' stroll in the afternoon. Use it to make sense of French history, culture and attitudes. Use it to discover a luxuriant hotel bar that you might stop in before taxiing off to a polished restaurant one evening, then to lure you into a downscale wine bar on your way to a neighborhood bistro the following evening.

Let this book inform you as to how France evolved, from chaos to kingdom, from monarchy to democracy, from Notre-Dame to the Eiffel Tower, from the marriage of Church and State to their separation. Let it lull you into lingering in the Luxembourg Garden and then tempt you to investigate the zones of sex and privilege in the Bois de Boulogne. Let it entice you into unknown quarters, knowing that you can always find your way back.

Wherever this book leads you, may each step bring you closer to feeling at home in Paris. Until one day we might be neighbors.

Bon Voyage. And many happy returns.

Gary Lee Kraut

Arrondissement Map

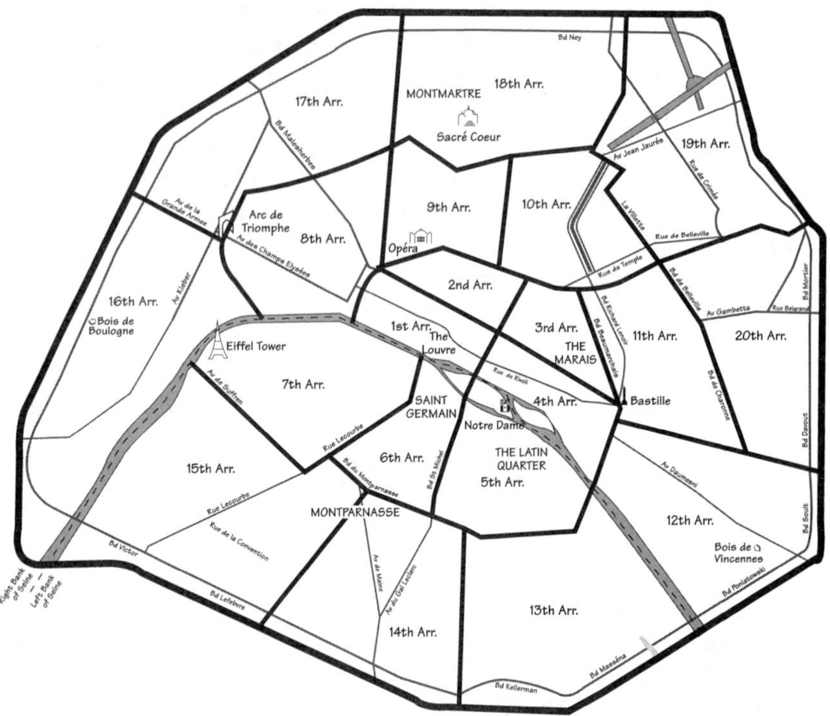

Paris has a population of 2.3 million—about 3 million on weekdays when those who come in from the suburbs to work or play are included. As the capital of a medium-sized country, Paris is at once France's New York City, Los Angeles and Washington, D.C. The greater Paris region, which includes the city and its extensive suburbs, is home to nearly 11 million people, almost one-fifth of the population of France.

The history of Paris is written in the form of concentric circles rippling out from Ile de la Cité, the City Island, in the Seine. Modern Paris is divided into 20 arrondissements, or districts, numbered clockwise and rotating out like a snail's shell beginning at the Louvre. Addresses in this book include their arrondissement number. When writing to any of these addresses, the arrondissement number is used as a part of the 5-digit postal code. Postal codes for the city run from 75001 (covering the 1st arrondissement) to 75020 (covering the 20th arrondissement).

THE KINGS OF FRANCE

Prior to Hugh Capet, the Frankish Merovingian (481-751) and Carolingian (751-987) dynasties ruled the land. The dates below note birth-accession to the throne-death. The name of the queen follows if historically significant.

Hugh Capet (father of the Capetian dynasty)
940-987-996
|
Robert II (the Pious)
970-996-1031
|
Henri I
1008-1031-1060
|
Phillip I
1052-1060-1108
|
Louis VI (the Fat)
1081-1108-1137
|
Louis VII
1120-1137-1180
m. Eleanor of Aquitaine, 1137
m. Constance of Castille, 1154
m. Adèle of Champagne, 1160
|
Philip II (Augustus)
1165-1180-1223
|
Louis VIII
1187-1223-1226
m. Blanche of Castille
|
Louis IX (St. Louis)
1214-1226-1270
m. Marguerite of Provence
|

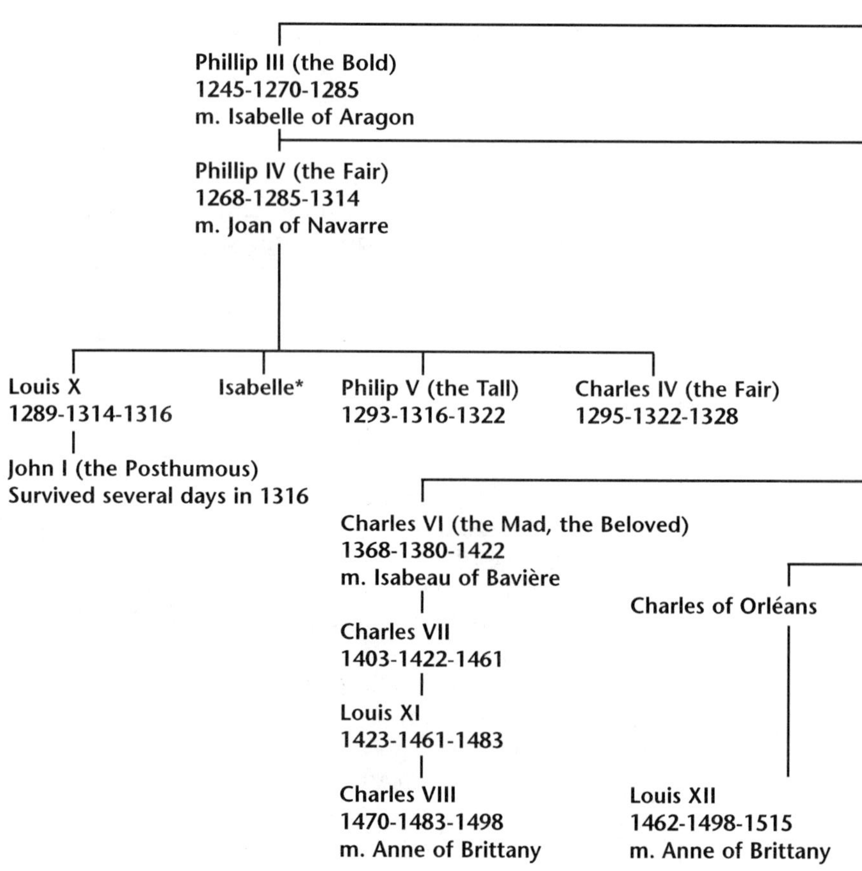

(The Bourbons)

Henri IV
1553-1589-1610
m. Marguerite of Valois
m. Marie de Médicis

Louis XIII
16-1-1610-1643
m. Anne of Austria

---

*Isabelle, sister of three kings, married Edward II of England. Their son, King Edward III of England, therefore, staked a claim to the French throne after Isabelle's brothers all died without a male heir.

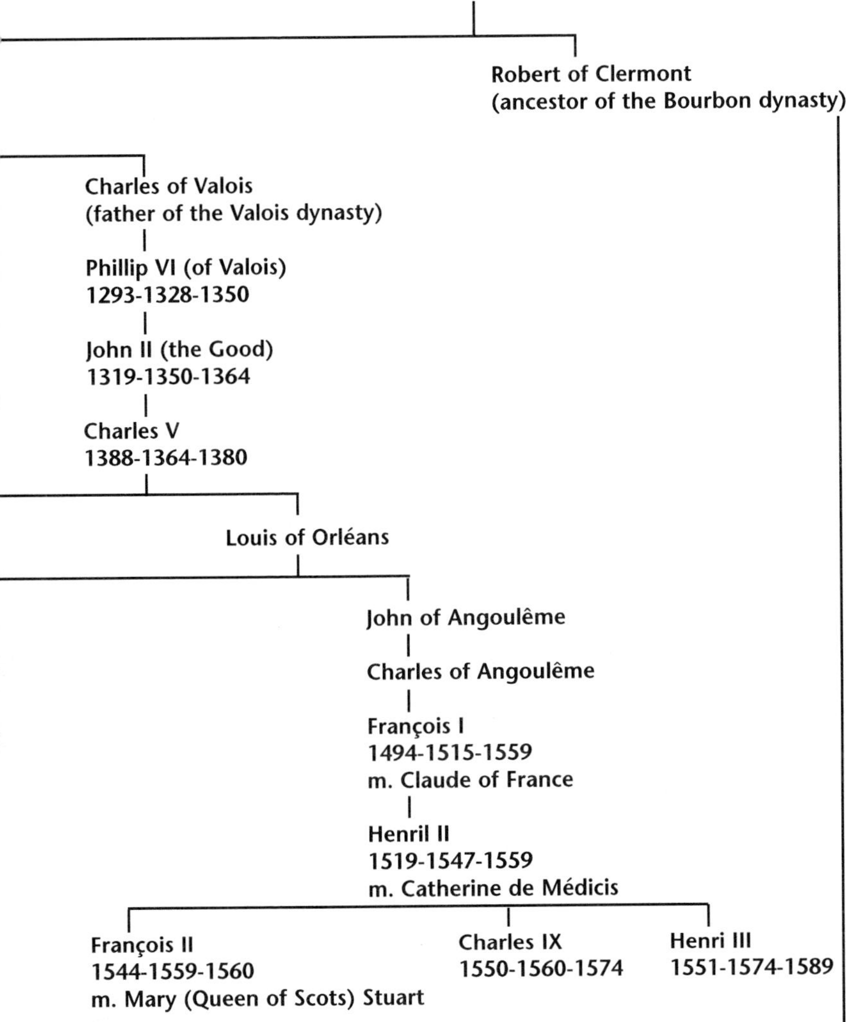

Robert of Clermont
(ancestor of the Bourbon dynasty)
Charles of Valois
(father of the Valois dynasty)
Phillip VI (of Valois)
1293-1328-1350
John II (the Good)
1319-1350-1364
Charles V
1388-1364-1380
Louis of Orléans
John of Angoulême
Charles of Angoulême
François I
1494-1515-1559
m. Claude of France
Henril II
1519-1547-1559
m. Catherine de Médicis
François II
1544-1559-1560
m. Mary (Queen of Scots) Stuart
Charles IX
1550-1560-1574
Henri III
1551-1574-1589

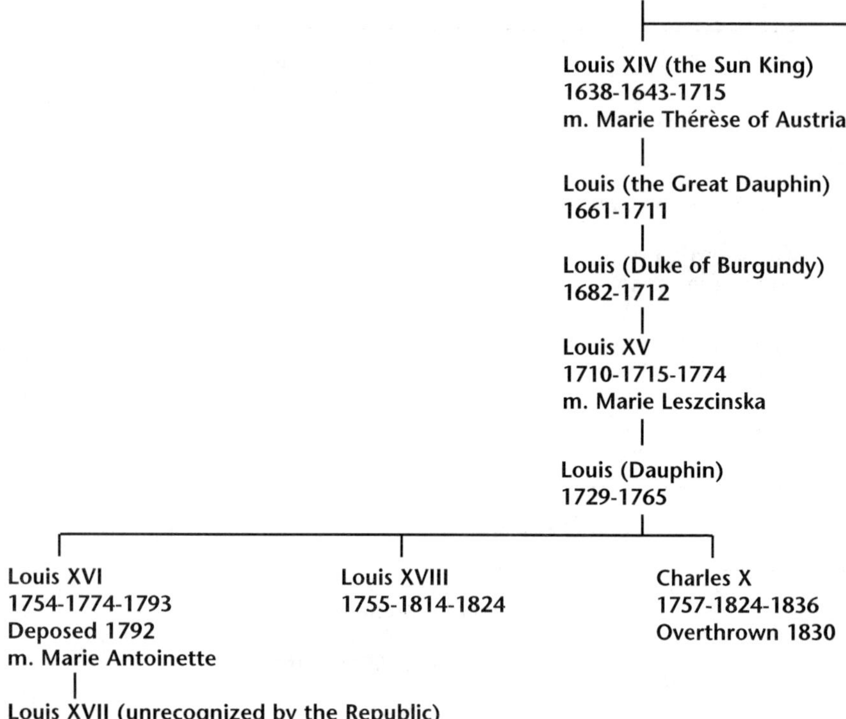

Rulers, Republics and Revolutions 1789 to present
Storming of the Bastille, start of the Revolution, July 14, 1789.

The Constituent Assembly, June 1789-Sept. 1791.
The Legislative Assembly, Oct. 1791-Aug. 1792.

1st Republic 1792-1799.

The Convention, 1792-1795. (The Terror, 1793-1794.)
The Directory, 1795-1799.
End of the Revolution, 1799.

The Consulate 1799-1804 (Napoleon Bonaparte, First Consul).

1st Empire, Napoleon I 1804-1814;1815.

The Restoration. Bourbon line restored with Louis XVIII and Charles X, 1815-1830.

Revolution of 1830.

Louis Philippe I, King of the French, 1840-1848.

Philip (Duke of Orléans)

Louis-Philippe I
1773-1830-1850
Abdicated 1848

Revolution of 1848.
2nd Republic 1848-1852.
2nd Empire, Napoleon III (nephew of Napoleon I) 1852-1870.
3rd Republic 1870-1940.
French Vichy State 1940-1944.
Provisional Government 1944-1946.
4th Republic 1946-1958
5th Republic Since 1958.
Presidents of the 5th Republic:
Charles de Gaulle 1958-1969.
Georges Pompidou 1969-1974.
Valéry Giscard d'Estaing 1974-1981.
François Mitterand 1981-1995.
Jacques Chirac since 1995. Second term ends 2007.

THE SIGHTS AND MUSEUMS OF PARIS

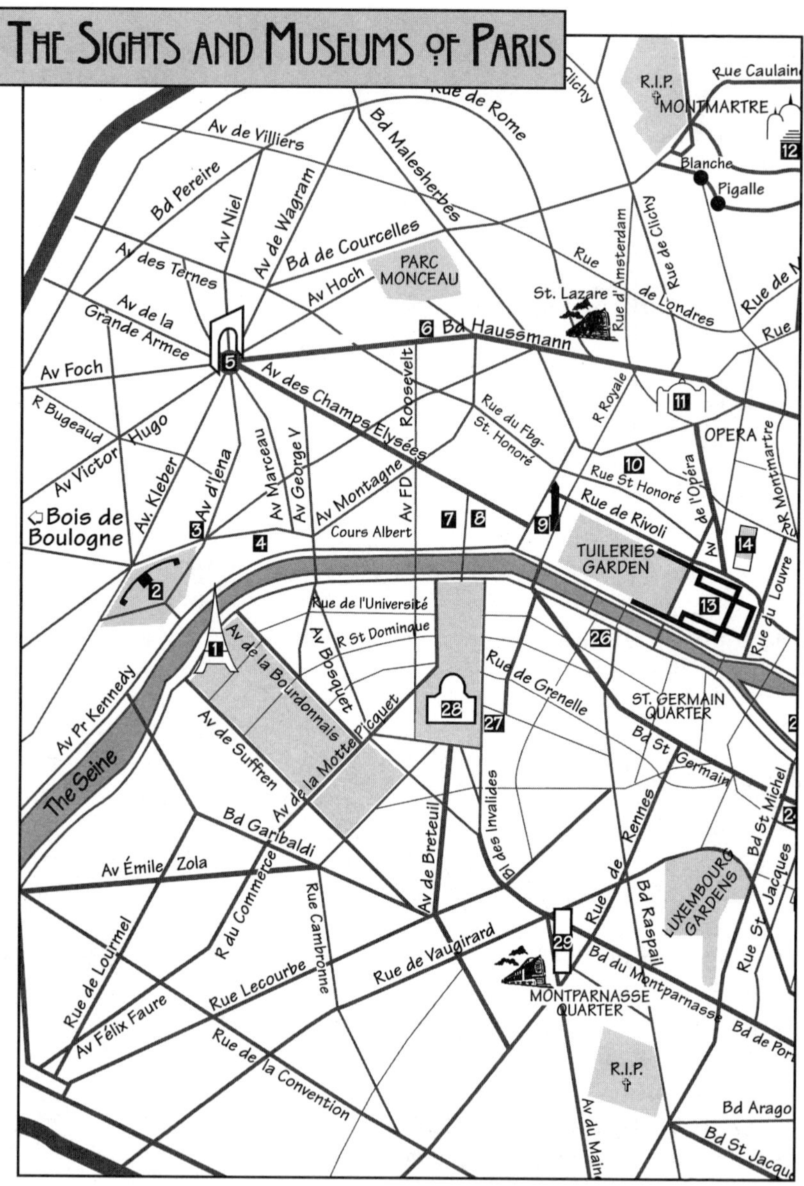

1 Eiffel Tower
2 Trocadéro
3 Guimet Museum of Asian Art
4 Museum of Modern Art (City)
5 Arc de Triomphe
6 Jacquemart-André Museum
7 Grand Palais
8 Petit Palais
9 The Obelisk
10 Place Vendôme
11 Garnier Opera
12 Sacré Coeur
13 The Louvre
14 Palais Royal
15 Hôtel de Ville (City Hall)
16 Pompidou Center

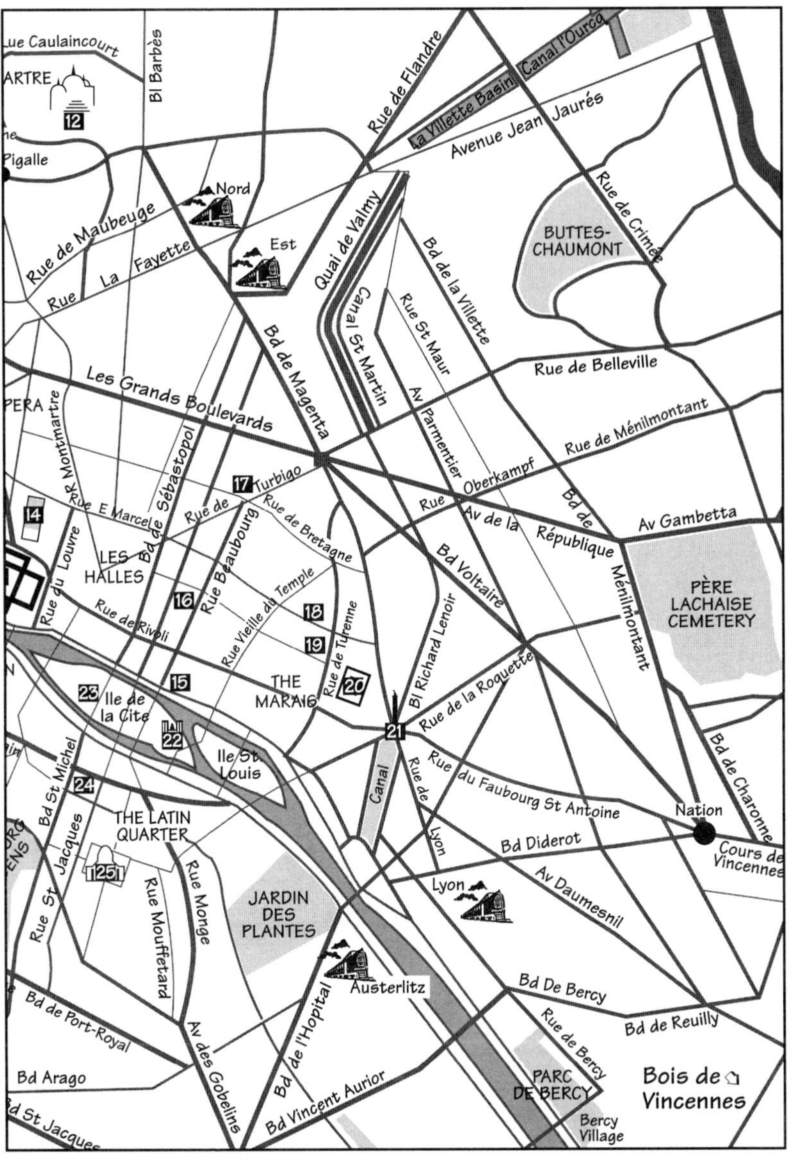

17 Musée des Arts et Métiers
18 Picasso Museum
19 Carnavalet Museum
20 Place des Vosges
21 Place de la Bastille
22 Notre-Dame Cathedral
23 Sainte-Chapelle
24 Cluny Museum of the Middle Ages
25 The Pantheon
26 Orsay Museum
27 Rodin Museum
28 The Invalides and Napoleon's Tomb
29 Montparnasse Tower

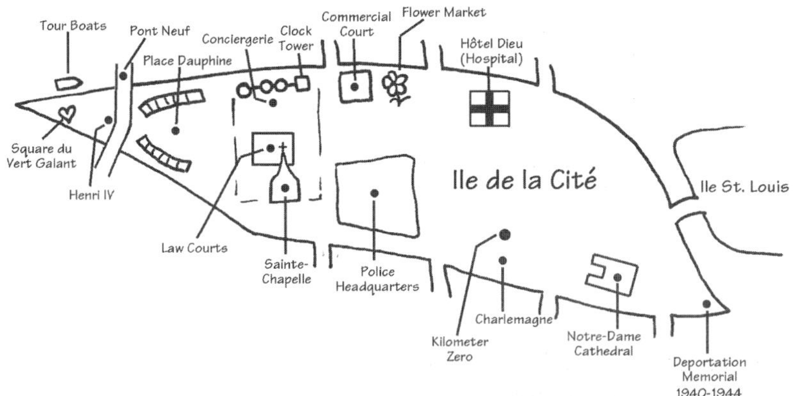

NOTRE-DAME AND THE ISLANDS

Read the map above left to right, west to east—from a park for lovers to a memorial of human horror, by way of major institutions of law, police, medicine and religion—and you'll see that Ile de la Cité, the City Island, is a fabulous allegory of life and death, individuality and society. And you thought you were just coming to visit Notre-Dame! Ile de la Cité also encapsulates much of the organization of France. It's only natural then that the square in front of Notre-Dame is marked with Kilometer Zero, the point from where all the roads leading to the capital are measured.

The Seine divides Paris into the Right Bank (*Rive Droite*) and the Left Bank (*Rive Gauche*), meaning to the right and left of the flow of the river. But it all started on an island in the middle. The history of Paris ripples out in concentric circles from there. It then ripples back, for this isn't only the historic center of the city but (along with City Hall nearby) Paris's administrative center as well.

A Celtic people called the Parisii settled here in the 3rd century B.C. making their livelihood from fishing. *Par* means boat in Celtic. Seine may derive from a Celtic term for "peaceful river." After the Roman conquest of Gaul, the Roman governors settled on the island. They set up their administrative palace on the west end of the island while a part of the east end was considered a sacred site. That east-west division between the spiritual and the temporal remains. The Paris Law Courts on the west side and Notre Dame on the east are direct outgrowths of the island's functions of 1900 years ago.

All that's really changed on the island is that it is no longer the residential heart of the city. Vestiges of the Gallo-Roman layout of the City Island are visible in the Archeological Crypt beneath the square in front of the cathedral. It takes an archeologist to understand or explain the rubble. But it takes little imagination to the see the importance of Ile de la Cité in the history and life of the French capital... and to be wowed by the sights.

NOTRE-DAME CATHEDRAL

***Metro** Cité, RER Saint-Michel. **Open** 8am-6:45pm, until 7:45pm Sat. and Sun. Closed Sat. 12:30-2pm. Free 45-minute organ concerts, played on France's largest organ, are given Sun. at 5:15pm. **Non-holiday mass schedule:** Sat. 8, 12, 6:30; Sun. 8, 8:45, 10, 11:30, 12:45, 6:30; weekdays 8, 9, 12, 6:15. **Religious information:** www.catholique-paris.com. Tel. 01 42 34 56 10.*

Notre-Dame's position at the center of the capital, with elbow room for impressive views on three sides, and its role in major events in French history place it in a category all its own. A harmonious solid block of early Gothic architecture, Notre Dame holds her head high at a site that long ago made sacred. Roman gods were honored here; a sculpture dedicated to Jupiter found beneath the cathedral is now in the Cluny Museum. Toward the end of the Roman period, a Christian basilica was built here, which followed the usual fate of being enlarged, pillaged, rebuilt and built again.

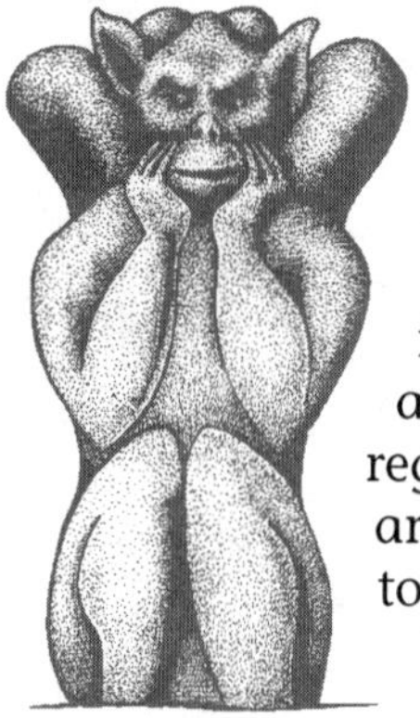

Bishop Maurice de Sully, wishing to see a cathedral worthy of Paris's and the Church's growing status, had the current cathedral started in 1163, shortly after the cathedral of Senlis (see *Châteaux of the Paris Region*).

Notre-Dame presents an important step in the development of a form of art and architecture that was growing out of the Paris region. It would come to be called "the French art," later known as Gothic, and would go on to triumph throughout France and much of Western Europe.

As one of the earliest of a new breed of cathedrals, Notre-Dame reveals a transition from Romanesque to Gothic architecture. But it stands mostly on the side of the latter. Specifically, the pointed arches, ribbed vaults, stained glass and decorative flourish here have gone a long way in taking over from the rounded vaults and arches and relative sobriety of churches begun less than 50 years earlier. With weight and strain displaced along relatively slender columns, and with adjoining and flying buttresses to counterbalance the outward thrust, the ceiling of the new cathedrals soared and the walls opened up to light. Like the Eiffel Tower, Notre-Dame was a precursor of architectural height. Vaulted at a height of 108 feet, it became the tallest church in Europe until the next generation of Gothic churches, designed a half-century later, reached their full height.

The art of stained glass developed and the great rose window was born. The rose of the western (front) façade hasn't budged since it was finished in 1225. Neither have the 1200 13th century oak beams, known as "the forest," that still form the frame of the roof. But over the centuries other parts of the cathedral have been less fortunate. Many of the sculptures and other windows have been replaced, though often with similar or exact copies, particularly during the 19th-century renovation that repaired the damage of time, weather and the Revolution.

Despite its modifications and replacements, we can afford to be generous travelers and accept Notre-Dame for its Gothic originality. Generously then we look on at the acrobatic roller skaters showing their skills nearby and at the pickpockets among the crowd out front as echoes of the traditional role of the cathedral as a gathering place, not only for prayer but also for performers, beggars, friends and thieves.

Places of Worship

France has some 45,000 Catholic churches, 1555 mosques, 1523 Protestant temples and 280 synagogues.

Hôtel Dieu (God's House), the hospital facing the square in front of Notre-Dame, is an outgrowth of hospice care organized by the Church. An earlier hospice was located near the statue of Charlemagne. Hôtel Dieu was so crowded during the medieval era that three people were said to lie to each bed: one sick, one dying, one dead.

The 12th and 13th centuries witnessed peaks of religious fervor during which kings led Crusades, a European-wide relic trade flourished, pilgrimage routes crossed the continent, and

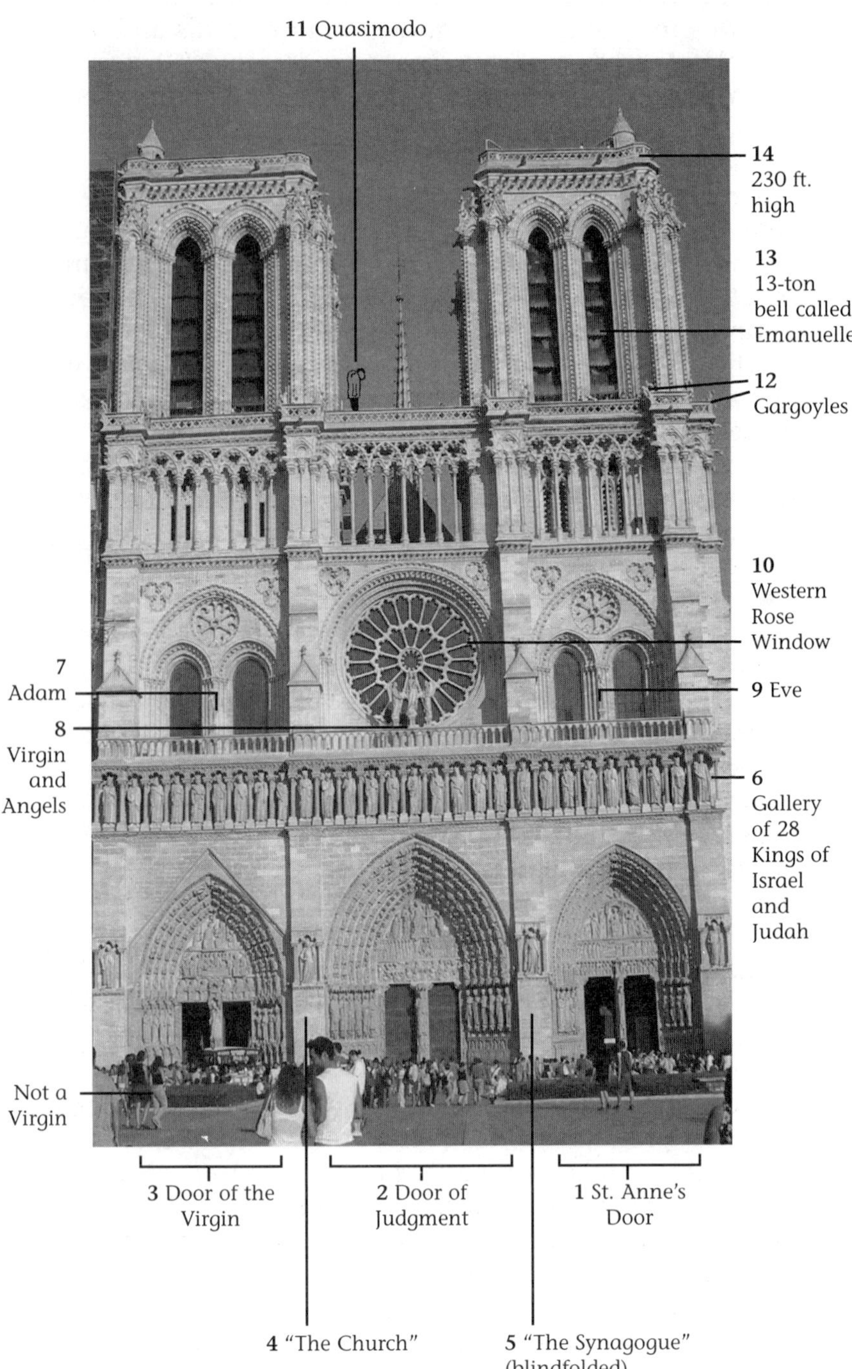

11 Quasimodo
14 230 ft. high
13 13-ton bell called Emanuelle
12 Gargoyles
10 Western Rose Window
7 Adam
9 Eve
8 Virgin and Angels
6 Gallery of 28 Kings of Israel and Judah
Not a Virgin
3 Door of the Virgin
2 Door of Judgment
1 St. Anne's Door
4 "The Church"
5 "The Synagogue" (blindfolded)

The Western Façade of Notre-Dame

1 Door of St. Anne. Mary in her majesty sits with baby Jesus. Below, scenes from the life of the Virgin and her parents, Anne and Joachim. They are surrounded by prophets, kings, angels and saints. Saint Marcel stands before the central pillar

2 Door of Judgment. Christ sits in judgment while below St. Michel weighs souls, sending those on the left to Heaven while those on the right are dragged off to Hell, with images of hellish torture and allegories of vice nearby. Below the weighing of souls, resurrection of the dead. Christ as teacher stands before the central pillar.

3 Door of the Virgin. Jesus receives Mary who is being crowned by an angel. Below, Mary is shrouded and an angel announces the Assumption while kings and prophet contemplate the mystery of the Virgin. Virgin and Child form the central pillar. Signs of the Zodiac are right and left of the door. To the left, Saint Denis, beheaded on Montmartre, holds his head while two angels stand beside him.

4 Allegory of the Church

5 Allegory of the Synagogue, blinded

6 Gallery of the Kings of Israel and of Judah dressed as medieval kings.

7 Adam

8 Virgin and Child surrounded by two angels

9 Eve

10 The western rose window.

11 Quasimodo pours molten lead on the people of Paris

12 Gargoyles and fantastic creatures

13 13-ton bell named Emanuelle

14 230 feet high

the Church and the Crown became intimate companions. All this enabled the bishops of Paris to collect funds to build the cathedral from the king, noblemen and influential clergymen and to obtain offerings from the entire population and high devotion on the part of the tradesmen involved in construction.

Notre-Dame is now owned by the state, which pays for and oversees restorations, while the Church pays for its own functioning from the $6 million or so that it receives from the sale of about 1.5 million candles, sales from the boutique near the exit, donations and collections (all monies accepted), and entrance to the treasury and museum.

The Notre-Dame time line

1160 Maurice de Sully becomes bishop of Paris. Decides on the construction of a new cathedral.

1163 Beginning of construction of Notre-Dame.

1170 Sculptures of the Door of St. Anne (right entrance).

1177-1782 Consecration of the choir.

1196 Death of Sully.

By 1220 Completion of first level of the façade: the three doors and the gallery of kings. Sculpture of the Door of the Virgin (left entrance) in place.

1220-1230 Modification of plans for upper levels and transepts influenced by further developments in Gothic architecture and decoration.

1225 Rose window of the façade in place—hasn't budged since.

1239 Much of Notre-Dame took shape within 75 years, allowing (Saint) Louis IX to leave the Crown of Thorns here until the Sainte-Chapelle was completed in 1248. The relic was again returned to Notre-Dame in 1806. Encased in a gold and crystal ring, it is locked away in the cathedral and watched over by the Knights of the Order of the Holy Sepulcher, who bring it out only on Good Friday.

1240 Completion of sculptures of the Door of the Last Judgment (central entrance).

By 1250 Both towers in place.

1270 Northern and then southern rose windows in place. The northern rose, where blue dominates, recounts scenes from the Old Testament with Mary and baby Jesus at the center. The southern rose, where red dominates, speaks of the

New Testament, with Christ sitting in glory at the center.

1310-1340 Construction and completion of chapels of the choir and reconstruction of flying buttresses.

1345 Completion of the cathedral.

1430 During the Hundred Years War between the French and the English, child King Henry VI of England was crowned King of France here. That was the same year that Joan of Arc took Charles VII, true heir to the throne, to Cathedral Notre-Dame of Reims, in Champagne, the traditional coronation site. Joan wouldn't make it much further as she was burned at the stake as a heretic in Rouen the following year. The trial to rehabilitate her was begun at Notre-Dame in 1455.

1572 Protestant Henri de Navarre married Marguerite de Valois (Queen Margot) while she stood in the choir and he stood at the door. He eventually ascended to the throne as King Henri IV but had to lay siege to the capital to fully conquer his kingdom. His conversion to Catholicism finally helped him gain the allegiance of his subjects. He famously said, "Paris is well worth a mass."

1638 Louis XIII dedicated the kingdom of France to the Virgin Mary after his queen of 23 years, Anne of Austria, finally gave birth to an heir to the throne, the future Louis XIV.

1630s-1707 Date of many of the large paintings that now decorate the side chapels. They were given to the cathedral in the annual tradition of gifts (known as *mays*) to the cathedral initiated by the Brotherhood of Goldsmiths in 1449.

1715 Marble sculptures created for the choir showing Louis XIII holding out his crown and scepter to Mary (in Pietà, 1723), while Louis XIV kneels to the other side.

18th century Modification and restoration throughout the cathedral, including washing of interior of its the polychrome decoration.

1792-1793 During the French Revolution, destruction or mutilation of lower sculptures representing royalty, of the Gallery of Kings of Israel and Judea on the second level of the façade, and of some stained glass. Notre-Dame lost its religious function and its spire and became the Temple of Reason. Some of the mutilated royal heads were recovered and are now in display in a room in the Cluny Museum of the Middle Ages (see "The Left Bank") along with other sculptures from the medieval cathedral safeguarded from pollution and weather. The row of kings along with many of the figures on the façade are 19th-century replacements.

1802 The Consulate, under Napoleon Bonaparte, restores the cathedral's religious function.

Dec. 2, 1804 Coronation of Emperor Napoleon I while the damage of the Revolution was hidden behind large tapestries and scaffolding.

1831 Publication of Victor Hugo's *Notre-Dame-de-Paris.* With or without revolution, Gothic architecture was far out of fashion by the start of the 19th century, but renewed interest came with the return of the Bourbon kings in 1815 and got a major shot in the arm when Hugo's bestseller brought both the author and the cathedral international fame through the story of the hunchbacked Quasimodo, the beautiful Esmeralda, and molten lead being poured through the mouths of gargoyles onto the people of Paris.

1845-1864 Major restoration of Notre-Dame. Eugêne Viollet-le-Duc (1814-1879) became the country's primary renovator of medieval monuments and had a hand in renovating religious monuments and castles throughout France. Notre-Dame became his masterwork. The vast restoration began after two years of detailed study of the damaged cathedral. Viollet-le-Duc assumed the mantel of savior of the cathedral and oversaw restoration and repair that brought it back from the brink of ruin. Stoneworkers, glassworkers and masons restored and replaced sculptures, gargoyles and stained glass and repaired structural and roofing damage. Viollet-le-Duc placed himself in the role as Saint Thomas (patron saint of architects) among the Apostles and Evangelists leading up to the spire; unlike the others who face out to the surroundings, he gazes up to admire his own work, a level in one hand. His likeness was also placed in the gallery of kings on the façade. Renovation of the cathedral took place at the same time as a major transformation of Ile de la Cité that cleared out remaining residences on the central part of the island. By 1890, the new hospital, Commercial Court and Police Headquarters had been built.

Aug. 26, 1944 Te Deum celebrating the Liberation from German Occupation.

1989 Placement of new alter.

1991-2002 Vast cleaning and restoration of facades.

The towers

The 380-step climb up the north tower takes stamina and a lack of claustrophobia but the reward is the Quasimado view from the heights of the cathedral, beginning with the fantastic gargoyles that greet you as you arrive. The visit to the cathedral's 13-ton bell can be skipped if there's a wait, but be sure to climb the narrow stairwell to the top of the southern tower, where you'll look out over the cathedral's roof, gargoyles, spire and flying buttresses to a magnificent panorama of the city.

Our Lady's behind

As impressive as Our Lady is from the front, the sweetest view is from the rear. That's where the full Gothic splendor of the flying buttresses supporting the choir comes into view. Sometimes you also get a glimpse of the small hawks (*falco tinnunculus*) that nest in the heights of Notre-Dame – their nests are indicated by the white line of droppings just below.

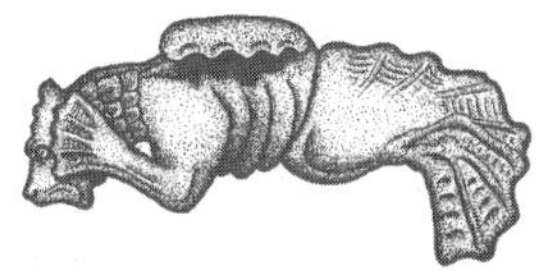

The Deportation Memorial, 1940-1944

The northeastern tip of the island holds a memorial to the 200,000 French deported 1940-1944. This crypt-like monument is to be discovered step by step as you descend from enclosure to enclosure to the Tomb of the Unknown Deportee and 200,000 points of light.

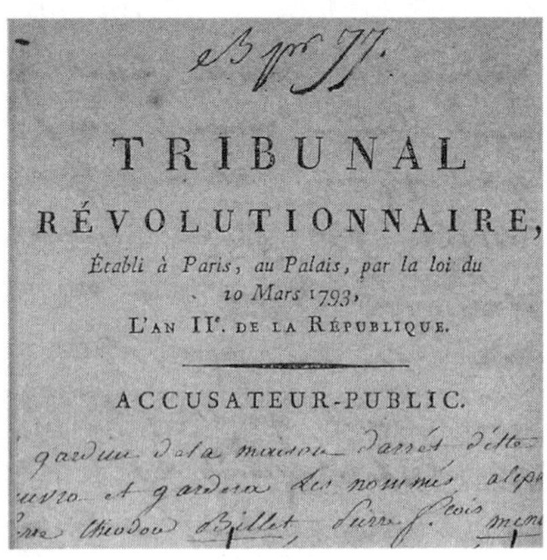
TRIBUNAL
RÉVOLUTIONNAIRE,
Établi à Paris, au Palais, par la loi du 10 Mars 1793,
L'AN IIe. DE LA RÉPUBLIQUE.

ACCUSATEUR-PUBLIC.

THE ROYAL PALACE OF THE CAPETIAN KINGS

Sainte-Chapelle and the Conciergerie

Along with Notre-Dame, the City Island presents two other major remnants of the Middle Ages, both dating from the time of construction of the cathedral:

- **the Sainte-Chapelle**, one of France's most brilliant Gothic gems, and
- **the Conciergerie**, showing the palace's medieval profile, which now mostly recalls its role as jail from which major figures of royalty and revolution were led to the guillotine.

They are the only visible portions of the former royal palace of the Capetian and first Valois kings who resided on the island. They are now surrounded by the Law Courts complex, which otherwise dates from the late-18th and mid-19th centuries. As usual, a bit of history best sets the scene.

The Capetian Kings: 987-1328

In 987, **Hugues (Hugh) Capet**, duke of the Franks, was elected king of France, signaling the full-fledged existence of the France and the beginning of the Capetian dynasty. By crowning his oldest son while still alive he created a truly hereditary dynasty that ruled France uninterrupted until the fall of Louis XVI in 1792.

Hugh Capet made Paris the seat of his power. He actually controled only a small territory surrounding Paris. Feudalism created powerful lords who protected the peasantry while taxing them and whose power depended primarily on the accumulation of land through war or marriage. Capet was little more than a wealthy lord. But little by little over the following eight centuries, various duchies and counties were incorporated into the French Crown, forming the territory of France as we know it today.

During a long reign from 996-1031, Hugh Capet's son **Robert the Pious** began the transformation of the City Palace, formerly site of the palace of the Roman governors, into a complex worthy of the seat of power of the French kings. From the 11th-14th centuries, his descendents would continue the task of creating a complex that would reflect the increasing power and territory of the French kings.

Paris itself grew steadily under the Capetian kings. The marshland (*marais*) that prevented building on the Right Bank began to be drained, and the city's extension, previously limited to the Left Bank, now continued on both sides of the river. As commerce along the Seine developed, so did the role of the guild of "water merchants." The symbol of their role in the city's development, a ship with a silver sail, remains the emblem of Paris.

As commerce along the Seine developed, so did the role of the guild of "water merchants." The symbol of their role in the city's development, a ship with a silver sail, remains the emblem of Paris.

During another long reign, that of **Philip Augustus**, 1180-1223, the territorial control of France increased while major work was undertaken to fortify and improve the capital, ringing the city with new ramparts to enclose the Right Bank, building aqueducts and public fountains, paving roads, constructing a defensive fortress and donjon called the Louvre. His grandson, **Louis IX**, then made a greater name for himself during his reign from 1226-1270.

Louis IX and the Sainte-Chapelle

The chapel is inside the Law Courts complex, so you need to pass through security before entering. Open 9:30am-6pm. Entrance fee. It's possible to purchase a combined ticket for both the Sainte-Chapelle and the Conciergerie. Evening concerts are occasionally held in the chapel.

While Notre-Dame is Paris's Gothic treasure, the Sainte-Chapelle is its most glittering gem. The chapel was built to house the most precious relic of all of Christiandom, Christ's Crown of Thorn, purchased by Louis IX in 1239. The relic is now in Notre-Dame, yet the Sainte-Chapelle remains a magnificent reliquary. The true sparkle comes from its stained glass windows, so the chapel is best visited on a sunny day.

Louis IX, eventually canonized as Saint Louis, reigned during relatively prosperous years during which the capital and the kingdom continued to grow, Paris's reputation as a major theological center began to extend far and wide (Thomas Aquinas taught at the University of Paris for a time), and Notre-Dame's magnificent western façade was influencing the many new churches and cathedrals then under construction.

As the relic trade flourished in Europe, Louis IX saw the opportunity to present himself as leader of the Christian world by purchasing pieces that, authentic or not, were considered the most holy relics of all, those of Christ's Passion, including the most precious of them all, the Crown of Thorns. In order to house the relics, he ordered the construction of the Sainte-Chapelle (the Holy Chapel) adjacent to his royal palace on Ile de la Cité. While Notre-Dame would take 175 years to complete, the Sainte-Chapelle, achieved in 1248, took less than 7.

Louis IX initiated major transformations of the City Palace, but none was more splendorous than this chapel. It is divided into two levels. The lower chapel, dedicated to the Virgin Mary, served as the parish church of the City Palace and was used by the palace staff. Its columns are painted with the royal fleur-de-lys against a royal azure background along with towers of Castille in honor of Louis IX's devout mother, Blanche de Castille.

The real glitter is in the upper chapel, intended for royal use. The king had direct entrance here from his palace. The upper chapel appears to be made of nothing but stained glass windows separated by statues of the 12 Apostles. Two-thirds of the 6,458 square feet of glass are original, providing a rare extensive display of 13th century stained glass. Reading from left to right, bottom to top within each lancet, the windows tell stories of the Bible, with those relative to Jesus presented in the apse. The relics themselves were placed in opulent reliquaries on the platform in the apse. The rose window was added in the 15th century.

Following the Revolution, the chapel, as other religious buildings, was converted for secular uses, in this case to store archives. It underwent major restoration beginning in 1846.

The Crown of Thorns, encased in a gold and crystal ring, is now locked away in a wardrobe of the sacristy of Notre-Dame.

Secure enough at home, temporarily at peace with the English, and royal leader of the Christian world, Louis IX led the (failed) 7th Crusade, 1248-1254. In 1270 he set out on the 8th Crusade but died of the plague in Tunis five months later. That would be the last major Crusade to the Holy Land of the Middle Ages.

Canonized a generation after his death, Saint Louis remains the most important figure in the marriage of Christianity and the French Crown. He is represented in statues and stained glass on churches throughout France. In Paris, Saint Louis and Joan of Arc, the other major figure of the Christian kingdom of France, stand watch by the entrance to Sacré Coeur on Montmartre.

The Conciergerie

Open *April-Sept. 9:30am-6:00pm.*

Viewed from across along the river, the three round towers and one square tower of the Conciergerie offer a glimpse of the medieval profile of the City Palace as distinct as the nose of the French kings who lived there. The square tower at the corner of the building by the Pont au Change, the bridge from Chatêlet, is embedded with Paris's first public clock, installed in the 14th century, replaced in 1585, and still ticking. The entrance to the Conciergerie is by the first round tower.

Tours given inside the Conciergerie are now mostly devoted to recalling its role as prison during the Revolution. The surviving portions of the royal palace, meanwhile, tell fewer stories but have more noteworthy architectural features. You can actually have a look at the guard room from the first half of the 14th-century without entering deeper since it's now occupied by the ticket area and museum shop. This is the old entrance to the Conciergerie, between the twin towers. Beyond the guard room lie the other major remnants of other Gothic rooms of the old palace, the enormous banquet room and, at its far end, the palace kitchen with four huge chimneys. These rooms have no furnishing to further spark the imagination. So here's a little local history to get you started before entering, as you stand near the Seine with view of the both the medieval towers and, diagonally across the river, Paris's City Hall.

The Conciergerie and the medieval city

In the 13th century the guild of water merchants, controlling movements along the Seine, adopted the motto *fluctuat nec mergitur*—it is tossed by the waves but does not sink. That remains the motto of the City of Paris. The water merchants formed a powerful corporation that the king allowed to oversee various functions of life in the capital. As representatives of the king in matters of commerce, they oversaw many aspects of trade in general, collected fines and ruled the main port, which was by the square in front of the current City Hall. Their important position led to the formation of a city council led by the provost of merchants, a mayor of sorts with economic, administrative and certain judicial authority.

The Capetian line ended in 1328 when Charles the Fair died without a son and the crown was inherited by his cousin Philip VI, who established **the Valois line**. Philip VI and his son John the Good continued to develop the City Palace as a royal residence. But domestic revolt led John the Good's son to move onto the Right Bank.

By the 15th century the Conciergerie had become a major prison. The *concierge* was the chief guardian of the entrance to the City Palace who could hand down justice himself in some matters.

In 1355, **Etienne Marcel** became provost of the merchants. He installed his command in a building by the main port, which has been the site of Paris's City Hall ever since. (City Hall, *Hôtel de Ville,* was rebuilt as a Renaissance palace in the 16th century; burned down with the fall of the Commune of 1871, it was reconstructed according to similar plans shortly thereafter.) Etienne Marcel's influence in the capital grew to the point that it rivaled that of the **King John the Good**. In 1358, in the midst of the Hundred Years War, while John the Good was being held prisoner by the English, Etienne Marcel seized the occasion to foment a revolt that overtook the royal palace. Under his orders two of the king's advisors were murdered. The king's son, the future **Charles V**, was in the palace at the time but managed to escape by boat. Marcel was killed soon after, but when Charles V finally returned to Paris as king in 1364 he settled not on the island, now considered unsafe, but on the Right Bank, sometimes in the Hôtel Saint-Pol (see *The Marais*), sometimes in the Louvre.

Aside from brief stays and official receptions, the City Palace was no longer inhabited by the kings after Charles V abandoned it as a prime residence. However, it remained central to the life of France and to Paris as the judicial and parliamentary functions of the royal government were there. Among its most important function was its judicial role. By the 15th century the Conciergerie had become a major prison. The *concierge* was the chief guardian of the entrance to the City Palace who could hand down justice himself in some matters. The Conciergerie was used as a prison during trials and sentencing or torture. Prisoners might be tortured on site but were usually carted off to the square in front of City Hall for execution by beheading, hanging, burning or quartering.

The Conciergerie during the Revolution

Systematic execution by beheading didn't take place until the Revolution with Dr. Guillotin's perfection of the machine that took his name. The National Razor, as it was also called, was mostly operational on Place de la Concorde (then called Place de la Révolution) and on Place de la Nation (then called Place de la Trône- Renversé, Square of the Overturned Throne). From March 1793 to May 1795 the Revolutionary Tribunal set up in the Parliamentary Hall of the City Palace handed down over 2700 death sentences. Under Robespierre, the easing of legal constraints, such as proof of wrongdoing and rights to a defense, made the Tribunal's job as signatory of the death sentence even simpler.

Prisoners were held in the Conciergerie temporarily while awaiting trial and execution. **Marie-Antoinette**, brought here from the Temple (see "The Marais: Carnavalet Museum"), was held at the Conciergerie for 10 weeks before she was sentenced to death and taken to Place de la Révolution on Oct. 16, 1793 to be guillotined. Her cell was transformed into an expiatory chapel by Louis XVIII, her brother-in-law, after he resumed power in 1815. **Charlotte Corday**, who murdered Marat in his bathtub, passed through the Conciergerie before being taken, along with other enemies of the Revolution and common criminals, to the guillotine. **Robespierre**, after a suicide attempt, was taken on the same route.

PLACE DAUPHINE AND PONT NEUF

The former garden of the royal palace was transformed into a charming triangular square at the start of the 17th century, at the same time that Pont Neuf, the bridge just beyond it, was being built. It's contemporary of Place des Vosges (see *The Marais*) but has lost some of its original harmony due to subsequent alterations.

Pont Neuf is Paris's oldest remaining bridge even though the name means New Bridge. It's novelty had to do with its being the first major bridge in the capital not to have apartment houses built on it. Decorated with 385 grotesque, grimacing faces above the arches, the bridge and the square date from the reign of Henri IV, who rides on horseback nearby. (See *Wine Bars: Bar du Caveau* for more about Place Dauphine.)

Boat Tours. Sit back, relax, and watch the city unfold, including wonderful views of Notre-Dame, the Eiffel Tower and the bridges of Paris. I recommend this for your first day in the city to get a feel for the layout and some of the highlights of Paris-on-the-Seine. Boats leave from several docking points in the city, but those departing from beside the Pont Neuf below the statue of Henri IV are the most conveniently located. Hearing the straight fact in several languages through the 45-minute tour can be annoying, but that's the heart of Paris you're passing through.

MARIANNE, FRANCE'S UNCLE SAM

From a kingdom devoted to Mary, France became a republic under the guidance Marianne. Marianne is the allegory of the French Republic, the French equivalent of our Uncle Sam. She leads the French into battle, soothes them with her confident, compassionate gaze, sustains them with pride, honors their dead. Her bust is present in town halls throughout France. Since the 1960s Marianne has been modeled after a series of celebrities whose beauty then represents the Republic. After Brigitte Bardot, Catherine Deneuve and Mireille Mathieu, the official bust of Marianne since 1999 has been modeled after top model Laetitia Casta. Town halls are not obliged to replace their busts each time a new model is produced.

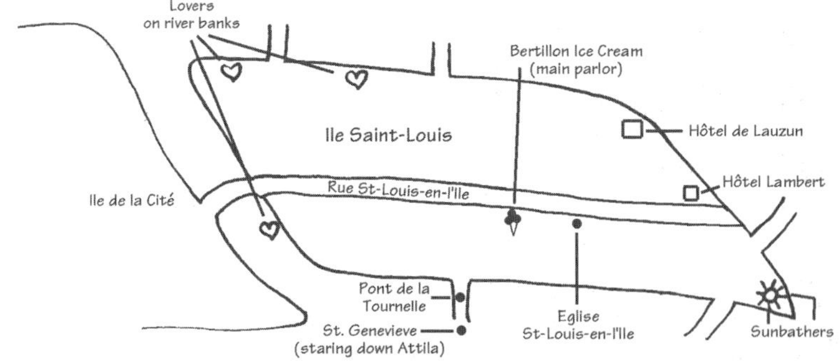

ILE SAINT-LOUIS: THE ISLAND OF CHARM

Beside the island of monuments awaits the island of charm. Ile Saint-Louis provides a sweet stroll even when crowded with visitors on a spring or summer afternoon, but its discreet seduction is best witnessed in the morning or off season. That's when it reveals itself to be a peaceable village of small and quaint commerce (novelty shops, food shops, cutesy galleries). There are several hotels on the island but there's no need to stay here, a brief visit is sufficient. Meanwhile, its stately mansions and apartments are among the most expensive real estate in Paris, reputed to be prized by wealthy Francophile Americans, international corporate executives, stars of classical music, and French heirs, few of whom you will ever see, particularly the latter whom I suspect are happy enough living elsewhere while renting to the former.

Formerly grazing ground through the Middle Ages, when it was known as L'Ile aux Vaches, Cow Island, Ile St-Louis developed in the 17th century along with the nearby Marais. The island now contains an ensemble of sedate 17th- and 18th-century mansions and apartment buildings, notably the **Hôtel de Lauzun** (17 quai d'Anjou) and the **Hôtel Lambert** (2 rue St-Louis-en-l'Ile), both on the northeast corner of the island. Since they can rarely be visited, what interior splendor exists can only be imagined by wrought iron balconies and shuttered windows. The butcher and cheese shops along the main street are the only sign that people actually live on the island. Eglise St-Louis-en-l'Ile (end 17th-beginning 18th centuries) is a noteworthy remnant from the Baroque and Jesuit era of the reign of Louis XIV. Along with the Counter Reformation, tennis was another sport of the time, and the hotel Jeu de Paume (#54) is actually built around the timbers of a former royal tennis court of sorts; the court is now the lobby lounge.

The island's main draw is **Berthillon ice cream and sherbert**, whose tasty little scoops draw crowds to a half-dozen stands. Join the back of the line and send someone from your group to make recognizance missions to check the available flavors on the board. The ice cream is great, but the sorbet is better. Berthillon's headquarters are at #31 on the main street; its own stand is closed Mon., Tues. and Aug., though others remain open then.

The cafés on the side of the island facing Notre-Dame and the restaurants along the main street have charm and calm to recommend them if not much else; they're pleasant enough without being outstanding. The cuisine throughout is strictly Franco-French with the exception of Isami, a little sushi hideway (see Restaurants: Foreign Cuisines/Japanese). Isami is by Pont de la Tournelle, the bridge that leads to Paris's most historic institution of haute cuisine, **La Tour d'Argent**, which always serves up a full glass of Notre-Dame.

Geneviève, patron saint of the city, stands high above the end of the bridge protecting a child as she faces east, toward the advancing Hun invaders. Her words and prayers are held to have saved the city from the impending invasion of Attila the Hun after he'd crossed the Rhine. The bridge also offers a superb view of Notre-Dame, with the Eiffel Tower in the distance. For a view back at Ile Saint-Louis go onto the terrace of the **Institute of the Arab World** (1987) across Pont de Sully, the next bridge upstream.

For more distant horizons stop in at the island's wonderful travel and trekking bookstore **Ulysses** (26 rue St-Louis-en-l'Ile; open Tues.-Sat. afternoons). Seasoned travelers and dreamers might check out the notice board at Ulysses if looking to hook up with someone planning a month-long climb in the Alps, a 6-month trek in Tibet, a sabbatical on a boat, or a three-year tour of the world.

Ile Saint-Louis itself, meanwhile, may not keep you occupied for more than 45 minutes, unless you take your loved one and your ice cream cones down to the cobblestones along the river for a long romantic pause.

THE LEFT BANK

The central Left Bank is comprised of three quarters that claim the Luxembourg Garden (see *Gardens*) as their back yard:

The Latin Quarter: The student-heavy quarter from Place Saint-Michel to the Pantheon to rue Mouffetard, with much history underfoot and the important Cluny National Museum of the Middle Ages along the way.

The Saint Germain Quarter: The charismatic quarter extending along the heart of boulevard and from the Seine to the Luxembourg Garden, popular with travelers not for its monuments but for its lifestyle, which begins with café culture.

Montparnasse: Below the tower with the grandest view of all, café culture is also alive and well in the celebrated cafés and brasseries along boulevard Montparnasse, still going strong since they drew together the cultural avant-garde of the 1920s.

THE BIRTH OF PARIS: FROM ROMAN LUTETIA TO FRANKISH PARIS

59-52 B.C. The Roman conquest of Celtic Gaul. Lutetia (Lutèce in French), a village on the Seine inhabited by a Celtic people called the Parisii, was conquered and burned to the ground.

1st-2nd centuries A.D. Growth of Gallo-Roman Lutetia. The Romans set up their administrative palace on the west end of the large island and a temple on the east, functions that continue to this day with the Paris Law Courts and Police Headquarters to one side and Notre-Dame to the other. The Romans expanded their city on the sloping left bank of the river. The right bank was less habitable as it lay low and was often flooded. Routes of communication and trade were developed as Roman civilization developed throughout Gaul. An arena, public baths, aqueducts and villas were built on Left Bank Lutetia. The outline of the arena and portions of the baths are still visible.

3rd-4th centuries. Spread of Christianity. Christianity began to spread through Gaul in the 3rd century, increasingly competing with Gallo-Roman cults. In the middle of the 3rd century Saint Denis, considered first bishop of Lutetia, was beheaded along with coreligionists on the hill to the north, eventually called Montmartre, Mount of the Martyrs. Constantine and Christianity triumphed in Rome in 312. Over the next two centuries Christianity replaced Gallo-Roman cults and the sites of Roman temples in Lutetia began receiving Christian prayers.

4th-5th centuries. Decline of the Roman Empire. With the Roman Empire under attack from the north and west, ramparts were built around the City Island. By the end of the 4th century Lutetia was left to fend for itself. It was pillaged by Vandals in 406. The population abandoned residences on the left bank of the river for safety on the island. After fending off a wave of attacks from the Franks, Julian, the Roman prefect of Gaul, was proclaimed emperor. Lutetia was increasingly referred to by the name of its inhabitant, the Parisii, as it gradually came to be called Paris.

5th century. Rise of the Franks. Even before the demise of the Roman Empire in the west in 476, parts had already fall away from Roman control following successive waves of invasion by Visigoths, Vandals, Franks (a Germanic tribe) and Huns that swept through Gaul.

In 451, **Attilla and the Huns**, pillaging their way across the continent, crossed the Rhine and began heading toward Paris. **Geneviève** (~420-502), daughter of wealthy Christian Frankish land owners, rallied the people of Paris to keep faith that God would not allow Attila to reach the town. Meanwhile a coalition of Romans, Visigoths and Franks (under their leader **Merowig**) joined forces to combat the Huns. The battle at the Catalaniques Fields (in the Champagne region) succeeded in pushing back Attila and his men.

Over the next several decades, while Geneviève's prominence as a moral force in Paris continued to grow, so did the dominance of **the Franks** in Gaul. Led by Merowig then his son Childéric then his grandson Clovis, they eventually held control of the lion's share of what had been Roman Gaul. But the Parisii continued to favor the (Christian) Romans over the (pagan) Franks and Geneviève led the opposition to Clovis taking control of Paris. But the face-off was untenable. Finally she and Clovis found the solution to an acceptable Frankish dominance: Clovis, having married Clotilde, a Christian, should convert. He was baptized at Reims (Champagne) in 496. Since then, with few exceptions, all French kings have been crowned at the cathedral of Reims. Clovis, founder of the **Merovingian dynasty**, then settled in Paris. (The name Clovis would evolve into the name Louis, the favored name of later kings.)

Geneviève, Clovis and Clotilde were all buried on the hill of the current Pantheon in a church that no longer exists. Geneviève, eventually canonized, became the patron saint of Paris. The hill took her name. In times of impending disaster (flood, disease, invasion), her reliquary would be paraded through the city. Her relics were mostly burned during the Revolution; however, what are held to be some of her bones were saved and are now in a reliquary in Saint-Etienne-du-Mont near the Pantheon.

THE LATIN QUARTER

Metro/RER *Saint-Michel.*

Once the heart of the Roman city of Lutetia, then abandoned in the face of invasions during the Dark Ages, this area of the Left Bank was reborn in the 13th century as a center for higher education, a vocation that continues to define life and travels in the Latin Quarter. A dozen major educational institutions—high schools, colleges, universities, research institutes—crowd within a quarter-mile's radius of the Pantheon. The Latin Quarter's student life makes it a natural attraction to young travelers. But this is truly a historical quarter where picturesque streets can make for a prolonged morning of wandering for anyone, from Place Saint-Michel to rue Mouffetard. Above all, two compelling sights—the Pantheon and the Cluny Museum of the Middle Ages—deserve attention for return travelers, particularly when staying in the nearby Saint-Germain Quarter.

Place Saint-Michel, rue de la Huchette and Eglise Saint-Séverin

There is no single approach to visiting the Latin Quarter, which begins just across the river from Notre-Dame. Yet everyone meeting in the quarter arranges to rendezvous at Place Saint-Michel by the statue of Michel slaying the dragon.

Rue de la Huchette and rue Saint-Séverin, two narrow pedestrian streets running east from Place St-Michel, give a picturesque glimpse of Paris of centuries past—at least they do when visited in the middle of the night or in the morning, when the inferior restaurants that otherwise mark the street are closed. On rue Saint-Séverin, Eglise Saint-Séverin is worth a visit at any time of day for the sight of its fabulous flamboyant Gothic forest of pillars and ribbed vaulting dating mostly from the late 15th century and for the light streaming in from a harmonious marriage of late-medieval and modern windows. After the church's windows have gone dark, the light gets smoky in the medieval basement of Caveau de la Huchette at 5 rue de la Huchette, an old haunt for jazz on Friday and Saturday nights, classic rock 'n' roll on weekdays.

The Cluny Museum of the Middle Ages and the Roman Baths

Address *6 place Paul-Painlevé, 5th arr. Metro Cluny.* ***Open*** *Daily except Tues., 9:15am-5:45pm. This isn't a large museum but there are enough details to keep you busy for an hour or two.*

Though often ignored by first-time visitors to Paris, the Cluny Museum of the Middle Ages deserves a place among the major monument-museums of the capital. It is a triple attraction for the quality of the collection, the splendor of the 400-year-old mansion that houses it, and the vestiges of the Roman baths alongside.

The Roman Baths: Around the year 200, Gallo-Roman baths (*thermes*) were built here, near the major crossroads of Lutetia. They were a meeting place for Parisii rich and poor. Vestiges of the tepidarium (tepid room) and of the caldarium (room for hot steam baths) are visible from boulevard Saint-Michel. Inside the museum, the frigidarium (room for cold water baths) and its 49-foot vaulted ceiling is the most impressive remnant, even though stripped of the marble and stucco that once adorned it. Nearby, rue Saint-Jacques traces the ancient cardo, the main Roman road running south from Lutetia. The aqueduct stood alongside it and fed the Thermes de Cluny and a larger bath complex that has disappeared beneath the Collège de France, two blocks away. The Roman Odeon was nearby, the Forum was just up the hill (currently rue Sufflot), the Arena was on the eastern edge of town.

The Hôtel de Cluny: In the 14th century the ruins of these baths were purchased by the Abbey of Cluny, based in Burgundy, so as construct a residence for its abbots when in Paris. Cluny was then the most influential abbey in Christiandom. It had spawned dependencies throughout Europe at a time when the continent was made up of fledgling feudal kingdoms. At its height, the Benedictine order directly oversaw 10,000 monks, while 1111 monasteries and priories were under its influence. Its influence waned as kingdoms of Europe gained in centralized authority and as the Church itself took to infighting, yet Cluny maintained enormous wealth (due to its land holding) until the French Revolution. Its pockets and prestige still fully intact at the end of the 15th century, the abbey rebuilt its Paris residence as the sumptuous mansion that now houses the Cluny Museum. The Hôtel de Cluny is one of only two remaining mansions in Paris from before 1600, the other being the Hôtel de Sens in the Marais, which served a similar function for the archbishops of Sens. Designed at the end of France's flamboyant Gothic era and on the cusp of the Renaissance, the courtyard of the Hôtel de Cluny deserves attention even without entering the museum. But since you've come this far...

The Collection: The religious medieval works in the museum aren't as self-explanatory as the art in the Louvre or the Orsay Museum, but they are an important complement to a visit to any medieval church in Paris, beginning with Notre-Dame. One of the first rooms in the museum presents original 13th century sculptures from the cathedral that come from a row of Kings of the Old Testament on the second level of the façade; because they represented kings, they were toppled after the guillotining started in 1793. Replacements were later made for Notre-Dame, but the original fragments, mostly heads, are here along with major sculptures from elsewhere on the cathedral and from other important religious monuments, safe from more recent assaults of weather and pollution. The museum also provides a close-up look at stained glass, sculptures, tapestries, tombstones, paintings, reliquaries, enamels and other decorative details from the Middle Ages, particularly from the 12th-15th centuries.

The Lady and the Unicorn: *The Mona Lisa* of the Cluny Museum is the famous series of six tapestries called *The Lady and the Unicorn.* Created at the end of the 15th centuries (less than 10 year before *The Mona Lisa*), it is among the masterpieces of late-medieval tapestry-making. The Lady and her Unicorn present the five senses: smell, taste, touch, sight and hearing. A sixth tapestry shows the Lady taking jewels out of a box and bears the inscription "A mon seul désir" (By my own desire), to say that the Lady's free will allows her to shun the attraction of earthly senses and pleasures in favor of a more spiritual life.

The Medieval Gardens: Medieval gardens have been recreated beside the museum along boulevard Saint-Germain. The gardens are a playful wink at aspects of medieval life, particularly as shown in this and other mille-fleurs (thousand-flower) tapestries: the Love Garden, the Heavenly Garden, the Medicinal Simples, the Kitchen Garden, and the Meadow, with a central brick path that bears the imprint of fantastic creatures of the forest who wandered about the medieval imagination.

From Cluny to the Louvre: In the chronology of the national museums of Paris, the Louvre takes over where the Cluny leaves off. Indeed, the medieval era in France can be said to end with the construction of the Hôtel de Cluny and with the spiritual illumination of *The Lady and the Unicorn* while the Renaissance begins with the transformation of royal palaces such as the Louvre and with the humanistic enigma of Da Vinci's *Mona Lisa.*

THE SORBONNE

Bordered by rues des Ecoles, de la Sorbonne, Cujas and Saint-Jacques, just south of the Cluny Museum. Best approached via Place de la Sorbonne.

The Latin Quarter's role as a center of higher education began with the founding in 1215 of the Theological University of France in the shadow of Notre-Dame. In 1257 Robert de Sorbon, chaplain to Louis IX, obtained land and funding from the king to found of a center for poor students and teachers of theology, which would eventually become Paris's most famous institution of higher learning, the Sorbonne. Other theological colleges followed, including the Humanist rival to the Sorbonne, the Collège de France, founded under royal sponsorship in the 16th century and located just behind it. The Sorbonne remained a major mover in theological circles until the Revolution, which brought an end to the official use of Latin in education (which had given the quarter its name) and eliminated the primary role of theological studies here and many other institutions in the area.

Despite the fame of its name, the Sorbonne is not among France's elite universities; it is instead the tip of the iceberg of the Paris university system which spreads throughout the city and suburbs. The massive Sorbonne complex dates mostly from the 19th century. Place de la Sorbonne leads to the main architectural interest of the Sorbonne, its 17th-century chapel. The view of the façade from the square outside the school is monumental, but the grander view is from inside the Sorbonne's main quadrangle, which can be entered at 17 rue de la Sorbonne. The chapel itself is rarely open for visits.

The Pantheon and the Separation of Church and State

***Metro** Maubert-Mutualité or RER Luxembourg. **Open** daily 10am-6:30pm (until 6pm Oct.-March). Since June 2002 it's been possible to climb to the top, offering a new panorama to the return traveler who has seen all others. Visit to top by accompanied group of 50, 10am-noon and 1:30-5:30pm.*

The significance of the Pantheon is enormous. The building may not be as impressive as Notre-Dame or the Eiffel Tower or stand out as much as Sacré Coeur or the Arc de Triomphe, but its complex history makes this one of the most telling sights in all of France. By itself it tells the story of a nation's successful struggle to separate Church from State. Whether or not you choose to explore the Pantheon from crypt to dome or just spot it from a distance, know-

ing that this impressive monument is here will give a greater understanding of how France made the transition from a Catholic kingdom to a secular republic.

Church of Saint-Geneviève: In 1744, Louis XV vowed during a serious illness that if cured he would rebuild the Church of Saint Geneviève, then falling into ruin at the top Mount Saint-Geneviève. The king did survive—and promptly ignored his vow, until it was deemed politically essential for him to show his interest in Paris and its religious leaders. He then asked the architect Soufflot to design the new Eglise Sainte-Geneviève. Construction began in 1764, with the king laying the first stone.

No sooner was the dome completed in 1790 than the revolutionary, anti-clerical ideals of the Revolution took hold. The Church, seen as having abused its privilege, repressed the people and subverted reason, was considered part of the axis of evil in the old regime and so its possessions were confiscated by the nation. Over the next decade many religious monuments would be abandoned, destroyed or converted for use as stables or warehouses, declared temples of reason or quarried for their stone.

Temple of the Nation: Church of Saint-Geneviève was one of the first to be converted. In 1791 the Constituent Assembly designated it as Temple of the Nation, the French Pantheon, dedicated to the great men of the nation.

Easy enough said, but what constitutes a great man for the nation? All republicans could agree that Voltaire and Rousseau, greats of the Enlightenment and both deceased in 1778, belonged in the French Pantheon, and so they were placed here respectively in 1791 and 1794. But the frequently changing winds of political favor during the Revolution and Terror turned the selection (and de-selection) of men to honor into a game of influence. In order to give some distance to the selection process, the ruling Convention decreed in 1795 that no one could be transferred to the Pantheon until he'd been dead for at least ten years.

> **The Pantheon is dedicated to the great men of the nation...Easy enough said, but what constitutes a great man for the nation?**

Meanwhile, inside and out, the building took on the appearance of a tremendous tomb. The lower windows were holed up and the upper windows were modified, transforming Sufflot's luminous domed church into a somber funerary monument. The religious virtues represented on the frieze were replaced by those honoring civic and military virtues. The Latin inscription dedicating the building to Geneviève was replaced with the words *Aux Grands Hommes La Patrie Reconnaissante*—To the Great Men the Grateful Nation.

The Pantheon-Church: Napoleon I, reestablishing a role for religion in the life of the nation but keeping it subservient to the needs of national (imperial) progress, restored the Pantheon to Catholicism in 1806 while maintaining the crypt as tomb for the greats. Reflecting his own sense of greatness, generals and statesmen who served the Empire were given place in the Pantheon over the next eight years. Though of certain importance during their time, few of their names are recognizable to the French today, much less to foreigners.

After the fall of Napoleon, Louis XVIII restored the entire building to its religious function. Eglise Sainte-Geneviève was back in business. Its role as pantheon ceased to exist, except to receive the remains of the architect Sufflot (1713-1780) in 1829. The inscription on the front was again changed to honor Paris's patron saint. The secular frieze, too, was torn down and the interior decorations repainted to reflect a continuity of religion and the Bourbon kings.

But after the Revolution of 1830 the Church was rededicated as Pantheon. Again the wording on the frieze was changed and the sculptural narrative redesigned (to their current appearance) by David d'Angers, the era's most renowned sculptor. But as a hot-button issue the building was otherwise abandoned by King Louis-Philippe and by the Second Republic.

Foucault's Pendulum: In 1851 Jean-Bernard-Léon Foucault created a public sensation when he provided visual evidence of the rotation of the earth. He had recently wowed men of science with his demonstration at the nearby Paris Observatory and now, beneath Sufflot's dome, he repeated the demonstration before the general public. He placed a brass sphere at the end of a rope attached from 250 feet high beneath the dome (i.e. a "fixed" point above the earth) and set the pendulum swinging. Lo and behold, the point at the bottom of the sphere traced lines in sand spread on the floor, proving that while the pendulum itself swings along a single axis the earth turns beneath it. A reproduction of the pendulum continues to swing beneath the dome of the Pantheon. The original brass sphere of Foucault's demonstration is at the Musée des Arts et Métiers (see *Museums*).

The National Basilica: The Catholic Church was not amused by the performance of science in a house of worship. Furthermore, in order to carry out his coup d'état later that year, Napoleon III needed Catholic support. He therefore decreed the church/pantheon the National Basilica, and religious services were reinstated. Even after his fall in 1870 Catholic statesmen under Third Republic ensured the building's continuation as a religious monument for almost a decade. The interior was decorated with frescoes celebrating the royal and Catholic history of France. These paintings remain.

To the Great Men [and Women] the Grateful Nation: The Pantheon's vocation as tomb of the greats of the nation was definitively proclaimed not so much by governmental decree as by the death of Victor Hugo in 1885 and his burial in the crypt of the Pantheon a week later. (This also signaled an end to the 10-years-dead rule). A million people lined the

Saint-Etienne-du-Mont

Paris churches can be impressive or imposing, Gothic or grotesque, Baroque or repaired, but they are never quirky and charming—with the exception of Eglise St-Etienne-du-Mont. This odd little church dates mostly from the 16th century, with a 17th-century façade. The interior is a strangely elegant mix of Gothic and Renaissance details.

*An ornate gallery runs across the church, separating the nave from the chancel. This is the rood screen (*jubé*) an addition to many churches in the 15th and 16th centuries reflecting an outlook in Catholicism of the period that called for a barrier between the priest's reading in the chancel and the congregation's understanding in the nave. The upper portion of the* jubé *also served as the rostrum from which sermons were given. Most rood screens were dismantled after an 18th-century revision of that point of view and this is now the only one in Paris (there are few elsewhere in France). Remains of St. Geneviève saved from the Revolution are in a reliquary in the chancel.*

route from the Arc de Triomphe to the Pantheon in a grandiose and moving procession honoring France's most famous literary figures of the 19th century, author of *Les Misérables* and *The Hunchback of Notre-Dame* as well as numerous poems, poems, essays and articles. He was also known as a militant defender and promoter of a republican form of government whose moral outlook needn't be governed by clergymen.

Since then the Pantheon has no religious function, though the religious symbols have been left intact, including the cross at the top. In the past century two dozen statesmen, presidents, scientists and authors have been "pantheonization," including the writer Emile Zola (1908); Jean Jaurès (1924), France's most celebrated socialist assassinated ten years earlier; Victor Schoelcher (1948), who was instrumental abolishing slavery in French colonies exactly a century earlier; professor Louis Braille (1952), transferred on the centennial of his death; resistance fighter Jean Moulin (1964); economist Jean Monnet (1988), a founding father of European union, and writer and statesman André Malraux (1996). Of the others, many ring only distant bells of historical memory, at most, for the average Frenchman and few will be known to foreign visitors.

A first woman joined the great men of France in 1995 when the remains of Marie Curie, discoverer of radium (which eventually killed her), winner of the Nobel Prize for Physics in 1903 and of the Nobel Prize for Chemistry in 1911, were moved here along with those of her husband Pierre, with whom she shared the 1903 prize.

Alexandre Dumas, author of *The Count of Monte Cristo, The Three Musketeers,* and other cinematographic novels, became the latest addition to the Pantheon when his remains were transferred here in autumn 2002.

The crypt of the Pantheon has space for 300 tombs, of which 227 remain empty. In other words, the Pantheon has a great future ahead of it—provided anyone can agree on whom to placed here.

Rue Mouffetard

Approached from behind the Pantheon or metro Place Monge.

La Contrescarpe: If cafés are the shared living rooms of Paris, then those on Place de la Contrescarpe, at the top of rue Mouffetard, are its collective verandas. Rue Mouffetard has long been a student hang-out of choice—cafés, bars, cheap restaurants, record stores, bookstores, a bowling alley—but you don't need a student ID to appreciate this village-like square set around a fountain, where few cars disturb the atmosphere. Hemingway lived around the corner at 74 rue du Cardinal Lemoine from 1922-1923.

If cafés are the shared living rooms of Paris, then those on Place de la Contrescarpe are its collective verandas.

Mouffetard Market: The bottom of rue Mouffetard becomes the heart of this "village" in the morning (especially Sunday), when locals stock up at the food shops and open-air stalls near Eglise Saint-Médard. Another outdoor market fills nearby Place Monge (metro Place Monge) on Wed., Fri. and Sun. mornings.

The Arena: Lutetia's Arena (near Place Monge) was built in the 1st century AD and was operational with theater and combats until the end of the 3rd century. The outline of the Arena outline can be seen. Its gladiator field and is now a playground for soccer and pétanque players.

The Botanical Gardens and the Mosque of Paris are nearby (see *Gardens*).

THE SAINT-GERMAIN QUARTER

Metro *Saint-Germain-des-Prés or Mabillon or Odéon.*

Why is St. Germain such a choice quarter for mid- and upscale travelers?

Lifestyle.

The Saint-Germain Quarter isn't about monuments, museums, history or even beauty. As it fans out from the Church of Saint-Germain-des-Prés to the Seine to one side and to the Luxembourg Garden to the other, St. Germain is all about lifestyle, living well, the charms of life in the City of Light and all associated myths and realities. Luxury and extravagance have their place here as do trendy and cool, yet charm is the operative word.

But you can't hang your hat on charm, so what's there to do in Saint-Germain?

Go to the café, examine the boutiques, go back the café, wander picturesque streets, see a couple of churches, return to the café, visit the Saint-Germain Market, see more boutiques, then go back to the café.

Come looking for more and you'll be disappointed, but look just for that and you'll know why 3- and 4-star travelers so love to stay in the Saint-Germain Quarter. (Also, it's very central: the Louvre, the Orsay Museum, Notre-Dame, the Seine, the Luxembourg, all an easy walk away).

Café culture: Café culture pervades all of Paris, but here in the Saint-Germain Quarter it reaches dizzying heights. In other quarters there are monuments to climb from which to gaze out at the city; in Saint-Germain you just takes a seat. For if there is one lesson to be learned about Paris it's that there is no such thing as good city living without a café close by.

The shops and jazz clubs and hotel bars may be smart enough, but the cafés are the real homes of *germanopratin* sophistication. *Germanopratin* is the adjective to describe things relative to the Saint-Germain Quarter. Knowing the word is a true sign of sophistication; using it in conversation is a sign of snobbery. Let that be your guide to staying on the right side of the track.

***Germanopratin* is the adjective to describe things relative to the Saint-Germain Quarter. Knowing the word is a true sign of sophistication; using it in conversation is a sign of snobbery.**

The cafés *Le Flore* and *Les Deux-Magots,* along with *Brasserie Lipp,* are celebrated hang-outs from the 50s. That's when St. Germain became known as the center of the French literary world, its own reputations heightened not only by the presence of a few Nobel Prize winners but also by the local congregation of publishing houses, bookstores, jazz clubs and artsy movie theaters and by the ebb and flow of students from the nearby the Latin Quarter. Did I mention the cafés?

All this literary grace and coffee drinking began at *Le Procope* (13 rue de l'Ancienne-Comédie). Calling itself the oldest literary café in the world, it is at least the oldest in Paris, founded in 1686. Le Procope's golden age was reached in the 18th century when the *Philosophes* (Voltaire, Rousseau, Diderot) met here, occasionally joined by commonsensical Benjamin Franklin during his years in Paris. But for well into the 19th century it remained a gathering place for writers and artists.

Le Flore and Les Deux-Magots remain the brightest stars of the vast constellation of cafés in this quarter and have retained their edge amongst writers and intellectuals, but there are no must-sits in St. Germain. Every café has its aficionados: *Le Bonaparte, La Rhumerie, Le Mabillon, La Pergola, Le Sauvignon, Le Buci,* and so many others. Drink what you will, and when it comes to having a bite keep expectations modest.

Between café stops the old streets of the quarter aren't for historical touring so much as for feel-good walks: rues Bonaparte, Jacob, de Buci, Furstemburg, de l'Echaudé, Saint-André-des-Arts—basically anywhere you step between boulevard Saint-Germain and the Seine has St. Germain charm written all over it, until the Latin Quarter takes over on boulevard Saint-Michel.

Ditto the streets between the boulevard and the Luxembourg Garden, though with more boutiques. **Boutiquing** is the activity of choice along rues de Rennes, du Four, du Dragon, de Grenelle and de Sèvres, which leads to Paris's classiest department store Le Bon Marché.

Saint-Germain-des-Prés: Eglise Saint-Germain-des-Prés (SG-in-the-Fields) is the historical centerpiece of the quarter. The church is a remnant of a powerful abbey that began to develop in the fields outside of Paris in the 6th century. Destroyed during the Norman invasions of the 9th century, the abbey church was rebuilt beginning about the year 1000, starting with the belfry, making it the oldest remaining tower in Paris. Portions of the church behind it also date from the 11th century, however most of the Romanesque architecture of the era was transformed by later Gothic-style additions, beginning with the choir, consecrated in 1163. The Benedictine abbey enjoyed much autonomy and influence until the Revolution, which spared little of the monastic complex other than the church and the abbatial palace behind it.

Saint-Sulpice: The quarter's other major church is the monstrous Eglise Saint-Sulpice (mid-16th–mid-17th centuries). Nothing was too ostentatious for royal and ecclesiastic leaders of the Counter Reformation in their attempt to reassert the kingdom's ties with Catholicism over Protestantism. Everything about Saint-Sulpice is super-sized: the monumental façade and portico, an interior nearly as vast as that at Notre-Dame, huge shell-shaped fonts, a tremendous organ. The enormous square out front is far too big for the quarter, except when the space is used for the occasional antique fair. Visconti's *Fountain of the 4 Bishops* seems lost in the middle of the square. Aside from a handful of faithful inside and several beggars on the portico, the church is often eerily empty, which is part of its attraction. That and some of its side chapels. Delacroix decorated the Chapel of the Holy Angels to the right of the entrance, painting scenes of *St. Michael Slaying the Dragon, Heliodore Driven from the Temple* and *Jacob Struggling with the Angel.*

The Delacroix Museum: Eugène Delacroix (1798-1863) began working on the chapel at age 50, when he was already a recognized master of Romanticism. Declining health made frequent trips to Saint-Sulpice increasingly tiresome from his home on the Right Bank, so he moved to the Saint-Germain Quarter to be closer to the project. His home and workshop at 6 place Furstemberg, behind Eglise Saint-Germain-des-Prés, are now the Delacroix Museum, which would be entirely for-

Jazz in Saint-Germain

The French first started tapping their feet to American music when they discovered ragtime at the Paris World's Fairs of 1889 and 1900. Jazz began to swing the Gallic soul in the 1920s, but it was in the 1950s, when the Saint-Germain quarter asserted itself as the intellectual center Paris, that night-owls at the basement clubs of the area claimed jazz as their own. Elsewhere in Paris, African, Caribbean, Latino and Brazilian rhythms may dominate, but Saint-Germain still favors jazz to nod to rather than music for dancing. The quarter's jazz traditions are maintained at small clubs on rue St-Benoît, such at Bilbouquet (#13). In the Latin Quarter, Caveau de la Huchette (5 rue de la Huchette) and Le Petit Journal (71 bd. Saint-Michel) are other classic jazz haunts. The bars of 4-star hotels in the Saint-Germain Quarter also occasionally have live jazz trios and quartets.

gettable if the setting weren't so quaint (open 9:30am-12:30pm and 2-5pm; closed Tues. and Wed.). **Place Furstemberg** itself is as cute a little square as you'll find anywhere in Paris.

Saint-Germain Market: The indoor Saint-Germain Market is between Saint-Sulpice and boulevard Saint-Germain. Near the market, the bakery of **pastry artist Gérard Mulot** (76 rue de Seine) is the pastry shop of choice in these quarters. Just visiting the shop is a sweet experience. Quiches and other light lunch dishes are available there along with pastries. Gérard Mulot is well known to Japanese visitors because of several shops in Japan that bear his name.

MONTPARNASSE

The Left Bank gradually slopes up to a hill once far outside the medieval city. Students from the Latin Quarter would come here to party; they called the hill Mont Parnasse (Mount Parnassus) after the mountain sacred to Apollo and the Muses. Little by little the city grew towards it and Montparnasse became the site for revelers of all ages drawn to its cafés and eateries, clubs and theaters. The name of the street rue de la Gaîté and its string of active theaters and sex shops are an echo of that time.

By the end of the 19th century the city had fully enveloped Montparnasse. And over the next generation the Montparnasse Quarter took over from Montmartre as the heart of international bohemian bustle while staking its own claim as center of the art world. Montmartre was old news, Montparnasse was new. Artists had once rallied around the workshops of the Bateau-Lavoir in Montmartre, now they only talked about La Ruche (Passage de Danzig, 15th arr.) in Montparnasse.

By the end of WWI Montparnasse had become the heart of Modernist bohemia: Chagall, Modigliani and Zadkine were joined in the cafés by Russian exiles Lenin and Trotsky, and the poetry of Apollinaire, Breton and Cocteau was in the air along with the music of Satie and Stravinki, while George Gershwin composed *An American in Paris,* and Prokofiev worked as a Russian in the City of Light (see *Restaurants: Foreign Cuisines/Russian*).

Montparnasse Cemetery: Some of the men and women of the arts associated with the Montparnasse and Saint-Germain Quarters lie in the Montparnasse Cemetery, including Charles Baudelaire, Guy de Maupassant, Jean-Paul Sartre and Simone de Beauvoir, Charles Garnier (architect of the opera), Tristan Tzara, César Frank, Saint-Saëns, Samuel Beckett, and the sculptors Zadkine (see below), Rude (*La Marseillaise* on the Arc de Triomphe) and Bertoldi (*Statue of Liberty*). The cemetery's entrance is from bd. Edgar Quintet.

The Montparnasse Tower

Metro *Montparnasse.* ***Open*** *April-Sept. 9:30am-11:30pm, Oct.-March 9:30am-10:30/11pm. Tickets for the 56th and 59th floor observation decks are taken from the square on the western side of the tower. A separate entrance and elevator goes to the restaurant Le Ciel de Paris (see Restaurants). The Montparnasse Mall is just in front of the tower.*

Construction of the 59-floor Montparnasse Tower and the mall nearby wiped out many of the deteriorating remnants of Montparnasse's heyday of 1905-1940, but in doing so it added a superb view over the city. Despite the historical pleasure of rising in the Eiffel Tower, the better view over Paris is from the Montparnasse Tower; not only is it more central, but from here you can fully admire the beauty of the Eiffel Tower and the carpet of grass leading to it from the Military Academy (*Ecole Militaire*). From the Eiffel Tower you merely suffer the eyesore of the Montparnasse Tower. It's a like living in an ugly 1970s apartment building and facing a decorative fin de siècle stone building: they've got the history, but you've got the view.

The great cafés and brasseries

Metro *Vavin.*

Remnants of old Montparnasse are visible in the first-generation metro entrances by Hector Guimard circa 1900-1910 and the second-generation signs circa 1924-1930. But what speaks most of the life of old Montparnasse, and what is most appealing today, are the ever-popular cafés, brasseries and bars that developed in the 1920s at the intersection of boulevard de Montparnasse and boulevard Raspail:

La Coupole, one of Paris's most famous and largest brasseries, which manages to draw both old-time Parisians and international tourists. The music in its basement dance-hall/nightclub is as up-to-date today as it was in the 20s;

Le Dôme, still serving a mean (and pricey) seafood platter along with its glitzy period décor;

La Rotonde, formally one of the top hot spots, now noteworthy mostly for its view of the intersection;

Le Select, an American favorite since it opened in 1924. Le Select remains Montparnasse's literary café par excellence if for no other reason than that people, often sporting facial hair, still write here in the morning, even if some of the scribbling is done on business documents.

One-man museums

A visit to the Montparnasse Quarter could consist of nothing more than a cup of coffee at the café Le Sélect and/or the view from the top of the Montparnasse Tower. But an extended itinerary could also include two worthwhile one-man museums, the Bourdelle Museum at one end of the quarter and the Zadkine Museum at the other.

Bourdelle Museum. ***Address*** *18 rue Antoine-Bourdelle, 14th arr.* ***Metro*** *Falguière or Montparnasse.* ***Open*** *Daily 10am-6pm except Mon. Free except during temporary exhibitions.* The expanded home and workshop of Antoine Bourdelle (1861-1929) displays the sculptor's admirable sense of form and balance as seen in his most well known work, *Hercules Archer*, as well as in models of some of his monumental pieces shown here.

Zadkine Museum. ***Address*** *100 bis rue d'Assass, 6th arr.* ***Metro*** *Vavin or RER Port Royal.* ***Open*** *Daily 10am-5:40pm except Mon. Free except during temporary exhibitions.* The Cubist and African influences on Ossip Zadkine's work, presented in the sculptor's workshop and garden, offer a delicious contrast with the rounded edges of Bourdelle's work. Zadkine (1890-1967) worked at the opposite side of Montparnasse from Bourdelle, between the great cafés of the quarter and the Luxembourg Garden. He lived, worked and taught in New York during WWII, and after his return to Paris he was frequently visited by American art students.

Americans in Paris in the 1920s

Ever since Benjamin Franklin and Thomas Jefferson came courting France to assist in the American cause, Americans have been fascinated by Paris more than by any other foreign capital. Paris: the very name had an aura of sophistication and savoir-vivre where one lived surrounded by art, architecture, philosophy and fashion (as well as revolution). And by the end of the 19th century Paris called to mind artistic experimentation and sexual freedom as well. But it wasn't until the end of World War I that Americans fully got into the act. British tourists had once set the tone for travel to the City of Light, but after WWI Americans began arriving in significant numbers and taking full advantage of the strong dollar/cheap franc.

Paris: the very name had an aura of sophistication and savoir-vivre where one lived surrounded by art, architecture, philosophy and fashion... artistic experimentation and sexual freedom.

Most were just visiting, but a sizeable expatriate community also developed. On the one hand Paris attracted artists, writers and musicians and on the other hand representatives of American wealth, heirs of 19th century industry. Some sought to integrate into local society, others stayed apart within the expatriate community, yet together they established an American love affair with Paris (and with the Riviera) that has been with us—and with the French—ever since.

For American artists born 1890-1900—what Gertrude Stein called the "lost generation"—Paris in the 1920s provided a distance from the United States from which they would reaffirm their very Americanness. Today their names are a roll call not only of those who experienced expatriate life in Paris when in their 20s and 30s, but of artists whose work would define American culture back home: Ernest Hemingway, Ford Madox Ford, F. Scott Fitzgerald, John Dos Passos, e.e. cummings, Aaron Copland, George Gershwin, Archibald MacLeish, Josephine Baker, Dorothy Parker.

Here are a some famous Americans associated with Paris in the 1920s.

Josephine Baker (1906-1975). In 1925, Baker rode into Paris on the wave of jazz and African-American music that thrilled Paris nightlife in the 1920s. She stood out in the *Negro Revue* at the Théâtre des Champs-Elysées, then became a celebrity with her wild and sensual *Banana Dance* performed at the Folies-Bergère. Having gained a respect that she felt would have been unavailable to her back home, she settled in France for the long run. Her reputation here goes beyond that of a black woman wearing bananas. Baker served in the French Red Cross and in the Resistance, using her professional travel as a cover for work as a military intelligence agent. She was subsequently awarded the Legion of Honor by Charles de Gaulle. After the war she founded a rainbow family by adopting 12 children of diverse ethnicity.

Nathalie Barney (1876-1972). Barney held a celebrated literary-artistic salon at her home at 20 rue Jacob from 1909 to 1968 that enjoyed its heyday in the 20s and 30s. She was one of a number of openly lesbian Americans involved in the expatriate literary and artistic community of the Left Bank.

Sylvia Beach (1887-1962). Creator of the lending library and bookshop Shakespeare and Company, Beach, with her lover Adrienne Monnier, formed a literary and business team that became central to British and American travelers and expatriates. Closely linked Modernist writers, Barney is above all associated with James Joyce, whom she championed to the point of publishing of his seminal novel *Ulysses* in 1920.

Janet Flanner (1892-1978). Flanner wrote her "Letter from Paris" for the New Yorker from 1925 to 1975 while living at the Hôtel Saint Germain des Prés, 36 rue Bonaparte.

Ernest Hemingway (1899-1961). Hemingway, who discovered Paris in 1918 at the age of 20, knew some of the best bars on the Right Bank (see *Bars: Harry's Bar and the Ritz*) along with his friend and rival Fitzgerald (himself a thoroughly Right-Bank man), but he otherwise did his drinking and writing on the Left Bank. A macho darling of the literary expat community, he frequently lived in Paris (in various Left Bank apartments) through the 20s and periodically thereafter, making sure that he was here in 1944 to take part in the liberation... of the bar at the Ritz.

Gerald (1888-1964) and **Sara** (1883-1975) **Murphy**. The archetype of wealthy American heirs in the playground of Paris and the Riviera in the 20s and 30s, the Murphys were major figures of expatriate life in France, both as generous patrons of the arts and as leaders in the movement to Americans summering in Antibes (at their celebrated Villa America). Gerald briefly revealed his own talents as a painter once in Paris while Sara nurtured and financed American writers (Hemingway, Fitgerald, Dos Passos) and artists and was also famously friends with Picasso. Gerald was heir to the Mark Cross luxury goods fortune while Sara and her sister Hoytie, another presence on the Paris scene, were heiresses to American industrialist Frank Wiborg. Returning to the U.S., the Murphys were influential in the development of artist colonies on Long Island, N.Y.

Winnie Singer, Princesse de Polignac (1865-1942). Heiress to the Singer sewing machine fortune, Winnie Singer, whose mother was French, spent much of her life in France and Italy. In 1893 she wed the Prince de Polignac, 30 years her elder, in a marriage of European aristocracy and American industry that flourished with mutual respect in which his boyfriends and possibly her girlfriends mingled at their high society parties. The prince died in 1901, but between her money and his title she had all doors open to her in Paris. Singer was a devoted and knowledgeable patron of the arts of dance and music who drew many of the greats of her time to the artistic salon she held until 1939.

Gertrude Stein (1874-1946). An imposing figure of the literary and artistic expatriatehood of the Left Bank, Stein was an art collector, an experimental writer, and a genius-in-residence of her own artistic salon, where she enjoyed the intellectual challenge of younger male artists and writers (e.g. Hemingway, Fitzgerald, Pound), whom she described as the "Lost Generation." She lived at 27 rue de Fleurus, just west of the Luxembourg Garden, from 1903-1938 before moving to 5 rue Christine, near the Seine. In 1907 she met **Alice B. Toklas** (1877-1967), who moved in with her three years later. They are buried together at Père Lachaise Cemetery.

NAPOLEON'S PARIS

Napoleon Bonaparte (1769-1821) is one of the most important and complex figures of French and European history. At once idolized and reviled, he was both a dictator and a major force in creating the modern civil French state, a man with a vision of Europe yet a terror to the continent, an heir to revolution and a domestic peacemaker. He remains a major object of study and fascination in France and abroad for historians, military buffs, aspiring soldiers, soldier-statesmen, and short men with large egos... as well as for us as we visit the sites described in this section.

The Rise and Fall of Napoleon (Bonaparte) I

1793-1798: Rise of the Little Corporal

Born in Corsica, to a family considered too pro-French for him to join the ranks of Corsican patriots, Napoleon Bonaparte set off to make his career in the French army, which became the Revolutionary French army by the time he was ready to rise through in the ranks. He got noticed through his actions in support of the Convention and then the Directory that governed the young republic, and before he was 30 Napoleon was leading the front.

1796-7: Italian campaign. In 1796 he led French forces on a military campaign in Italy that unified and strengthened the French army and revealed the Little Corporal to be both a brilliant strategist and an inspiring leader. From his victorious return from Italy in 1797 until his final exile in 1815 he was the dominating factor in Europe, the last Frenchman to make the English and German armies tremble.

1798-9: Egyptian campaign. He then struck the British Empire via Egypt, furthering his reputation as a hero in France and a danger in Europe. Elsewhere in Europe the French were meeting with mixed success, while back at home, coup d'état followed coup d'état in Paris and royalist and peasant uprisings left pockets of civil war in the young republic.

1799-1804: First Consul

Bonaparte returned to France in November 1799 and joined the political fray head on in a coup that placed him among a troika in charge of the government. December saw the establishment of a new constitution creating the Consulate, and Bonaparte became First Consul.

Declaring an end to the "romance or revolution," he set about creating viable administrative, legal, accounting and banking structures that steadied the country and solidified the groundwork of the modern French state. Despite his autocracy, promotion by merit, the separation between Church and State, educational opportunities, and conditions amenable to free enterprise all took shape during his reign as First Consul Bonaparte and then as Emperor Napoleon I.

1801: The Concordat. Forging a compromise between the atheistic heritage of the Revolution and the Catholic heritage of the Ancien Régime, a concordat arranged between Bonaparte and Pope Pius VII regulated relations between France and the Vatican, thereby quelling the inflammatory demands of the clergy and their followers while ensuring religious freedoms.

1802: Creation of the Legion of Honor, awarded for military valor and civil service, thereby placing an emphasis on merit rather than birth and privilege.

1803: Sale of Louisiana to the United States. The French possession of Louisiana, a great swath of largely undeveloped land around the Mississippi Valley, had been ceded to Spain in 1762 but was returned to France in 1800. Intent on concentrating resources and energy on its European aspirations, Napoleon sold the 800,000-square-mile possession to the U.S. for $15 million, doubling the size of the U.S.

1801-1814, 1815: Emperor Napoleon I

By 1804, Napoleon, increasingly dictatorial since becoming First Consul, held full control of the country and was crowned Emperor Napoleon I by Pope Pius VII at Notre-Dame, creating the (First) Empire and an imperial court.

Civil achievements: Notwithstanding his domestic dictatorship and military terrorization of Europe, he fully assumed the role of righting France's administrative and legal systems that had been overturned by the Revolution and continued to create the civil systems of a modern state, giving him a historical role in France that extends well beyond the battlefield. He brought to fruition the Civil or Napoleonic Code that has formed the basis of French law ever since. He allowed the development of civilian rule, but having risen through the military he would eventually fall through his military endeavors.

Master of continental Europe: Victory after victory gained ground for the French empire in Europe (although his blockade of England failed) mounting towards a stirring victory over Russian and Austrian forces at Austerlitz in 1805. By 1808 Napoleon I was the master of continental Europe. His brothers sat on the thrones of Holland and Westphalia, with other family members and loyal marshals in power or heirs to power from Italy to Spain to Sweden. He briefly created a form of European unity well before its time. The pope, too, was forced to bend to his will. And when the emperor's son was born he was immediately called the King of Rome. Napoleon appeared invincible. But by 1809 France was overextended in Europe, and the strain soon began to be felt.

1812-1813. The Russian Campaign and Defeat. In 1812, Napoleon's decision to gather French and allied forces into a *grande armée* to bring Russia to its knees proved disastrous. He managed to reach Moscow, but the Russian campaign not only devastated Russia but his own army as well, and the defeat was accentuated during the autumn retreat, which further decimated the Grande Armée. This was followed by an alliance between Russia and Prussia and a further defeat in Austria in 1813. By March 1814 the coalition against the

French Empire was knocking at the gates of Paris.

1814-1815. First abdication and exile. Deposed by the Senate, Napoleon abdicated on April 6, 1814 (see *Châteaux: Fontainebleau*) and went into exile on the Isle of Elba, off the coast of Italy. The throne was offered to Louis XVI's brother, Louis XVIII, who then returned from his own exile in England to restore the Boubon dynasty and a modified version of the *ancien régime*. The coalition against France forced the nation back to its borders of 1792.

March-June 1815. The Hundred Days. Less than a year after his abdication, Napoleon, in the "Flight of the Eagle" from Elba, returned to France, where the army quickly rallied behind him. Louis XVIII again fled the country. Napoleon and his army then set off to retake Belgium. At Waterloo Napoleon met his final defeat when he encountered a coalition of armies, mostly English and Prussian, led by the Duke of Wellington. Again forced to abdicate, he was exiled to the remote South Atlantic island of St. Helena, a British possession, where he died in 1821. His remains were returned in a grandiose ceremony in 1840 and he was eventually entombed at the Invalides.

Napoleon's Wives

In 1796 Napoleon I married Josephine de Beauharnais (1763-1814), whose first husband had been guillotined during the Revolution. Napoleon had the marriage annulled in 1809 on the basis of her inability to bear him a child (she'd had two children with her first husband) so that he could marry the much younger Marie-Louise (1791-1847), daughter of Francis I, Austrian Emperor, formerly the last Holy Roman Emperor. Marie-Louise gave birth to a son in 1811 (see Napoleon's Tomb).

THE ARC DE TRIOMPHE

Metro/RER *Charles-de-Gaulle Etoile.* ***Open:*** *daily 10am-11pm, until 10:30pm Oct.-March.*

At first glance the Arc de Triomphe is merely monumental and neither very original nor particularly French, and it isn't especially old, only now approaching its 200th anniversary. Still, it is one of the most remarkable and important monuments in the city and has retained its symbolic value since it contains the Tomb of the Unknown Soldier.

Construction: The powers that be had wanted to put some monumental marker on this hill on the edge of the city for half a century before Napoleon I took a firm stand. In 1806 he commanded that an arch be built in true Roman fashion, only bigger, to glorify his victories and honor his generals and armies. Its feet had barely been set in place when Napeoleon's second wife, Marie-Louise, was due to enter the city, so a trompe l'oeil arch was thrown up with scaffolding to greet her. It had yet to be completed when Napoleon was forced into exile. His successor, Louis XVIII started work up again in 1823, but the arch wasn't completed until 1836, in time for the dramatic return of Napoleon's remains in 1840.

Parades and Ceremonies: The Arc de Triomphe has

become a major passage on the parade route through Paris, most noteworthy upon the return of Napoleon's own remains from exile and those of Victor Hugo on his way to entombment at the Pantheon—19th century reflections of French military glory on the one hand and cultural glory on the other. The arch took on even greater significance on Nov. 11, 1920, when one of 1.4 million Frenchmen who had been killed during the Great War was placed in the Tomb of the Unknown Soldier. He was one of a total of 9 million casualties of WWI, another of which became The American Unknown Soldier buried at Arlington National Cemetery. The Flame of Remembrance at the tomb is rekindled daily at 6:30pm. The president lays a wreath on the mornings of May 8 (V-E Day), July 14 (National Holiday), and Nov. 11 (Armistice Day).

Hitler and his men marched through the arch to show their strength as an occupying force during WWII. Charles de Gaulle and his men marched this way to mark the end of their occupation; a statue representing the general descending the Champs-Elysées stands at the base of the Champs-Elysées by the Grand Palais. Today, the July 14 military parade in honor of the French national holiday passes solemnly around it, and several days later the Tour de France races in front of it on its final stage. Daily, some of the 1.6 million cars that circulate in Paris and on its ring road make it around the circle with limited damage.

Decorations: Allegorical sculptures decorate the front and back legs of the arch, the most dramatic and famous being that on the front right when facing the arch from the Champs-Elysées, *Departure of Volunteers in 1792*, also known as *The Marseillaise*, by François Rude. Napoleon is seen being crowned as Roman-style emperor on the left leg of the arch. The names of generals and battles from 1792-1814, i.e. from the birth of the republic to the fall of Napoleon I, are engraved on the monument. The avenue leading out of the city from the Arc de Triomphe is named for Napoleon's Grande Armée.

Visiting the arch: To reach the monument, take the underground passage from the top of the Champs-Elysées. If you intend to go to the top of the arch take a ticket by the stairs at the end of the tunnel. Otherwise just go up to the ground level. The top is accessible by stairs only, though older or handicapped visitors may be able to convince the elevator operator to take them on the lift. At 164 feet, the top offers a fabulous view of the city as you look down the twelve radiating avenues that give the circle its name Etoile, meaning Star. Come also to learn the number one lesson in driving before renting a car in France: the car coming from the right has the right of way.

La Marseillaise

The French national anthem was composed in 1792 by an officer based in Strasbourg on the eve of war against Austria and was originally known as "The Battle Song of the Army of the Rhine." But its fame came from its being sung by volunteer soldiers of the Revolutionary army from Marseille. It was adopted by the government on July 14, 1795, but as a revolutionary song of the republic it was banned under Napoleon I and his successor Louis XVIII and again by Napoleon III. It was finally adopted as the national anthem in 1879. Official and semi-official attempts have occasionally been made to modify its militaristic and bloody lyrics.

The Champs-Elysées

***Metro** Charles-de-Gaulle Etoile, George V or Franklin D. Roosevelt. The Paris Tourist Office is toward the top of the avenue at #127.*

Avenue des Champs-Elysées rises with a flourish from Place de la Concorde and radiates in triumph at the arch at the top of the hill. From there the perspective leading out from the Tuileries continues along the avenue de la Grande Armée, named for Napoleon's allied forces, and eventually out of the city to the business suburb called La Défense, which has its own arch to draw the eye even further west, tracing a line toward Saint-Germain-en-Laye, birthplace of Louis XIV. The avenue and the perspective recall the glories of France; the nation's setbacks, such as Hitler's parade down the avenue, aren't forgotten so much as overshadowed.

But despite its monumental status and its role as a site for parades and celebrations, the Champs-Elysées is above all a thoroughfare, a walkway, a shopping mall and all the mundaneness that implies. Palatial hotels, high fashion shopping, top-notch restaurants, multinational corporations, international law firms, private residences representing exceptional wealth, and the people behind all of those are found or hidden on the streets and avenues radiating out from the Champs, particularly those running south, leaving the avenue itself to show the more common side of commercial success.

Origins: Originally an alley for royal promenades beyond the Tuileries Garden in the 17th century, the path up the hill became known in the early 18th century as the Champs-Elysées, the Elysian Fields, the happy home of the good after death in classical mythology. Nobles began building mansions out beyond Place de la Concorde—Thomas Jefferson lived at what is now #92 on the avenue from 1785 to 1789 while ambassador to France—but even when the Arc de Triomphe was built in the early 19th century the avenue was little more than a suburban stretch for general distraction. Over the next century, though, the avenue and its surrounding streets became famous for their spacious airs of luxury.

The Mall: The Champs-Elysées may have once deserved the title of "The most beautiful avenue in the world" but its offerings now make it indistinguishable from any other grand avenue in Europe or America, Planet Hollywood and all. There are some special touches here and there, but the Champs can easily appear as an international version of a highway outside Anytown, USA, bordered by fast food outlets, car dealerships, shopping centers, blockbuster movie houses. Nevertheless, like a strip mall leading to the Grand Canyon, it retains a certain grandeur and we are happy to be footloose in Paris: here we are strolling along the famous avenue, here we are on a sidewalk café, here we are admiring the expanse up and down the Champs, here we are people-watching in one of the great tourist melting pots in the world.

The Chic: Champs-Elysées the imperial takes over from Champs-Elysées the commercial at the Rond-Point des Champs-Elysées (metro Franklin D. Roosevelt), where avenue Montaigne breaks off on a most discreet jaunt into the territory of haute couture. The Champs may not in itself be star-studded, but the streets and avenues flow-ing from the southern sidewalks are dripping in it.

The Perspective: Beginning at the Rond-Point, the lower portion of the avenue is bordered by trees and gardens interrupted only by theaters and fine restaurants. Next stop, Place Clemenceau (metro Champs-Elysées Clemenceau), where Charles de Gaulle is seen striding down the symbolic avenue as he re-entered the freed French capital in August 1944. Place Clemenceau offers another one of those wonderful perspectives that Paris has managed so well to create over the centuries. This perspective leads with heart-aching grandeur to the golden dome of the Invalides by way of Paris's most elegant bridge. The Alexandre III Bridge, completed in time for the World's Fair of 1900, was built in honor of the Russian czar with whom France had signed an alliance several years earlier. French and Russian river nymphs face the river on either side, while bronze cherubs and candelabra decorate the railing, and gilt Pegasuses struggle to take flight from the pillars.

Avenue Winston Churchill, leading to the bridge, is bordered by the Grand Palais and the Petit Palais, also remnants of the World's Fair of 1900. The Petit houses a permanent collection of art from the 18th and 19th centuries. The Grand, one of the city's major temporary exhibition spaces when its magnificent glassy and steel roof isn't falling apart, is undergoing extensive renovation that could last until 2007. Nevertheless, portions remain open for major temporary exhibits. The dramatic sculptural flights of horses from the roof of the Grand Palais have meanwhile been removed. But even without them to draw the eyes across the river, the lure of the expanse to the Invalides is tough to resist. That's the problem with perspective: don't have enough and you just follow the pack, have too much it's hard to decide which way to turn.

While considering your next move, turn your back to the Invalides to glimpse, beyond the park and the black gate, the Palais de l'Elysées, the official residence of the President of the Republic.

PLACE DE LA CONCORDE

***Metro** Place de la Concorde.*

Day or night, Place de la Concorde offers one of the great ah-Paris views of the city. An entire guidebook of monuments comes into view: the Eiffel Tower, the Arc de Triomphe, the Invalides, the Obelisk, the National Assembly, etc. At sunset, the view from the Tuileries side of the square is pure enchantment as the sun passes below the horizon along the Seine and lights go on at the numerous monuments within view and, voilà, Paris by day becomes Paris by night.

The square is the hinge where the east-west perspective from the Arc de Triomphe du Carroussel near the Louvre to the Arc de Triomphe on the hill meets the north-south perspective from the National Assembly to the Madeleine—all four of these monuments due to Napoleon.

The octagonal square itself, completed in 1775, was created by Louis XV's architect Jacques-Anges Gabriel to open the city out to the west. The two palaces on the square date from that time; the one on the right now serves as the Ministry of the Navy, the one on the left is partially occupied by the top-end Hôtel Crillon. The American ambassador's residence and consulate are respectively to the left and right when facing the palaces.

As a royal square, it originally offered a rich frame for a statue of Louis XV that was placed at the center. But its royal splendor faded with the fall of the ancien régime; the statue was removed, the square was renamed Place de la Révolution, and the guillotine was set up to execute the sentence of Louis XVI on Jan. 21, 1793 (see *Death in Paris: The Guillotine*). Initially placed on the northwest corner, the guillotine was soon moved to the eastern side of the square, nearer the Tuileries. Queen Marie-Antionette was executed there on Oct. 16 of the same year. The beheadings accelerated during the Terror, 1794-1795, which reigned until Robespierre and his advocates passed beneath the "national razor" on July 28, 1795.

The square's renaming as Place de la Concorde indicated the arrival of more domestically peaceful times. Napoleon ordered the construction of the Church of the Madeleine to the north of the square as a further connec-

Napoleon and the Louvre

While emperor residing in the Tuileries Palace, Napoleon I ordered major work on the Louvre. He set out to renovate the old revolution-weary palace and transform it into Europe's greatest museum-palace. The Louvre already housed hoards of works of the former royal collection. To them Napoleon added the war booty that flowed into France following the victories of his armies, particularly from Italy. Near the Louvre, at the entrance to the Tuileries Palace, he ordered the construction of the Arc de Triomphe du Carrousel, celebrating his victories, and topped it with famous horses taken from the Saint Mark in Venice. Though France was obliged to return vast amounts of artworks after the final fall of Napoleon, including those horses, his successors remained attached to his vision of the Louvre as the world's greatest museum.

Napoleon and Egyptomania

Napoleon's initial Egyptian campaigns of 1789-9 kindled a fascination with Egyptology that included the enigma of the Rosetta stone, a stone brought back by one of the Little Corporel's capitains, Jean-François Champollion. The stone was inscribed in 196 B.C. with an edict whose Egyptian hieroglyphics couldn't be deciphered. In 1822 Champollion finally broke the code of hieroglyphics for the modern world. His discovery sparked another bout of Egyptomania that would give rise to the Louvre's Egyptian collection, overseen by Champollion himself. In 1829, the Viceroy of Egypt offered France the 3300-year-old Obelisk from the Palace of Luxor, whose hieroglyphics were then readable on Place de la Concorde.

tion between his empire and the glories of classical antiquity. The Palais Bourbon across the river already existed as a palatial home of high nobles. It was confiscated during the Revolution and renovated to eventually serve as the Chamber of the Deputies, now called the National Assembly, the major chamber of French parliament. Napoleon merely transformed the façade to put it in harmony with that of the Madeleine.

The statues surrounding the square represent eight cities of

France. The 3300-year-old Obelisk at the center was a gift from Egypt in 1829. Copies of the famous Horses of Marly (originals in the Louvre) open the way to the Champs-Elysées. Two winged horses lead the way into the Tuileries Garden. (see *Gardens: The Tuileries* if continuing in that direction.)

The Invalides and Napoleon's Tomb

Metro/RER *Invalides or Metro Latour Maubourg or Varenne. (The Rodin Museum is near the Invalides and might be visited with it. See Museums.)*

Like the Arc de Triomphe, the Invalides is dedicated to the honor of the French military, and particularly to the emperor himself, whose tomb is in the back. It was created, however, by another authoritarian with many victories under his belt: Louis XIV. It was constructed under orders of the Sun King in the 1670s to accommodate "all officers who are crippled, elderly or frail," i.e. *les invalides*. Beyond the bronze canons, Louis the Great on horseback greets visitors at the entrance to the building, surrounded by symbols of power, strength, justice and the sun.

A portion of the building continues to served as a convalescence center for wounded and disabled soldiers but the Invalides now mainly houses the **Museum of the Army**, which displays one of the world's foremost collections of the military arts through the ages, particularly from the Middle Ages until after World War II. Once a dusty old hangout for military aficionados, the museum is now inviting for all. Brief descriptions in English provide sufficient assistance in each section. The collection is far too large to tarry at every display case. Nevertheless, a visit to the museum and Napoleon's Tomb can last 1.5 hours.

The section of medieval armor is always a crowd pleasure, but those concerning the French military from the 17th-19th centuries, on the western side of the museum, and the section of relief maps on the top floor of the eastern side will be noteworthy mainly to military history buffs. The exception to this is the exhibit of Napoleon I memorabilia such as a portrait of the defeated emperor on the eve of his fall, his horse Vizir, which he took with him to exile on St. Helena and which returned to Paris via the taxidermist, and the emperor's death mask. Also of interest due to its relation to our own history are the portions concerning the First and Second World Wars; the displays are naturally intended to honor the French army, not ours.

As a former military hospital there is also "the Soldiers' Church" named for the crusader-king Saint-Louis. It is a simple church of clean lines whose sole decoration was left to the traditional hanging of banners captured from enemy forces. A second church, the former royal church called the Church of the Dome, contains Napoleon's Tomb and is directly behind it. The courtyard of the Invalides and Eglise St-Louis may be visited without actually entering the museum.

Napoleon's Tomb

Without its gilt dome, the Invalides might be viewed as little more than a palatial military complex. With it, this becomes one of the most glorious monuments of the capital. Louis XIV may have had little interest in setting foot in Paris once he moved out to Versailles, yet he gave his city some splendid touches (Place Vendôme, Place des Victoires, front of the Louvre) and none more stunning than this belated addition of 1706 to his Invalides, culminating at 350 feet and outlined with 26 pounds of gold. Napoleon lies beneath, in a tremendous sarcophagus in an open crypt.

Shortly after the Pantheon began honoring the great men to whom the nation was grateful, Napoleon raised Louis XIV's royal church to the ranks of another pantheon, this time to military glory. The Church of the Dome was marked as a military pantheon in 1800 when Napoleon ordered the transfer of the remains of the Grand Turenne, field marshal under Louis XIII and XIV, who was considered the greatest military strategists of the 17th century. But its full consecration came 40 years later with the arrival of the remains of the emperor himself.

Napoleon was originally buried on St. Helena. In 1840 his mortal remains were exhumed and brought to France. On Dec. 15 of that year they were carried in a national funeral of extraordinary pomp and emotion through the Arc de Triomphe, down the Champs-Elysées, and across the Seine to the Invalides, where they then awaited creation of the tomb, a lengthy process finally completed in 1861, during the reign of the emperor's nephew Napoleon III.

The large red porphyry sarcophagus lies on a green granite pedestal and is decorated with laurels and inscriptions recalling Napoleon's victories. It is surrounded first by marble relief sculptures showing the emperor's achievements on behalf of the nation. Napoleon I is invariably shown here, and in most representations, monumentally, imperially, in full glory. He is then surrounded by tombs and monuments of several illustrious names of the military and by his own titled family, including:

• Napoleon II (1811-1832), his son, known as L'Aiglon, the Eaglet. He was born with the title King of Rome, became Prince of Parma at age 3, and Duke of Reichstadt at age 5 but never ruled over anything. In 1814, Napoleon actually abdicated in favor of his son, and Bonapartists therefore considered him as Napoleon II. But once his father went into final exile the boy was never allowed to leave Austria, where he died of tuberculosis. On Dec. 15, 1940, 100 years to the day after the return of his father's remains, the Eaglet's remains were transferred to France, a gift from Adolf Hitler. They were finally placed near his father's tomb in 1969.

• Joseph and Jérôme Bonaparte, Napoleon's brothers.

• Vauban, the 17th-century military architect who designed fortifications around the kingdom under Louis XIV. His heart was placed here in 1846 in a funerary monument bracketed by figures representing Science and War.

• Field Marshall Lyautey, Minister of War during WWI.

• Field Marshall Foch, a important WW1 commander.

Arsenic and Old Ulcers

After six years in exile, Napoleon died on St. Helena at the age of 51. His death mask can be seen in the Museum of the Army in the Invalides. An autopsy performed immediately after his death concluded that Napoleon, who had long had a chronic perforated ulcer, died of stomach cancer, as his father had. But in the 1960s the analysis of locks of his hair, saved as keepsakes, revealed traces of arsenic. Medical debate and conspiracy theories have raged ever since. Was he intentionally poisoned? If so, by whom? Did the arsenic level in his body come from a chemical used in making the decorative elements on his green wallpaper? Could that have killed him or merely made a sick man sicker? Did doctors unwittingly give a man already dying with stomach cancer a substance that precipitated his death?

LATE 19TH-CENTURY PARIS:

LUXURY, FASHION, ENTERTAINMENT AND ART

The sights and quarters visited in this section mostly bear the memory of the period from 1871-1914, from the end of the Franco-Prussian War to the start of World War I, from the completion of the Opera to the completion of Sacré Coeur, from Impressionism to Cubism, from an era of grand dukes and struggling artists to an era of struggling dukes and grand artists. The lasting fame of these quarters comes from their reputation as centers of luxury, fashion, entertainment and art during those years. But the groundwork for all this was laid a generation earlier, during the reign of Napoleon III. Before entering these quarters, then, a bit of imperial history sets the stage.

NAPOLEON III AND THE SECOND EMPIRE: 1848/1852-1871

Napoleon III gets far less attention than his uncle Napoleon (Bonaparte) I, who played a pivotal role in French and European history from 1799 to 1815. He is often seen as a lesser Napoleon with a goatee, a fashion-conscious dictator who engaged France in a disastrous war with Prussia. You will rarely come across his name as you travel in the provinces. Yet the cityscape of Paris today owes more to the reign of Napoleon III than that of any other emperor or king. He oversaw an enormous transformation of Paris that he pursued for two decades. A tremendous amount of changes took place in the capital during his reign as president of the Second Republic then as emperor of the Second Empire: Paris's annexation of neighboring villages and the city's division into 20 arrondissements, the creation or makeover of boulevards and avenues, squares and parks, monumental buildings and train stations, the founding of the haute couture and luxury industries on the central Right Bank, the birth of the palatial hotel, the development of the Woods of Boulogne and Vincennes as leisure centers, the vast extension and renovation of the Louvre, the movement of artists, the working and serving classes to Montmartre, the opening of cabarets and theaters and cafés, the construction of the Garnier Opera.

1848-1852. The Second Republic. The Revolution of 1848 caused the abdication of Louis-Philippe, the last of the kings, and gave rise to the Second Republic and to the presidential election of **Louis-Napoleon Bonaparte (1808-1873)**. (The first republic followed the fall of Louis XVI in 1792 and lasted until Napoleon I declared the first empire in 1804.) The second would be an illusory and short-lived republic. Louis-Napoleon, having spent his youth in exile and having twice attempted coups from without (1836, 1840), organized a coup d'état from within the government and had himself ratified as Emperor Napoleon III, thus instating the Second Empire.

1852-1870. Napoleon III and the Second Empire. After putting down the initial riots that followed his coup, Napoleon III managed a certain harmony within the country. Economic progress sufficiently masked his dictatorship during the first half of his reign: expanding empire, developing railway system, growth of the banking and luxury industries, free trade treaty with Great Britain, inauguration of the Suez Canal, fading of royalist claims, contentment of the imperial aristocracy (see *Châteaux: Compiègne*). When his popularity began to slip in the mid-1860s he gave greater leeway to his government to develop more liberal policies: right to strike, educational reform, more freedom to the press.

In foreign affairs, his attempt to install a pro-French

The Transformation of Paris

Napoleon III looms large in the cityscape of the capital—but the name most associated with many of these transformations is that of ***Baron Haussmann*** *(1809-1891). Baron Haussmann, the prefect of Paris during the emperor's reign, was given the task of overseeing urban planning within the capital. He oversaw the transformation of the medieval city into a modern capital of large boulevards and wide avenues interrupted by major squares and bordered by vast apartment and office buildings constructed in a monumental style known as Haussmann-style. Paris, now defined by those avenues and boulevards, remains a 19th-century city just as New York, defined by its skyscrapers, exemplifies the 20th-century city.*

The creation of Paris's boulevards had already begun under Louis XIV with the removal of ramparts that were no longer necessary for the growing city. Their development as major thoroughfares accelerated under Haussmann's project, which also cut through various quarters of the old city. The traces of former ramparts are visible on the city or metro maps, notably on the Right Bank (line 8 between Madeleine and Bastille, line 2 between Nation and Etoile), but also on the Left. Portions of the old city were heavily occupied by the underclasses, who were then pushed to the northern and eastern edges of the city, further favoring the implantation of the entrepreneurial class and banking and luxury industries on the central Right Bank. The boulevards and avenues had the added advantage of providing the space necessary for troops to maneuver through the city in case of civil unrest of the type that had rocked the city in 1830, 1848 and 1852. They would soon be called into play when the government forces put down the insurrection of 1871.

regime in Catholic Mexico to counterbalance Protestant Anglo-America, in defiance of the Monroe Doctrine, evaporated following a series of interventions (1861-1867), yet France furthered its interests in southeast Asia, North Africa and the Caribbean. Like Napoleon I, Napoleon III sought to assert France's power within Europe, but with neither the force nor success of his uncle... and without counting on the awakening of a militarized Prussian/German state.

1870-1871. The Franco-Prussian War. Provoked by the Prussian quest for dominance in a German empire and Bismark's wider European politics, Napoleon III played into Bismark's hand by declaring war on Prussia on July 19, 1870, only to find France standing alone against the heavily militarized German states. Within six weeks Napoleon III and his troops had been encircled at Sedan (northeastern France). The emperor was then deposed and a Government of National Defense established in Versailles as the Prussian army advanced on Paris. The Prussians lay siege to the capital from Sept. 19, 1870 to Jan. 28, 1871, holding positions on the hill of Montmartre as well as elsewhere surrounding the city.

The proclamation of the German Empire at Versailles on Jan. 18 and the surrender of Paris marked the final maneuvers of the war. While the government negotiated a peace treaty by which France would lose Alsace and most of Lorraine and be required to pay heavy compensation, and while much of the country favored an armistice, more radical groups in Paris refused to disarm. Opposed to the conservative government and to a humiliating peace, a loose group comprised of republican radicals, socialists, anarchists and communists seeking economic and political reform, gathered strength in Montmartre and other working class quarters of the city to form an insurrection known as the Commune of Paris. The Communards, as they were called, quickly took control of the city but within three months they were violently put down by government forces from Versailles. The Bloody Week of May 21-28, 1871 ended with the massacre of militant Communards, but not before City Hall (Hôtel de Ville) and the Tuileries Palace had been burned to the ground and the Napoleonic column on Place Vendôme pulled down.

1871. Birth of the Third Republic. The Franco-Prussian War gave way to the Third

Republic in France and to the German Empire, setting the stage for a chain of events that would eventually lead to the outbreak of WWI. But for a time France lived in relative peace with its neighbors, and Paris led the world in major evolutions in luxury, fashion, lifestyle and the arts. This is what we've come to explore.

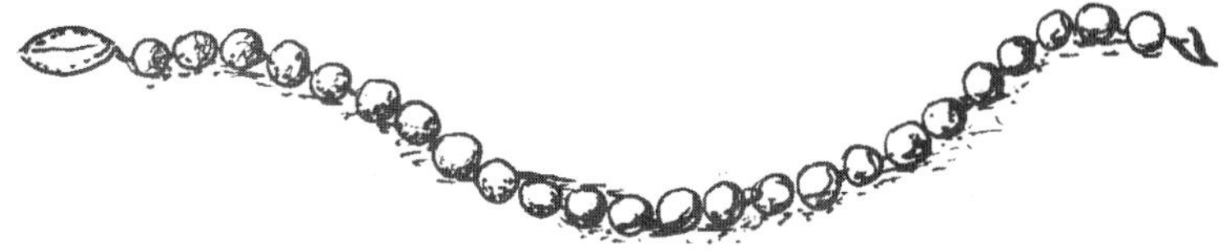

PLACE VENDOME, LUXURY AND THE PALATIAL HOTEL

Metro *Tuileries or Concorde.*

Britain and France were enemy superpowers of Europe for centuries. But ever since Napoleon I's defeat at Waterloo in 1815 their differences have been confined to the spheres of diplomacy and culture, to the sports arena, and to mutual mockery—the English are still as happy calling the French Frogs as the French are calling the English Rosbif (Roastbeef). Even their colonial rivalry remained polite with an entente codiale. And the English have long appreciated France's land and culture, as they still do, from the French-speaking royal family to hoards of English campers.

The Second Empire

British aristocracy defined international travel in Paris from 1850-1914 and played a significant role in the development of the palatial hotel, haute couture and luxury goods industries between rue de Rivoli (bordering the Tuileries Garden and the Louvre) and the Opera. They and other well-heeled visitors stayed at the **Meurice** (opened in 1835), the **Westminster** (to which the duke of same lent his name in 1846), the **Hotel du Louvre** (1855), the **Grand Hotel** (1862), and other palaces. Briefly, there had been Texans here, too; from 1842-1843, 1 place Vendôme, served as the **embassy of the Republic of Texas**, a short-lived sovereign state (1836-1845) that France, in 1839, was the first country to recognize (see *Hotel: Hôtel de Vendôme* for more).

The British, however, were only a portion of the clientele of the budding luxury industry in this quarter near the Tuileries Palace. It developed primarily to serve the needs of Napoleon III and Empress Eugénie and the fashion-conscious imperial court. The needs of the Napoleonic aristocracy for the latest in fine garments and accessories was a major impetus in the birth of the **haute couture** industry as we know it today.

Ex-Empress Eugénie

Napoleon III and Empress Eugénie were exiled to England following France's defeat in the Franco-Prussian War. Napoleon III died there in 1873 and his only son was killed while serving in the British army. Eventually, Eugénie (1826-1920), a wealthy but powerless aristocrat unthreatening to the Third Republic, was allowed to return. She was a striking women of Spanish nobility who, as an elderly ex-empress, still stood for elegance and high fashion as she had when she held court at the Tuileries Palace. Eugénie now stayed at what has become the **Intercontinental** (rue de Castiglione), enjoying grand promenades and endless dinners along with her friends of the French and British aristocracies, who set up camp within a quick stroll or carriage ride of the Tuileries, the Champs-Elysées and the Opera. They were joined by other European aristocrats, high officials, giants of banking and industry, and little by little their American counterparts (see *Left Bank: Americans in Paris.*)

Place Vendôme

Place Vendôme, Louis XIV's royal development project, has been a lap of luxury since it was completed in the early 18th century. The solid unity of the Classical facades on the square is in sharp contrast with the troubled history of the **column** at the center. Befitting its origins as a royal square, an equestrian statue of Louis XIV was first set here but was pulled down during the Revolution. It was replaced in 1806 by a bronze column, made with canons melted down from Napoleon I's voctorious battle at Austerlitz. Its spiraling bas-relief tells tales of Napoleonic glory. A statue of the emperor dressed as Caesar was place on top, but it was toppled along with Napoleon I himself. The Restoration (Louis XVIII) placed royal symbols on top, but eventually Napoleon was returned to the place of honor, first dressed as his diminutive self, and then, under Napoleon III, with a copy of the original Napoleon-as-Caesar. The entire column was pulled down during the Commune of Paris, but it was soon uprighted.

The Belle Epoque

Once the royalist-bonapartist question had been resolved by a long run of the Third Republic, the area by the Tuileries Garden pursued its development as the center for high-style living and travel. The **Hôtel Ritz** opened on Place Vendôme in 1898, followed shortly thereafter by the jeweler **Cartier**. The entire area took on the face of Belle Epoque opulence that marked fashion, art, entertainment and architecture at the turn of the century. **Maxim's** opened its doors on rue Royale to dukes and counts of all nations to luxuriate in the restaurant's effusive Art Nouveau style, not far from the expanding tea room and pastry shop **Ladurée**, while the tearoom Angelina (see below) also attracted the *grandes dames Parisiennes* with its more staid fin-de-siècle style.

Haute couture, meanwhile, continued to make its statements on **rue de la Paix**, the most expensive street on the French Monopoly board, leading from Place Vendôme to the Opera. **The first metro line**, with its Art Nouveau entrances by Hector Guimard, opened in 1900, passing along rue de Rivoli and up the Champs-Elysées. The **Crillon** joined the flock of luxury hotels in 1909 when took over a portion of one of the palaces on Place de la Concorde.

Post-WWI

Increasingly, after WWI, international fashion and luxury expanded on the side streets surrounding the Champs-Elysées (Monopoly's second most expensive property), with the creation of more palatial hotels in that zone. While fashion boutiques still line rue du Fauboug St-Honoré nearby, the flagship homes of haute couture are now on avenue Montaigne, off the Champs-Elysées.

Paris's palatial hotels, simply called *les palaces de Paris* in French, still have their share of French upperclassmen and chin-high Brits (and it is surprising to know just how many officially or unofficially titled persons still circulate in Europe along with the euro), but these hotels are now naturally heavy

Angelina:
Paris's Premier Home for Hot Chocolate

Address *226 rue de Rivoli, 1st arr.* **Metro** *Tuileries.*

Everyone's a character at Angelina: the Japanese women gesticulating at the pastry tray, the American couple lucky enough to speak the other international language, the three posers on their cell phones (at the same table), les dames parisiennes keeping up tradition, me writing up notes after visiting a nearby palace-hotel—in short, anyone who might walk beneath the arcades of the Rue de Rivoli in search of sweet comfort in the middle of the afternoon. Upscale, downscale, pretentious, unpretentious, tourist, local, chic-shoed or sneakered, the wonderful thing about Angelina is that it is accessible to all while maintaining the mystique of 1900 elegance.

This is deservedly Paris's most famous tea room—rather, hot chocolate room, for the teatime drink of choice is Angie's bitter-rich stand-a-straw-in-it hot chocolate sweetened with dollops of whipped cream. In addition to its celebrated hot chocolate, the pastry of choice is the mont blanc, a cool, megarich chestnut cream, pastry cream, and meringue dessert. You'll see plenty of other tempting pastry choices on display at the entrance or being paraded by on trays, but someone at the table's got to order the mont blanc. The chocolate and the pastry are too much for a single person to handle; the hot chocolate is filling enough on its own, while the mont blanc goes down better with tea. (Ordering coffee at Angelina is considered ultrachic.) Travelers who got good grades in pre-school should each order one and then share. As a sign of the richness of it all, this is a rare Paris eat&drinkery where the waitresses (themselves characters one and all) serve water without you having to ask.

As one of Paris's prime 4-5 o'clock settings, there is often a line at Angelina's door in the middle of the afternoon. Don't be put off by the queue, it moves quickly enough. In crowded times you may be asked if the non-smoking section is acceptable—well it isn't! You may want to relax your principles because on a crowded afternoon non-smoking here is a euphemism for "the room in the back."

in Americans, oozing with Saudis, rampant in Russians, courteous to Japanese, etc.

"The more things change the more the stay the same," say the French. Indeed the recent arrival of Tati Or (a jewelry shop opened by the discount department store chain Tati and therefore a tweak at haute everything) (1994), the entrance of luxury jewelers into the portfolios multinational corporations (1990s), and the opening of the Hilton (2002) may represent the chaining of Right Bank luxury, but it is a gold and diamond-studded chain nonetheless, only less unique.

Meanwhile, the Justice Ministry on Place Vendôme is given scant attention, even by the French government.

THE GARNIER OPERA

Metro **Opéra.** ***Open*** *daily for visits and ticket sales 10am-5pm.*

The Garnier Opera is a temple of lyrical music and ballet that has much in common with Notre-Dame Cathedral. Its rooftop green beret topped by a lyre recalls Notre-Dame's green spire topped with a Cross. And like the cathedral, the opera house is a dramatic presence from every angle. Approach it as you wish:

✦ **The regal approach** along avenue de l'Opéra from the Louvre,

✦ **The sophisticated approach** as you round the corner from rue de la Paix,

✦ **The sudden splendor approach** as you emerge from the Opéra metro station (exit/*sortie* Place de l'Opéra/Avenue de l'Opéra), a magical metro exit that is second only to that from the Pont Neuf station.

Baron Haussmann's transformation of the Right Bank left a hole for the crown of the new city to be filled with all the eye-catching opulence that architect Charles Garnier and the Second Empire could muster. The Garnier Opera, so pompous that it's also known as the Garnier Palace, is a delightfully excessive mix of marble and majesty, built at a time when minimalism was what one did for the poor.

Designed in 1860, it defines its era so much that it is *the* monument to the Second Empire. Though it wasn't inaugurated until 1875, five years after the fall of the emperor, it has Napoleon III and Empress Eugénie written all over it, from the ramps on the left side wide enough to receive their imperial carriage to the N's and E's along the brow of the façade.

Having stopped to admire the sculptural work on the outside, particularly the joyous *Dance* to the right of the entrance, the return traveler enters for a tour of the opulence of another era. Visit on your own or on periodic guided tours: the grand staircase, the profusion of marble, the chandeliers, the lounge areas, the crypt-like basement, the theater. Chagall's ceiling (1964) above the theater's tremendous chandelier is the only part of the house that contrasts with the marble and sheen, but it's nonetheless festive.

Since the opening of the Bastille Opera in 1989, the 1991-seat Garnier Opera has been mainly devoted to ballet and light opera. A boutique for opera and dance buffs is in the lobby, as is the ticket booth. Ticket information and the schedule of performances at both opera houses are available on the site www.opera-de-paris.fr.

Café views: Across from the Opera, the **Café de la Paix** is the historic grand café from which to experience the avenue and inhale the exhaust of passing cars and buses. Recently renovated, the café and the Grand Hotel are themselves monuments to late 19th-century luxury and its evolution to date. However, for a spectacular angled view of the façade of the Opera, nothing beats an upstairs window seat at the café/restaurant L'Entracte around the corner on rue Auber. **L'Entracte** (meaning "the intermission") is a wood-paneled, wine-proud café serving respectable bistro fare, where the imaginative traveler can easily spend an hour seeing carriages stopping before the Garnier Opera and letting out men and women dressed to the nines.

Just as Notre-Dame also should be viewed from behind, so too the Garnier Opera. The restaurant and terrace on the top floor of the department store Galeries Lafayette offer a grand view of the back from beneath the store's stunning dome of 1912.

LES GRANDS BOULEVARDS

***Metro** Opéra, Richelieu-Drouot or Grands Boulevards*

Everything is grand around the Opera: the Grand Hotel out front, the *grands magasins* (French for department stores) out back, the *Grands Boulevards* to the east. The French word *boulevard* comes from bulwark, a type of rampart, and came to refer to the wide thoroughfare that developed when ramparts were dismantled. The word now has more general use, which we have inherited, yet Paris's Grand Boulevards, running from the Garnier Opera to Place de la République, return us to the source.

Replacing ramparts that were dismantled in the 17th century, these boulevards were gradually transformed, like the word itself, into something well trafficked, high spirited, too lighthearted to be snobbish, too popular and entertaining to be sophisticated. By the early 19th century *le boulevardier*, Paris's man-about-town, had been born. And during the Second Empire, sporting a goatee and a top hat, the boulevardier and his girl or his pals promenaded along the now-grand boulevards, shopped in the covered passageways that connected boulevards and side streets, attended the theater, spent like sports in the eateries. This became, and remains, Paris's main theater district, where *le théâtre du boulevard*, light comedy, with or without music, was and still is the mainstay of French theater. Many of the theaters still in use are 19th-century houses: the *Opéra Comique* on boulevard des Italiens, the **Folies-Bergères** on rue Richer, the Théâtre des Bouffes-Parisiens, the Théâtre de la Renaissance on boulevard St-Martin. Meanwhile, cafés as we know them today were developing during the Second Empire and become a major presence along the boulevards by the turn of the century, which is why the traditional Parisian café is often imagined as having a Belle Epoque or Art Nouveau décor.

The department stores **Printemps** and **Galeries Lafayette**, on boulevard Haussmann behind the Opera, are both late-19th-century institutions that continued to expand as up-end shopping bazaars at the turn of the century. Printemps added a cupola in 1911 and Galeries Lafayette topped that with its own in 1912.

After WWI the high-end reputation of the Grand Boulevards began to wear off as the entertainment and shopping in the area were increasingly democratized. There is still much that's grand about the boulevards surrounding the Opera. The theaters here are still (subsidized) crowd pleasers. And the boulevards, having played an important role in the birth of cinema, have a concentration of **movie theaters**, from the multiplexes on bd. des Italiens to the city's most imposing movie theater (and concert hall), the Rex, on bd. Poissonnières (metro Bonne Nouvelle). Leaving the Opera Quarter, though, the Grand Boulevards are anything but extraordinary; unlike the boulevards further north they aren't even sufficiently sordid to be alluring. The cafés are overpriced and mundane, the restaurants are unremarkable (however, see *Restaurants: Brasseries/Julien*), and the shopping is of little interest. Still, all of the boulevards have a fair amount of good chi as they bear witness to the life of a nervous city and the strut of the modern-day boulevardier.

MONTMARTRE

Metro *Anvers, Blanche or Pigalle*

Imagining Montmartre 1871-1914

Montmartre is an easy place to visit, its sights and entertainment flamboyant, brash and direct, from Sacré Coeur to the stomping grounds of artists to the Moulin Rouge. As you visit, a little imagination will go a long way. So imagine Montmartre in the last quarter of the 19th century.

Imagine it: Montmartre has been annexed to the capital. The ramparts outlined by lines 2 on the metro map have been torn down. The city has been transformed by Napoleon III and Baron Haussmann's enormous urban renewal project that has torn through the medieval city and created wide boulevards, wiping out many cheap rents along the way. Members of the working and serving class, dissidents, artists, entertainers and prostitutes move up to this hill north of the new boulevards of Clichy and Rochecouart, crowding the former village of Montmartre. The tunnels of former quarries have made the subsoil on top of the hill unstable, sparing it from large-scale development.

Imagine Paris after May 1871: The capital has capitulated, the Prussian army has gone, and the Commune of Paris, born on Montmartre, has been crushed. Montmartre is part of the capital yet removed enough to give it the atmosphere of a large village, an air of rebellion and of bohemia. Manet and Monet have been working against the grain of conventional art. In 1874, Impressionism is born. And Catholic leaders are making plans for a basilica they'd vowed to build if the city were saved from Prussian advances; Sacré Coeur then begins to rise from the top of a hill.

Imagine the last quarter of the 19th century: Artists, writers and composers have favored the area in previous generations, but there is something about the atmosphere now that makes this a bouillon of culture and entertainment attractive to Renoir, Pissarro, Degas, Cezanne, the American Mary Cassette, and others. Van Gogh lives and paints on Montmartre for two years before moving south; he meets Gaugin here. The center for the city's art and nightlife has moved north—not the art and nightlife of the upper bourgeoisie and the aristocracy near the Opera and along the Grand Boulevards, but of the middle and lower classes: new dance halls and cafés and cabarets are opening on the hill and along the northern boulevards. Degas moves between classes as he captures the color, the movement, the life of the city: the laundresses of Montmartre, the dancers and musicians at the Garnier Opera, the joy of the outdoor dance hall at the Moulin de la Galette, the horses and riders at the Longchamps racetrack.

Imagine the Belle Epoque: Mills (*moulins*) have dotted the hill of this former agricultural village for hundreds of years, though increasingly fields and vineyards are being erased by the expanding city. On Place Blanche, beneath a red mill, the Bal du Moulin Rouge raises its curtain—and its skirts—in 1889. Toulouse-Lautrec is here to record the high and low life of Montmartre. The Belle Epoque is alive and well, as it is in the Opera Quarter, but racier and less opulent here. For the artists this is indeed bohemia, *la vie de bohème*, where squalor and artistic hope and despair excite the palette.

Imagine the turn of the century: Montmartre has already become a legend. A new generation of artists has come to stew in Parisian inspiration. The metro is beginning to pass this way, its entrances marked by Hector Guimard's Art Nouveau wrought iron. Picasso has visited several times as a young man between 1900 and 1902 and in 1904 he settles into a studio at the Bâteau-Lavoir, a miserable stirring pot of experimental art, where George Braque, Juan Gris and many others are also painting. The death of Cézanne in 1906 heightens their awareness of his special approach to perspective in terms of volumes. In 1907 Picasso's *Les Desmoiselles d'Avignon* (in NYC's MOMA) is destined to become a defining moment in art history. In 1908, a critic mocks Braque for reducing everything to cubes—hence Cubism—while Modigliani, Utrillo, Dufy, Bonnard and Vuillard, all restlessly settled in Montmartre, are working in other directions. Meanwhile, Sacré Coeur is reaching its final height.

This is the Montmartre we come to visit, Montmartre 1871-1914. By WWI, Cubism's initial energy had worn thin, Sacré Coeur had only to be consecrated, and bohemia had moved to Montparnasse.

Sacré Coeur

Sacré Coeur represents Montmartre in the way that the Mosque of Al-Aqsa represents Jerusalem: its bright and beautiful dome is necessary for the photograph, a splendor to the eye, but unless you're praying there the true interest of a visit is the street, the people, the lifestyle, the yearning.

According to the text of the National Vow to the Sacred Heart, adopted in 1871: "In the face of the misfortunes that are desolating France and the greater misfortunes that may yet to threaten her... We recognize that we have been guilty and rightfully punished... We promise to contribute to the erection in Paris of a sanctuary dedicated to the Sacred Heart of Jesus." Catholic leaders, having raised their vow to a nationally subsidized cause, would have their prayers fulfilled of setting the basilica on the highest part of the city, where it

1848-1905 in Museums

The Orsay Museum is the perfect complement for an exploration of the area covered in this section. It covers not only the art of the era, some of which originated in Montmartre, but also presents architecture and interior design at the turn of the century, including a large model of the Opera Quarter at the time. Displays at the Carnavalet Museum (see The Marais*) present a political overview of this period.*

Mount of the Martyrs

The top of Paris's northern hill has long been a religious site. The Romans built a temple here that was very much in favor when Denis, first bishop of Paris, and two coreligionists attempted to evangelize the area in the middle of the 3rd century. The authorities responded to their politics with their own, ordering them decapitated. Hence the name Montmartre, the evolution of Mont des Martyrs, Mount of the Martyrs. The decapitation is said to have taken place at the site of the small Eglise Saint Pierre around the corner from Sacré Coeur. That church, built on the ruins of the Roman temple, stands on the foundations of a chapel consecrated in 1147, the area's sole remnant of the abbey of Benedictine nuns that occupied the hilltop through the Middle Ages.

Legend has it that Saint Denis, once decapitated, picked up his head, stopped to wash it in a fountain behind the hill, then carried it 10 miles north to the site that would become the town of Saint Denis. The Basilique St-Denis (Metro St-Denis) later became the necropolis of the kings of France. Occasionally from the 6th century then in unwavering tradition from the 10th century, the kings of France were buried there. Design of the basilica predates that of Notre-Dame by almost 30 years and is considered primitive Gothic as it is one of the first churches to implement the new awareness of the architectural possibilities of pointed and crossed arches. The tombs, meanwhile, reveal the evolution of sculpture through the Middle Ages and into the Renaissance. Denis can be seen on the left entrance to Notre-Dame Cathedral holding his decapitated head in his hands.

would be visible to all. They would also see their prophecy of "greater misfortunes" realized even before the basilica could be consecrated. Indeed, though the bright white basilica of Sacré Coeur was built as an act of national hope and atonement following the Franco-Prussian War, it wasn't consecrated until after World War I.

The neo-Byzantine basilica, with King/Saint Louis IX and Joan of Arc standing at the entrance, is impressively showy, but the first temptation when you reach the basilica is to look back down at the city. (Wherever your attention is drawn, beware of the pickpockets that circulate among the crowds in front of Sacré Coeur and by Place du Tertre). Unfortunately, the western part of the city is blocked by buildings and trees. The more startling, if cramped, view of the low, dense capital is from the height of the dome, open 9am-7pm, 5pm in winter. One of the world's largest ringable bells, the Savoyarde, is here. On the way down you'll have a glimpse inside the basilica from its central dome. The crypt is without interest unless you've a special fondness for crypts.

The interior isn't particularly beautiful—it's surprisingly somber in contrast with the bright white exterior—but its atmosphere is far more solemn and soulful than any other Catholic church in the city, including Notre-Dame. The shuffling feet of tourists hasn't prevented Sacré Coeur from staying faithful to the perpetual adoration of the Sacred Heart. This remains an important pilgrimage destination.

PLACE DU TERTRE

Place du Tertre, the central square of village Montmartre, known to millions of travelers as "the place where the artists gathered," is fully given over to tourism. At street level the square and neighboring streets are reminiscent of Main Street Disney, which attempts to capture the same era in small-town U.S.A., except that you can drink all you want here and employees don't smile as much.

But the buildings atop Montmartre truly do recall the village of the late 19th century. Despite first impressions, all is not glossy tourism up here: the Sunday tea dance at La Bohème du Tertre, the corny dinner-cabaret show at La Bonne Franquette (subject of a painting by Van Gogh), the glimpses of Sacré Coeur looming nearby. In fact, there's much appeal (in small doses) to the touristy area, especially in the morning when it's less crowded—and in winter when it's easier then to imagine Van Gogh in an unheated garret writing to his brother for more paint. And nightfall on the steps of Sacré Coeur offers a moment of romance and unction that is the stuff of dreams of lonely backpackers, non-communicating couples, doubting Catholics and cynical travel writers.

Climb and Descent

There are a number of possible approaches to Montmartre and Sacré Coeur. But there is no resisting the monumental approach, beginning from metro Anvers and proceeding up rue de Steinkerque; from there either take the funicular (which uses a metro ticket) or walk up through the garden.

Since a traveler must never return the way he came—that being a law of nature—you have no choice but to discover less Disney-like portions of the hill as you wind your way down.

HILLSIDE MONTMARTRE

Outside of its hilltop attractions, Montmartre is a wonderful mix of an area, a jumble of all that's sleazy, strung out, artistic, bourgeois, contemporary and nostalgic, a blend of pay-attention-to-me and leave-me-alone, between closing the door to outsiders and welcoming anyone in—your basic big-city village, yet one that's particular Parisian.

Along with Sacré Coeur and Place du Tertre, much else remains of the vision of Montmartre 1871-1914 described earlier. You'll come across these remnants by roaming the hillside as you descend the southern slope toward Place Blanche and the Bal du Moulin Rouge.

First, though, a brief walk down the northern slope along rue des Saules brings you to **Montmartre's vineyard**, a half-acre plot planted in 1932 in the name of tradition, after urban development and phylloxera lice had killed off the once extensive vines that even at the turn of the century were producing healthy amounts of wine. The gamay and pinot noir grapes are harvested in early/mid-October and pressed and placed in vats in the basement of the district hall of the 18th arrondissement. The 500 bottles of Montmartre wine are then sold at auction to the benefit of local charities, the entire process taking place with much folklore and celebration. Some of that folklore is celebrated daily except Monday in the little **Montmartre Museum**, at 12 rue Cortot, behind the vineyard. Across from the vineyard is the famous old **cabaret Lapin Agile**.

On the southern slope, let **rue Lepic** be your guide part of the way as it curves along the two remaining windmills of Montmartre, most notably the higher mill, **Moulin de la Galette**, whose neighboring café-dance hall (now gone) was most famously painted by Renoir.

Rue Lepic runs into **rue des Abbesses**, whose cafés are an upbeat gathering places for locals and visitors. In particular they gather near the Abbesses metro station. The station's entrance is itself a turn-of-the-century artifact; Hector Guimard's original Art Nouveau wrought ironwork is topped by one of the rare remaining glass canopies. The café-bars **Le Saint Jean** and **Le Sancerre**, 23 and 35 rue des Abbesses, retain the convivial spirit of old Montmartre, where everyone seems to have a philosophy, an art, a limp, heartache, very big plans, or a lot of wine in them, often several at once, and no amount of tourism will deter them from their appointed rounds.

Upstairs from the **Place des Abbesses** make a detour to pretty Place Emile Goudeau, another "artists' square," but without easels. The studios of the **Bâteau-Lavoir** that once stood by the square were made famous by the artists who worked there a century ago: Picasso, Braque, Gris. The Bâteau-Lavoir burned down in 1970 and has been replaced by new studios. There are still many active studios and artist types (including those of the 7th art) in Montmartre.

Return to rue Lepic to continue the descent—many food shops along the way—to Place Blanche.

Travelers on the cemetery tour (see *Death in Paris*) may continue over to the western base of the hill, where **Montmartre Cemetery** has Stendhal, Berlioz, Nijinsky, Degas and François Truffaut among its illustrious dead.

MOULIN ROUGE

Address *82 bd. de Clichy (Place Blanche), 9th arr.* ***Metro*** *Blanche.* ***Tel.*** *01 53 09 82 82.* ***Site*** *www.moulin-rouge.com. Small and large groups may also wish to contact www.parisrevisited.com for organization of Paris-by-night arrangements.*

The Broadway of Paris is not its concentration of theaters around the Grands Boulevards but its cabarets and dinner-shows. The Bal du Moulin Rouge was one of a handful of cabarets that flourished along the boulevards de Clichy and de

Rochechouart during the Belle Epoque. From the Moulin Rouge at Place Blanche to the clubs around Place Pigalle to the concert hall at Metro Anvers, these upper boulevards continue to have an active nightlife that is at once touristy, hip and sleazy.

Moulin Rouge, the temple of can-can that Toulouse-Lautrec so loved, opened in 1889 beneath the red mill (*moulin rouge*) that gave it its name. The international cabaret revues of Paris from the Belle Epoque inspired both Broadway and Las Vegas. Ziegfield came to the Moulin Rouge, where he was inspired for his Broadway follies—and Broadway shows to follow.

The frieze at the Pantheon symbolizes the crowning achievements of the patriot and declares: *Aux grands hommes la patrie reconnaissante* (To the great men the grateful nation). In a wink at the subversive nature of sexual seduction the Pantheon is parodied inside the Moulin Rouge in a mock frieze showing dancing girls and the words: *Aux petites femmes la nation est reconnaissant* (To the little women the nation is grateful).

Shows begin at 9pm and 11pm and run about 1.5 hours. The 9pm show can be combined with dinner at 7pm. See website for dinner menus and prices. Though dinner at the Moulin Rouge prior to the show can be practical in terms of timing and logistical convenience, I recommend just coming for the show. Admission to the show includes a half-bottle of Champagne per person.

Other major cabarets

Lido, *116 av. des Champs-Elysées, 8th arr. Metro George-V. Tel. 800-227-4884 (North America). Site www.lido.fr.* Paris's other major cabaret show and Moulin Rouge's rival on the big-time cabaret stage is the Lido, which opened in 1946, its reputation assured by post-war fervor and American soldiers. This is now a glitzy international revue of Bluebell Girls and Lido Boys playing to a 1100-seat theater. I prefer the Moulin Rouge for its sense of history. Yet the Lido is conveniently situated for those staying in the large 4-star hotels of the Right Bank.

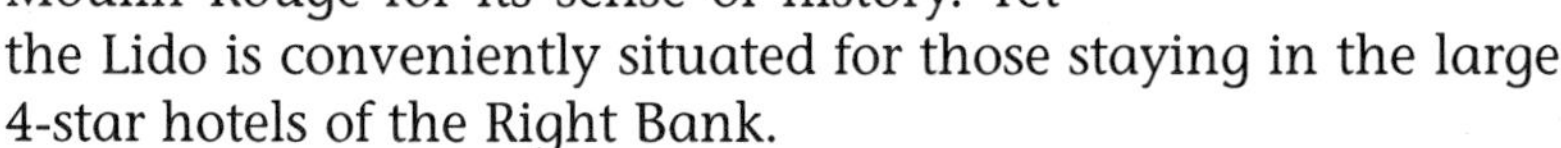

Crazy Horse Saloon, *12 av. George-V, 8th arr. Metro George-V. Tel 01 47 23 99 04. Site www.lecrazyhorseparis.com.* Making its mark on the Paris scene in the 1950s inspired by the American striptease and saloon concept, the Crazy Horse later moved away from its loose striptease act, but sex-'n-swivel appeal is still at the heart of the glossy, fleshy cabaret show in this bar-theater-saloon. Dinner, when booked with the show, is arranged with nearby restaurants of equal sheen.

Michou, *80 rue des Martyrs, 18th arr. Metro Pigalle. Site www.michou.com.* Celebrated transvestite show near Pigalle.

PIGALLE: WHERE ROMANTICISM MEETS EROTICISM

The hub of the literary and artistic life of Paris moves from generation to generation, and in the second quarter of the 19th century it settled in the quarter just south of boulevard de Clichy, which became known as New Athens. This was the era of Romanticism in France, when writers and artists emphasized imagination and emotion over reason.

The Museum of Romantic Life *(Musée de la Vie Romantique, 16 rue Chaptal; metro Pigalle or Blanche; closed Mon.) is a forgettable little museum that honors that period. However, its courtyard tea room beneath the trees is charming and romantic enough. The museum occupies the home of the painter Ary Scheffer, who frequently welcomed gatherings of artists and writers. Along with his own works and possessions, the museum is devoted to the memory of the Parisian novelist George Sand (1804-1876), famous for her writings, her independence, her cross-dressing, her sexual freedom, and her relationship with three leading men of the Romantic period: the composer Frederic Chopin, the artist Eugène Delacroix, and the writer Alfred de Musset.*

Romance has now fully given way to eroticism along boulevard de Clichy. France didn't invent sex and sensuality any more than you did, but much of its savoir-faire is displayed along these boulevards, which is where you'll find the **Museum of Erotic Art** *(72 boulevard de Clichy; metro Blanche; open daily 10am-2am). The Musée de l'Erotisme is a private museum devoted to sex and sexuality in all its pleasure, humor and fantasy. The 2000 objects displayed on seven floors swing between kitsch, curiosity, eroticism, art, and pornography. For the libertine in all of us!*

A FRESH LOOK AT THE EIFFEL TOWER

A letter protesting the construction of the Eiffel Tower was published in Paris on February 14, 1887, less than three weeks after Gustave Eiffel broke ground on the tower that would far overtake the Washington Monument as the world's tallest manmade structure.

The letter was signed by dozens of "personalities from the world of arts and letters," and though many of the signatories were little known or merely fashionable artists of the day, the letter did carry the weight of such respected voices as Charles Gounod (composer of *Faust*), Charles Garnier (architect of the Opera), and the writers Guy de Maupassant and Alexandre Dumas fils.

The artists, declaring themselves "passionate about the beauty hitherto intact of Paris," denounced the planned 300-meter/1000-foot tower as "useless and monstrous," "a horrendous column of bolted sheet iron." They claimed that it would "profane" and "dishonor" Paris to have the city government associate itself with "the mercantile imaginings of a constructor of machines."

"Not even commercial America would want it," they said. And they were right.

Eiffel's project was monstrous. The tower would dominate the low, dense skyline of the City of Light, and do so for no other reason than to demonstrate to what heights it was possible to build with iron and to attract visitors to the World's Fair of 1889.

They were right that the tower would eclipse Paris's glorious monuments of decades and centuries past and that the "beauty hitherto intact of Paris" would be changed in ways hitherto unimaginable. They were right that the tower's stature would command attention to the point of becoming the very symbol of Paris. And how could Paris be Paris if symbolized by a useless pile of iron? Didn't beauty and history demand that the French capital be represented by religious monuments such as Notre-Dame or Sacré Coeur (then under construction on the city's highest hill), or by monuments honoring national glory through war, such as the Arc de Triomphe or the Invalides, or at the very least by the Louvre, a monument to both government and art?

Didn't beauty and history demand that the French capital be represented by a religious monument, war memorial or government building?

They were right that commercial America wouldn't even have wanted something as frivolous and meaningless as a 1000-foot tower in 1887. At the time, Las Vegas had barely heard of the Can-Can! It would be another 110 years before it got an Eiffel Tower.

They were right about Eiffel's tower being profane.

But they were on the wrong side of history—and progress. And Gustave Eiffel stood clearly on the other side.

Gustave Eiffel

Gustave Eiffel (1832-1923) was already a successful engineer at the head of an engineering firm of international renown by the time he embarked on the tower. Bridges and viaducts were his company's specialty, built in response to enormous growth of railway networks, while the company also designed the metal framework for a variety of structures. In Paris, Eiffel's company designed the framework for the

Eiffel Tower Practical Information

Metro/RER *The classic starting point for visiting the ET is with the view from the terrace of the Palais de Chaillot by the Trocadéro metro station. The tower can also be approached via the Ecole Militaire metro station or the Champs de Mars-Tour Eiffel RER station.* ***Tel.*** *01 44 11 23 33.* ***Site*** *www.tour-eiffel.fr.* ***Open*** *From June 22-Sept. 1, elevators and stairs are open 9am-midnight. Otherwise, elevators run daily 9:30am-11pm, while stairs are no longer accessible after 6:30pm. The top level closes 30 minutes before the rest. Opening times may be modified if weather conditions require.* ***Distant views*** *The most distant view can generally be had just before sunset; a haze sometimes hinders the morning view. Yet there isn't much to see in the far distance, since the tower's most interesting views are from the first and second levels, where you overlook Paris's grey slate and zinc rooftops. Return travelers sometimes tell me, slightly embarrassed, that they've never actually gone up the tower. But that's no great shame. The most impressive view is looking up.* ***Tower attractions*** *Several attractions provide multimedia and educational distraction while visiting the tower.* ***Restaurants*** *Altitude 95 (brasserie) on the first level, tel. 01 45 55 20 04; Jules Vernes (gastronomic) on the second level (direct access from the South pillar), tel. 01 45 55 61 44; snack bar on first and second levels.* ***Post office*** *Stamps and cards may be purchased on the first level, and mail deposited on the tower will cancelled with a special Eiffel Tower stamp.* ***Tourist office*** *Information booth at the base of the tower.*

church of Notre-Dame-des-Champs (6th arr.), the synagogue on rue des Tournelles (3rd arr.) and the Bon Marché department store (7th arr.). The company carried out major projects throughout France as well as in Spain, Portugal, Romania, Egypt, Hungary and Latin America. Eiffel's company also designed the metallic structure that supports the Statue of Liberty.

In 1884 Gustave Eiffel patented plans for a 300-meter/1000-foot tower standing on four pillars 125 meter/410 ft. apart, doing so in the names of his collaborators Emile Nourguier and Maurice Koechlin and himself. There was no actual project to build the tower when Nourguier and Koechlin (long-forgotten names) drew up the original plans, though Eiffel was well aware that the government intended to approve plans for Paris to host a World's Fair in 1889. And the possibility of such a colossal structure did grasp the imagination.

In addition to his engineering skills and the reputation of his company, Eiffel was a wise businessman who knew how to play politics, deal with financial institutions, communicate with the press, take risks and get things done. He knew how to convince the organizers of the Fair that his tower was just the thing that was needed to draw attention to the event and demonstrate the industrial potential of the host nation.

In 1886, the organizers launched a competition for plans to built a 300-meter tower, mostly of iron, with a square base 125 meters wide. The competition was obviously rigged to allow Eiffel to built his tower.

Construction

The Eiffel Tower, as it was soon called, was completed on time and within budget in 2 years, 2 months, 5 days. Though practical solutions needed to be found along the way, particularly in preparing the foundations for the pillars on the sandy Seine side of the structure, Eiffel wasn't a man to embark on a project he wasn't sure would succeed. In response to complaints from distant neighbors, his company assumed all risks of the tower's falling during construction.

In 1884, the Washington Monument had topped out at 600 ft. and became the world's highest manmade structure. Five years later, the Eiffel Tower, reaching 1023 ft., took over as number one. It wasn't height alone that set the two apart, but, just as importantly, weight. The Washington Monument made for a fine monument of masonry, but weighing in at 90,000 tons, it was a construction of the past. The future was in metal and alloys. The iron of the Eiffel Tower weighed in at a mere 7,300 tons, so light for its size that if placed in a box large enough to enclose it, the tower would float at sea. It remained the highest manmade structure from 1889 until 1930, when the Chrysler Building in New York briefly took over the mantle at 1046 ft., before the Empire

The Eiffel Tower for Geeks

Construction time: 2 years, 2 months, 5 days
Weight of the metallic structure: 7,300 tons
Total weight: 10,100 tons
Distance between pillars: 125 meters/410 feet
First level: 57 meters/187 feet
Second level: 115 meters/377 feet
Third level: 276 meters/905 feet
Highest point: A new antenna installed in 2000 puts it at 324 meters/1063 feet. The original height upon completion in 1889 was 312 meters/1023 feet.
Number of steps to the top: 1665
Record ascension on foot: 8 minutes, 51 seconds
Distance visible on a clear unpolluted day: 55 miles.
Number of rivets: 2,500,000, about 1.4 million of which were installed on girders prefabricated in Eiffel's workshops in Levallois-Perret, a northwestern suburb of Paris.
Number of girders and other iron pieces: 18,038
Paint: The Eiffel Tower is repainted every seven years with a bronzish paint called Eiffel Tower Brown, with the latest paint job being completed in February 2003 by 25 acrobatic painters. Actually there are three shades of Eiffel Tower Brown, with the lightest at the top and the darkest at the bottom in order to offset the optical effect of distance. The most recent paint job used lead-free paint for the first time, 60 tons of it.
Tilt: Sun causes the tower to tilt more than wind does since heat swells the legs of the tower receiving direct sunlight more than those in shade. A maximum tilt of just under 6 inches has been recorded.
Broadcasting tower: The tower's use for radio communications beginning in 1925 was followed up by its initial use in television broadcasts in 1935. The tower now serves to broadcast 6 TV channels and 30 radio stations.
Lighting: 336 sodium lamp projectors annually consuming 680,000 kW. All but the 8 at the top are yellow-orange.
Number of visitors: Nearly 2 million visitors ascended during the 6-month Fair of 1889. About 6 million now visit each year. About 200 million people have visited since 1889.

State Building rose even higher.

The organizers of the World's Fair of 1889 had originally required that the tower be built only with French materials, but when it came to creating the elevators no French company was experienced enough to take the risk of an elevator that would cover the variably inclined middle portion. Therefore the American elevator company Otis was invited to construct the hydraulic elevators running from the base to the second level.

Also, the original plans called for no decorative elements, but in the end a decorative trim was added in the form of small arches beneath the first level, and just above the arches were placed the names of 72 French scientists famous for their role in scientific advancements from 1789 to 1889.

Even without decoration, Eiffel had argued in his response to the protest letter in February 1887, "the Tower will have her own beauty." "Her curves...will give a great impression of strength and beauty." (A tower is a feminine noun in French; the Eiffel Tower is therefore also known as *la Dame de Fer*, the Iron Lady.) "Furthermore," he wrote, "the colossal has an attraction, its own charm, to which ordinary theories of art are hardly applicable."

The skyscraper was born.

The World's Fair of 1889

Paris hosted World's Fairs (*Expositions Universelles*) at regular intervals in the second half of the 19th century—1855, 1867, 1878, 1889, 1900—but none was more important for the image of France than the Fair of 1889. In deciding to hold the *Exposition Universelle* de 1889, the French government wished for it to fulfill several purposes. It would commemorate the centennial of the French Revolution, demonstrate France's complete recovery from the debacle of the Franco-Prussian War of 1870-1871, and display the capacities and possibilities of a country fully involved in the industrial age. Finally, it would be a feather in the cap of French democracy, then represented by the Third Republic.

France's First Republic (1789-1799) was revolutionary, its the Second Republic (1848-1852) quickly morphed into Napoleon III's dictatorship, but the Third Republic, after a shaky start in 1871, had wings. Those wings were still wobbly in the in the mid-1880s. They were weighed down by monarchist and Bonapartist attempts to restore a hereditary system of government, while hard-line Catholics resisted religious integration and lay institutions. Yet France managed to keep its anti-democratic forces in check while it composed a colonial empire and harvested the fruits of the industrial revolution and the transforming power of modern engineering. Paris itself was becoming the center of the art world through the influence of the Impressionist then Post-Impressionist movements, while the luxury industry was flourishing in the capital as never before (see *Late-19th Century Paris*). France's political stability was still only relative, but it was indeed a democracy, unlike its neighbors, all still ruled by emperors and kings.

Due to the Fair's association with revolutionary France, its opening was boycotted by all of the royal and imperial courts of Europe, except Belgium. No diplomats representing England, Austria-Hungary, Russia or Germany attended the opening in May 1889. But the Fair was too successful and the tower too extraordinary to ignore, and by June, royalty, too, were climbing the tower, beginning with Edward, Prince of Wales, the future Edward VII of England.

With the Eiffel Tower as the Fair's centerpiece, exhibition halls were erected throughout the surrounding area: in the Trocadero Garden across the river, on the Esplanade in front of the Invalides, and along the river. The most important technological exhibitions were installed in a series of glass-and-iron hangers constructed on the Champs de Mars, the lawn running between the Eiffel Tower and the Military School. Among the industrial achievements of the era that visitors could see there were Edison's photograph, Singer's sewing machine, typewriters, railway equipment, electrical-powered machines, weaving machines and a gas-powered automobile.

While Edison was in Paris representing American innovation, Buffalo Bill Cody was in town representing American entertainment.

Thomas Edison ascended the tower and presented Gustave Eiffel with one of his phonographs. (Eiffel's office at the top of the tower now recreates the scene in which Edison visited Eiffel there.) While Edison was in Paris representing American innovation, Buffalo Bill Cody was in town representing

American entertainment. Cody had brought his show of cowboys and Indians and Annie Oakley to Paris that summer to take advantage of the crowds drawn to the World's Fair. The World's Fair of 1889 also introduced Paris to American ragtime, of which Parisians would get a greater earful at the World's Fair of 1900.

Two million visitors ascended the tower by elevator or stairs during the 6-month Fair. Due to its success, Eiffel's one-year lease on the tower was extended to 20 years, after which it would belong to the city to do as it wished, including dismantle it.

Eiffel and the Panama Affair

Eiffel and his firm were at their height in 1887 when construction on the tower began, but Eiffel didn't intend for the tower to be his defining achievement. That same year he signed an agreement with the Panama Canal Company to take over as chief engineer in the French attempt to build the Panama Canal. But the operation began to unravel the year of the World's Fair. The cause of failure of the French canal project wasn't engineering difficulties—in fact, Eiffel had been successfully designing important elements of the early stages of the canal system—but corruption. The Panama Canal Company was a corrupt organization that corrupted all levels of government, business, banking and the news media before it fell apart in a storm of scandals. Its successor, the New Panama Canal Company, fared little better.

The crash of the Panama Canal Company led to the Panama Affair, which broke out in 1890 when it was revealed that 150 members of the National Assembly (France's Congress) had taken payoffs to keep the company moving forward despite the project being bled of its finances left and right. The eventual result of the company's failure was that the Panama project was relinquished to the United States. Among the flurry of court cases that arose from the corporate failure, Eiffel was found guilty of misusing funds, and though the decision against him was overturned on appeal, the Panama Affair brought about Eiffel's public downfall.

The Eiffel Tower for City Planners

The Eiffel Tower was completed on time and within budget. Gustave Eiffel, through his company, assumed all risks of the tower falling during construction. The City of Paris, which has owned the tower from the start, financed 20% of the construction cost. The rest was financed by Eiffel's company and by the managing company founded by Eiffel and three financial institutions. Nearly the entire investment was earned back in the first year it was open. Eiffel originally had a one-year lease that was then renewed for 20 years.

The Eiffel Tower is now operated by the Société Nouvelle d'Exploitation de la Tour Eiffel (SNTE), a company that is owned 30% by the city and 70% by SAGI, a development company heavily involved in public building and housing projects and of which the city has a minority holding. The entire Eiffel Tower operation employs about 500 people, half of which are employees of SNTE, the other half employed by the various business and public institutions in and around the tower (restaurants, shops, police, post office, etc.).

The Eiffel Tower is one of the only public monuments in France not receiving public funding that makes a direct profit. In recent years it has earned an annual profit of about $5 million, the large majority of which goes to the City of Paris.

Eiffel in retirement

Following his entanglement in the Panama Affair, Eiffel retired from his company, yet he remained on the forefront of engineering techniques for the next twenty years. From the start he had promoted the tower as a place for meteorological and astronomical observations and for studying the wind. After his retirement as a builder, he continued to promote his tower for its use in research into the budding technologies of aerodynamics and wireless communications. Aside from his personal scientific interests, he wished to demonstrate the tower's utility should the city seek to dismantle it at the end of his 20-year lease.

In 1898, initial trials of wireless telegraph created a link between his tower and the Pantheon. In 1903, Eiffel financed more extensive research into using the tower as a true wireless telegraph relay. Five years later, the Army, convinced of the tower's utility, installed a military radiotelegraph station underground beside the tower. Messages could be transmitted and received as far away as Berlin and Casablanca. In 1909, the Navy used the tower to conduct early research into wireless telephone.

While others conducted the communications research, Eiffel turned his personal focus to studying aerodynamics, of which he is considered a founding father. As of 1903, he studied the movement of objects through the air by dropping them from a specially designed system from the second level of the tower. Then, with the birth of the airplane, he turned his attention to the study of self-propelled objects and set up an aerodynamics laboratory at the tower's base in 1909. Three years later he moved his experiments to a wind tunnel that he created in Auteuil (now a part of Paris). That aerodynamics complex is still in operation. From there he assisted the pioneers in aviation in testing their designs. Gustave Eiffel and airplane designer Glenn Curtis were awarded the second Langley Gold Medal of the American Smithsonian Institute in 1913, three years after the Wright Brothers received the first.

The Eiffel Tower revisited

By the time Eiffel's lease was up on the tower, there was no doubt that, in addition to its military role, it had become an essential part of the cityscape of Paris. The "horrendous column of bolted sheet iron" came to signify more than its early dissenters had imagined. It signified human achievement, technical know-how, progress. It meant that the modern city need not be dominated or symbolized by religion, the military, a royal or imperial past, or even by government at all. Progress would suffice. And like a bridge that spans a void, the tower was constructed without anything having to be destroyed.

The importance of the Eiffel Tower lies in its triple role as a precursor to skyscrapers, communications towers and city symbols. By the end of the 20th century, it would seem that a modern city couldn't be considered dynamic or a country didn't deserve a place on the map if it didn't have a tower monument of its own: Toronto's CN Tower, Japan's

Eiffel Tower meal stops

There's something about the Eiffel Tower that gives visitors an appetite. But descend from the tower and look around and you'll find no restaurants in sight. You may choose to eat in ***Jules Verne****, the gastronomic restaurant on the second level, a destination in itself, if you've reserved well enough in advance. You can enjoy a seat at the brasserie* ***Altitude 95*** *on the first level restaurant on a shorter reservation or settle for a bite at one of ET's* ***snack bars*** *on a whim. But having thoroughly explored the Iron Lady you may be ready to return to earth.*

Across the river at ***Trocadéro****, behind the Palais de Chaillot (a remnant of the 1937 Fair of Arts and Technology), you'll find an array of café-brasseries. The simple café-restaurant* ***Le Totem****, in the right part of the Palais de Chaillot (when facing the tower), has a terrace that shares the post-card view of the tower; Le Totem serves simple fare and does not take reservations. But you may have begun with that view and don't wish to return up the hill.*

In that case, head east from the tower and two streets back from the Seine. The area has a good variety of choices for a meal, with or without a reservation, as well as an eerie view of the tower in winter when it disappears into the fog and a surrealistic view in summer when it looms bright overhead.

Au Bon Accueil*, 14 rue de Monttessuy, 7th arr. RER Pont de l'Alma. Tel. 01 47 05 46 11. Closed Sat., Sun. A charming little bistro serving mildly contemporary classics with kind professionalism. Au Bon Accueil has gained a sizable reputation in the past two years (and can therefore afford to push the envelope on prices) so reservations are recommended for lunch, though not always necessary if arriving by 12:15.*

Cafés, Brasseries, Bakeries *Several café-brasseries are situated near Au Bon Accueil along rue de la Bourdonnais. The two closest to the tower, by the corner of rue de Monttessuy, are* ***Le Royal Tour*** *(#23), a classic tourist café-brasserie, and the smaller* ***Le Relais de la Tour*** *(#27). More café-brasseries as well as bakeries and food shops are found by proceeding further up rue de la Bourdonnais then turning onto rue Saint-Dominique or rue de Grenelle. A lengthy afternoon walk along rue de Grenelle would allow you to discover the breadth of the 7th arrondissement.*

Tokyo Tower, Berlin's Fernsehturm, Aukland's Sky Tower, Shanghai's Oriental Pearl Tower, Uzbekistan's Tashkent Tower, and so on around the globe. When we think of 9/11, our sense of horror comes not just from the number of victims but from the demise of the Twin Towers, the great-grandchildren of the Eiffel Tower. But that's another century.

A metallic precursor of the computer, built with its own form of binary code: 1, 0, on, off, girder, space, girder, space.

The significance of the Eiffel Tower in the late 19th century is somewhere between that of the Gothic cathedrals designed in the 12th century and that of computers designed in the late 20th. The Eiffel Tower is actually the link between the cathedral and the computer. You can stand in the transept of Notre-Dame, Our Lady, gaze up at the rose windows facing north, south and west, and imagine the glory and drama of the human spirit. You can stand beneath la Dame de Fer, the Iron Lady, gazing in and through the towers rising from pillars pointing north, south, east, and west, and imagine the same. As an icon of progress during the industrial age, the Eiffel Tower is also a metallic precursor of the computer, built with its own form of binary code: 1, 0, on, off, girder, space, girder, space.

The Eiffel Tower is the most recognizable symbol not only of Paris but of France. And it doesn't take Gallic pride to see that the Eiffel Tower, overshadowing city and national symbols across the continent, has become a foremost symbol of Europe itself.

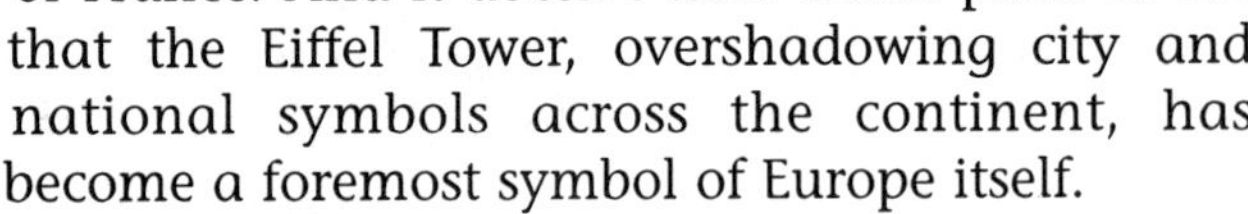

As to "the beauty hitherto intact of Paris," it remains.

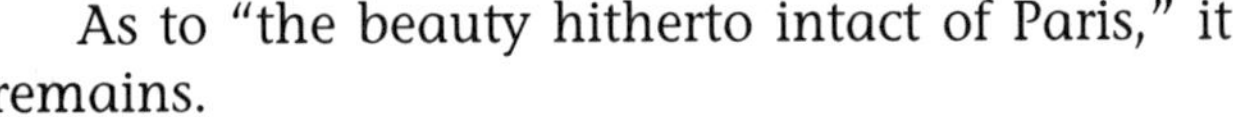

THE MARAIS

The Marais is one of Paris's great gifts to the city stroller. Once the most fashionable quarter in the capital, the playground of nobility in the 17th century, the Marais has entered the 21st as one of the most engaging quarters of Paris. From the aura of its 350-year-old mansions and the unique museums they house to boutiques and eateries seeking the perfect pitch between cute and cool, and from gay bars to Jewish bakeries to contemporary art galleries, the Marais has in recent years become a great stroll-way for Parisians and foreign visitors alike–its status as an increasingly dear residential quarter only enhanced in the process.

The Marais now earns an honorable place on the to-do list of first-time visitors to Paris: somewhere between "Visit if time

The Marais consists of four distinct yet inseparable sections:
- **Noble Marais and the Museums**
- **Gay Marais**
- **Jewish Marais**
- **Artsy Marais and the Galleries**

on day 4," "Read up on this," and "Brad and Sue say to get a guide here." The return traveler, meanwhile, writes THE MARAIS in thick letters, underlined twice, near the top of his must-explore list—and Brad and Sue's advice is still worth considering.

Actually, the Marais moves up on a few notches that first-trip list for travelers who identify with any of the four major affiliations associated with the Marais: museum-goers, gallery mavens, gays and Jews. He who identifies with two or more will feel blessed here. This chapter explores those four separately. But you don't need a label to enjoy the animation, art and architecture of the Marais. You need only the desire to wander the streets, to pay attention to details, to peek into courtyards, to glimpse history, to look into shop windows, to explore eloquent museums, to observe or meet people... and stroll.

The Noble Hôtel

The mansions of the Marais are called hôtels *in French, a term used since the late Middle Ages to designate the city residences of nobles, later also applied to the townhouses of society's upper crust, titled or not.*

The old Marais

By the middle of the 17th century the Marais had became Paris's most fashionable quarter as counts, dukes, cardinals, marquises, royal advisors, royal ministers and all manner of nobility called upon the major architects and decorators of the day to design and embellish their town mansions (*hôtels*). Though decorative developments and occasional building continued into the 18th century, the construction boom in the Marais slowed substantially after Louis XIV officially moved the Court out from Paris to Versailles in 1683. And by the end of his reign high nobles were already eying large plots in the Faubourg St-Germain (7th arr.) and in the Faubourg St-Honoré (8th arr.) for the construction of their new city palaces.

The Marais nevertheless maintained its aristocratic airs until July 14, 1789, when the noble Marais was fully overshadowed by the ignoble Bastille, the fortress-cum-prison nearby. By the end of the Terror, in 1794, with its titled owners and renters either executed or in exile, the noble homes of the Marais slumped in a decline that would continue for the next 160 years; seen another way, the ascent of the working class in the quarter was underway. While some buildings were saved by their purchase by the city of Paris or by the national government, others gradually fell into ruin or were demolished or converted to apartments, workshops, warehouses and stores.

The new Marais

An interest in restoring the noble homes of the Marais emerged in the 1950s, paralleling the initial post-war efforts throughout France to rehabilitate and regild the nation's past – and therefore present – glories. The creation in 1965 of a preservation zone in the 3rd and 4th arrondissements marked a turning point in the history of the Marais, and over the next two decades, noble mansions were restored throughout the area.

Restorations have continued but the modern Marais was fully born in 1985. That same year the Hôtel Salé opened as the Picasso Museum, a part of Marais fully asserted itself as the visible center of gay life in the city, rue des Rosiers noticeably attracted Jewish tourists, and space on several streets was eyed for contemporary galleries and mod boutiques.

The Marais has come to be called "the Left Bank of the Right Bank."

Altogether those developments signaled the renewal of the Marais and its increasing gentrification, which, while naturally attractive to the foreign traveler, has eliminated the working class life of the quarter, inexorably pushed to the edges of the city. Now exuding a quaintness and prosperity and stroll-appeal that long ago defined the Saint-Germain quarter, the Marais has come to be called "the Left Bank of the Right Bank." Only a lack of luxury hotels and restaurants (with notable exceptions on the Place des Vosges) has held back the gears of international tourism. For now, foreign travelers blend in with the Parisian residence and visitors. The quarter has gained such popularity that even homophobic, anti-Semitic high-brows and low-brows are conflicted by their refusal to set foot here. On Sunday afternoon, when other quarters fall into dominical slumber, the Marais draws visitors from far and wide; that, then, is the best time to take part in the strolling life of the Marais. But for a quieter, more workaday walk, there's nothing like a semi-aimless exploration on a weekday.

THE NOBLE MARAIS: PLACE DES VOSGES AND THE MUSEUMS

Whether you've come to examine the nuances of 17th and 18th century architecture and interior design or simply want glimpses of details of the rich and famous of that era, one piece of advise: keep your eyes open and wander, entering courtyards wherever there's an open door.

The Marais covers a wide area between the Seine and rue de Bretagne, where you'll come across dozens of noble mansions both great and small, entire and partial, courtyards open or closed. For a briefer, nevertheless extensive, tour of the noble Marais, concentrate within the zone between rue des Francs-Bourgeois, rue des Archives and rue de Turnenne, while also making sure to include (preferably begin with) the Hôtel de Sully and Place des Vosges

An eclectic range of museums crowds this area, from the major Picasso and Carnavalet Museums to the charming Cognacq-Jay Museum of 18th-century decorative arts and the handsome Hunting Museum. The Museum of the Art and History of Judaism is described with "The Jewish Marais."

PLACE DES VOSGES

The good life first reigned in the Marais in the 14th century under **King Charles V**, who served as regent 1356-1364 then reigned until 1380. Having witnessed rebellion in the heart of the capital and wary of being trapped on Ile de la Cité, he was the first king to move royal affairs onto the Right Bank, camping in either the Hôtel Saint-Paul in the Marais on the eastern edge of the city or the fortress castle of the Louvre on the western side. To protect his residence in the Marais he ordered the construction of a fortress that came to be called the Bastille. Little remains of that first noble building boom, which took advantage of the complete draining of the marshland (*marais* in French) that had earlier described the zone.

The Hôtel Saint-Pol was eventually torn down and a second royal residence, the Hôtel des Tournelles, built on the current site of Place des Vosges. Jousting tournaments were then held nearby, by the wide road leading from the Bastille (rue St-Antoine), the eastern entrance into Paris. **King Henri II** was taking part in one such tournament in 1559 when his opponent's joust splintered and mortally wounded him in the eye. The medieval Marais died with him. His widow, Queen Catherine de Medicis, abandoned the Hôtel des Tournelle then ordered it demolished as she began plans for the Tuileries Palace near the Louvre.

Henri IV (reigned 1589-1610) had to conquer both his crown and his capital but in doing so he brought an end to a long era of civil and religious conflict. At the turn of the 17th century he oversaw a period of peace and prosperity during which he set about embellishing Paris. He created Place Dauphine and the Pont Neuf and expanded the Louvre, yet his major gift to the capital was the royal square, one of the first in the kingdom, that he ordered created on the site of the former Hôtel des Tournelles. Place Royale, as it was then called, was the centerpiece of a major development project by which 36 identical facades of brick and stone with slate roofs were to be built, along with two higher pavilions, the King's Pavilion to the south and the Queen's Pavilion to the north. The nobles who bought into the development were then given free rein to develop their pavilions to individual taste.

Place Royale was inaugurated in 1612, two years after Henri IV's death, with a ceremony that celebrated the engagement of his son, **King Louis XIII**, with Anne of Austria, Infanta of Spain. Paintings in the Carnavalet Museum illustrate the carousel and the great pomp of the event. The equestrian statue of **Louis XIII** stands beneath the horse chestnut trees at the center of the square, while orderly lindens now frame the lawns.

The square's inauguration and the advent of Louis XIII signaled the start of a 75-year building spree that reached its height in the middle of the century, during the pre-Versailles days of **Louis XIV**. Embellished by hundreds of noble hôtels, the Marais became the most fashionable quarter of the capital.

The Middle Ages had also seen the development of religious communities in the Marais, and religious structures continued to hold their own in the area as the Counterreformation set about reaffirming a preeminent role of Catholicism in the kingdom. **Eglise Saint-Paul-Saint-Louis** (99 rue Saint-Antoine), built 1627-1641, displays the full orchestration of the French Baroque. As a sign of its importance, the hearts of Louis XIII and Louis XIV were placed here.

When King Louis XVI lost his head, Place Royale lost its name. It was renamed Place des Vosges in honor of the department of Vosges, the first department (similar to a county) to pay its revolutionary taxes.

Victor Hugo, one of France's major literary figures of the 19th century, author of *Les Misérables* and *The Hunchback of Notre-Dame*, lived at #6 from 1832 to 1848. His apartment is now the **Victor Hugo Museum** (closed Mon.), its rooms recreated as when he lived here. Befitting this former royal square, the most discrete of the top restaurants of Paris, **L'Ambroisie**, hides beneath the arcades at #9 (tel. 01 42 78 51 45; closed Sun., Mon., Aug.). Along with the noble heights of its cuisine, its reputation as one of the most difficult reservations in the capital has long been assured.

Its facades fully restored in the 1990s, Place des Vosges exudes elegance nearly four centuries after its creation. The beautiful repetition of its arcades, the grace of its brick and stone architecture, and the majestic proportions of its park refuse to go out of fashion.

MAJOR MANSIONS AND MUSEUMS

Hôtel de Sens

Address *1 rue du Figuier*

It wasn't until 1622 that Paris was raised to an archdioceses. Previously the archbishop of Sens (Burgundy) had overseen the diocese of the capital. In the last quarter of the 15th century, with expanding resources and power, the archbishop of the time therefore saw fit to build a great pied-à-terre in Paris. That residence, the Hôtel de Sens, is the oldest existing hôtel in the Marais, one of Paris's two remaining mansions from that period, the other being the Hôtel de Cluny in the Latin Quarter, built as Paris residence for the abbots of Cluny.

The heart of the noble Marais is most directly approached from Metro Saint-Paul or Bastille, but one can also begin at Metro Pont Marie for a glimpse of the Hôtel de Sens. The Hôtel de Sens is best viewed in all its Gothic flamboyance from the inner courtyard. The hôtel now houses the Forney Library (closed Sun., Mon.) specializing in documentation relative to decorative arts, including an important collection of historic wallpaper.

Hôtel de Sully

Address *62 rue Saint-Antoine*

The most impressive introduction to the noble homes of the Marais begins with the Hôtel de Sully. This great mansion, built in the 1620s and therefore one of the earliest after the creation of Place des Vosges, is fittingly occupied by the National Service for Historical Monuments and Sites. The front and back courtyards are freely open to visitors as is the bookstore devoted to books about sites and monuments throughout France.

The Hôtel de Sully shows the typical construction of the noble residences of the 17th century in the Marais: entered through a passage large enough for carriages, these homes were built in the form of a U around a cobblestone courtyard, with a garden out back and the entire property surrounded by high walls. Some of the homes in the Marais were built with the main body directly on the street, but the major hôtels are built between courtyard and garden.

The facades of the front courtyard of the Hôtel de Sully are decorated with sculptures representing the elements of air, fire, water and earth, along with representations of autumn and winter. Spring and summer decorate the back façade, facing the simple garden. The large orangery or citrus greenhouse at the back further attests to the palatial quality of these noble homes. A passage from the back corner of the garden leads directly to Place des Vosges.

Madame de Sévigné (1626-1696)

For the quality of her collected letters, Madame de Sévigné has become a major figures of 17th-century French literature. Beyond Parisian, she was a true Maraisian, devoted as she was to the quarter where she was born. Born in a pavilion on Place Royale (Place des Vosges), orphaned at 7, widowed with two children at 25, she lived in eight different homes in the Marais, but is primarily associated with the Hôtel Carnavelet, which she rented for the last 20 years of her life. The several thousand letters that have been collected since her death show her to be a keen observer of the details, dramas, comedies and affections that she lived or witnessed or heard about secondhand. As such she provides a valuable record of both her life and her times. Portraits of Madame de Sévigné can be seen in the Carnavalet Museum and a room has been restored as she may have known it, but in any of the decorative rooms, even those from other eras, one can imagine Madame de Sévigné seated at her desk, writing away.

The Carnavalet Museum of the History of Paris

Address *23 rue de Sévigné.* ***Metro*** *Saint-Paul.* ***Open*** *10am-6pm. Closed Mon.* ***Free entrance*** *(excluding temporary exhibits).* ***Visiting time:*** *1-2 hours, depending on interest.*

Visiting the Carnavalet is like flipping through a magnificent coffee-table book about the history of Paris. As much as the Picasso Museum reveals the sweep of life of a great artist, the Carnavalet Museum presents that of a great city. Entrance is free, so there's no excuse to not step beyond the courtyard and its sculpture of Louis XIV for a quick look inside. The only problem is that a quick look is impossible. You're more likely to emerge an hour or two later imbued with the sense that the history of Paris is made of one decorative style and revolution after the next.

The Carnavalet Museum occupies the Hôtel Carnavelet (built in 1548, modified in 1655) and the adjoining Hôtel Le Pelletier de Saint-Fargeau (1686). For the short version of a tour of the museum, concentrate on the portions presenting rooms that were installed here after being dismantled from various noble mansions throughout the Marais. These begin on the ground floor but mostly cover the second and are **a wonderful complement to an architectural tour of the Marais.** The rooms chronologically display decorative styles and developments through the noble years of the Marais, from the 16th through the 18th centuries, including much beautiful wood paneling. This is the only place in Paris to find such an important range of styles through the reigns of Louis XIII-XVI; you'd need to go out to the chateaux of the region to find a fuller view of these periods.

Try to quit the museum after the decorative sections and you're likely to find yourself so lost as room spills into room and stairwell leads to stairwell that you'll have no choice but to continue visiting. Anyway, **it would be a shame, this close to the Bastille, to skip the rooms that present the history of the French Revolution.** When the Bastille was torn down in 1789, blocks of its stone were sculpted into miniatures of the fortress-prison that were then sent around France as a reminder of the injustice of the *ancien régime*. One such miniature is in the Revolutionary section of Carnavalet.

The storming of the Bastille in 1789 signaled the start of the Revolution but not immediately the end of Louis XVI. The king lost power to the Constituent Assembly by successive steps. On the night of June 20-21, 1791, he and the royal family attempted to flee the country, only to be captured and brought back to Paris, where, in September, he accepted his role in a constitutional monarchy. But his resistance to and veto of decrees of the Assembly led to an untenable situation and on Aug. 10, 1792, the Tuileries Palace was overrun and the king taken prisoner, thus marking the fall of Louis XVI.

The royal family were then imprisoned in the Dungeon of the Temple, part of a fortified religious complex that was located several blocks north of the Hôtel Carnavalet. A reconstruction of the room in which they were held is shown in the museum. Louis was put on trial for treason four months later, and on Jan. 21, 1793 he was taken from the Temple to place de la Concorde to be executed. The Temple complex was already progressively being dismantled when, in 1808, Napoleon I ordered demolition of the dungeon in order to prevent royalists from using the site of Louis XVI's imprisonment as a rallying point against his rule.

Those with little basis in French history may be a bit lost among the twists and turns of fashion, politics and revolution presented in the 19th- and 20th century sections, but presumably, if you just keep moving forward in history, you'll eventually find an exit.

Art and the Law of Dation

A 1968 law allows heirs to pay their inheritance taxes with works of art if the works are deemed to be of value to the cultural heritage of France. Known as dation, *the law has been useful in keeping significant works from certain collections united and in France; if put on the open market they would undoubtedly be spread around to wealthier museums and collectors overseas. The most famous application of this law has involved the Picasso estate whose taxes were paid with some 203 paintings, 158 sculptures, 88 ceramics, and a load of other valuables, including drawings, sketchbooks, prints, and 50 other works that Picasso had collected from other artists (Braque, Renoir, Cézanne, Matisse, Derain). This original* dation *of 1979, the taxman's answer to Picasso's death in 1973, was followed by the* dation *of 1990, in consideration of the death of Jacqueline Picasso, his widow, in 1986, which enriched the museum with dozens of works, particularly from the last decade of the artist's life. Meanwhile, the Picasso heirs have fully taken advantage of their rights to exploit the artists' name, likeness and works, making him a formidable "commercial" artist even today.*

The Picasso Museum (Hôtel Salé)

***Address** 5 rue de Thorigny. **Metro** Saint-Paul. **Open** 9:30am-5:30pm (Oct.-March)/6pm (April-Sept.). Closed Tues. **Visiting time:** 1.5+ hours for a full view.*

Picasso is the ideal subject for a chronological exploration, and whether your interest is the life of an artist or the art of a lifetime–inevitably both–the Picasso Museum is the best biography of an artist that Paris has to offer. Though Spanish, Pablo Picasso (1881-1973) spent most of his life in France, first settling in Montmartre, later living on and off in various section of Paris (mostly on the Left Bank at 7 rue des Grands-Augustins) and along the French Riviera.

When Picasso's work is seen individually in other museums, his assembled and disassembled figures tend to appear above all as intellectual expressions of a "modern"artist. But taken together and chronologically–Blue Period, Rose Period, Cubism; Eva, Olga, Marie-Thérèse, Dora, Françoise, Jacqueline; Bathers, Minotaurs, bullfights, sculptures, ceramics, prints; Spain, Paris, the Riviera, Vallauris–the emotional side of the work emerges, revealing his evolving loves, needs, rejections, desires, frustrations. The museum as a whole is therefore accessible to the unstudied visitor despite the difficulties of individual pieces.

Explanations in English in each room tell of the influences and innovations during given periods beginning with a small collection from the Blue, Rose, pre-Cubism periods and then Cubism, whose initial flame was extinguished during WWI. While all periods of the artist's life are covered, the museum is especially rich in works of the 20s and 30s. One effect of this is that, having presented the early developmental and more formal searches as an artist, a major body of work here speaks directly of his loves and passions and politics as they accompanied and reflected his artistic evolution. This is a large museum and it can be both intellectually and visually tiring, in part the natural consequence of a vast retrospective of such a long, productive life. By the time you've reached his later works you may wish that he would just put down his tools and go play with his grandchildren, or that you yourself might take a café break and then return, but the master keeps working away... and you keep climbing and descending stairs.

The museum occupies the Hôtel Aubert de Fontenay, built in 1656. The mansion became known as the Hôtel Salé since de Fontenay's enormous wealth came from his position as royal administrator in charge of the salt tax. *Salé* means salty or salted relative to food as well as stiff or steep relative to prices.

Only the façades, front and back, and the grand staircase of this imposing mansion recall its noble era. It is otherwise fully given over to the presentation of the works of Picasso. De Fontenay's own life of luxury in the Marais was brief. In 1663, in the wake of the fall of Finance Minister Nicolas de Fouquet (see *Chateaux: Vaux-le-Vicomte*), de Fontenay, too, fell into royal disgrace and his belongings were seized by the crown.

Cognacq-Jay Museum (of 18th-century Decorative Arts)

Address *8 rue Elzévir.* ***Open*** *daily except Mon. 10am-6pm. Free entrance (except for temporary exhibits). Visiting time: 20-30 minutes.*

The Hôtel Denon reveals its own late-16th-century origins in the stark elegance of its courtyard and painted ceiling beams in some room, otherwise it is devoted to the precious charms of 18th-century decorative arts: paintings of rosy-cheeked ladies in fine garments, sculpted cherubs, vases, wood paneling, parquet, pill boxes, smelling salt boxes. Room guards sometimes outnumber visitors here but you may luck upon a gathering of well-dressed Parisians and listen in on their conversation to pick up a French vocabulary of decorative oohs and ahs: *ravissant* (ravishing), *charmant* (charming), *exquis* (exquisite). *Exquis* indeed!

Hôtel de Soubise and Hôtel de Rohan (the National Archives)

Soubise: ***Address*** *60 rue des Francs-Bourgeois.* ***Open*** *weekdays (except Tues.) 1:45-5:45pm and weekends 10am-5:45pm.*

Rohan: ***Address*** *87 rue Vieille-du-Temple.* ***Open*** *daily (except Mon.) noon-6pm during temporary exhibition.*

The Hôtels de Soubise and de Rohan are the most majestic of the noble homes of the Marais, built by members of the same family beginning in 1705 in the last major explosion of construction in the greater during its noble heyday. The properties are now united via their gardens since both are part of the National Archives complex, which covers the entire block.

Soubise is the most palatial mansion in the Marais, an elegant Classical building set back from a spacious front courtyard surrounded by a portico. The tremendous façade is decorated with sculptures of the Seasons above the first floor and the reclining figures of Glory and Magnificence above the pediment. Inside, the princely apartments circa 1735 can be visited. A Gothic entrance of 1380, a unique above-ground remnant of the first noble building boom in the Marais, was integrated into the side of the Hôtel Soubise and can be seen along rue des Archives.

The Hôtel de Rohan, also called the Rohan Palace, holds temporary exhibitions relative to the archives of France. Even without entering the building you might step into the second courtyard (entered through the first), formerly the courtyard of the stables, for a look at the famous bas-relief sculpture of the *Horses of the Sun.*

OTHER MAJOR HOTELS

Hôtel de Libéral Bruant (Locksmith Museum)

Address *1 rue de la Perle.* ***Closed*** *Sat. and Sun.*

At the corner near the Picasso Museum, this mansion of 1685 houses the Locksmith Museum, displaying locks and keys from antiquity through the 20th century.

Hôtel Guénégaud (Hunting & Nature Museum)

Address *60 rue des Archives. Closed Mon.*

Designed in 1651 by François Mansart, a major architect of the first part of Louis XIV's reign, the Hôtel Guénégaud houses the Hunting and Nature Museum: trophy rooms, hunting weapons, sculptures, paintings.

Hôtel de Lamoignon (Historical Library)

Address *24 rue Pavée.* **Closed** *Tues.*

The Hôtel de Lamoignon was built in 1584 and now contains the city's Historical Library. Its back is visible across the street from the Hôtel Carnavalet.

Hôtel Amelot de Bisseuil

Address *47 rue Vielle-du-Temple*

The courtyard of the Hôtel Amelot de Bisseuil (mid-17th century) is closed to visitors but that shouldn't stop you from admiring the wood carving of Medusas on the massive doors and the sculpted figures of War and Peace on the pediment. From 1776 to 1788 the hôtel was rented by Caron de Beaumarchais who wrote his play *The Marriage of Figaro* here and also operating a company set up to enable the transfer of funds to the American colonies for the War of Independence.

Hôtel de Beauvais

Address *68 rue François Miron*

This is one of the latest hôtels to be restored. In 1654 Queen Mother Anne of Austria, regent during the minority of Louis XIV, selected her chambermaid and confidante, 40-year-old Catherine Bellier, to initiate the 16-year-old king in the pleasures of love. This assured Catherine, nicknamed Cateau la Bornesse (i.e. One-Eyed Catty, for she was blind in one eye), and her uncomplaining husband Pierre Beauvais elevation to the status of baroness and baron, along with a noble income that enabled them to build their Marais mansion. Despite ridicule from many of her new peers, Catherine's consecration came in 1660 when high members of the Court joined her on the balcony of her new home to witness the entrance into Paris of Louis XIV and his bride Maria Teresa as they passed along the street on their way to the royal palace.

Seven-year-old Mozart stayed here a century later during his time in Paris (1763-4), during which he was taken to Versailles to wow the Court of Louis XV.

A portion of the 13th-century Gothic basements on which the Hôtel de Beauvais and others in the area were built can be seen by entering the headquarters of the Association for the Preservation of the Historical Marais at #44 on the same street. Access to the basement is free to the public.

MARAIS FOR THE HUNGRY TRAVELER

You'll never go hungry in the Marais. Along with the more sectarian restaurants affiliated with the Gay Marais and the Jewish Marais (see below), lunch, snack and dinner possibilities abound throughout the Marais and along the main streets and squares that surround it. The quarter's main market street is ***rue de Bretagne****, and from there the park benches of the Square du Temple are just a block away. The pleasure of sitting at an outdoor tables on the cute little* ***Place du Marché St-Catherine*** *(between rue de Turenne and rue de Sévigné) far outweighs the ordinariness of the restaurants there. Also see the Restaurants chapter for descriptions of the* ***Le Dôme du Marais, Little Havana*** *(Cuban) and* ***Bofinger*** *(brasserie).*

THE GAY MARAIS

You don't have to look very hard to find what's gay in gay Paree. Paris's main concentration of gay bars, cafés, restaurants and shops occupies choice territory in the very heart of the city. You could well come across the gay portion of the Marais by chance: on your way to the Picasso Museum, or after visiting the Museum of Modern Art at the Pompidou Center, or by merely crossing the street after having admired the neo-Renaissance City Hall, seat of Mayor Bertrand Delanoë, who happens to be gay.

But Paris's main gathering of gay eateries and drinkeries is too well known to just stumble upon. The Marais as a whole, once largely ignored, even by Parisians, now attracts visitors from near and far, both gay and merely glad to be here. The evolution of gay life and business in the Marais has gone hand in hand with the overall renewal of the quarter in the past two decades–even leadin the way for much of the 80s and 90s. The Marais would never have drawn visitors so fast without its position as a gathering place for the loose gay community that has claimed certain streets as its own. (Lesbians may identify with the Marais as well but are far less present.)

The Marais is Paris's second-generation gay quarter. An initial concentration of gay-oriented businesses grew up in the late 1970s near the Opera quarter, around rue Sainte-Anne.

That street is now largely branded as Little Japan due to the many restaurants, shops and agencies catering to Japanese business and leisure travelers. Nevertheless, remnants of the city's previous gay center hold their own in that area, including the granddaddy of gay restaurant/bars, **Le Vaudeville** *(14 rue Thérèse, 1st arr.; tel. 01 42 96 27 23)*, whose low ceiling, miniscule bar and campy waiters continue to give it the smoky air of 70s semi-hideaway. Two blocks away is **La Champmeslé**, the *grande dame* of lesbian bars, *(4 rue Chabanais, 2nd arr.; closed Sun.)*. Nearby, the gay discotheque **L'Insolite** *(33 rue des Petits-Champs, 1st arr.)* is now surpassed by larger, more voguish and racier clubs in other quarters, yet dancing and flirting in this ancient vaulted cellar remain a particularly Parisian experience.

By the mid-1980s several gay businesses had begun venturing into a corner of the Marais that was then a quarter neither here nor there behind the Pompidou Center. Among the enduring businesses that anchored a gay presence in the Marais are the **gay/lesbian bookstore Les Mots al la Bouche**, the hotel/bar Le Central, and the bar/piano cabaret Le Piano Zinc. While the latter two are now past their prime, the bookstore remains an important fixture in the quarter.

The area soon got the nod from the larger gay community, which had recently gotten the nod from the French government itself. Homosexuality, which had been criminalized by the wartime Vichy government in 1941, was fully decriminalized in 1982. In 1985 the Socialist government adopted a **law against discrimination** in employment, housing and services based on sexuality. The age of sexual majority in France was set at 15 years for any forms of consensual sexual activity (though the law considers that someone older than 18 who has sexual relations with someone 15 to 17 may be accused of corrupting a minor).

Since the Marais had only just begun to develop as a gay center at the time that AIDS entered the scene, the disease didn't stunt the quarter's development as it did in more established gay quarters in the United States, such as the Castro or in the West Village. Furthermore, the Marais wasn't at the time a place where gays lived, only where they gathered. There was, therefore, only one way for it to grow: up.

And grow it has. By vaguely heading across the street from City Hall (the metro station Hôtel de Ville), behind the department store BHV, you need only follow your nose along rue des Archives, rue Saint-Croix de la Bretonnerie and rue Vieille du Temple, as it leads past:

the café terrace of Les Marronniers, *(18 rue des Archives),*
the bookstore Les Mots á la Bouche *(6 rue St-Croix-de-la-B.),*
the old corner bar Le Central *(33 rue Vieille-du-Temple),*
the classic cruiser Quetzal *(10 rue de la Verrerie),*
the clone-bar Le Cox *(15 rue des Archives),*
the mixed sex Mixer Bar *(23 rue St-Crois-de-la-B.),*
the watch-them-all-go-by Open Café *(17 rue des Archives)*
and points in between.

Other gay bars, clubs, and restaurants congregate along Rue des Lombards in the nearby Les Halles quarter, from:

the self-explanatory Bear's Den *(6 rue des Lombards)* to
the basement dance club London *(33 rue des Lombards)* to
the buoyant restaurant L'Amazonial *(3 rue St-Opportune).*

Places specifically oriented towards women are more spread out. Among them:

the café-bar Unity Bar *(176 rue Saint-Martin, 3rd arr.),*
the café-bar L'Utopia *(15 rue Michel-le-Comte, 3rd arr.),*
the bar Les Scandaleuses *(8 rue des Ecouffes, 4th arr.),*
the bar La Champmeslé *(4 rue Chabanais, 2nd arr),*
the nightclub Divan du Monde *(75 rue des Martyrs, 18th arr.) and*
the restaurant L'Accent *(93 rue de Javel, 15th arr.; tel. 01 45 79 20 26)*

Free publications available in bars provide details of specific events and other addresses. For information on GLBT associations and news, visit the website of **Paris's Gay and Lesbian Center** (Centre Gai et Lesbien) at www.cglparis.org.

Beyond the Marais

Paris–at once France's New York, Los Angeles and Washington, D.C.–is naturally the country's GLTB mecca. While the concentration of gay businesses in a corner of the Marais makes that the center of gay life in the city, gay nightclubs, sex clubs and bathhouses are found in the surrounding area as well as elsewhere on the Right Bank. The city's many sex outlets thrive without stigma–though visitors should note that Paris is intimately familiar with HIV and other STDs.

Sex clubs aside, two dance places stand out for their generous effort at maintaining French traditions:

Le Tango (dancehall)

Address *13 rue au Maire, 3rd arr.* ***Metro*** *Arts et Metiers.* ***Open*** *Fri. & Sat nights.*

Le Tango, in an alley at the northwest corner of the Marais, is an old-fashioned dancehall/nightclub, where on Friday and Saturday nights you'll find two men or two women pair-dancing to a tango, a passo and various French and Latino cha-chas and oom-pahs before midnight, followed by an eclectic mix of music from the past three decades. It is one of the rare clubs where gays and lesbians actually mix and is also the kind of place gay travelers shouldn't hesitate to bring along their straight friends.

Chez Raymonde (dinner + dance)

Address *110 av. Parmentier, 11th arr.* ***Metro*** *Parmentier or Goncourt.* ***Tel.*** *01 43 55 26 27.* ***Closed*** *Mon.*

Chez Raymonde, further afield, is a treat for a party of four or more. Come for a late dinner (9-10ish) of basic bistro fare, then stay on as this mild-mannered restaurant becomes a small dance-hall where the sound of an accordion draws onto the dance floor men with men, women with women, women with men, oldsters with youngsters, any size with any shape, and anyone from your table with anyone from their table. Thursday through Saturday tend to be best but it all depends on the crowd–and your willingness to join in.

Tolerance à la française

Tolerance al la française begins with the twin notions of privacy and indifference. While the American sense of diversity broadly speaks of "the right to be different," the French speak of "the right to indifference," meaning that an individual can expect others to be indifferent to his or her private life. Privacy laws – which prohibit tabloid-style scandal sheets–reflect and reinforce this cultural point of view. Consequently, private matters such as

... an individual can expect others to be indifferent to his or her private life.

the sexuality, religious practice and family life of public figures are rarely directly mentioned either politically or in the media. The public confession – a common statement of rebirth in America–is not only rare but is frowned upon. In a certain respect this instills a kind of cultural "Don't ask – Don't tell" policy, though one that hasn't prevented social progress.

Au contraire. In 1999, France adopted a domestic partnership law creating the **Civil Pact of Solidarity**, known by its French acronym as PACS. While falling short of marriage, the PACS recognizes partnership rights (inheritance, housing, health coverage) and obligations (joint taxes, shared debts) of non-married couples, regardless of sex.

That same year, the French Government Tourist Office in New York, an arm of French Tourist Ministry, first promoted France as a gay-friendly destination. The FGTO then put out a magazine entitled "Gay Friendly France," with the subtitle *Liberté, Egalité, Diversité,* a modification of the French motto of *Liberté, Egalité, Fraternité,* championing France as a great place to be out... and about. For men, at least; women were largely ignored in the magazine, there being no such thing as lesbian chic in Mediterranean countries.

[Nevertheless, a fascinating guided tour can be made that retraces the footsteps of **the literary lesbians of the Left Bank** who were an important force in expatriate life and literature in Paris from 1905-1935: Nathalie Barney, Gertrude Stein and Alice B. Toklas, Sylvia Beach, Djuna Barnes, Hilda Doolittle, Radclyffe Hall and Margaret Anderson. The tomb of Stein and Toklas is an important pilgrimage site at Père Lachaise Cemetery as is that of Oscar Wilde, who also died in Paris (see *Death in Paris*).]

Paris is a very tolerant city, and "the right to indifference" means that gay couples should feel at ease in the hotels noted in this book. Anyway, there are no gay hotels of particular interest. As for restaurants, those in the gay portion of the Marais serve basic French comfort food; they are undoubtedly gay-friendly but not much more friendly than that.

Outside of the Marais, it remains uncommon to see two men or two women linked in the kinds of embraces that Paris is known for, but that doesn't keep hundreds of men from stripping to their skivvies on warm sunny days and lying on cobblestone "beaches" along the River Seine in the very center of the city. Furthermore, for generations, if not centuries, the

Seine-side terrace of the Tuileries Garden by the Louvre has been recognized as a soft-cruising ground.

Pick-Clops

***Address** 16 rue Vieille du Temple, 4th arr. Corner of rue du Roi-de-Sicile. **Metro** Saint-Paul or Hôtel de Ville.*

There are four distinct leanings for the cafés, bars and restaurants in the Marais: gay/lesbian/gay-friendly, Jewish/Jewish tourist, noble/mainstream tourist, and it's-cool-to-go-to-a-straight-place-near-the-gay-bars. And then there's the Pick-Clops, now an old standard, quietly living its life as a heterogeneous café-bar at the corner of rue Vieille du Temple and rue du Roi de Sicile. Run by a bunch of guys who appear to take pride in working here, the Pick-Clops is a nice place for lunch or for a late-afternoon pause when you don't feel like being categorized. Actually, the Pick-Clops does have a category, if you wish, that of clean-cut-rocker-downloading-classic-and-French-rock, which sounds like a fair compromise.

THE JEWISH MARAIS

The gay bars of the Marais abruptly start/stop at rue des Rosiers, where the falafel stands of the Marais's old and enduring Jewish quarter end/begin. Round the corner and everything changes. Or so it seems. It may first appear that the two communities–gay and Jewish–have little in common outside of their antagonism to and from far-right leaning citizens and other natural predators and demagogues. But as they exist in the Marais the two communities are in fact clear reflections of each other's joyful minority status: the one promoting safe sex and AIDS awareness, the other promoting donations to Jewish charities; the one offering beer and peanuts, the other falafels and Coke; the one selling clubwear, the other selling bar-mitzvahwear; each with a major community bookshop; each catering not only to the local community but to visitors from throughout Paris, France, and beyond. Furthermore, the cultural "Don't ask–Don't tell" of French discretion equally applies to both the religious and the sexual experience.

The Jewish presence in the Marais, which has existed since the 15th century, has remained strong and pronounced ever since Jews were granted civil rights during the French Revolution. Traditional (more or less orthodox) religious institutions, practice and culture flourish within courtyards and passages, however the façade of rue des Rosiers, in keeping with real estate developments throughout the Marais, clearly presents the more gentrified face of Judiasm and Jewish tourism, with increasingly trendy tourist-minded boutiques and eateries catering to visitors from well beyond the old *pletzl.*

Sunday is the day for crowds and atmosphere along the rue des Rosiers, while a visit on a weekday afternoon reveals more of the day-to-day life of the Jewish Marais.

Noshing on Rue des Rosiers

The entrance to the restaurant/delicatessen Jo Goldenberg (7 rue des Rosiers) still bears the wounds of a terrorist attack in 1982 that killed 6 people. As victim to terrorism and as homage to Ashkenasic eats, the restaurant stands out as symbol of an enduring community and anchor of rue des Rosiers. As such it attracts, along with its usual customers, politicians and others seeking acceptance in the Jewish community. For a simple meal of Ashkenasic-Israeli fare, I prefer the restaurant Chez Marianne (46 rue des Rosiers). But the falafel stands and pastry shops are more in keeping with the noshing nature of the wandering Jew, or Gentile, in the Marais.

The Museum of Jewish Art and History

***Address** 71 rue du Temple, 3rd arr. **Metro** Rambuteau. **Open** Mon.-Fri. 11am-6pm, Sun. 10am-6pm. **Closed** Sat. and Jewish holidays. **Site** www.mahj.org.*

Past its courtyard, the Hôtel de Saint Aignan has little to show for its 1645 origins. That may be appropriate considering that its primary historical narrative recounts the life of a community whose members rarely set foot in the Court of the Kings Louis. The Jewish Museum, as it is often called, opened in 1998 as an important addition to the Marais's cultural landscape. It offers an exploration Jewish art and history in terms of Diaspora, the Jewish bourgeoisie, the Jewish working class/immigrant, and the meaning of holidays.

Much of the museum is dedicated to presenting Jewish practices and migrations, yet as fascinating as this can be–and the beauty of 17th- and 18th-century religious objects notwithstanding–it will be more revealing to non-Jewish than to Jewish travelers, who may already know a thing or two about Hanukah and Passover. The audioguided tour provides informative commentary, but the visual appeal of the museum is limited.

As to its emotional appeal, the most significant section of the museum is that which introduces, through photographs and brief biographies, the Jews who lived in this building prior to 1942—a time when the Marais was largely defined as a working class neighborhood, when noble mansions were the homes of scores of immigrant and French Jews, among others—and their eventual deportation to the concentration camps. This on-site link with the less distant past is the museum's most important contribution to the city.

✡✡✡

Two synagogues

Gustave Eiffel, later of tower fame, designed the inner ironwork of the synagogue (1875) at 21 bis rue des Tournelles. The arch of its roof can be seen beyond the slate roofs on the eastern side of the place des Vosges.

Another celebrated builder, **Hector Guimard**, whose wife was Jewish (and American), designed the synagogue at 10 rue Pavée, seen when approaching the Marais from Metro Saint-Paul. Designed in 1913, this was one of the last structures built in Paris in the Art Nouveau style. Though the curves of its façade are not as exuberant as those of Guimard's famous green metro entrances, they are clearly recognizable as his handiwork. The synagogue was dynamited by occupying German forces on Yom Kippur 1940 and restored after the war.

✡✡✡

A brief history of Jews in Paris

The Jewish Diaspora followed in the footsteps of **the Roman conquest** of Gaul in 52 B.C. Arriving in Lutetia (Paris), a Jewish community initially settled on the Left Bank of the Seine, now the Latin Quarter, but successive waves of barbarian invasions led the Jewish community and other residents of the Left Bank to crowd onto the Ile de la Cité. Among the narrow old streets indicated by cobblestones in front of Notre-Dame (and unearthed in the archeological site beneath) is the **street occupied by Jews in the 12th century**. By the end of that century, Jews were found throughout much of France, including towns and villages in Provence and other southern regions that were relatively hospitable territories for

Roundups and Deportations

As of 1940, Jews were given special status excluding them from the normal advantages of citizenship in German-occupied Paris. In collaboration with Germans and on their own, the French government (based in Vichy) along with local and state French police began rounding up Jews in 1941, first primarily foreign Jews, then increasingly French Jewish men. The roundup of July 16-17, 1942, when nearly 13,000 Jews were corralled at the winter cycling stadium (Vélodrome d'Hiver) known as the Vél d'Hiv that then stood just beyond the Eiffel Tower, has come to represent the injustice and horrors of deportations throughout the period.

The event was exceptional not only for the number of Jews that were arrested in a single roundup but for also the fact that it embodied a clear shift in policy to the deportation of women and children along with men. From there they were moved to the transit camp at Drancy, northeast of the city, and then by train to Auschwitz. In ways both personal and organized, some French came to the aid of remaining Jews after the roundups of the summer of '42. Nevertheless, more than half of the Jews of the Marais perished in the camps. About 180,000 of France's 300,000 Jews in 1939 survived the war.

The Memorial to the Unknown Jewish Martyr, at 37 rue du Turenne in the Marais, adjoins a documentation center containing archives from the period. The Memorial to the Deported at the tip of Ile de la Cité, behind Notre-Dame, holds the Tomb of the Unknown Deportee and honors the 200,000 French, irrespective of affiliation, who were sent to the Nazi death camps.

Public acknowledgement of France's role in sending Jews to the concentration camps was finally made official in 1995 when, on the anniversary of the roundup of Vél d'Hiv, President Jacques Chirac recognized the responsibility of the French state in its treatment of Jews during the war.

the Jews, and their numbers increased, augmented by waves of emigration from Spain.

From the 12th through the 15th centuries, as the European

states coalesced, typically around a central religion, Jews were periodically expulsed from various territories. In the kingdom of France, **expulsions by royal decree in 1182, 1306 and 1394** were echoed by local pogroms such as those following accusations that Jews were causing the Black Plague of 1348. From 1394 to 1790 Jews were officially forbidden to reside in France, though Jewish communities survived and eventually flourished in enclaves of Provence, namely the papal states of Avignon and the Comtat Venaissin (i.e. possessions of the Pope and fully administered by the Catholic Church, therefore out of reach of French decrees). Despite the successive expulsions, Jews, who were perpetually forced to follow shifting winds of repression and tolerance, did manage to trickle back into France, and by the 15th century a Jewish community had settled in the Marais.

The French Revolution granted civil rights for Jews, providing them full status as French citizens. By 1791 they were again allowed to live in Paris and throughout the country. This was the beginning of 150 years of growth, expansion and assimilation of the Jews of France and of the immigrants that would join them. The Marais, particularly around rue des Rosiers, became the *pletzl*, the little gathering place for Jews.

Taking up the question of religion in the wake of anti-clerical Revolution, Napoleon I saw to a new definition of the place of the Catholic and Protestant Churches with respect to the French state, then turned his attention to the Jews. In 1806 he called for a meeting of a kind of Jewish parliament in Paris to appraise the commitment of the various communities to French laws. Reassured as to their patriotism, he then saw to the formation in 1808 a governing body of Jewish groups, **the Consistoire Central des Juifs de France**. This consistory remains the country's main organizational body for Jewish institutions (www.consistoiredefrance.org).

The growth of the number of Jews in Paris, at all levels of the economic spectrum, accelerated in the last quarter of the 19th century. Jews arriving from Alsace and Lorraine, annexed by Germany following the defeat of France in the Franco-Prussian War (1870), were followed by waves of immigrants from Eastern Europe from 1880-1914, as in the United States. The Marais, increasingly established as a center of Jewish life in Paris, became the major landing point for Ashkenasic Jews as new arrivals swelled the population along rue des Rosiers, rue des Ecouffes, rue Ferdinand-Duval and

Other Jewish quarters

Return Jewish travelers interested looking for a fuller view of Jewish life in Paris than that provided along rue des Rosiers should consider venturing into two other quarters with a clear Jewish presence.

In the middle of the 19th century, Askenasic Jews also formed a thriving community along and at the intersections of ***rue du Faubourg-Montmartre, rue Geoffroy Marie and rue Richer*** *(between metro stops Grands Boulevards and Cadet). This is a part of Le Sentier, home to the textile industry in Paris, and therefore displays far more of the daily hustle and bustle of city life than rue des Rosiers. This Jewish quarter of the 9th arrondissement now has a distinctly Sephardic accent, and therefore many of its kosher restaurants serve North African fare. Two major synagogues in the area are the Synagogue Buffault, 28 rue Buffault, and the Synagogue de la Victoire (known as the Rothchild synagogue), 44 rue de la Victoire, built in 1877 and 1874, respectively, to serve an expanding community.*

A more recent, nonetheless historic, quarter for the Jewish community is around ***boulevard de Belleville*** *(between metro stops Belleville and Couronnes). Belleville, a traditional landing-ground for immigrants, received a sizable population of Arabs and (Sephardic) Jews from North Africa beginning in the mid-1950s. Its mix of Jews and Muslims was formerly more pronounced, but the Jewish presence in the area has been in decline since the 1980s as Jews have moved up the economic scale and moved away from immigrant status. The Arab population is far more visible while the more recent trend in Belleville is as home to Asian immigrants.*

other streets of the Marais, adding a distinctly Yiddish accent to the quarter.

The defeat of 1870, financial scandals implicating Jews and the influx of Jews from Eastern Europe were among the factors that some French latched onto as anti-Semitic views gained terrain and became increasingly vocal, paving the way to **the Dreyfus Affair**. In 1894 Captain Dreyfus, a Jew, was falsely accused of treason by allegedly spying for the Germans and found guilty on the basis of evidence fabricated by upper levels in the military hierarchy. A second trial in

1899, inspired by activists condemning the military conspiracy (notably Zola's public accusation of the powers that be, *J'accuse*), nevertheless resulted in a second finding of guilt. But the tide had already turned against the politics of anti-Semitism, and in 1906 Dreyfus was rehabilitated.

The law of 1905 ended any overt religious practice by the State and delineated a separation of Church and State that would still be considered radical by many American accustomed to hearing the prayers of faith-based militants and politicians. In 1936 Léon Blum became France's first Jewish prime minister.

For centuries France had received **Sephardic Jews** exiled from Spain and Portugal, and others began to arrive from French colonies or protectorates beginning in the 19th century, but Sephardim mostly arrived in Paris from the mid-1950s to the mid-1960s as Morocco, Tunisia and Algeria gained independence from France. France is now a rare country outside of Israel to have such sizeable numbers of both Askenasic and Sephardic Jews. American Jews, for example, are largely of Eastern European decent.

France is now a rare country outside of Israel to have such sizeable numbers of both Askenasic and Sephardic Jews.

As a result of France's strict separation between Church and State and in response to lists of Jews kept during the war, religious and ethnic affiliation is not permitted in census questionnaires. It is nevertheless estimated that there are **currently about 600,000 Jews in France, the largest number in Europe**. Half of these live in Paris and the surrounding region.

✡✡✡

ARTSY MARAIS: NoMA AND THE CONTEMPORARY GALLERIES

The Marais hit its economic stride in recent years with a jump in real estate prices and a throng of new boutiques and food shops, while simultaneously bringing out a new group to affiliate with the quarter: the art crowd. The Marais has now fully earned a place for itself on the Paris art scene, though it is still far from rivaling the quarter between boulevard Saint-Germain and the Seine as the center of the art trade in Paris (aside from the auction houses). Yet the Marais is clearly devoted to contemporary art whereas the galleries near the Seine offer a wide mix of visual and decorative arts, contemporary and antique. Twenty-some galleries have now found space on the streets north of the museums and government buildings of the Marais: NoMa, to put a New York spin to the zone, as in "No, Ma, I'm not gay, I'm an artist."

Most galleries in this quarter are closed Sunday and Monday.

Just north of the Picasso Museum:

- Galerie Cent8, Galerie Xippas and Galerie Yvon Lambert. These three occupy various spaces around the courtyard at 108 rue Vieille-du-Temple. Other galleries crowd nearby.
- Galerie Thaddaeus Ropac, Thaddaeus Ropac, 7 rue Debelleyme.

North and northeast of the Pompidou Center:

- Galerie Nathalie Obadia, 5 rue du Grenier Saint-Lazare,
- Galerie Anne de Villepoix, 43 rue de Montmorency,
- Galerie Daniel Templon, 30 rue Beaubourg,
- Galerie Marian Goodman, 79 rue du Temple,
- Galerie Bernard Jordan, 5 rue Chapon,
- Galerie Philippe Casini, 13 rue Chapon,
- Galerie Zarcher, 56 rue Chapon.

Contemporary galleries in other quarters:
6th arrondissement: Major and minor galleries crowd within several blocks of the Seine, particularly near the Ecole des Beaux-Arts along:

- Rue Bonaparte,
- Rue des Beaux-Arts,
- Quai Voltaire.

8th arrondissement:

- Galerie Jérôme de Noirmont at 36-38 avenue Matignon,
- Galerie Lelong, 13 rue de Téhéran. Gallery upstairs. Posters on the ground floor. Among this gallery's sidelines, is its role in selecting the artist who is commissioned each year to produce the work that will appear on the annual poster and t-shirts for the Roland Garros (French Open) tennis tournament. the artful fan may purchase posters here.

Galleries near the new National Library:
13th arrondissement:

The contemporary gallery scene has also recently taken up residence near the National Library, metro Chevaleret or Bibliothèque François Mittérand.

PLACE DE LA BASTILLE

They danced around the ruins of the Bastille on July 14, 1790, to celebrate the first anniversary of the taking of the infamous fortress-prison, and they still dance around here today... and gather in the cafés, applaud at the opera, hold demonstrations, and raise elbows in the bars, forks in the restaurants, feet in the nightclubs. The party (and traffic) goes on and on round and round the square. Meanwhile the Bastille has retained its symbolic appeal. The very name recalls popular uprising against injustice and consequently *liberté, egalité, fraternité,* the motto of the French Republic.

The outline of the Bastille is marked along the ground of the square, in front of Café Français and at the start of rue Saint-Antoine, the former entrance to the city. The Bastille was built as a fortress in the 14th century to protect Paris from outsiders approaching from the east but was often a favored target for civil war and civil uprising. In the 17th century, the noble era of the Marais, the Bastille also served as state prison, and as such it came to symbolize the arbitrariness of the law and of a despotic regime; in particular, the *lettre de cachet,* an order under the king's private seal, authorized imprisonment without trial. But despite its reputation, the Bastille was a relatively cushy prison for the time, more like living under house arrest than in dungeon depths.

Louis XVI's firing of his popular finance minister Jacques Necker on July 11, 1789, was the spark that pushed angry and frustrated Parisian mobs to rush to arms (stolen at the Invalides) then to attack the Bastille. When the Bastille was finally taken after a day-long siege on July 14, only seven prisoners trickled out, yet that was enough for revolution to have been born. Later that year it was dismantled in great revolutionary fervor. Stones from the fortress-cum-prison were carved into miniature Bastilles that were then sent to the provinces as a reminder of despotism and the ancient régime. One of these sculpted blocks is displayed in the Carnavalet Museum.

The column now at the center of the square commemorates not the events of 1789 but the victims of another revolution, that which toppled Charles X in the Revolution of July 27-29, 1830. A crypt beneath **the Column of July**, which can't be visited, contains the bodies of those who were killed during that revolt, which became known as "The Three Glorious Days."

There's also said to be an Egyptian mummy in the crypt. The mummy story goes as follows: The Egyptian collection of the Louvre had developed following Napoleon's Egyptian campaigns a generation earlier and it continued to grow and to be organized through the reign of Charles X. Among that collection was a mummy that, because it had become damp, was set out into the courtyard of the Louvre to dry in the summer heat. A major point of clash during the Revolution of 1830 took place in front of the Tuileries Palace, the royal abode across from the courtyard of the Louvre, and when the bodies of combatants were collected after the battle the mummy was carted along with them–and placed in the crypt.

There's also said to be an Egyptian mummy in the crypt.

Those bodies were later joined by victims of the Revolution of 1848 that saw the fall of the last of the kings and the brief rise of the Second Republic.

The column is topped with the graceful gilt **Spirit of the Bastille**, a splendid symbol of liberty.

The Bastille Opera

The Opéra de Paris Bastille, inaugurated during the bicentennial celebration of 1989, is France's premier opera house, having taking over the role formerly held by the smaller Garnier Opera. However, when Parisians speak of "the Opera" or "the Opera Quarter" they're referring to the Garnier Opera and its surroundings rather than to the Bastille.

Celebrating Bastille Day

The French national holiday, which we call Bastille Day, is simply called le Quatorze Juillet–the 14th of July–in French. Dance balls are held in certain squares and streets and in local firehouses (the traditional Firemen's Ball) throughout Paris on the evening of the 13th. On the morning of the 14th, the President of the Republic places a wreath at the Tomb of the Unknown Soldier beneath the Arc de Triomphe. A military parade then proceeds down the Champs-Elysées and flies overhead. That afternoon the president hosts a Garden Party for thousands of officials and invited guests at the Presidential Palace and sits for an hour with three journalist for a now-customary television interview about the state of the republic. That evening, beginning at about 10:30pm, fireworks are shot from in front of Trocadero, with prime (crowded) viewing from near the Eiffel Tower and along the Seine.

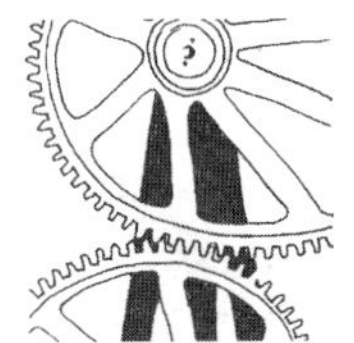

THE LOUVRE, THE ORSAY
AND OTHER MAJOR MUSEUMS

The wealth and variety of the museums of Paris are enough to make you wish for stormy weather—or to visit off season. But even after a week's worth of rain there'd still be much left to see. You could spend a week in the Louvre alone, or split that week with the Orsay. After those two world-leading museums, a wide array of top-notch museums calls for attention. Return travelers have their work cut out for they before they can profess to having seen it all. And nowhere in the traveler's bible does it say that you can't see something twice.

In fact, once you think you have seen it all twice, there's sure to be something new on the horizon. The museumscape of Paris continues to be renovated, shifted around and expanded. The Musée de l'Orangerie, whose collection includes Monet's monumental *Nymphéas* (Water Lilies) will reopen after extensive renovation in 2004. In 2005, a new major museum will open its doors with the inauguration of the Musée du Quai Branly, a national museum of the arts and civilizations of Africa, Asia, Oceania and the Americas (some of its works currently form a section of the Louvre); visit www.quaibranly.fr for continued updates.

The museums of Paris are listed below according to their relative significance. My star-ratings will not necessarily conform to your particular interests. Not all of the museums on this list are covered in this particular section. Some are described in other chapters; those *chapters: sections* are noted in italic.

★★★★★ **The Louvre:** Western art (painting, sculptures, objets d'arts, etc.) dating from the Middle Ages up to 1848. Also the art (particularly sculpture and objets d'arts) of antique civilizations that proceeded and influenced Western art: Oriental, Egyptian, Greek, Etruscan, Roman.

★★★★★ **Orsay Museum:** Western (mostly French) art from 1848 to 1914: Neoclassicism, Realism, Impressionism, Postimpressionism and other isms. Painting and sculpture with some architecture and furniture displays.

★★★★ **National Museum of Modern Art (Pompidou Center):** The Pompidou Center, France's main temple of 20th century art and culture, prides itself on housing Europe's most important collection of art from 1905 to the present.

★★★★ **Cluny Museum of the Middle Ages:** French stained glass, sculptures, tapestries, tombstones, paintings, reliquaries, enamels and other decorative details from the Middle Ages, particularly from the 12th-15th centuries. Also contains vestiges of the 2nd-century Roman baths of Lutetia. See *The Left Bank: The Latin Quarter.*

★★★★ **Musée des Arts et Métiers:** The national museum of technical innovation, also known as the Louvre of Technology, showing actual and scale models of innovations of the industrial era, mostly 19th and 20th centuries, in the fields of materials, construction, communication, energy, mechanics and transportation.

★★★★ **Picasso Museum:** Hundreds of paintings, sculptures and ceramics by Pablo Picasso (1881-1973) displayed in a major mansion in the Marais. See *The Marais: The Noble Marais.*

★★★ **Museum of the Army:** A vast military museum in the Invalides, behind which lies Napoleon's Tomb. See *Napoleon I's Paris: The Invalides.*

★★★ **Carnavalet Museum:** Two adjoining noble mansions dedicated to the history of Paris. A sequence of rooms shows decorative evolutions in the homes of nobility in Paris from the 16th through the 18th centuries. Also presents a collection of various objects and paintings that tell the history of Paris from 1789 on. See *The Marais: The Noble Marais.*

★★★ **Jaquemart-André Museum:** The mansion-museum of a couple in the late 19th century who were devoted to collecting paintings, furnishings and decorative works of 18th-century France and Renaissance Italy, along with some Dutch and Flemish masters.

★★★ **Rodin Museum:** Museum and gardens displaying the sculptures of Auguste Rodin (1840-1917).

★★★ **Guimet Museum of Asian Arts:** Sculpture (with some painting and ceramics) from various eras over the past 2000 years representing the arts and cultures of India, Afghanistan, Thailand, Cambodia, China, Korea and Japan. The museum is especially rich in works from southeast Asia, including the foremost collection of Kmer sculpture outside of Cambodia.

★★ **Modern Art Museum of the City of Paris:** Covering the same period as the Modern in the Pompidou Center through a less monumental collection with fewer major works. Nevertheless, a noteworthy collection of works from 1905-1935.

★★ **Museum of Jewish Art and History:** Religious and cultural objects recounting the history and culture of the Jews of France, housed in a building in the Marais that was inhabited by Jews deported to the death camps during the Holocaust. See *The Marais: The Jewish Marais.*

★★ **Marmatton Museum:** Best known for its major collection of Monets, this was the home of art historian Paul Marmottan, himself primarily a collector of European Primitives and Napoloenic (Empire) works. See *Gardens: Giverny.*

★★ **Bourdelle and *Zadkine Museums:** Two one-man sculpture museums in their former workshops in Montparnasse. See *The Left Bank: Montparnasse Quarter.*

★ **Cognacq-Jay Museum:** A charming little mansion displaying 18th-century decorative arts. See *The Marais: The Noble Marais.*

★ **Victor Hugo Museum/Home:** Memorabilia of the writer and poet Victor Hugo (1802-1885) in the townhouse he occupied from 1832 to 1848. See *The Marais: The Noble Marais.*

★ **Delacroix Museum:** A quaint but forgettable museum in Delacroix' former home and studio. See *The Left Bank: Saint-Germain Quarter.*

Museum Closing Days

Closed Monday: *Orsay, Museum of Modern Art (of Paris), Arts et Métiers, Carnavalet, Rodin, Cognacq-Jay, Marmottan, Bourdelle, Zadkine, Versailles, Museum of the Army and Napoleon's Tomb (first Mon. of each month), Victor Hugo.*

Closed Tuesday: *Louvre, National Museum of Modern Art (Pompidou Center), Cluny, Picasso, Guimet, Delacroix, Fontainebleau.*

General information

Admission to national and other non-city operated museums is generally 6-8€. There are often reduced rates for students under 26 and seniors over 60. Admission for children under 18 is generally free. Most major museums are free the first Sunday of each month. Museums operated by the City of Paris (Carnavalet, City Museum of Modern Art, Cognac-Jay) are free, except for temporary exhibitions.

When considering the closing times given here, note that rooms or sections begin to close 15-30 minutes earlier and that ticket sale ends 30-45 minutes prior to final closing.

Museum Pass

If you plan to visit several museums over a few consecutive days, the Paris Museum Pass is well worth considering. Passes are available at the participating museums, most metro stations and the Paris tourist office.

Museum passes are valid for 1 day or for 3 or 5 consecutive days beginning with the day of first use. They give free entrance to 70 museums and monuments in Paris and the surrounding region. They are especially practical because they allow you to avoid ticket lines, which can be long at the major museums and sites, particularly April-Sept.

The pass includes entrance to the Louvre, the Orsay Museum, Versailles and Fontainebleau (valid for general admission, not tours), the towers of Notre-Dame, the roof of the Arc de Triomphe, Napoleon's Tomb, the Pompidou Center, the Picasso Museum, the Rodin Museum, and many other museums and monuments. A complete list is provided in the brochure that accompanies the pass. The pass is not valid for temporary exhibitions in these museums. Of the major monuments of Paris, only the Eiffel Tower is not included with this pass.

The official site for the Museum Pass, www.intermusees.com, provides further details. Other websites selling the pass typically add a 20-30% surcharge.

THE LOUVRE

__Address__ Musée du Louvre, 1st arr. __Metro__ Palais Royal-Musée du Louvre. __Tel.__ 01 40 20 51 51, recorded info in 5 languages. __Site__ www.louvre.fr. __Open__ Daily except Tues. 9am-6pm; open until 9:45pm Mon. (partially) and Wed. __Entrance__ Main entrance via the pyramid. If there's a line at the pyramid and you have a Museum Pass or a ticket already, quick access is possible via Passage Richelieu, the passage through the northern wing of the Louvre. Entrance is also possible via the Carrousel du Louvre, the underground shopping mall between the two wings. __Tickets__ Your ticket is valid for the entire day, so it's possible to leave and return—not that anyone ever does that. Entrance fee is one-third off after 3pm (and lines are often shorter then). Tickets may be ordered in advance via the museum's website. __Map__ Pick up a free museum map at the information booth before entering. __Audioguides__ Available for rental. __Coat check__ You must show *your museum ticket or pass in order to check coats and bags.* ***Tours*** *Guided tours in English are scheduled daily; telephone 01 40 20 52 09 for times and themes or inquire upon arrival.* ***Lunch/Snack/Café*** *The Carrousel du Louvre mall has a basic food court. Café Marly facing the pyramid makes for an inviting photo in glossy magazines but having been treated with distain by the waiters I can't recommend it. Other cafés are situated across rue de Rivoli.* ***Visiting time*** *In about 4 hours of continuous walking you can catch a glimpse of every section—which isn't necessarily a worthy objective. Anyway, headache sets in after 2.5. The Louvre shouldn't be approached as an endurance test. How long are you willing to sit through a good movie? That's how long you should time your visit in a major museum.*

It's a shame that you aren't allowed to jog through the Louvre, running along surrounded by paintings and sculptures the way you might run through enchanted woods. What a wonderful jog through time and place that would be—past Mesopotamia and Etruria and pharaonic Egypt, into ancient Greece and Rome, north and south through Europe, a long stretch of the Renaissance, a wide expanse of France through the ages, and a confusion of signs pointing to *Mona Lisa, Vénus de Milo, Winged Victory*, etc. And after you've made your way through these enchanted woods, you could then jog over to the Orsay Museum, which picks up the national collection where the Louvre leaves off, in 1848.

Enter with the vague idea of *doing* the Louvre and you'll soon have the impression that its single ambition is to be the largest and most treasure-laden art museum in the world.

Enter with the vague idea of *doing* the Louvre and you'll soon have the impression that its single ambition is to be the largest and most treasure-laden art museum in the world. As a matter of fact, those are its ambitions, and they have been ever since Napoleon Bonaparte designated a portion of the Palace of Louvre as the main repository for his war booty 200 years ago. One of your goals, then, must be to visit without being overwhelmed—unless, of course, your objective is to be overwhelmed, as though attending an all-night rave party. Once you've accepted that you can't consume it all in a single visit, or even on a return visit, you'll need to devise a personal plan to explore the Louvre.

Begin by picking up a free map of the collection at the central information booth beneath the pyramid. From there, make a few basic choices according to your interests. The vast entrance hall, beneath the pyramid, offers three choices of an entrance and from there four separate levels. The map indicates the various sections as well as the placement of the most sought after specific works. You can aim for specific works, eras, styles, empires or nations. Keep your list short, because once you've started your visit you'll find yourself tugged by beauty, nudity or curiosity in numerous directions along the way. Simply heading for *Mona Lisa* is enough to set you on an hour or two of artful wandering.

The Louvre as palace

Long before becoming a museum, the Louvre was a palace of the kings of France. The Louvre is now fully devoted to its life as a museum, but keep an eye open for its history as a palace as you visit. You'll catch glimpses of that in stairwells, frescoes, stuccowork, marble flooring, galleries, as well in rooms that have been restored to their royal or imperial glory and in a display of several Crown jewels themselves. The exterior, meanwhile, remains that of the palace, with the exception of the pyramid entrance.

The Sully wing leads into the earliest portions of the palace. A short medieval circuit takes you past the earliest visible remnants, where you'll see the base of the dungeon of about 1200 and the surrounding walls of the original fortress. That fortress was built to protect the City Island from attacks coming upstream from the west. Its transformation into a fortress-castle began in 1364, when Charles V deemed the royal palace on the City Island too dangerous in case of civil uprising of the kind he had been forced to flee as a child. Vestiges of his Gothic additions are visible along with a model of the fortress-castle as it appeared at the end of the 14th century.

In the 15th century, during the Hundred Years War with the English, Paris itself was too dangerous for the French kings, who mostly resided in the Loire Valley. François I, whose reign (1515-1547) fully introduced France to the Renaissance, returned the royal eye to the Louvre. He ordered the destruction of the medieval dungeon and the Louvre's reconstruction as a Renaissance palace. The ornate inner facades of the courtyard began under his reign and continued under his son Henri II. Since François I, nearly every ruler of France has left his mark here; most recently, President François Mitterand initiated an enormous renovation and reorganization project called the Grand Louvre of which the pyramid entrance is the tip of the iceberg.

The kings and emperors who modified or expanded the palace and museum "signed" their work by having their initials placed as part of the decoration. As you walk around the exterior, look for the various H's for Kings Henri II, III and IV, the L's for Louis XIII and XIV and the N's for Napoleon I and III.

By the end of the 16th century, the Tuileries Palace, a more "modern" royal abode, had taken shape near the Louvre. The Tuileries Palace, which no longer exists, would eventually stretched from what are now the tip of the two wings of the Louvre. It was begun in the 1560s, with the Tuileries Garden (see *Gardens*) landscaped as its backyard. The Arc de Triomphe de Carrousel, which now appears to lead into the Tuileries Garden, was actually an arch that Napoleon I had built to make for a grandiose entrance to the Tuileries Palace. (Horsing exhibitions called carousels were once held in the courtyard of the extended Louvre.)

Soon after the Tuileries Palace was built, it seemed reasonable to want to connect it to the Louvre. This was the Grand Design of Henri IV (reigned 1594-1610). In 1857, after 250 years of on-again off-again expansion, Napoleon III achieved the final link between the palaces. He then set about reconstructing various other portions of the Louvre and harmonizing certain facades, creating an appearance of unity in a structure that was hundreds of years in the making. The interior opulence of the Napoleon III's Second Empire style can be seen in the ministerial apartments upstairs in the Richelieu Wing. A painting on the ceiling there shows the emperor placing the final link between the Tuileries Palace and the Louvre. However, in 1870, within three years of his renovation of the Louvre, Napoleon III was deposed. In May 1871 the Commune of Paris, having briefly taken over Paris, was put down by government forces, but not without burning down the Tuileries Palace, leaving the Louvre with two extended arms, but no palace to reach out to.

The Mona Lisa

Some paintings and sculptures are so famous that seeing them "in the flesh" is like a return visit in itself. It's sometimes surprising, though, to find that the actual image is not at all as you imagined. *The Mona Lisa,* for example, is fleshier in person than in reproductions. Her cleavage and the roundness of her cheeks tend to get lost in photographs. Needless to say, you don't find enigmatic smiles on skinny chicks.

Leonardo da Vinci's painting has been a star even since it was painted in about 1503. The subject of the portrait is presumed to be Monna del Giocondo. In English we refer to her by her first name, while the French, more formal by nature, refer to her by her last. They call the portrait *La Jaconde.*

The mystery created by the smile, the "perfection" of the human form, and the contrast between her flesh and her gown are intensified by the deeper contrast between her fleshy humanity and the lack of humanity in the background. The only human touch behind Mona is a stone bridge crossing a wild river that runs though a desolate landscape, while the infinite distance is enveloped in what, five centuries later, we might call a post-nuclear haze.

The painting was one of three that Leonardo da Vinci (1452-1519) brought to France from Rome in 1516 when he accepted the invitation of King François I to live near the royal château at Amboise in the Loire Valley. Leonardo also brought with him his painting of *Saint Anne,* which can be seen near *The Mona Lisa* and which is its clear echo. The third painting, *Saint John the Baptist,* was completed in Amboise.

François I, who decisively brought the Renaissance to France, had befriended Leonardo during his Italian campaigns and wished to further honor the Renaissance man par excellence, a genius painter, sculptor, architect and engineer. He provided him with the handsome manor of Clos Lucé, a half-mile from the château, and a no-strings-attached pension that allowed the genius-in-residence to work and create as he pleased. During that time, the king visited him frequently to discuss Leonardo's projects and ideas. Presumably during that time he purchased *The Mona Lisa.* Leonardo lived at Clos Lucé for the last three years of his life, and was buried at the chapel of the château.

François I later undertook the creation of Fontainebleau (see *Châteaux*), *the* royal château of the French Renaissance, and placed *The Mona Lisa* there. He also ordered the transformation of the Louvre from a medieval castle to a "modern" palace. So it is only appropriate that 500 years after its creation, the most famous painting in the world holds a place of honor in the most famous museum in the world.

The Louvre as museum

The royal collection of sculptures, paintings, drawings and antiquities had been organized museum-style as early as the reign of Henri IV (1589-1610), when lodgings were also set aside in the palace for artists. Art shows were even held here after Louis XIV had freed up space by moving the Court to Versailles in 1682. Louis XIV added a monumental front to the palace but he then left it to the French Academies and courtly hangers-on and to general neglect. During Louis XV's reign the idea was hatched to open some of the royal art collection to the larger public in the long galleries of the Louvre that ran along the Seine. This was finally accomplished by the Revolution, whose leaders gathered other artworks from the royal and noble abodes and from possessions of the Church. The museum was officially opened in 1793.

Napoleon can be most credited with starting museum-mania in France. In 1801, he ordered the creation of two dozen museums throughout the country to display pieces from the imperial collection, works seized from nobility during the Revolution, and booty from his various military campaigns throughout Europe and North Africa. For a brief time, the greatest artworks of Europe were displayed here. But after Napoleon's defeat at Waterloo, the victorious allies demanded the return of most of the war booty. Nevertheless France had gotten a taste of the glory of a great museum, and so subsequent governments pursued the march to enormity.

In addition to their interest as works of art, many of the works you'll see in the Louvre are intimately related to the history of France. The story of how they came to be here will further enhance your visit and make it slow going. There isn't sufficient place here to tell their stories, so I leave it to you to discover those stories through audioguides or real guides or explanatory panels.

The Orsay Museum

Address *62 rue de Lille, 7th arr.* ***Metro*** *Solférino.* ***RER*** *Musée d'Orsay.* ***Open*** *Daily except Mon., 10am-6pm; opens at 9am on Sunday and from 6/20 to 9/20; open until 9:45pm on Thurs.* ***Ticket*** *Available for the entire day. Major exhibitions relative to the period 1848-1914 are held at the Orsay and a separate ticket is required for those.* ***Map*** *Pick up a free map at the entrance, but even with it it's easy to get balled up on the upper floors.* ***Audioguides*** *Available for rental.* ***Hand-held explanatory panels*** *Available in certain sections of the museum.* ***Lunch/Snack/Café*** *The ornate restaurant upstairs to the front of the museum is open for lunch 11:30am-2:30pm and serves as tea room 3:30-5:30pm. The café/snack bar upstairs on the Seine side is open 10am-5pm, Thurs. until 9pm.* ***Visiting time*** *In 2.5-3 hours you could cover most galleries at a mildly attentive pace—but if approached that way you'll exhaust yourself. Give yourself 2 hours then call it quits.* ***Site*** *www.musee-orsay.fr.*

From 1848 to 1914 France was at the top of its game in the world of art. French and foreign artists in France led currents and movements from neo-Classicism to Impressionism and from post-Impressionism to the first steps of Modernism, and many isms in between. An astounding number of major works of that period can be seen in the Musée d'Orsay.

Many of the names and the works here are so familiar to us that visiting the Orsay can be like visiting your local grocery store, where, for better or worse, we're attracted to certain brands and packaging and only occasionally by others: Ingres, Delacoix, Manet, Monet, Renoir, Degas, Pissarro, Van Gogh, Gaugin, Saurat, Cézanne, Rodin, Toulouse-Lautrec, Bonnard, Vuillard; *Whistler's Mother, Déjeuner sur l'Herbe, L'Absinthe, L'Eglise d'Auvers-sur-Oise,* etc. That best-of aspect of the Orsay makes it at once an important "commercial" art center and an artist's art museum, the occasion for a cultural quickie or for a prolonged trance. You're choice.

One of the great things about the museums in Paris is the diversity of the buildings that house them. The Orsay was built as a train station in 1900. It was given more esthetic considerations than other train stations of the era because it was to be within view of the Louvre and the Tuileries Garden just across the river. Its metallic structure is therefore hidden behind stone facades, making it look more like a neo-Baroque cathedral then a train station, with the ornate clocks standing out like rose windows on the side. Its similarities to a cathedral continue inside as you take in the view of the tremendous nave of the station, which displays an alley of sculptures down the middle and the currents of painting in "chapels" on either side.

The Orsay station was the end of the former Paris-Orléans line, hence the initials PO on the façade along with the names of cities reached from here. Within 40 years of its inauguration, the station proved too short for electric trains. It then lay more or less dormant for several decades, and there were suggestions of tearing it down. In the late 1970s the idea of transforming it into a museum saved the structure. The Musée d'Orsay opened in 1986.

The ground floor displays works from the period 1848-1870s, particularly the art currents of Neoclassicism and Realism and the countercurrents of Romanticism and Orientalism. The central alley presents sculptures of the period, including the work of Carpeaux whose celebratory *Dance* once decorated the front of the Garnier Opera. A scale model of the Garnier Opera and its surrounding quarter as it appeared prior to 1914 are shown in the far end of the central alley; they represent the architectural culmination of the period covered by the museum (see *Late 19th-Century Paris,* particularly *Garnier Opera* for more). Also note the early Eiffel Tower souvenirs around the corner—scarcely different from those of today.

The upper levels of the museum are given over to Impressionism and Postimpressionism. The major rooms of the Impressionists offer a magnificent view over the Seine and out to major monuments of the Right Bank: the Louvre, the Garnier Opera, Sacré Coeur. Otherwise, the layout of the upper floors is less inviting than the ground floor; the space is more cramped and the sequence of rooms can be confusing. Or so it seems, because museum fatigue begins to set in by the time you reach the Impressionists. Let that be a warning not to wear out your artistic sensibilities on the ground floor if it's the Impressionists and Postimpressionists that truly interest you. Unlike museums where you can relax your focus in some rooms and merely scan a few walls, the density of familiar and famous works throughout the Orsay means that there's no downtime. Nearly every piece calls for attention. If you've rented an audioguide you'll have to be selective about the works you choose to hear about.

Because of that density and because of the labyrinthine layout of the museum, the crowds at the Orsay are more likely to detract from the museum experience than in the expansive Louvre. Furthermore, from April through September there is often a long line to go in (except with the museum pass). As must-see fabulous as the Orsay is, it can also be tiring. Kudos to the off-season traveler.

The Pompidou Center & The National Museum of Modern Art

Address *Rue Beaubourg, 4th arr.* ***Metro*** *Rambuteau or Hôtel de Ville.* ***Open*** *Daily except Tues., 11am-10pm; museum and exhibits close at 9pm.* ***Tickets*** *There are separate tickets for the museum and for the individual temporary exhibits; for a thorough Pompidou experience you may purchase a one-day pass valid for entrance throughout the center. If on a mission, there is indeed enough going on here to keep you busy for a good part of the day.* ***Site*** *www.centrepompidou.fr.*

The colored tubing of the Georges Pompidou Center announces the entrance to France's main temple of 20th century art and culture. Known locally as Beaubourg, for the name of the downtrodden quarter it leveled, the center is a stew of contemporary culture with an air of officialdom about it. It has been a huge draw ever since it opened in 1977. In addition to housing the National Museum of Modern Art on two floors, the center contains several spaces for tempo-

rary exhibits as well as auditoriums, projection rooms, an industrial creation space, a children's workshop, an acoustic research institute and a public library.

The Pompidou wears its arteries and intestines on the outside, with each color corresponding to its basic needs: white for support, blue for air, green for water, yellow for electricity, red for you. The inside then can be divided at will, making it as malleable as a cartoon; its only decoration is functionalism itself, which would have all the charm of a trade show hall were it not for the quality of the museum and exhibits and for the view of the surrounding city as you move from level to level along the exterior escalators. The city blossoms around you as you rise, culminating in a spectacular view from the top (6th) level. The view there is particularly Parisian in that you stand just above the zinc rooftops as you perceive monuments and towers and the grey-blue sky.

While the Orsay makes you want to be a collector of promising young outsiders, a visit to the Pompidou makes you want to retire and create things on your own.

The rooftop café-restaurant, **Georges** (as in Pompidou), allows you to enjoy (at museum prices) a portion of that view with a seat, though window seats are hard to come by. Meanwhile, back on the ground, **Café Beaubourg**, next to the center, is a must for subtly fashionable intellectuals. Joyous **Stravinsky Fountain** by Niki de Saint-Phalle (colors) and Jean Tinguely (black) plays in the basin to the right of the center. Several laidback (if not terribly friendly) lunch places are appealingly set beside fountain.

Musée National d'Art Moderne. Modern art means works of the 20th century, and the national museum at the Pompidou Center prides itself on presenting Europe's most important collection of works from 1905 on. The collection picks up more or less where the Orsay leaves off. While the Orsay makes you want to be a collector of promising young outsiders, a visit to the Pompidou makes you want to retire and create things on your own.

Entrance to the museum is on the building's 4th level, which covers works after 1955. The 5th level covers the period 1905-1955. The museum can therefore be visited chronologically be starting upstairs once inside the museum. However, since the later works are more challenging due to their relative lack of familiarity, you might just as well start with the 4th before turning back in time for the 5th. Use of the audioguides may be helpful, particularly if arriving innocent of the 20th century. This is a large museum, though, so with or without the audioguides you'll have to find the right pace to keep your tour under two hours.

Other Contemporary Venues in Paris

The Pompidou Center is the main space for exhibitions of all kinds relative to art, architecture and culture since 1950. The addresses of several other major venues for contemporary exhibitions in Paris are noted below. Also see *The Marais: Artsy Marais* for addresses of contemporary art galleries throughout the city.

Cartier Foundation (Fondation Cartier de l'art contemporain). ***Address*** *261 bd. Raspail, 14th arr.* ***Metro*** *Raspail.* ***Open*** *Daily except Tues., noon-8pm.*

Jeu de Paume. ***Address*** *1 place de la Concorde, 1st arr.* ***Metro*** *Concorde.* ***Open*** *Daily except Mon.* The former tennis court of the Tuileries Palace in the Tuileries Garden, now a space for single artist exhibits.

Palais de Tokyo. ***Address*** *13 av. du Président-Wilson, 16th arr.* ***Metro*** *Iéna or Alma-Marceau.* ***Open*** *Daily except Mon. noon-midnight.* ***Site*** *www.palaisdetokyo.com.* You can't blame the creators of this self-congratulatory grunge museum for the missed opportunity—they managed to receive a good amount of public funding along with a 30s building to trash. It may actually be possible to chance upon a stimulating exhibit among the several going on at one time at this mildly interactive "site of contemporary creation," but better check the website before considering a detour. The café resembles a high school cafeteria after a riot, which can indeed make someone feel creative.

Modern Art Museum of the City of Paris.
Address *11 av. du Président-Wilson, 16th arr.* ***Metro*** *Iéna or Alma-Marceau.* ***Open*** *Daily except Mon. 10am-5:30pm.* ***Tickets*** *Free except for temporary exhibits.*
The city's Museum of Modern Art (not to be confused with the national museum at the Pompidou Center) is a bit out-of-date in its presentation and lighting, but that's part of its charm. It provides a manageable overview of modern, i.e. 20th century, art beginning with Fauves of 1905 and ending with video art of the 1990s. The collection has a mid-century hole from 1937 to 1960. Its most notable works are pre-WWII, in tune with the building itself, a remnant of the 1937 Fair of Arts and Techniques, as is the Palais de Tokyo next door.

Rodin Museum

Address *77 rue de la Varenne, 7th arr.* ***Metro*** *Varenne.* ***Open*** *Daily except Mon. April-Sept. 9:30am-5:45pm, park closes at 6:45pm, Oct.-March 9:30m-4:45pm, park closes at 5pm.* ***Site*** *www.musee-rodin.fr.* ***Audioguide*** *Available for rental.* ***Visiting time*** *About an hour, plus a pause in the garden café-tearoom which serves sandwiches, desserts and beverages.* ***In the area*** *The museum is around the corner from Napoleon's Tomb at the Invalides. Government ministries are located throughout this corner of the 7th arrondissement, including the prime minister's residence Matignon, several blocks down rue de Varenne.*

In 1908, Auguste Rodin (1840-1917) was a leading sculptor when he set out to make the mansion known as the Hôtel Biron his museum. It has become one of Paris's most pleasurable museum settings, both for the garden that gives breathing space to major works of the master and for the museum building itself, a mansion of 1730 that displays the full flourish of France's Rococo period.

The visit should begin inside, starting with early works such as the Greco-Roman-like *Man with a Broken Nose* and the precious clay *Young Woman with Flowered Hat* (both 1865). Rodin reached his maturity as an artist with the draped torso of *The Age of Airain* (1877), whose plaster cast was so life-like that he was accused of having molded it directly on the model. He followed that up with the full nude in bronze, naked even of his lance. The expressive nature of Rodin's work moved to the forefront as he revealed his attachment to the works of Michelangelo in *Saint Jean-Baptist* (1880) and *Adam* and *Eve* (both 1881).

In 1880 Rodin received a commission for a door to a museum of decorative arts. That commission would be his famous *Gate of Hell*, a sculptural translation of Dante's eight circles of decent of *The Divine Comedy*: "You who enter, abandon all hope." *The Gate of Hell* would take 15 years to complete, and during that time it became a gathering place for a number of Rodin's major works, reproduced in miniature. The door stands in the front garden, across from Rodin's most celebrated work, *The Thinker*. On its own, *The Thinker* represents the inward-looking individual, where muscle, flesh, bone, toes, strength and beauty are visible to the spectator yet turned within. *The Thinker* also has a place on *The Gate of Hell*. Sitting there with less balance, just below *The Shadows*, *The Thinker* becomes Dante himself in contemplation of the world of the damned. Other copies of *The Thinker* exist, including one on Rodin's tomb at Meudon, a suburb southwest of Paris.

Other major works with a place in *Hell* are found in the museum or in the garden, including the *Falling Man*, the couple *Paolo and Francesca*, and *Ugolini and his Children*. The large version of the latter occupies the center of the basin at the back of the garden, where Ugolini is seen starving along with his dying children whom he is destined to eat.

The Bourgeois of Calais is another major piece in the garden. It is the product of a commission that Rodin received in 1885 to honor the surrender and sacrifice of the town leaders of Calais in 1347. Under siege by the English during the Hundred Years War, a deal was made by which the town would be saved if the town leaders (burghers or bourgeois) would give themselves over to the enemy. Here, the six men are seen walking barefoot to their death, attached to a rope, each bearing a different expression and position of surrender. The hands alone express the drama of the scene. In fact, hands became part of Rodin's signature, as in *The Hand of God* (1896), *The Cathedral* (1908) and *The Secret* (1909), all seen inside the museum.

Marbles and bronzes through the museum reveal the strength, movement and expression in his individuals and fragments of individuals, e.g. the tenderness of *The Young Mother* (1885), the force and sensuality of *The Kiss* (1889).

Following Rodin's wishes, the works of the sculptor Camille Claudel (1864-1943) were given a room of their own. The two met in 1883 when she was his student, and before long she was also his lover and studio assistant. She created the bust of Rodin (1888) seen here. Their mutual influence and support turned sour after 1893 though they maintained a deteriorating relationship until 1898. Her own masterpieces were produced from 1890-1900: *The Waltz* (1895), a work full of passion, adoration, peace and movement; *Maturity* (1898), a vision of the destiny of age; *The Implorer* (1900), an image of abandonment (by Rodin). Though she continued to work for several more years, her mental health declined over the next decade, including bouts with paranoia, and in 1913 she was committed to a mental institution, where she remained until her death 30 years later.

The rooms upstairs in the mansion are among the most fascinating for visitors interested in the creative process as they reveal the stages of development and composition of several of Rodin's major works: *The Gate of Hell*, *The Bourgeois of Calais* and the statues of *Balzac* and of *Victor Hugo*. The room presenting preparatory works for Rodin's monumental sculpture honoring the writer Honoré de Balzac is the most telling as it shows the ways in which Rodin decorticated, sketched and fathomed his subject as he worked towards creating the final sculpture.

Jacquemart-André Museum

Address *158 boulevard Haussmann, 8th arr.* ***Metro*** *Miromesnil or St-Philippe-du-Roule.* ***Open*** *Daily 10am-6pm.* ***Restaurant-tearoom*** *Open 11:30am-5:30pm; lunch served 11:30am-3pm: salads, pastries, some hot dishes.* ***Audioguide*** *Free.* ***Site*** *www.musee-jacquemart-andre.com.*

The Jacquemart-André Museum has just the right amount of splendor, is just the right size and has just the right tearoom to make it just right for rounding out the itinerary of a return traveler. You needn't crave the sight of 18th century French art and furnishings, 15th century Italian works and the paintings by Flemish and Dutch masters to partake in its luxuriance, for one doesn't come here to visit a museum so much as to be the guest in the home of its creators, Edouard André (1833-1894) and his wife Nélie Jacquemart-André (1841-1912).

With unlimited resources, no children, nothing so mundane as a job to tie them down, and a knowledgeable passion for the work they set out to collect, the Jacquemart-Andrés became major collectors of their era. This museum is very much the product of their collective lives.

The mansion was originally designed as the showy society bachelor pad of Edouard André, heir to a banking fortune who also had an interest in government affairs. His home would become one of the major markers of the luxury-minded Monceau quarter, which developed in the 1860s during the reign of Napoleon III as Baron Haussmann laid out major boulevards in the area. Monceau immediately became one the prime residential quarter of the imperial gentry and of the upper bourgoisie, particularly for those in the banking industry. (The atmosphere of the museum can carry over into a walk north of the Jacquemart-André mansion to Parc Monceau; see *Gardens*)

One doesn't come here to visit a museum so much as to be the guest in the home of its creators.

The André house was built on a rise with its back to boulevard Haussmann and entered by a driveway curving around to the front. Like the Garnier Opera, it was designed during the reign of Napoleon III but wasn't inaugurated until 1875, five years after the emperor's fall. By that time its destiny had already changed. After Edouard André and Baron Rothchild helped collect funds to pay off the war indemnity that Bismark posed as a condition for ending the siege of Paris during the Franco-Prussian War, André ended his relationship with the Third Republic and devoted the rest of this life to the accumulation and promotion of the arts.

As a young woman Nélie Jacquemart was a society portraitist. She met André in 1872 when he commissioned her to paint his portrait. After their marriage in 1881, their collection and its presentation in the home became their shared focus. For their sense of upper-crust living, the couple was on the forefront of their era, but they were anything but collectors of contemporary works. André's original interest was in bringing the taste for the 18th century into the home by collecting French paintings and furnishings (Louis XV and XVI) from the period. Nélie, though she gave up her own work as portraitist, also had a fine eye for the intimate portraits of the preceding century. The ground floor is largely devoted to that passion and also presents their collection of Flemish and Dutch masters, among them several Rembrandts.

They then turned their attention to decorating the upper floor, originally planned as Nélie's studio. Since she no longer painted, that became their "Italian museum," where they displayed their rich collection of works of the Italian Renaissance. Past the winter garden, a monumental marble staircase decorated with a Tiepolo fresco, which appears to have been created for the space, leads to their presentation of works of the Italian Quattrocento. The Jacquemart-Andrés amassed a collection that had conservators of the Louvre knocking at their door. In fact, their buying budget was far greater than that of the Louvre at the time.

The audioguide is an excellent companion during your visit, giving helpful explanations of the couple's buying interests and elevated social position. We learn that theirs was a "marriage of reason" and are left to assume that the reason had something to do with the complementarity of his passion for Venetian art and her preference for Florentines.

The couple traveled extensively about half of each year, especially to Italy as well as to Egypt, and those travels would be the occasion for enormous buying sprees. After her husband's death, Nélie traveled even wider, from England to India to the Far East, while continuing to devote herself to the collection and its presentation here. The couple bequeathed their home and collection to the Institut de France, which opened it as a museum. When possible, their possessions have been left as they were displayed by Nélie.

The restaurant-tearoom, which occupies the mansion's vast dining room, is very much a part of the Jacquemart-André experience. Along with the restaurant-tearooms at the Orsay and Rodin Museums, this offers one of the finest museum pauses in Paris. As such it is also a favorite lunch spot for those who work in the area; it's often crowded between noon and 2pm and there can be a wait to get in. But even when crowded, it exudes the sense of artful luxury that the couple's home was, and still is, all about.

Musée des Arts et Métiers
National Museum of Technical Innovation

***Address** 60 rue Réaumur, 3rd arr. **Metro** Arts et Métiers. The copper shell of the metro station on line 11 sets the tone for the visit here. **Open** Daily except Mon. 10am-6pm, until 9:30pm Thurs. **Demonstrations/Tours** Free demonstrations and general or thematic tours are given hourly 11am-5pm in various sections of the museum. Though in French, they're worth joining for the demonstrations.*

This may well be the greatest of the unsung museums of the city. If you aren't immediately attracted to the theme of technical innovation, you should at least be aware that this brainy museum is the best of its kind. That's why it is often called the Louvre of Technology or the Pantheon of Technical Innovation. I'm no industrial tech-head either, but the objects themselves are as beautiful now as they were innovative when designed. It's almost as though one were visiting a sculpture museum. There's also the pleasure of enjoying the grandeur of a large museum with hardly a visitor in sight.

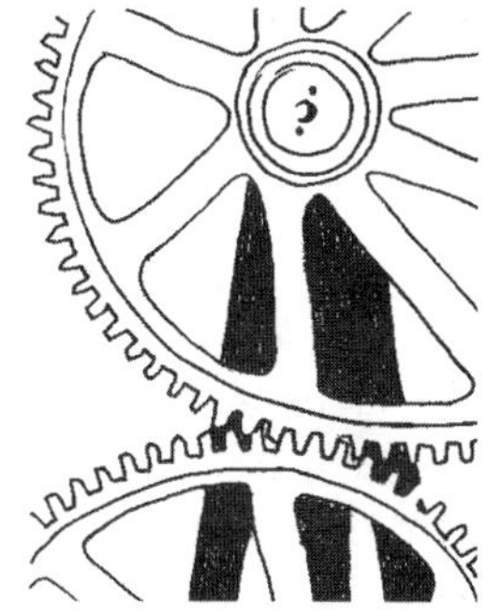

In 1794, revolutionary priest Abbé Grégoire presented the Convention, then ruling revolutionary France, with a proposal to create "a conservatory for arts and trades [*arts et métiers*] where all of the tools and machines that are newly invented and perfected shall be brought together." The former Abbey of St-Martin-des-Champs was consecrated to just such a plan in 1798. The abbey church itself would become a veritable church of progress. Adjacent buildings still serve as a school of technology. The old tracks along which machines were trollied to be demonstrated through the 19th century are still visible in the museum.

From *The Dulcimer Player* (1784), an automaton that once belonged to Marie-Antoinette, to 18th-century chain-making machines, from a steam "automobile" (1800) to Foucault's pendulum (1851), from an Edison phonograph (1877) to a Lumière brothers film projector (1895), from a model of a high speed train to that of an atomic accelerator, the museum and the school are France's main repository for original machines of innovation. Beyond the vast collection presented here, tens of thousands of objects remain in storage.

The circuit begins in the attic with a presentation of scientific instruments. From there, the museum is organized in seven sections: materials, construction, communication, energy, mechanics (including choice figures of the museum's automaton collection) and transportation. There are enough descriptive notices in English to keep you informed without going over the head of the layman. And touch screens provide visuals of the inner workings of the certain machines and technologies.

The circuit ends with the holy of holies, the former abbey church that has been beautifully restored and is now dedicated to technical know-how. Foucault's pendulum, from the first experiment to provide visual proof of the rotation of the earth, hangs from the ceiling in the 12th-century chapel (see *The Left Bank: The Pantheon* for more on the pendulum). In the nave, an early flying machine hangs overhead like an angel, while at the far end the original plaster model of the *Statue of Liberty* stands like the Virgin herself, bearing not Child but Flame. Sacrilege? No, science.

Guimet Museum of Asian Arts

Address *6 place d'Iéna, 16th arr.* ***Metro*** *Iéna.* ***Open*** *Daily except Tues. 10am-6pm. Audioguide Free.* ***Site*** *www.museeguimet.fr.*

From a Cambodian Harihara to an Afghan Buddha to a Tibetan Pachen Lama, from Brahma to Vishnu to Shiva's cosmic dance, the national collection of Asian art at the Guimet Museum is as beautiful as it is meaningful. The museum can serve as a magnificent introduction to Asian sculpture or further the appreciation of those already initiated in the arts and culture of the region from India to Japan by way of Afghanistan, Thailand, Cambodia, China and Korea.

This national museum developed from the collection of the industrialist Emile Guimet (1836-1918), whose initial interest in foreign art was to demonstrate the universal morality he believed to be at the basis of all religions. Over time Guimet's focus turned from world religions to Asian art in particular. The collection benefited from major French expeditions in the region in the late 19th and early 20th centuries and from the French presence in Indochina at the time.

The Guimet Museum is especially rich in works from southeast Asia, including the foremost collection of Kmer sculpture outside of Cambodia. While the beauty of the objects is readily visible, the audioguide is a valuable source of information to better understand their religious and/or historical significance. The building was restored and the collection reorganized several years ago. The museum is now nothing short of stunning.

THE GARDENS OF PARIS

Rush through the Louvre, stay at the foot of the Eiffel Tower, shun the Champs-Elysées, yawn in gastronomic restaurants... but linger in the gardens and parks of Paris and the gods of travel will smile upon you. Among the great monuments of Paris and the surrounding region, none offers a more relaxed, romantic and civilized vision of French culture than its monuments to nature. Disregarding them would be an affront to both leisure travel and urban nature.

The Paris region covers 2.2% of France's continental territory while housing 18.5% of its population (11 million out of 61 million). But don't let those numbers fool you into believing that the capital and its immediate surroundings have been completely abandoned to concrete, metal and stone. Nature—albeit tamed nature—still plays an important role in urban and suburban life. Though its soil, slopes, waterways and woods have been combed over and modified for centuries, Paris has allowed itself the space for a wonderful array of "natural" urban landscapes.

Paris's gardens, parks, grassy squares and tree-lined cemeteries collectively go under the heading of *espaces verts*, green spaces. Together, they testify not only to the history and growth of the city but to its ongoing life as well. This even holds true for the cemeteries (covered in *Death in Paris*). First-time travelers tend to view the gardens as paths between sights. The return traveler knows them to be destinations in themselves. You'll undoubtedly linger longer in gardens under blue skies, but they aren't just for sunny-day strolls. Even on gray days they reveal their romance and charm. Every major sight and quarter of the city, along with each of the châteaux of the surrounding region, is associated with its own green space, so you could just as well prepare an itinerary of gardens and parks and woods as an itinerary of museums and monuments.

The surrounding region abounds in nature that is both tame, as at Versailles and other great châteaux, and less tame, as in the Woods of Vincennes and Boulogne, known as the lungs of the city, or in the Forest of Fontainebleau, a hiker's delight. Further afield, no one goes to Giverny to visit Monet's home, they go for his gardens. Commentary on gardens continues in the chapter *Châteaux of the Paris Region*; after all, the glory of Versailles radiates from its gardens as well as from its architecture and décor.

For weary museum-goers these green spaces mean that a seat in the park is just around the corner, for market-goers that means a picnic bench is right nearby, for budget travelers that means you can always have the best seat in the house, for lovers that means the perfect backdrop for a kiss. For all travelers these green spaces are a special angle from which to partake in French culture. So loosen your itinerary and head for the green.

Green Acres

Green spaces (a term uniting gardens, parks and tree-lined cemeteries) in Paris total 832 acres, to which can be added the 4,940 acres of the lungs of the city, the Woods of Boulogne to the west and of Vincennes to the east.

The Medieval Garden at the Cluny Museum

The National Museum of Medieval Art, also known as the Cluny Museum, is Paris's major museum of the Middle Ages (see The Left Bank: The Latin Quarter*). Whether or not you enter the museum, garden lovers—or simply lovers—should take note of the medieval garden that has been recreated beside it, at the intersection of boulevard Saint-Germain and boulevard Saint-Michel. The garden is a playful wink at medieval life, particular as shown in the tapestry* The Lady and the Unicorn, *which is the centerpiece of the Cluny Museum. Beneath chestnut and oak trees, the garden is planted only with species that existed in the Middle Ages in France, particularly flowers from the millefleur tapestries, mille fleurs meaning a thousand flowers. The Garden of Cluny is divided into five sections representing different uses of plants and flowers during the Middle Ages, particularly for the nobility and/or clergy. You'll find the Love Garden full of roses, the Heavenly Garden, the Medicinal Simples (i.e. medicinal plants), the Kitchen Garden (i.e. vegetables), and the Meadow. The brick paving of the central path bears the imprint of the fantastic creatures of the forest that may have wandered about the medieval mind at night.*

Le Nôtre and The Tuileries Garden

There was a time in the 17th century, while the gardens of Versailles had yet to emerge from the surrounding swampland and most of America was but a glimmer in colonial eyes, when nobles and Parisians of note strolled the paths of the Tuileries Garden as though they had returned, fully and elegantly dressed, to the Garden of Eden. There was a purity to the garden, a perfection to the labyrinths of precisely trimmed hedges and the alleyways of pruned trees, a playful rationalism to the diverse geometry found throughout the park. This was no Biblical garden of innocence conceived in order to be spoiled. This was a pure work of man: intelligent, rational, civilized, nature-taming man. And it bore the imprint of André Le Nôtre, the most accomplished garden designer France has ever known.

The Tuileries is the great-great-grandfather of city parks in France, stretching out in the heart of the modern city. Some of its 17th-century elements are missing or have been redesigned, the armies of gardeners to tend to the space are gone (though the city and national payrolls ensure its well-being) and the activities that took place here – the gallant promenades, the Baroque parties – have long disappeared, replaced by other walks of life. Yet the basic elements of Le Nôtre's vision remain: the horseshoe ramps along the western edge, the terrace overlooking the Seine River, the large octagonal basins, and above all the great perspective leading out along what has become the Champs-Elysées. While Louis XIV, the Sun King, submitted France to his royal will, Le Nôtre tamed the land and brought about the golden age of the formal French garden.

Nowadays we visit the Tuileries to escape the density of the city into more natural surroundings. If Parisians use the cafés as their livingrooms, they step into the gardens and parks as their backyards. But the Tuileries predates that view of the city. At the end of the 16th century, the time of the creation of the original garden of the Tuileries Palace, one needed merely to step outside the city walls to be in the countryside. These grounds themselves were an outpost of the city where clay was dug up to be baked into roof tiles, *tuiles* in French. At the far end of the *tuileries* were the city ramparts, beyond them fields then woods, to the side the muddy slopes of the river. So when Catherine de Medicis purchased this land, she was not in search of a breath of raw nature, rather she sought a bit of private, organized nature on the edge of the countryside.

Eglise St-Roch, Burial Place of André Le Nôtre

One block north of the Tuilieries on rue Saint-Honoré, the beautiful Baroque church of St-Roch pays homage to the talents of André Le Nôtre, who is buried here. A bust of France's premier classical gardener bears the inscription: *Il n'a point eu de concurrent qui lui fut comparable* (He had no competitor who could be compared to him). Over the centuries Saint Roch, which was built during Le Nôtre's lifetime, has become known as the church for ceremonies honoring the death of artists.

Catherine de Médicis and the Tuileries Palace

Catherine de Medicis (1519-1589) is best known as the queen mother of three kings, who, with her sons, alternately extinguished and fanned the fires of a turbulent period known as the Wars of Religion. This was a time when the struggle for freedom of worship and the political rights of the French Protestants, Huguenots, intersected with a struggle for power among the high nobles of France. Here at the Tuileries Garden, though, she is also recalled as the widow of Henri II, who, following a mortal injury of her husband (1559) during a jousting tournament in the Marais, abandoned the royal palace there and in 1563 ordered the construction of a new palace across from the Louvre. Behind the area set aside for the palace, Catherine also purchased the large parcel of land called the *tuileries*, a name then inherited by the palace and its garden.

The original garden was cut into numerous parterres, i.e. garden plots on which plants are set into geometric patterns like arabesque embroidery *(parterres de broderie)*. The nobility took to the setting. Little by little the garden of the Tuilieries Palace became a place for the French Court to stroll about in fine robes, a promenade during which they'd admire delicate embroidery of boxwood, an intricate labyrinth of hedges, trees imported from faraway lands. The noble gardens of 16th century France were initially inspired by the gardens of the Italian Renaissance (Catherine herself was Italian by birth), though in place of the slopes of her native Florence the Tuileries was adapted to the flat ground of the Seine Valley. By the 17th century the development of the French garden was underway.

Basins and fountains were eventually added as the play of water was introduced. Fashion and economics also altered the landscape. During the reign of Henri IV (1588-1610) an alley was raised on the northern side of the Tuileries for an orchard of white mulberries, whose leaves were used to feed silk worms in order to produce the fabulous fabric, originally brought from China, that had become a fashion symbol of the Renaissance. No self-respecting aristocrat or ambitious bourgeois would be seen without silk.

THE GARDEN BOOKSTORE

Just inside the garden's entrance from the place de la Concorde, near a bust of André Le Nôtre, there's a great garden and gardening bookstore, including a section of children's books about nature. Proper toilets are also found by that entrance.

Le Nôtre and the grand perspective

André Le Nôtre grew up in that primitive Italian-cum-French garden. His grandfather had worked there under Catherine de Medicis, his father had been chief gardener for

Tuileries Flora and Fauna

Due to its placement in the heart of the city, the Tuileries attracts millions of foreign travelers, but keep your eye out for more indigenous species and expatriate flora. These include the horse-chestnut, a species originally from the Balkan Mountains and first brought from Constantinople in 1612, now a common sight in Paris parks, along with lindens and plane trees; all three dominate in the Tuileries. Elms, lindens and maples also grow on the terraces. You'll also find well-fed carp in the basins, swallows and swift visiting from April to October, magpies, black crows and wood-pigeons descending from their tree-top nests and nuthatches and blue tits peeking out from trunk holes. Sparrows and swallows, meanwhile, have made homes for themselves in the upper niches in the Arc de Triomphe du Carrousel ever since 1808 when that triumphal arch was built under orders of Napoleon I to serve as the imperial entrance to the Tuileries Palace.

Louis XIII (reigned 1610-1643). Le Nôtre's two sisters married gardeners, both of whom worked at the Tuileries. And Le Nôtre himself would eventually succeed his father as royal gardener.

Unlike later gardens where Le Nôtre would conceive of most or all of the elements of the space, his task at the Tuileries in 1664 was to redesign rather than create a garden. Yet it fully bears his imprint as a master of the interplay of garden and landscape elements, using the full language of the formal French garden: alleys, borders, parterres, trimmed yews and hedges, flowerbeds, basins, terraces, and, above all, balance and perspective. Furthermore, he placed the French garden on a scale of vast proportions that would reflect the nobleman or king who owned such civilized nature. The Tuileries Palace, meanwhile, was being enlarged by the architect Le Vau, who provided the architectural accompaniment to Le Nôtre's gardens at Vaux-le-Vicomte and Versailles.

Le Nôtre created the horseshoe ramps at the far end of the park and built up the terrace on the Seine side of the garden. It would balance the northern terrace that had begun to take shape in his grandfather's time with the creation of Henri IV's alley of mulberries. During Le Nôtre's father's era, in 1628, Marie de Médicis had called for a long path leading out from the garden, but it was Le Nôtre who extended the perspective to majestic proportions by planting trees along the route that would become the Champs-Elysées. In pushing out the western edge of the capital Le Nôtre was calling for the eye to follow the route over the hill (on which now stands the Arc de Triomphe) and on toward the setting sun.

It so happened that the sun set in the direction of the birthplace of the Sun King himself, for this was the straight route into Paris from the royal palace of Saint-Germain-en-Laye, 20 miles west, where Louis XIV was born and spent much of his youth. Since that distant perspective was created from the point of view of the former Tuilieries Palace (destroyed in 1871), it now seems askew when viewed from the pyramid of the Louvre. Near the pyramid, therefore, a statue of young Louis XIV on rearing horseback now indicates the point with which that perspective lines up: a line going beneath the Arc de Triomphe du Carrousel, through the Tuileries Garden, past the Obelisk on place de la Concorde, between the Horses of Marly at the entrance to the Champs-Elysées, up the avenue, through the Arc de Triomphe, and over the massive Arch of La Défense, before fully disappearing over the horizon.

Slugs and Cabbage

The garden-landscaper André Le Nôtre was eventually knighted by Louis XIV in 1675. He remained a modest man. When the king invited him to choose a coat of arms, he chose three silver slugs, a head of cabbage and a spade.

Perspective, one of the central tenets of the Renaissance, was of utmost importance for the formal French garden. The 17th century saw the birth of France's Age of Reason. Réné Descartes, the metaphysician and mathematician, founder of polynomial algebra and cofounder of analytic geometry, laid out the principles of optic geometry. Decartes's "I think therefore I am" confirmed the existence of the world through man's rational, doubting eye. The shape of the kingdom itself became geometric; the French refer to their continental territory as "the hexagon." By adding man's sense of balance, equilibrium, perspective and symmetry to the landscape, by taming and controlling it, nature itself, transformed by powerful men, appeared more civilized, and so, too, the kingdom.

The French garden was not intended to bring nature to the French Court, nor an attempt to capture the beauty of nature, rather a blatant attempt to improve upon it. The Tuileries Garden and the gardens that followed sought to demonstrate not only a mastery of water, earth and plants but man's triumph over them. (For more on Le Nôtre and his influence on the development of the French garden see *Châteaux of the Paris Region*, particularly Vaux-le-Vicomte and Versailles.)

The modern Tuileries

Ironically, it was Louis XIV, the most absolute of France's rulers, who opened the garden not just to the nobility but to a larger public as well. He could afford such generosity because he, himself, rarely set foot in his Paris palaces once he and the Court had moved to Versailles (1682). Before long, the Tuileries Garden had became a highly civilized and reasoned setting for controlled public gathering and exchange.

The Revolution naturally further opened the garden to the masses. Statues taken as public property from the parks and gardens of nobility outside of Paris were brought here. The fabulous *Horses of Marly* were set at the entrance to the Champs-Elysées (copies are there now, the originals are in the Louvre).

A decade of work through the 1990s on a project called "Le Grand Louvre," which included the rejuvenation of the Tuileries Garden, has succeeded in restoring much of the popular yet regal air to the Tuileries by replanting, sprucing up,

removing dying trees, cleaning blackened sculptures, covering over a street, installing new cafés. It has not fully recreated the Le Nôtre's garden, though, since doing so would be like playing waltz music at a discotheque: what would we do with it?

Don't miss the Ferris wheel

The Tuileries Garden's most impressionistic view comes as the setting sun shimmers on the Seine and on the city as seen from atop the Ferris wheel that turns in the Tuileries in the spring and fall. Seize the occasion!

Today we ask that our city parks and gardens serve as breathing space away from the concrete, cars and commerce of urban life. The 15000+ plants and flowers the gardeners place in this soil each year are largely an impressionistic touch to accommodate our modern needs for color and nature in a bustling city. Reflecting this modern view of the garden, a roomful of the Impressionist Monet's famous *Water Lilies*, along with other late 19th-early 20th-century works, can be found in the former royal orangery or citrus greenhouse on the garden's southern terrace (closed for renovation until 2004). Temporary contemporary exhibits occupy the former *jeu de paume*, the indoor court of an aristocratic game played in the 17th-19th centuries that was a precursor to modern tennis. Both buildings date from the final heydays of the Tuileries Palace in the mid-19th century.

After 300 years of periodic development of the palaces of the Louvre and the Tuileries, the two were finally connected during the reign of Napoleon III. But following the fall of Napoleon III, the Tuileries Palace was burned to the ground in 1871 in an insurrection known as the Commune de Paris, and all traces were later removed. Only the garden remains.

Garden of the Palais Royal

The storming of the Bastille on July 14, 1789, signaled the end of the power of Versailles and the birth of the French republic. Dissent and revolution, however, had already been in the air in the parks and gardens of the capital. And nowhere was the air more charged than in the garden of the Palais Royal. But the excitement and depravity of that revolutionary garden have long gone, leaving this garden as an oasis of calm in the center of the Right Bank.

History of the Palais Royal

Once the property of Cardinal Richelieu (prime minister under Louis XIII), and thus originally called the Palais-Cardinal, the palace, facing the Louvre, was bequeathed to Louis XIII in 1642, whereupon it became the Palais-Royal or Royal Palace. A generation later, Louis XIV awarded the palace to his younger brother Philippe d'Orléans in apanage, i.e. to be passed on to Philippe's eldest male descendants. It was one of those descendants, Louis-Philippe d'Orléans, Duc de Chartres, who decided in the 1770s to develop three sides of his garden in a vast money-making venture. Earlier he had set about developing the area around the Parc Monceau (see below). Such development projects were not unusual for nobles in need of funds to support their lifestyles, there being

The Marriage of Old and New

The buildings and garden of the Palais Royal are a great monument to Classicism, but the first thing one sees upon entering the palace's court of honor is the modern archisculptural unit by artist Daniel Buren. Entitled The Two Plateaus *but generally referred to as* Buren's Columns, *the black and white columns were the Paris art scandal of the mid-80s that served as a warm-up for the debate over the pyramid of the Louvre: what role can modernism play in centuries-old patrimony? It's an argument that old nations are forced to confront as their cities evolve; because of the important role that the French state plays in developments in and around historical monuments here, no country engages in to such debates with more passion than France. A hundred years earlier, the Eiffel Tower had set the same polemics in motion.*

In 15 years of passing through the Palais Royal, Buren's Columns have grown on me in a way that Pei's Pyramid of the Louvre, which leaves me indifferent, has not. Perhaps that's due to the essential difference between art (the columns) and architecture (the pyramid), but the pyramid clearly begs for acceptance and now appears as nothing but an entrance, whereas the columns ask for a playful appreciation of space.

Buren's work nonchalantly take up the stripes of the window awnings and the Classical columns of the court of honor of the Palais Royal and then goes about filling and ordering its own space; the surrounding buildings, having been questioned, are left to fend for themselves. Buren's work gives rise to excitable and restless communication between visitors as they shout to or photograph each other from the columns or walk about them as though trying to fathom the players of an unfathomable game of checkers. A metal grid reveals the passage of a stream beneath the plateaus. There are those who try to throw coins onto a column that stands in the middle of a stream–only to have their dreams fished out by children with string and magnet.

no other suitable jobs for their title. Louis-Philippe's development would help pay for the high life he led and for the construction of two theaters, the Comédie Française (at the time, the Théâtre Français), on the southwest corner and the Théâtre du Palais-Royal on the northwest corner. Victor Louis, celebrated architect of the Grand Théatre in Bordeaux, designed the project with its arcades and Corinthian capitals. The park itself was divided into a private part behind the palace and a public part further back.

And the public did come, making this a focal point of debate and debauch in the years leading up to the Revolution. The arcades and garden were alive with cafés, gaming rooms, pawn shops, brothels, dance and music halls. By the summer of 1789 the garden of the Palais Royal was a hotbed of civil discontent, frequented not only by all manner of riff-raff but by orators and gazetteers come to hark their ideas and editorials. Louis-Philippe d'Orléans was himself involved in the ideals of the new society and so dropped his noble name in favor of the name Philippe-Egalité (Philip-Equality). He later became a member of the revolutionary Convention.

July 12, 1789. Among the numerous cafés beneath the arcades was the famous Café Foy where Camille Desmoulins, a statesman and journalist, stood on a table in the garden and called for the gathering crowds to take up arms against the government.

July 13, 1789. A mob broke into the military storage rooms at the Invalides.

July 14, 1789. Storming of the Bastille.

1793. Despite his conversion to the ideals of the Revolution, Philippe-Equality, the former duke and owner of the Palais Royal, was beheaded.

1794. Camille Desmoulins, too, was led to the guillotine.

1814. With the fall of Napoleon and the return of the Bourbon monarchy, the Palais Royal was given to Philippe-Egalité's son, Louis-Philippe. He would complete the work that his father had begun on the buildings and

add the double portico that separates the garden from the court of honor.

1830. Louis-Philippe was crowned King of the French (kings of the Old Regime had been crowned King of France), reigning until the revolution of 1848 forced his abdication in favor the Second Republic.

An oasis of calm

There are no external signs of the garden of the Palais Royal. On damp days it has the quiet of a secret garden, innocent of the major arteries of the Right Bank close by. Of course, everyone know it's here, beginning with those who work in the area. They pass through on their way to work or stop by to eat a sandwich or to have a smoke.

On hot summer days, the garden becomes a French version of an Islamic garden: the surrounding arcades, with their Corinthian capitals decorated with laurel, oak, olive and acanthus leaves, keep out the desert (read: city) while visitors sit around the fountain at the center. (It is believed that the first Roman thermal baths of Lutetia were on this spot, as a villa and a large basin were found here.) Almost everything is circles and right angles in the garden of the Palais Royal, in a word: harmony.

The cannon of the Revolution

Paris was the center of the world in the 18th century, with the meridian of Paris cutting through the heart of the city to prove it. The meridian passed through the Palais Royal on its way to the North and South Poles. In 1786, soon after the completion of the galleries surrounding the garden, a clockmaker began signaling the noon hour, using a magnifying glass to light a wick that would set off a small cannon.

Over the next few years, the firing of the cannon became so identified with the dissenting voices of the garden that it became a symbol of the Revolution. In 1799, the canon was moved onto the grass, where it was set off daily until 1914, when the powder was requisitioned for war. (Not uncoincidentally, the death knoll of Paris as the center of the world can be considered to have occurred in 1911, when France adopted the Greenwich meridian.) The cannon is inscribed with the words, "I count only happy days."

The tradition of the cannon was brought back at the end

of the Revolution's bicentennial year, on July 13, 1990. Shortly before noon, as the first sandwiches of functionaries from the Ministry of Culture are unwrapped on the neighboring benches, a garden keeper prepares the little brass cannon—placing the wick, taking out a rag that's been stuffed into the cannon, pouring in the black powder, then stuffing the rag back—then lights the wick and holds her ears. The cannon pops, the rag flies halfway across the lawn, and someone may shout *Vive la République,* "Long live the Republic!"

Springtime and the Silver Linden

The silver linden has for centuries been a favored tree of European cityscapes, such as Berlin's Unter der Linden. The linden is an orderly, upright tree that's easily pruned. Schoolyards throughout France are planted with a checkerboard of lindens. Part of the romance of Paris in the springtime stems from the linden tree. Palais Royal and Place des Vosges are two prime examples.

The branches of the linden are sharply pruned in February and they begin to bud in March, but it's as their leaves unfold with the arrival of spring that the romance begins. April is a rainy month here; as Audrey Hepburn famously says to Humphrey Bogart in Sabrina: *"Never an umbrella in Paris... and rain the very first day." But after a day or two of walking around in the drizzle with your head down, you look up to find the linden's young, pale green, heart-shaped leaves against a blue sky. Like love itself, one half of each leaf is always longer, the other half always wider. By May the branches are casting full shadows–while the black swallow returns from wintering in Africa to make its home there for the next six months. In June, the linden's yellow-white flowers blossom, releasing a strong sweet fragrance. The shade of summer then gives way, in September, to the brief flush of coloring of the Paris autumn.*

A wonderland of collectibles

The garland of tiny shops beneath the arcades of the Palais Royal seem never to have any customers. The displays of collectibles in the window appear to have been lying there undisturbed for generations. There are shops for collectors of old pipes, stamps, military decorations, antique clothes, antique accessories, antique furniture, antique jewelry, antique table settings, figurines, old post cards, autographs, manuscripts, music boxes. Those that aren't already promoting old things sell objects such as stuffed animals, linens and perfumes that are waiting for customers to buy them a ticket for the journey from gift box to bedroom to closet to attic—and from there to the window of a collectibles shop. There's a wonderfully strange quality to these shops, many of which are open only several hours in the afternoon. By late afternoon, when the office workers have passed through on their way to the metro home, an eerie silence invades the garden, which the garden keepers then lock in behind the golden tips and tassels of the gate.

...

Restaurant: Le Grand Véfour

Address *17 rue de Beaujolais.* ***Tel****. 01 42 96 56 27.*

The timeless beauty of Paris has its echo in the ageless restaurant Le Grand Véfour, at the far end of the garden of the Palais Royal. Le Grand Véfour comes in and out of high fashion from year to year but always remains one of France's premier institutions of fine dining. I find it one of the most romantic of the grand restaurants of the city. While more radical spirits of the populace gathered elsewhere around the garden in the late 18th-century, monarchists continued to feel at home at Le Grand Véfour—and the restaurant has maintained the delicately effusive Louis XVI-style décor ever since. The cuisine fully matches the décor's sense of play and luxury. The service is excellent without being uptight. The price is naturally top end. Of course, you can always just stand on you toes to catch a glimpse of the décor.

...

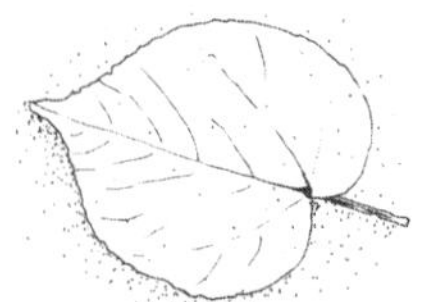

The Endless Joys of the Luxembourg Garden

The Luxembourg Garden is Paris's most poetic, diverse and livable garden. In contrast with the strict if theatrical rationalism of the Tuileries, the Luxembourg has contemporary ambitions, leaning down this alley to sport, behind these bushes to playfulness, around this corner to studiousness, over here to romance, over there to politics. The Luco, as it is called by students in the nearby Latin Quarter, also offers a clear display of what the French mean when they call themselves individualists: not the sort of individuality that we, as Americans imagine, inviting each person to parade his difference, rather an individuality by which every citizen may sit or stroll in a private reverie and be obliged to notice no one.

There are plenty of outlets for sport, play and hobby here—tennis, chess and dominoes, *pétanque* (bowls), bee-keeping, fruit-growing—yet the Luxembourg is above all the perfect setting for a Left Bank pause, rivaling the café terraces of Saint-Germain for the day-to-day joy and melancholy and reflection of an outdoor sit. In fact, staying on the Left Bank without coming for a sit in the Luxembourg is as much a waste of a destination as visiting the Saint-Germain quarter without stopping into a café. And once is not enough.

Within its gate of gold-tipped lances, the Luxembourg is a multifarious setting in constant change and movement. There are a surprising number of goings on here: from reading and pastry eating to postcard writing and making out, from space for playing tennis and pétanque to plots for studying bees and fruit trees. Come weekends, the Luxembourg is a veritable amusement park for well-dressed Left Bank kids, treated by *maman* and *papa* to pony rides, tricycle rides, puppet shows, slides and jungle gyms. At the center of the garden, children with sticks run around the octagonal basin following their rented sailing ships, an echo of the colorful regatta that once delighted the courtly garden parties at Versailles and elsewhere. The children lean over the edge to push their ships back toward the center, where the single spurt of the fountain flows down the arms and backs of three rusting cherubs and pushes the ships back to the edge.

Hundreds of chairs surround the basin, overlook terraces and spread along the garden paths, and most are occupied on a sunny day. The very diversity of activities and plants allows the Luxembourg to offer the truest sense of the seasons in Paris, yet I can't help but agree with a certain Madame de Grippée who declared that "If Paris had but one season, they would call it Luxembourg." Perhaps that's an old-fashioned way of what Gertrude Stein, who lived just west of the garden (27 rue de Fleurus), meant when she wrote "A rose is a rose is a rose."

Marie de Médicis' palace and garden

The origins of the Luxembourg Palace and Garden as we see them today date from the time of Marie de Médicis (1573-1642). After the assassination of her husband, King Henri IV, in 1610, she sought out a setting that would be more comfortable and intimate than the royal palaces of the Louvre or the Tuileries. The land she purchased for her new home had once been on the edge of the Gallo-Roman town of Lutetia and still lay, at the turn of her century, just outside the ramparts of the Paris. Part of the property had belonged to Duke François de Luxembourg, whose name would remain linked with the queen's palace. The duke's mansion of the mid-16th century is, in fact, still here though expanded in the 18th century and now the official residence of the president of the Senate. The park and gardens themselves belong to the Senate, France's second house of parliament.

Numerous monastic cloisters and complexes surrounded the outer walls of medieval French cities. Here, the ruins of a fortified castle had been given to a group of monks because it was believed that the place was haunted. Marie's property abutted the wall of the Carthusian monastery. Unable to get the monks to move so that she could extend her garden to the south, she was forced to have the main axis of her garden lie not north-south, in direct line behind the palace, but east-

The Alpha Women of the Luxembourg Garden

Marie de Médicis stands stolid and inexpressive among the 20 "Queens of France and Illustrious Women" that ornament the semi-circular terraces surrounding the central portion of the Luxembourg Garden. The limestone figures, with needles sticking out of their heads to keep off pigeons, present an eclectic 19th-century collection of historical Alpha women. Among the most famous are:

Geneviève (423-512), the patron saint of Paris. *Geneviève is credited with having saved the city from imminent attack by the Huns by rallying the people of Paris to keep faith that Atilla and his men, who had been pillaging their way across the continent, wouldn't reach the city. In 451, at the Catalanque Fields in the Champagne region, a coalition of Romans, Visigoths and Franks did in fact halt the invasion. The hill on which the Pantheon now stands came to be called Mount Sainte-Geneviève in her honor.*

Mary Stuart (1542-1587), tragic queen of France and Scotland. *Mary Stuart became queen of Scotland at the age of one week but much of her childhood was spent in preparation of becoming queen of France, as she was destined to be married to the future François II. By the age of 16 she was Queen of France and Scotland and, in the eyes of some, rightful Queen of England. After only one year on the French throne, François II died in 1560 at the age of 16, and Mary then left France to assume her eminent role in Scotland. But the Catholic queen was increasingly opposed by an ever more Protestant country and she was forced to abdicate in 1567. She then sought refuge in the England of her Anglican cousin, Elizabeth I, who locked her up for 19 years before having her beheaded.*

Anne Marie Louise d'Orléans (1627-1693), Duchess of Montpensier. *Known as the Grande Mademoiselle, she was the dynamic daughter of Gaston d'Orléans, brother of Louis XIII. She and her father took part in the Fronde, a revolt against Mazarin, who led the kingdom during the minority of Louis XIV.*

Blanche de Castille (? - 1252), Queen of France. *More significant than her role as queen was her role as queen mother and regent of Louis IX. Her ruthlessness helped incorporate the regions of Toulouse and Provence within the French crown.*

Marguerite d'Anjou (1429-1482), French queen of England, wife of Henry VI. *Henry VI lost England's possessions in France in the final phases of the Hundred Years War. Marguerite remained at his side and more or less at the helm of England as royal authority was challenged in the Wars of the Roses, while the king fought not only with his enemies but for his own sanity. Finally, they and their descendants lost their throne. Here she is seen in a commanding pose as her young son hugs her skirt. At their feet it is written: "If you don't respect an exiled queen/Respect an unhappy mother."*

west. An alley of plane trees and an orangery recall the shape of her garden.

The Luxembourg Garden's major perspective now runs off toward the south, thanks to the Revolution, which sent the monks packing and led to the dismantling of the monastery. The longitudinal sight line from the Paris Observatory passes along that axis.

Marie de Médicis became a powerful regent during the minority of her son Louis XIII, who was 9 at the time of his father's death. At 15 she arranged his marriage to Anne of Austria, the Infanta, 14-year-old daughter of the king of Spain. Marie's hand in affairs of state was slapped when, two years later, Louis XIII had her choice of prime minister, an Italian, Concini, assassinated. Concini was succeeded by Cardinal Richelieu, with whom the queen mother came into direct conflict over the management of the kingdom. Marie de Medicis and Louis XIII had a stormy relationship of exile and reconciliation, as might be expected between a teenage king and his mother, though here it echoed a series of large and small rebellions of high nobles. In 1621, at a time when she was in favor with the king, she ordered as decoration for her palace a series of 24 monumental paintings from the Baroque master Rubens illustrating her heroic and glorious life as queen and regent. After a final attempt to oust Richelieu in 1630 she was forced into exile where she remained until her death in 1642 without ever seeing her kingdom or her son again. The paintings are now presented in a specially designed gallery in the Louvre.

The Médicis Fountain

The central line of Marie's garden originally ended with the Médicis Fountain (1620), which was later moved to the northeastern edge of the garden. The basin of water from the fountain, inhabited by large goldfish and bordered by tired plane trees and Médicis vases, appears to actually slope down toward the fountain. The fountain is presented as a dripping grotto-style stone, recalling Marie's own memories of her childhood in Florence at the Pitti Palace and its Boboli Gardens. It presents a scene of the story of the Cyclops Polyphemus. We see him here as he discovers Galetea, the sea nymph he loves, in the arms of Acis, a Sicilian shepherd whom the Cyclops then killed out of jealousy and whose blood turned into the Sicilian river that bears his name. Marie de Médicis' arms are presented beneath the pediment.

The modern Luxembourg

For its mix of romance, discovery and sociological tourism, the entire garden merits exploration. Along the way you'll come across the "Queens of France and Illustrious Women" and much 19th-century sculptural kitsch. Of the latter, none is more excessive than the tribute to the painter Eugene Delacroix erected by his admirers. A bronze scale reproduction of Liberty, shown at Paris's World Fair of 1900, stands on the western edge of the park. **An American oak has been planted nearby in memory of the victims of 9/11.**

Along with providing all kinds of leisure activities to locals and breathing space for students and travelers, the Luxembourg Garden has the double vocation of teaching apiculture (beekeeping) and arboriculture (the cultivation of trees and shrubs). Classes on both are open to the public upon preregistration. In the southwest corner of the garden, you may come upon a group of budding apiculturists dressed in protective gear gathered around smoked beehives. The Luxembourg's famous collectioin of fruit trees is in that same corner. The history of fruit growing on this land goes back to the era of the monks, whose nursery was said to be of great quality. Courses in fruit growing have been given here for 200 years, ever since the trees were replanted following the

Revolution. The nursery has been at its current site on the southern edge of the Luxembourg Garden since 1866. It now contains 1000 plants, trees and shrubs and is especially reputed for its 600 varieties of apple and pear trees, pruned into flat shapes that are best adapted to small gardens.

Parc Monceau and the Upper Bourgeoisie

There is a natural and intimate luxuriance to Parc Monceau that comes not only from its leafy paths but from the surrounding neighborhood, unwaveringly home to the upper bourgeoisie for over two hundred years.

Monceau reveals the life of the quarter the way the Luxembourg reveals the life of its own. You either come alone for a solitary stroll, or you come in pairs – classmates, lovers, friends, mother with child, nanny with stroller. This is one of the favored jogging parks of the capital, and often joggers, too, come in pairs. Even elderly women feed the birds together, standing side by side like sculptures on a fountain as sparrows rise to take bread crumbs then drop to the ground.

A Natural Fact

With a circumference of 23 feet, a tired old Oriental plane tree in Parc Monceau holds the record of Paris's thickest tree trunk.

Previous to developing the area behind the Palais Royal in the 1770s, Philippe d'Orléans was well on his way to creating an ambitious project here, just outside the old city, near a village called Monceaux. Breaking with earlier, formal notions of the French garden, Parc Monceau is a "folly" garden, a shady enclosure given over to exoticism and illusion intended to transport visitors to distant lands. Theatrical elements include a colonnade of Corinthian columns in partial ruin, the oval pond of a naumachia (the basin Romans used for mock naval battles), a Chinese bridge over a stream, an Italian grotto, an Egyptian pyramid. Together they present a mix of luxury and ancient ruin as might be seen in the works of 18th-century French painters Watteau, Fragonard, Lancret and Bouchet in the Louvre. A rotund at the western end of the park recalling the Roman Pantheon served as a tollgate into the city at the end of the 19th century. It is now the entrance to the park from the Monceau metro stop, charging a toll only for use of the toilets.

The theatrical décor of Parc Monceau is now too quaint to carry us anywhere but into the lap of the upper bourgeosie, particularly that of the second half of the 19th century. The area greatly developed as the upper classes of the Second Empire (Napoleon III, 1852-1870) built their stately mansions in the area surrounding the park. Abutting the park, the pretty **Nissim-de-Camondo Museum** (63 rue de Monceau; closed Mon., Tues.), displaying 18th-century furnishings, and the **Cernusci Museum** (7 av. Vélasquez; closed Tues.), devoted to Chinese art, are two examples of such homes. But to have a true feel for the splendor sought by wealthy collectors of the time, combine your visit to Parc Monceau with a tour of the **Jacquemart-André Museum**, several blocks away (see *Museums*).

Bois de Boulogne: Sex, Privilege and Bagatelle

Getting there: *Bagatelle can be reached by taking the metro to the Pont-de-Neuilly stop. From there, take bus 43 or walk. Or take a taxi from the hotel. Bagatelle is open March-Sept. 8:30am-7pm and Oct.-Feb. 9am-5:30pm. Guided tours are given periodically in flowering seasons. For information call 01 40 71 75 23.*

The Champs-Elysées rises up to the Arc de Triomphe, and from there most travelers head back down. But on the opposite side of the arch, avenue Foch can lead you, if you let it, into contact with the diverse flora and fauna of the Bois de Boulogne, where the offerings of sex and privilege peacefully coexist. The sex trade begins midway down Avenue Foch. From there to deep into the woods, every manner of physical exchange—some involving money, some not—has its territory: young men for hire, young women for hire, mutually consenting men meeting behind trees, men and women interlaced on blankets, and, most famously, a confusion of transvestites, transsexuals and less-operated women from every continent.

During the day and into the long evenings of spring and summer, the sex traders share the woods and the paths with picnickers, rollerbladers, cyclists, joggers, equestrians, dog walkers. (Only the sex traders stay into the night, for safety's sake you shouldn't.) But there is much more. The Bois de Boulogne also boasts two race tracks (Longchamps and

Auteuil), an exceptional restaurant (Le Pré Catalan), several chic café-restaurants and exclusive sporting, equestrian and polo clubs. The Roland Garros complex, home of the French Open tennis tournament, is nearby.

The mix of sex and privilege in these woods goes back several hundred years, to when a lodge served as a royal love nest. In 1777 that house of royal pleasure was purchased by the Comte d'Artois, Louis XVI's brother. Marie-Antoinette, the count's sister-in-law, bet him that he couldn't rebuild the old lodge within two months. He did—and the result, to Marie-Antoinette's delight, was the charming Bagatelle and its garden. The queen was always the object of scandal, and some members of the Court rumored that she was romantically linked to her brother-in-law.

Bagatelle has maintained its aristocratic airs over the past two centuries because it has always found favor with people of note: Napoleon I enjoyed it; the Comte d'Artois, who had escaped the guillotine by going into exile, returned as owner and was crowned King Charles X in 1824; Romanticism romanticized it; aristocrats of the mid-19th century took to the woods and saw to the development of its various clubs; British owners kept Bagatelle alive later in the century. The various clubs, the gardens of Bagatelle, the lakes, the overall pleasures of the setting and of course the sex trade have kept it popular with the right crowd ever since.

The Bagatelle Garden remains a privileged place for an enchanting stroll, a lush treat for the return traveler come for the range of tulips in April and May and for the celebrated rose gardens from June to September. Ostensibly, Bagatelle attracts visitors exercising privilege not sex, but where there is one in the Bois de Boulogne the other is never far away, for Bagatelle is not only Paris's most luxuriant garden but its most aphrodisiac well.

Botanical Gardens & Tearoom of the Mosque

Getting there: *The closest metro stop to the Botanical Gardens is Gare d'Austerlitz, though they can also be approached from the Jussieu stop or following a walk through the sculpture garden along the Seine.*

The Botanical Gardens (*Jardin des Plantes*) in the 5th arrondissement are a treasure chest of flora and fauna that should be visited as aimlessly as a flea market. A labyrinth, an alpine garden, rose and iris gardens, three greenhouses (Mexican, Australian, tropical/winter), a menagerie, paleobotanical and paleontological galleries and the National Natural History Museum make this a setting for any time of year, any set of natural interests. This has been a site for serious study and whimsical wandering since it was laid out in 1626 by Louis XIII's doctor to grow and study medicinal plants. Reflecting major developments of these gardens in the 18th century, a number of 200+ year-old trees are found here.

The Natural History Museum (open daily except Tues.) is a glossy museum that was renovated several years ago and presents educative displays on evolution, natural selection, natural diversity and human effects, beginning with a parade of animals in the main gallery. There's a comfortable tea room/snack bar upstairs.

But a more ambient place for mint tea and honey-laden pastries (loukoums, baklavas, makroutes, mamouls) is across the street at the **tea room of the Mosque**–sunny days out by the dripping fountain, cool and rainy days on the cushions inside. The tea room is but a small part of the Mosque complex. For further relaxation, consider a few hours of steam and message at the *hammam*, the steam baths of the mosque complex. The *hammam* is open for men only Fri. and Sun., for women only Mon., Wed., Thurs., Sat.

The mosque complex was built in the mid-1920's as part of a project initiated as a sign of Franco-Arab friendship honoring the participation of North African colonies and protectorates in the French army during WWI. About 8% of the population of France is Muslim by heritage.

The Floral Park

The Floral Park on the edge of the Vincennes Woods presents hundreds of varieties of flowers. The major seasons of bloom are those of irises (until early June), followed by geraniums and hortensias (until early September), and finally the dahlia festival toward the end of September. The Floral Park is reached by taking the metro to the Château de Vincennes stop. The park is just beyond the Castle of Vincennes (see Châteaux*).*

Monet's Gardens at Giverny

Where do old Impressionists go when everyone starts talking neo and other isms? Claude Monet (1840-1926) went to Giverny, on the edge of Normandy, where he remained loyal to Impressionism–and to his gardens–until the end. From 1883 until his death, he lived here in a two-story pink stucco house with green shutters on an estate with lush gardens and water lily ponds that would become a major source of inspiration for his paintings. From the 1872 work Impression, Rising Sun that earned the movement its name to the Water Lilies that brought him worldwide fame, Monet's exploration of the interplay of water and light would be his great legacy.

At Giverny, poor reproductions of some of the *Water Lily* paintings and other works are shown in the large studio where he worked on them. That studio is now the Monet Foundation shop, where you'll catch glimpses of water lilies on everything from dessert plates to ties to barrettes. Commerce threatens to overrun nature here, but if you avoid weekends from May to September you can still get a clear, if peopled, impression of the gardens the master created.

The gardens would certainly have been wilder under Monet's ownership, as there was no need to channel visitors then, but the palate of color, water, movement and light is more or less as he knew it, and the lily ponds are indeed those he painted. From the moment the gardens are open to the public in early spring to their closing in mid-autumn, the flowers and foliage and shimmering pond are in constant change.

Inside, the house would also be familiar to Monet–as would the hens and turkeys clucking away by the side entrance. Adorning many of the pastel walls of the house are his collection of Japanese prints, an art that influenced the Impressionist and neo-Impressionist movements. More reproductions of the artist's work are presented in his living room-studio. The warmest, most appealing rooms, however, are the sky blue kitchen and the sunflower yellow dining room, where one can imagine the master surrounded by gatherings of friends and family.

Americans at Giverny

It's no recent fad that brings Americans to Giverny. A first wave of Americans had come to France in the decade following the American Civil War, thereby encountering the initial surge of the Impressionist movement. France was the center of the art world at the time, and since Monet was becoming a major figure in that world, a colony of American painters came to the village to be inspired by the master. That historical tourism combined with contemporary tourism inspired the creation in 1992 of the American Museum of Art a few steps away from Monet's home. The works of American Impressionists are shown here as well as more contemporary works presented in temporary exhibits. This is a thoroughly honorable, modern museum, but its true appeal is that there's nothing else to do in Giverny once you've spent an hour at Monet's.

Practical tips for Giverny

Giverny is about an hour's drive west of Paris. The châteaux of the Paris region make for far more worthwhile daytrips, but those driving to Normandy may as well stop at Giverny since it's on the way. From A13 take exit number 14 or 15, direction Vernon, then follow signs to Giverny. By train from Paris's Saint-Lazare station, buy a ticket for Vernon (on the line to Rouen), then take a bus or taxi from the station. It's also possible to rent bicycles at the station; Giverny is an easy ride of a few miles from Vernon and the bikes can also be used to explore some of the countryside.

Monet's home and gardens: ***Open*** *Daily 9am-6pm, April-Nov. 1 only.* ***Site*** *www.foundation-monet.com.*

Museum of American Art: ***Open*** *Daily except Monday 10am-6pm, April 1-Nov. 30 only (also closed Tues. And Wed. in Nov.).* ***Tel.*** *02 32 51 94 65.* ***Site*** *www.maag.org.*

Major Monets in Paris

The Marmottan Museum has the world's most extensive collection of Monets, many of them inspired by his gardens at Giverny. The museum occupies the home of art historian Paul Marmottan, who was actually a collector of European Primitives and Napoloenic (Empire) works. The museum's Impressionist and post-Impressionist collection developed with a first donation in 1957, followed in 1966 by the gift bequeathed by Monet's son Michel of dozens of his father's works. Among them is *Impression, Rising Sun,* the 1872 work that inspired the term Impressionism. Subsequent donations have further enriched the museum in late 19th-century works and in medieval illuminations. ***Address*** *2 rue Louis-Bouilly, 16th arr.* ***Metro*** *La Muette or RER Boulainvilliers.* ***Open*** *Daily except Mon. 10am-6pm.* ***Site*** *www.marmottan.com*

The **Musée de l'Orangerie**, the former citrus greenhouse of the Tuileries Garden, houses in a specially designed room the collection of monumental *Nymphéas* (Water Lilies) that Claude Monet gave as gift to the nation following WWI. The museum will reopen after extensive renovation in 2004.

In the larger context of the mid- to late-19th-century, Monet's place in art history is apparent when visiting the **Musée d'Orsay** (see *Museums*), whose choice pieces by the master include *Le déjeuner sur l'herbe, Le cathédrale de Rouen* and *Les dindons* (The Turkeys).

DEATH IN PARIS

Every trip of a lifetime is enhanced by a brush with death. And there's no better city in which to survive an assortment of near-death experiences than Paris. Overindulging in 3-star restaurants, crossing the traffic circle to the Arc de Triomphe, and requesting service in a shop without first saying *Bonjour* are several ways of getting there. Visiting the tombs and memorials explored in this chapter is another.

Other tombs and memorials are described in the following section: The Tomb of the Unknown Soldier in *Napoleon I's Paris: The Arc de Triomphe*; Memorial to the Deported in *Notre-Dame and the Islands*; Napoleon's Tomb in *Napoleon I's Paris: The Invalides*; The Pantheon in *The Left Bank: The Latin Quarter*. During your daily wanderings you'll also come across plaques on walls indicating where famous or once-famous men and women lived and/or died. Other plaques tell where resistance fighter were shot by German forces during WWII. Monuments in train stations and in other public buildings honor the dead of the World Wars.

Death and the French Revolution

The Guillotine

The "modern" history of death in Paris begins with the Revolution—and that means with the guillotine.

There was little consensus as to the best way to carry out an execution in France before the Revolution, so in 1789 the Constituent Assembly sought a uniform manner of carrying out the death penalty. Decapitation was agreed to be the most efficient and least barbarian, therefore the Academy of Medicine was commissioned to propose the optimal method of beheading. In a report drawn up by a certain Dr. Louis, the Academy chose a machine designed by Dr. Joseph Guillotin, by which an 88 lb. blade angled at 45 degrees falls on a vertical drop of 7.5 feet to slice the neck of the condemned.

Originally, the execution machines was called the Louison or the Louisette, after Dr. Louis, but it soon became popularly known as the guillotine. The "e" was added to Dr. Guillotin's name to form a feminine noun since the French word for machine is feminine. The guillotine was a timely idea that was put into service in April 1792, just four months before the first public political executions of the Revolution.

Several thousand people were guillotined in Paris over the next two years and thousands more in cities throughout the young republic, which also referred to it as "the widow" or "the national razor." Executions took place at various sites in Paris as the guillotine was set up for several days or weeks on different squares. It was particularly active in Place de la Nation, then called Place de la Trône- Renversé (of the Overturned Throne), and on Place de la Concorde, then called Place de la Révolution.

The guillotine was used in France until the death penalty was abolished in 1981.

Death in Paris: 1792-1795

1792

April 25. The guillotine is used for the first time for a public execution, on a common thief.

Aug. 10. Three years after the start of the Revolution, Louis XVI is finally overthrown. The royal family is imprisoned at the Temple (see *The Marais: Carnavalet Museum*).
September. Prison massacres in hysterical response to advancing Prussian troops, which were soon pushed back.
Sept. 21. Abolition of royalty and proclamation of the Republic.
December 11. The deposed king is put on trial for treason. He would be found guilty and sentenced to death.

1793

Jan. 20. Le Peletier, a nobleman and judge who voted the death penalty for the king, is assassinated.
Jan. 21. The guillotine is set up for the first time on Place de la Révolution for the execution of Louis XVI.
March 10. Creation of the Revolutionary Tribunal to judge anti-revolutionary crimes.
April 6. Creation of the Committee on Public Safety, initially set up for the defense of the nation. Danton takes charge.
June 2. Fall of the Girondins, who supported continental war and sought a major role for the provinces rather than total control from Paris. The Revolutionary government is then dominated by the Montagnards (among them Marat, Danton and Robespierre), who seek unlimited power to control and promote the Revolution.
July 13. Marat is assassinated in his bathtub by Charlotte Corday, a young royalist.
July 17. Feudal rights are completely abolished.
September. The Committee of Public Safety becomes the central arm of the law, installing the Reign of Terror. The Law of Suspects allows for arrest of anyone opposing the Revolution.
Oct. 16. Execution of Marie-Antoinette on Place de la Révolution.
Oct. 31. Execution of leaders of the Girondins.
Nov. 23. Government decree to close all churches.

1794

Feb. 4. Abolition of slavery in French colonies.
April 5. Execution of Danton who sought to moderate the Reign of Terror.

June 10. Law fully turning the Revolutionary justice system into a machine for passing the death sentence by increasing the number of Revolutionary tribunals and denying any rights of defense to the accused. Robespierre becomes dictator of the Terror as a 7-week period of incessant activity of the guillotine begins.
July 27. Fall of Robespierre.
July 28. Execution of Robespierre, who passes beneath the national razor face up. End of the Reign of Terror.
August. Repeal of the Laws of Suspects and of radical revolutionary justice.

1795

Feb. 21. Freedom of worship restored but with separation of Church and State.
May 31. Revolutionary Tribunal abolished.
June 8. Death of 10-year-old Louis XVII, nominal king after his father's execution, of scrofula (tuberculosis of the lymph nodes), after three years in the prison of the Temple (see *The Marais: Carnavalet Museum*).
Oct. 5. Napoleon Bonaparte, commanding troops protecting the Directory against a royalist uprising, orders that cannons be fired into the crowd, a stepping stone on his rise to power four years later.

THE EXPIATORY CHAPEL

Address *Square Louis XVI, off boulevard Haussmann, 8th arr.*
Metro *Saint-Augustin.* ***Open*** *Thurs.-Sat. 1-5pm.*

Louis XVIII settled into power after the Napoleon I's second abdication in 1815 and, 22 years after the beheading of his brother Louis XIV, installed a period known as the Restoration. One of Louis XVIII's first acts was to remove the remains of Louis XVI and Marie-Antoinette from the mass grave where they'd been buried, along with 1300+ others who had been guillotined on Place de la Concorde, and to entomb them in the Basilica of Saint-Denis, north of the city, the official burial place of the kings of France. On the site of the mass grave he then ordered the construction of this Expiatory Chapel as a way for the kingdom to make amends for the death of the royal couple and others. The neo-Classical chapel receives few visitors and indeed isn't worth a detour. Just knowing it's here is enough.

CEMETERY OF PICPUS

Lafayette and Franco-American friendship

Address *35 rue de Picpus, 12th arr.* ***Metro*** *Nation or Picpus or* ***RER*** *Nation.* ***Tel.*** *01 43 55 18 54 for guided tour.* ***Open*** *winter Tues.-Sat. 2-4pm, summer Mon.-Sat.* ***Closed*** *July 14-Aug.* 15.

The other main site of executions during the height of the Terror was by the columns that now stand beside Place de la Nation. From June 14-July 27, 1794, the guillotine claimed the lives 1306 people here, including many nobles and clergy. Their bodies were placed in a mass grave several hundred yards away in the Garden of Picpus that is now overseen by a religious community.

The site also includes several marked graves. Among them is that of the Marquis de Lafayette (1757-1834), though he did not die during the Revolution. In July 2002, Congress designated Lafayette as an honorary citizen of the United States, reaffirming his importance to the causes of American liberty and Franco-American friendship at a time when some voices are prepared to consider France as being in the enemy camp.

Lafayette served the American cause on both sides of the Atlantic—as a nobleman lobbying Louis XVI for arms and money and as an officer fighting alongside George Washington. In 1776, when only 19, he went overseas, befriended Washington and fought on the forefront of the American War of Independence. A decade later he was involved in the politics of his own country. He eventually gave Thomas Paine the key to the Bastille for him to present to Washington. With the French Revolution underway, the marquis favored overthrowing the *ancien régime* with a bloodless revolution that would bring about a constitutional monarchy. While in favor of the abolition of feudal privilege, he also sought to defend the king. He served as a commander in the Revolutionary Army in 1792, but sensing that his position as a moderate and as a nobleman were untenable he fled to Belgium. There he was immediately imprisoned by the

Prussians and Austrians who considered him dangerous as an anti-monarchist. The United States failed to help win his release and he spent the next five years in prison despite his having earlier been made an honorary citizen of Virginia and Maryland. In recently naming him an honorary U.S. citizen, Congress formally apologized for that failure.

Returning to France under Napoleon's rule, Lafayette again entered political life. In 1824 he was invited to tour the U.S. where he was greatly honored as a hero of the American Revolution. He lived long enough to play a role in yet another revolution, the 1830 overthrow of Charles X, and died in Paris on May 20, 1834. An American flag has flown over Lafayette's grave since the end of World War I.

Thomas Paine (1737-1809)

Thomas Paine isn't buried in Paris, but he deserves mention for being as much a defender of liberty in France as he was in America. Paine was an outspoken militant for the cause of freedom on both sides of the Atlantic. Born into a Quaker family in England, Paine moved to the American colonies in 1774 at the suggestion of Ben Franklin. In Philadelphia he worked as a journalist and soon became famous for his critical writings, beginning with African Slavery in America *(1775), a condemnation of slavery, followed up by his bestseller* Common Sense, *calling for American independence, then by the* American Crisis *papers that he published throughout the War of Independence. A hothead too extreme for a political career in the United States, he return to England to throw himself into politics there.*

Paine's writings in support of the French Revolution, Rights of Man *(1791), earned him the accusation of treason in England. He escaped to Paris where he received a hero's welcome, became a French citizen, and was elected to the National Convention as a Girondin even though he didn't speak French. When the Montagnards took power he was sent to prison. There he wrote* The Age of Reason, *honoring the Englightenment and countering the unreasonable nature of religion.*

Paine didn't die in Paris, but he may well have. He returned to the United States in 1802, destitute, battle-weary and either ignored, forgotten or considered as too much of a freethinker to be honored as one of our great defenders of liberty.

Princess Di and the Flame of Liberty

***Metro** Pont de l'Alma*

Another symbol of Franco-American friendship, a replica of the Flame of Liberty, is now also shared by the memory of Princess Diana. Princess Di died with Dodi Fayed on Aug. 31, 1997, after the car in which they were riding crashed into a pillar in the tunnel beneath a replica of the Flame of the Statue of Liberty. The Flame, a gift of Franco-American friendship from donors from around the world, including the American Chamber of Commerce in Paris, now also serves as the unofficial memorial to the late princess. Di-mania originally transformed the Flame into a gilt post for notes, flowers, photos and graffiti left by mourning and admiring fans. The Flame has since been cleaned and chained off, to be admired from afar—sometimes like liberty itself.

The Catacombs

***Address** 1 place Denfert-Rochereau, 14th arr. **Metro/RER** Denfert-Rochereau. **Open** Wed.-Sun. 9am-4pm, Tues. 11am-4pm; closed Mon.*

Halt, here is the empire of Death!

So warns an inscription engraved in stone at the entrance to the Catacombs as you decend the 90 steps that lead to the enormous necropolis 42 feet underground. When you've had enough of tombs and want to get to the bone of the matter, come to one of Paris's more unusual tourist attractions: the subterranean necropolis installed in the 2000-year-old tunnels of Gallo-Roman quarries.

Even before the Revolution added several mass graves to the landscape, the parish cemeteries of Paris were a health hazard bursting at the seams by the end of the 18th century. That's why work had already begun in clearing out those cemeteries by removing the bones to the Catacombs. The former rock quarries were used as an ossuary from 1785 to 1805 when some six million skeletons were removed from cemeteries throughout the city. About two million of them came from the Cemetery of the Innocents at Les Halles, which for a thousand years had been the main burial site in the capital. Expect to do a lot of walking as you visit the well-arranged piles of bones in this romantically morbid setting.

PERE LACHAISE CEMETERY

Entrance *Boulevard Ménilmontant between Metro Père Lachaise and Philippe Auguste. Or rue des Rondeaux near Metro Gambetta.* **Open** *Daily 8am-6pm, from 8:30am Sat., from 9am Sun. and holidays, closed 5:30pm Nov. 6-March 15.* **How to visit** *There is no single itinerary for visiting the 100-acre cemetery. Maps are sold at newsstands and flower shops around the cemetery for about 2€. Pick one up and aim for the names that interest you. I recommend entering at the central alley off boulevard Ménilmontant and exiting at the central alley onto rue de Rondeaux. There are toilets near the two main entrances. Count on 1.5-2 hours of hilly walking on cobblestones.*

Père Lachaise is the most prestigious cemetery in Paris—among the most famous in the world—and offers the setting for one of the most curious and fascinating strolls in the capital. Along with the cemeteries of Montparnasse and Montmartre, it holds the remains and remembrance of a who's who of artists, scientists, politicians, generals and aristocrats who lived and/or died in Paris. They include men and women known not only in France but throughout the world.

At 100 acres, Père Lachaise is also the largest "green space" in Paris, aside from the Woods of Boulogne and Vincennes. It is as much a sculpture garden as a cemetery. You'll come across a magnificent array of sculpture, bas-reliefs and mausoleums from the late 19th century, an era whose funerary arts have inspired horror stories and horror movies ever since.

The beauty of Père Lachaise lies in its diversity, both in terms of those funerary arts and in terms of reverence to those buried here. Père Lachaise draws various forms of pilgrimage and homage. Visitors leave flowers, place stones, rest kisses, venerate names, leave notes, recount stories, ask questions, contemplate, pray, sigh, dream, laugh, admire, regret, vow, hold hands. Musicians seek guidance at the tombs of Bellini and Bizet or before the urn of Maria Callas; artists seek inspiration at the tombs of Pissarro, Ingres, Delacroix, and others; writers visit the graves of Proust and Balzac or the ashes of Richard Wright; Poles pay homage to the tomb of Frederic Chopin; actresses honor the tombs of Sarah Bernhardt and Rachel; followers of the Spiritualism gather around the dolmen-tomb of Allan Kardec; rock-until-you-die fans contemplate the life and death of Jim Morrison; gay and lesbian travelers pay homage to Oscar Wilde and stop at the tomb of Gertrude Stein and Alice B. Toklas; descendents of slaves, particularly from the Caribbean, stand before that of Victor Schoelcher, a major anti-slavery activist. Many other well-known, lesser or unknown names and tombs cause visitors to pause along the way.

Yet Père Lachaise Cemetery wasn't an immediate success, either for visitors or for potential buyers. At the turn of the 19th century, people were accustomed to burial in or near churches; they had little interest in cemetery grounds that were without ancestral history or religious significance. The area had been occupied by a Jesuit order and by the home of Father (*Père*) Lachaise, Louis XIV's confessor, but that was only history enough to give the cemetery its name.

In order to attract Parisians to buy plots, city developers transferred the remains of several famous figures here in 1817. The remains of legendary 12th-century lovers Héloïse and Abélard were placed on the western side of the cemetery. The major 17th-century writers Molière and La Fontaine were placed in the middle. Little by little Père Lachaise began to attract buyers, then mourners, and by 1850

Creating the major cemeteries

By 1801 most of the bones of the parish church cemeteries had been placed in the catacombs. For sanitary reasons, a municipal decree put an end to burials within the city limits, with exception made for religious figures who could be entombed in the churches. In 1804, three major cemeteries were then created on the outskirts of the city: Montparnasse to the south, Montmartre to the north, Père Lachaise to the east. The city has since grown around them.

it was on its way to becoming *the* Paris cemetery of note. Many major sculptors of the day were commissioned to decorate the tombs of illustrious and/or wealthy deceased.

People are still dying to get in. Plots still come available. Also, Père Lachaise has Paris's only functioning crematorium. The funerary wonderland has increasingly found its way onto the mainstream tourist map. However, there are also visitors who's friends and relatives are buried here, so a certain amount of respect is required.

The Père Lachaise A-list

A list of some of the most famous names and fascinating tombs in the cemetery appears below. They are buried or inurned along with 70,000 others. You'll find other famous names on cemetery maps that can be purchased in flower shops and newsstands near any of the entrances. Some names are naturally more famous to the French then to us. Often the high points of theirs careers are engraved on the tomb—being buried in Père Lachaise has always been good for a person's reputation. You'll also frequently see *Ci-gît* or *Ici repose*, both meaning Here lies.

The cemetery is divided into 97 divisions; the division number is indicated below in parentheses beside each name. Even knowing the division it can be difficult to find the tombs, so some searching is necessary. Therefore they're presented here in a rough itinerary that they might be visited in an extensive walk through the cemetery beginning at the main entrance on boulevard Ménilmontant.

Colette, 1873-1954 (4). French novelist.
Louis Visconti, 1781-1853 (4). French architect of portions of the wings of the Louvre constructed under Napoleon III. The Louvre is shown here in bas-relief. He also designed the tomb of Napoleon I.
Rossini, 1792-1868 (4). Italian composer. His remains were later returned to Florence.
Alfred de Musset, 1810-1857 (4). French poet and playwright. He is one of the novelist George Sand's three lovers buried in the cemetery, the others being Delacroix and Chopin.
Baron Haussmann, 1809-1891 (4). Prefect under Napoleon III who transformed Paris into a modern capital (see *Late 19th-century Paris*).

Félix Faure, 1841-1899 (4). French president from 1895 until his death of a stroke while in the arms of his mistress.

Monument to the Dead (4).

Géricault, 1791-1824 (12). French painter. He is seen on his tomb reclining above a bas-relief of his masterpiece *The Raft of the Méduse* (in the Louvre).

Jacques-Louis David, 1748-1825 (56). French neoclassical painter.

Bellini, 1801-1835 (11). Italian composer.

Cherubini, 1760-1842 (11). Italian composer.

Chopin, 1810-1849 (11). Polish composer. One of the most visited tombs due to its appeal to musicians, music lovers and Poles. A white marble Muse sits atop the tomb.

Héloïse and Abélard (7). Famous 12th-century lovers, the Romeo and Juliette of France. Abélard was a theologian, teacher and poet. In 1118 while lodged on Ile de la Cité at the home of Fulbert, a canon of the church, Fulbert asked him to teach his niece Héloïse, 20 years Alébard's junior. The two fell in love, Héloïse became pregnant, and the couple married in secret. In search of revenge to the affront to his family, Fulbert and several accomplices caught Alébard and castrated him. Abélard went on to found his own monastery while Héloïse became a nun, but the two remained true to each other's love. Héloïse eventually headed a convent that Abélard founded. After his death she had his remains brought there. At her own death many years later she was buried alongside him. Their remains were transferred to Père Lachaise in 1817.

The Gothic-style tomb of Héloïse and Abélard is near the original Jewish portion of the cemetery that hugged its western wall. The cemetery is no longer segregated by religion.

Jim Morrison (Dec. 8, 1943-July 3, 1971) (6). American musician, singer of The Doors. Morrison came to Paris to flee his image of as a sex symbol as well as the American justice system, which was after on charges of public indecency. He succeeded by becoming a hefty alcoholic with plans for a literary future. He was soon found dead in his bathtub, apparently from a mix of drug and alcohol, though some believe his body was carried there from a nightclub. The inscription on the tombstone means "According to his spirit." Morrison's otherwise unadorned tomb is embellished by the presence of a constant stream of pilgrims and visitors. The cemetery has been known to be closed on his birth and death dates to keep out hoards of pilgrims to his grave.

General Foy, 1775-1825 (28). Monument to one of Napoleon I's top generals.

Marshal Ney, 1769-1815 (29). Ordered by Louis XVIII to arrest Napoleon I upon his return to France from exile on the Isle of Elba, Ney ended up siding with Napoleon's cause and was later sentenced to death when Louis XVIII returned to power after the Hundred Days.

Beaumarchais, 1723-1799 (28). French playwright, author of *The Marriage of Figaro*. He helped channel French funds to the American colonies during the War of Independence.

Anna de Noailles, 1876-1933 (28). Poet and countess. Next to her portrait she is quoted as saying *Je n'étais pas faite pour être morte*, "I was not made to die."

Richard Wallace, 1818-1900 (28). English aristocrat who donated green drinking fountains to Paris, many of which are still in place throughout the city.

David d'Angers, 1788-1856 (37). A leading French sculptor of his era, author of many of the cemetery's early works.

Parmentier, 1737-1813 (37). French chemist and pharmacist credited with the spread of potato cultivation in France, which has earned him a notable place in French history.

Molière, 1622-1673, and **La Fontaine**, 1621-1695 (25). Celebrated 17th century writers. These may not in fact be their remains, but their tombs here set the tone for Père Lachaise as the final resting place for deceased in the field of the arts.

Camille Corot, 1796-1875 (24). French landscape painter often associated with the Barbizon school. His works are found in the Orsay Museum.

Ingres, 1780-1867 (23). French neoclassical painter, student of David. Many of his works are in the Louvre, some in the Orsay Museum.

Victor Schoelcher, 1804-1893 (50). A foremost anti-slavery activist whose efforts contributed to the abolition of slavery in French territories in 1848. His remains were transferred to the Pantheon in 1949.

Eugène Delacroix, 1798-1863 (49). French painter.

Gérard de Nerval, 1808-1855 (49). French poet.

Félix Beaujour, 1765-1836 (48). French diplomat now less famous than his huge phallic-shaped tomb.

Honoré de Balzac, 1799-1850 (48). French writer, author of *The Human Comedy* and *Père Goriot.*
Georges Bizet, 1838-1875 (68). French composer of *Carmen.*
Alan Kardec, Oct. 3, 1804-March 31, 1869 (44). Founder of the Spiritualist philosophy whose tomb receives the most flowers of any in the cemetery and probably the second largest number of visitors after that of Jim Morrison. The dolmen shape of the tomb recalls his association with ancient Druids; he believed to have been a Druid in a former life. The Spiritualist motto is written on the front of the dolmen: "Be born, die, be reborn and progress always, such is the law." The tomb is inscribed with the words: "All effect has a cause, all intelligent effect has an intelligent cause. The power of the cause is by reason of the greatness of the effect." His birth and death dates are major pilgrimage dates. He regarded Spiritualism as a philosophy, not a religion, and he didn't want people praying before his tomb.
Sarah Bernhardt, 1844-1923 (44). Legendary French tragic actress. During a suicide scene played in 1905 she was supposed to fall off stage onto a mattress but the mattress wasn't in place. The injury to her knee eventually led to the amputation of her leg in 1914, but she continued to act, her fame furthered by her appearance in several silent films. She was said to occasionally sleep in a coffin to prepare herself for eternity. An effigy of a casket is part of the tomb's decoration.

Montparnasse and Montmartre A-lists

Montparnasse Cemetery, the second largest cemetery in Paris, contains the tombs of the writers Charles Baudelaire, Guy de Maupassant, Jean-Paul Sartre, Simone de Beauvoir and Samuel Beckett, Charles Garnier (architect of the Opera), the sculptors Rude (La Marseillaise on the Arc de Triomphe) and Bertoldi (Statue of Liberty), Boudelle and Zadkine (their museums may be visited in Montparnasse), the composers César Frank and Saint-Saëns, and Alfred Dreyfus (the wronged Jewish captain at the center of the Dreyfus Affair). Montparnasse also has some interesting sculptural work.

Montmartre Cemetery has its own stars, including Stendhal, Berlioz, Offenbach, Nijinsky, Fragonard, Degas and François Truffaut.

Marcel Proust, 1871-1922 (85). A major figure in French literature, author of *Remembrance of Things Past*, a vast panorama exploring memory, love and art against a backdrop of the lives of the aristocracy and the upper bourgeoisie.

Columbarium and crematorium (87). Père Lachaise remains a functioning cemetery, especially through its crematorium, the oldest in France (1889) and the only one in Paris. It was recently expanded in view of the fact that a quarter of Parisians now choose cremation. Among the thousands of niches of the columbarium are the urns of Maria Callas (#16258), Isadora Duncan (#6696) and Richard Wright (#848).

Victor Noir, 1848-1870 (92). Journalist assassinated by a cousin of Napoleon III for his support of democracy near the end of the reign of the last emperor. When his recumbent statue was placed here two decades later, his fame as a young man murdered for his defense of democracy was soon rivaled by his having become a symbol of virility and fecundity. That second line of fame is due to the hyperrealism of the statue—it not only shows the impact of the bullet that killed him but also a healthy bulge beneath the buttons of his pants, the top one of which is undone. The desire to touch his groin gave rise to the myth that women wishing to become pregnant should rub it for luck. Some also leave notes of prayer.

The desire to touch his groin gave rise to the myth that women wishing to become pregnant should rub it for luck.

Amadeo Modigliani, 1884-1920 (96). Italian painter who might have drunk himself to death if tuberculosis hadn't gotten there first. His pregnant wife committed suicide the following day.

Edith Piaf, 1915-1962 (97). Celebrated French singer. She is buried with her husband and her daughter, who died at the age of two.

Monuments to those deported to the death camps (97). A series of monuments dedicated to those who perished in various camps: Auschwitz, Buchenwald, Mauthausen and others. *Wall of the Federates*. Monument to the "Fédérés," fighters of the Commune of Paris of 1871 who were killed along the wall by division 97.

Gertrude Stein, 1874-1946 and **Alice B. Toklas**, 1877-1867 (94). Famous expatriate writer and couple.

Oscar Wilde, 1856-1900 (89). English writer, author of The *Portrait of Dorian Gray* and *The Importance of Being Earnest.* Married and father to two sons and the most famous writer of his time, his homosexual relationship with Lord Alfred Douglas (a.k.a. Bosie) led to his criminal condemnation and two years in prison, during which he wrote *De Profundis.* Destitute, in ill health and unable to see his children, he moved to Paris upon his release from prison. He lived at a (then) cheap hotel at 13 rue des Beaux-Arts on the Left Bank until his death. The sphinx with open wings that decorates his tomb was the gift of a wealthy old English lady "as a memorial of her admiration for the Poet." Puritans continued to attack Wilde after his death—the sphinx itself has been emasculated. It is customary to leave lipstick marks on the tomb in appreciation for his efforts on behalf of sexual alternatives.

CHATEAUX OF THE PARIS REGION

The region that surrounds Paris, though home to 9 million people, abounds in forests, rivers, châteaux, gardens and parks that recall the splendor, style, politics, pleasures, sport and loves of the French kings, emperors and high nobles. Versailles, the consummate reflection of royal glory under three kings named Louis, is typically a first choice of a daytrip from Paris. Versailles is deservedly, if overwhelmingly, a madhouse of international tourism. But there is much else to choose from in Ile de France, as the greater Paris region is called. Fontainebleau and Vaux-le-Vicomte can each stake a claim as "the one you've to see" and, for the energetic traveler, they can actually be seen on the same day. Each of the châteaux in this section offers a unique glimpse into the life and times of the rulers and high nobles of France.

No château here truly represents a single era; the architecture, décor, furnishings and gardens evolved from generation to generation as a reflection of fashion, progress, personality and/or politics. Most were stripped of their furnishings and in more or less dire need of restoration by 1794, following the events of the French Revolution and Terror. Little by little over the past two centuries they've been restored – magnificently and with great national or associative pride – and refurnished with original pieces or pieces from the same period that have been (and continue to be) tracked down through auction houses, given as donations or, more recently, inherited by the state as a form of estate tax.

Although these châteaux have too much history to represent a single man or century, I present them, when logistically possible, in a certain chronology, so that these pages can be read with a sense of historical evolution:

- **Fontainebleau**: 16th-19th centuries.
- **Vaux-le-Vicomte**: 17th century.
- **Versailles**: 17th-18th centuries.
- **Chantilly**: 18th-19th centuries.
- **Compiègne**: 19th century.

The Renaissance (16th century) château of Ecouen and the medieval town of Senlis are described just after Chantilly, which is in the same general area north of Paris.

The Castle of Vincennes, with its 14th century dungeon and chapel (and 17th century additions) should actually go first in this chapter because it is the oldest of these as well as being the closest to Paris. I've placed it at the end, however, since the dungeon is closed for restoration until 2007. The beautiful Gothic chapel remains open.

Chateau vs Castle

A château can literally be translated as a castle, yet the terms can also be used separately in English as a way of distinguishing fortified medieval castles – protective, functional, habitable fortresses – from luxury castles of the French Renaissance (16th century) and beyond – elegant, stylish, decorative châteaux.

FONTAINEBLEAU

Fontainebleau has come to be synonymous with luxuriant leisure throughout the world. For three centuries it meant the same thing to the rulers of France. The current château is a composite of architectural and decorative splendor from the 16th through the 19th centuries, i.e. from the start of the French Renaissance to the overthrow of the last emperor. Yet a medieval tower stands as a reminder that Fontainebleau had served as prime hunting and leisure grounds for the kings of France since the 12th century. At least 30 kings and emperors of France entered the Forest of Fontainebleau to sojourn here, typically during the autumn hunting season.

As you walk around the exterior, passing courtyard after courtyard, wing after wing, you'll get an idea how vast the royal complex truly is. Here, as at the Louvre, another palace that was modified and expanded over centuries, you'll spot the architectural signatures of the sovereigns involved in its construction; there are the H's of the kings Henri and the L's of the kings Louis, yet Fontainebleau above all recalls the reigns of François I (r. 1515-1547), symbolized by the fire-breathing salamander (also the letter F), and of Napoleon I (r. 1804-1814), symbolized by the imperial eagle holding a thunderbolt in its claws (as well as by an N and by bees).

Fontainebleau and the Renaissance

Despite successive developments, Fontainebleau is a Renaissance château at heart, the Paris region's first royal palace to fully reflect France's entrance into "modern" times. The end of the Hundred Years War with the English in 1475 was followed by a period of relative peace and prosperity during which the French kings turned their attention to securing and expanding border on all sides through military campaigns, feudal claims, treaties and marriages. A succession of Italian campaigns under Charles VIII (r. 1483-1498) and Louis XII (r. 1498-1515) failed to win control over the coveted regions of Naples and Milan, nevertheless it gave them a first taste for the (Italian) Renaissance at a time when France was still mired in Gothic flamboyance.

François I's military campaign in Italy resulted in no lasting strategic success but it did consecrate France's acceptance of the arts and architecture of the Renaissance. A man of taste with an interest in style and the arts, François I invited Leonardo da Vinci, the Renaissance man par excellence, to live near the king in the Loire Valley, where the kings and high nobles had gathered during the Hundred Years War. The king also brought other Italian architects and designers to France. With the heavily defensive needs of the fortress castle now a thing of the past, castles were transformed or razed to build open, decorative châteaux. Moats became ornamental or completely disappeared, artificial lakes were created, pleasure gardens were designed, figures of Greek and Roman mythology began to decorate gardens and interiors.

This initial burst of the French Renaissance, France's so-called First Renaissance, found a home for itself in the Paris region when François I decided to raze most of the castle at Fontainebleau to develop a château that would be a French center for the arts of the new era. (In 1541 he also began to transform the Louvre from a fortress castle to a royal palace.) If Fontainebleau's exterior appears relatively plain compared with those of the same period in the Loire Valley, that's largely because the stone of this region is less easily sculpted than the tuffeau stone along the Loire. The work of the First Renaissance is most evident on the main façade with its horseshoe staircase. Evolving styles of the period are seen in two other courtyards: the Cour de la Fontaine, behind the central façade, and the Cour Ovale, further around the back, past the brilliant Gilded Door.

On your way around the exterior you'll see various aspects of royal gardens over the centuries. The first garden comes into view past the mirror-like Carp Pond. The original Renaissance garden was redesigned in 1645 by André Le Le Nôtre as a young man. Though spacious and regal, the garden lacks the intricacies and subtleties of perspective of French gardens as Le Nôtre would develop them at Vaux-le-Vicomte nearby and then at Versailles. On the opposite side of the château, the Garden of Diane, named for the mythological huntress who stands above one of the basins, is the most inviting and expressive of Fontainebleau's gardens. Note the rectangular building at the far end of that garden; this is Henri IV's *jeu de paume* (1601), a forerunner to the modern indoor tennis court and a sport of kings. Henri IV was also accomplished in another sport of kings, that of having an official mistress; his mistress Gabrielle d'Estrées was a familiar guest at Fontainebleau, as had been Henri II's mistress Diane de Poitiers.

The interior

Fontainebleau has been magnificently restored over the past dozen years and now offers visitors eyeful after eyeful of the rich decorative styles of the kings and emperors who sojourned here. From the intricate parquets to the frescoes and the furnishings and from the paintings and arches to the stucco-work of the ceiling, the décor is so rich and lavish that it can make you dizzy. It's a high-energy kind of place, better visited in the morning when the mind is more accepting of the onslaught of detail rather than after hours of touring elsewhere.

Among the major galleries of Fontainebleau, the long François I Gallery, connecting the two main parts of the château, is one of the masterworks of the Italian decorators the king brought here; it can be considered as a precursor to Versailles' Hall of Mirrors built 150 years later. A Second Renaissance, more distinctly French than the first, developed under his son Henri II (r. 1547-1559). The high life of his Fontainebleau and of the Fontainebleau School of decorative arts is most visible in the Henri II Ballroom.

Fontainebleau is a time capsule that transports visitors from era to era: the Stags Gallery of Henri IV (r. 1589-1610), designed not for stag parties of the horny but for the horns of stags, the exhaustingly Baroque chapel where Louis XV married Marie Leszczynska in 1725, Marie-Antoinette's boudoir and gilt bed, the Napoleon rooms (see below) and others. Most of the château can be visited with an audioguide, but certain rooms may be only visited on a live tour.

Napoleon at Fontainebleau

Napoleon I was intimidated by the royal authority and grandeur that Versailles and its association with the kings Louis represented. He preferred Fontainebleau, considering this "the home of the centuries, the true residence of the kings"—a phrase that reflects his own endless quest for legitimacy. His imperial eagle decorates the main entrance gate to the château, an eagle that recalls the eagles of the Roman empire and of the empire of Charlemagne, two sources of inspiration for the Little Corporal. The bee, another symbol on the emperor's arms, also appears on decorative elements inside.

A frequent visitor to Fontainebleau, he set about renovating what had been destroyed during the Revolution and stationed a special military school here. The town of Fontainebleau began developing at that time. The throne room and royal suites, including Empress Josephine's effusive bedchamber, evoke Napoleon I's imperial reign. One wing of the château contains a museum in his memory.

In 1814, having been deposed by the Senate, Napoleon I signed his abdication at Fontainebleau, leaving France to Louis XVIII, brother of beheaded Louis XVI. The main entrance courtyard, the Court of the White Horse, is also known as the Court of Farewells (*Cour des Adieux*) because it was here that the emperor bid farewell to the imperial guard after that first abdication, before leaving for the Isle of Elba. A year later, Louis XVIII responded to the "flight of the eagle" from Elba by fleeing France as Napoleon I rallied the army and returned to power, only to be defeated at Waterloo by the coalition against France one hundred days later. After Napoleon's second abdication he was exiled to St. Helena.

The Forest of Fontainebleau

The town of Fontainebleau is limited in its expansion by the national forest that nearly completely surrounds it. Like the forests near all of the royal châteaux explored in this chapter, the Forest of Fontainebleau was a favored hunting grounds for the kings and emperors of France. That age having passed, the Forest of Fontainebleau has become a choice setting for a variety of outdoor adventures, from romance to sport to picnic. The unique natural forestscape of sandy and chalky paths, rounded and fissured boulders, and oak, beech and pines makes these favored grounds for hikers, rock climbers, horseback riders, mountain-bikers and picnicker from the entire region. These natural adventures are all available to return travelers willing to loosen their cultural schedule for a hike into the woods. For a brief promenade you need only park in any nook off the roads through the forest. A list of equestrian clubs and bicycle rental shops can be obtained, along with other local information, at the Fontainebleau tourist office: 4 rue Royale; tel. 01 60 74 99 99; open Mon.-Sat. 10am-6pm, Sun. and holidays 10am-12:30pm, 3-5pm.

Practical Tips for Fountainbleau

The château is open June-Oct. 9:30am-6pm, Nov.-May 9:30am-5pm. Tel. 01 60 71 50 60.

Fontainebleau, 40 miles southeast of Paris, is reached by train from Paris's Gare de Lyon station in 40 minutes. The château is 1.2 miles from the station. Buses and taxis go between the two, though if time and weather are on your side you might go by foot at least one way. The town, whose main development began in the 19th century with the arrival of Napoleon I, is sufficiently well-heeled and well-touristed to offer inviting cafés and pastry shops along with way.

By car, Fontainebleau is about a 70-minute drive from Paris; on the return, avoid rush hour traffic, 5-7pm. Parking is available just in front of the château. With a car, it's possible to visit Fontainebleau and Vaux-le-Vicomte in a full, well-timed day. If so, I suggest beginning with Fontainebleau. Fontainebleau can also be visited in combination with the town of Barbizon, five miles towards Paris. Barbizon is a pleasing, gallery-strewn town famous for the pre-Impressionist Barbizon School of painting (Corot, Rousseau, Millet and others) that developed here in the 1850s and 1860s, taking its inspiration from the surrounding light and sky and fields and forest. Paintings of the Barbizon School are in the Musée d'Orsay—as well as reproduced on postcards and posters in town.

VAUX-LE-VICOMTE

The monstrous beauty and historical significance of Versailles naturally place the palace of the Sun King atop most lists of excursions outside of Paris. The return traveler is then ready to set his or her sights 35 miles southeast of Paris on the remarkable château and gardens of Vaux-le-Vicomte.

Vaux-le-Vicomte, affectionately known as Vaux, displays the noble drama of 17th-century architecture and its echo in the most flawless of monumental French gardens. So seamless was Vaux's splendor inside and out that Louis XIV and his prime minister Colbert saw both the estate and the man who would dare finance such a project, Nicolas Fouquet, as a threat to the very power and prestige of the throne. Three weeks after throwing a 4-day celebration in honor of the king and to inaugurate his home, Fouquet was jailed and eventually sentenced to life in prison. And Louis XIV, having witnessed the brilliance of Vaux-le-Vicomte, whisked off Vaux's creators to blow its harmony to bloated proportions in creating Versailles. Vaux decisively announces what would become known as Louis XIV style.

Fouquet's rise

Nicolas Fouquet (1615-1680) was a man approaching the heights of personal and professional glory when he began construction on the château at Vaux-le-Vicomte in 1656. In 1653, after several years of loyal service to Mazarin, regent of young King Louis XIV, he was appointed Superintendent of Finance, i.e. minister of the treasury. Enriched by inheritance, his career and especially by his new position, he set out to build a palace at Vaux-le-Vicomte to reflect his sense of personal and public worth.

Fouquet gathered the day's three rising stars of the château industry to accomplish the project: the architect Louis Le Vau, the painter-decorator Charles Le Brun and the landscape gardener André Le Nôtre. Individually and in coordination, the three would display the full extent of their talents at Vaux. Five years later, in 1661, the masterwork of the era was nearly complete, a château of imposing elegance and a monumental garden that would reveal le Nôtre as France's master landscape gardener.

The climbing squirrel

Fouquet's self-confidence was expressed in the motto inherited from his father: *Quo non ascendet*, To which height he shall not rise. That was further reflected in the family coat of arms: a squirrel (*fouquet* means squirrel in the regional language of Anjou, where the family came from), standing as though about to climb a tree, surrounded by two lions, themselves symbols of royal protection. The squirrel and lions are symbols found throughout Vaux, on the façade, in decorative elements inside and in sculptural elements of the gardens.

Fouquet's fall

To unveil his new residence, Nicolas Fouquet threw a garden party in honor of the king on Aug. 17, 1661. It was a tremendous party, complete with fireworks shot off from the top of the château, theater, balls, ballet and feasting. Unfortunately for Fouquet, 1661 was also the year that Louis XIV, then 23 years old, assumed full control of his kingdom following the death of his minister Mazarin. Mazarin had been France's veritable ruler during much of the king's minority, as well as an ally to Fouquet. It had been Fouquet's ambition to succeed Mazarin as prime minister. But it was Colbert who fully gained the ear of the king, and Colbert recognized a threat to his own position as well as to that of Louis XIV's absolute control of the kingdom.

No wonder Louis XIV would feel threatened at the sight of Vaux's splendor and signs of power. Even though Fouquet had no direct designs against the king and considered himself a loyal aid, one view of the central perspective of the garden, reaching off as far as the eye could see, could only mean that the very grasp of the man who owned it stretched so far. At the far end of the garden, Hercules leans at ease against his club in a classic pose of power. Hercules was a personal symbol of Fouquet—there is also a Hercules room in the château. As to Louis XIV, he identified with Apollo, god of the sun. Here, in Fouquet's garden, it was as though Hercules was showing up Apollo himself. Colbert was quick to call the king's attention to the threat that Fouquet represented and to point out the construction of Vaux as evidence of the man's excessive ambitions and the fact that he had both hands in the nation's purse. The Crown was not amused.

Immediately following the garden party, he denounced Fouquet for misuse of royal funds and three weeks later the king ordered his arrest, which was carried out by d'Artagnan, the famous musketeer. During the three years necessary for the trial, Fouquet was imprisoned in the Bastille. He was then condemned for his misdeeds, some real, some trumped up (of course Fouquet's misappropriation of public funds wasn't unique) and sentenced to banishment from the kingdom. However, the king found that insufficient punishment and ordered the sentence changed to life in prison. Fouquet died 16 years later, in the fortress of Pignerol in the Alps, having never again seen the château and grounds that are among the masterpieces of mid-17th century architecture, decoration and landscaping. Meanwhile, the furnishings, tapestries, paintings

Royal Bed-hopping

During the Middle Ages, when the kings rarely stayed in a single castle very long, it was customary for high nobles to install a royal apartment in case royalty came calling. Châteaux built into the 17th century continued to have such rooms, just as a palatial hotel might have a presidential suite. Louis XIV never did sleep at Vaux, however. On the eve of Fouquet's garden party he stayed at home, at Fontainebleau.

and garden sculptures were confiscated by the king and taken to the Louvre and to Versailles.

A private château

Vaux has been in the hands of various families since it was confiscated from Nicolas Fouquet. Returned to Madame Fouquet twelve years after her husband's downfall, then inherited by their son, it was sold in 1705 to the Maréchal (Field Marshal) de Villars. In 1764 it was sold to the Duc de Choiseul-Praslin, and after several generations in that family's hands it was purchased by Alfred Sommier, an industrialist who made his fortune in the sugar refining business. Certain rooms inside naturally reflect the decorative style of owners subsequent to Fouquet, but much has been restored to reflect its former, if brief, glory. Vaux-le-Vicomte is now the only major château in the region that is still in private hands. It belongs to Sommier's great-grandson, (Count) Patrice de Vogüe, a dynamic senior citizen who received Vaux from his father as a wedding present. M. and Mme. de Vogües reside in some of the outbuildings, while the château itself is open to the public.

The château

A long alley bordered by plane trees signals the entrance to the domain of the château, then the château suddenly appears behind a tremendous gate, sitting on a slight rise and surrounded by an ornamental moat. With grey sandstone at its base and lighter limestone above the stairway, the front (northern) façade, is certainly imposing, yet the true elegance of Vaux is seen from the back side, where the golden limestone shines in the sun.

Inside the château, against the backdrop of Le Vau's architecture, Le Brun's decorative elements announce the Baroque style that would flourish under Louis XIV. Rent an audioguide in English for a detailed description—tapestry by tapestry, marble by marble—of the château's beautifully restored and refurbished rooms. One of the novelties of Vaux was that originally visitors had a view from the entrance across the grand salon on the back side of the château and into the gardens beyond. The painting designed by Le Brun for the copula of the grand salon was never done, though a drawing of what was intended can be seen in the room. Unlike other major châteaux where visitors have the impression of being herded along from room to room, at Vaux you can explore at your own pace. Versailles is naturally far more luxurious than Vaux-le-Vicomte, yet one feels much less like a pawn visiting Vaux than one does at Versailles, making this a more noble, even intimate experience.

The rooms recall various occupants from the 17th century to the start of the 20th century, though main rooms such as the king's bedroom and Fouquet's bedroom remain clear examples of the original era. Period music from Fouquet's time often accompanies the visit. The château can be visited from top to bottom, from the intricate framework of the dome and its view over the domain down to the original kitchen in the cellar, refitted by Alfred Sommier and in use until 1956.

The gardens

The château is a treat in itself, but the gardens are the true reflection of Vaux's noble joie de vivre. This is no impressionistic or semi-wild garden but rather nature tamed into garden theater, the rational drama of the monumental French garden.

Unlike the Tuileries, Fontainebleau and several other palace gardens which had been designed and redesigned for several generations before André Le Nôtre took over, Vaux-le-Vicomte offered him the possibility to create a major palace garden nearly from scratch. Fouquet had purchased an old château here in 1641 and in the years before Le Nôtre arrived to begin designing the garden, in 1653, a sloping platform had already been roughly landscaped at the juncture of two small rivers. On that platform, Le Nôtre gave birth to the monumental French garden. Le Nôtre, less well known than Le Brun or Le Vau at the start of the project, would emerge as the recognized master of his art. He had demonstrated his talents before Vaux, but it was here that he revealed his genius.

Begin your exploration outside by standing at the top of the stairs out back of the château facing the garden, directly south. (You might also glance over your right shoulder to the château's top left dormer, where Le Nôtre may have stayed while overseeing work on the garden in its later stages.) The woods now hug the garden tighter than was originally planned—overgrowth, deer, rabbits and snails are a gardener's enemy at Vaux—yet one can easily imagine Louis XIV standing here, with Fouquet to one side and Colbert to the other, taking in a similar view of the land as it dips down across parterre squares then rises up toward Hercules before flying off into the distance. It would seem at first glance that this view commands every element of the garden, yet Le Nôtre is only playing with us, preventing us from taking it all in at once.

A stroll around the grounds of Vaux-le-Vicomte is garden entertainment, a 17th-century version of going to an exclusive country club.

As we come down from the stairs of the terrace, cross the drawbridge and walk between the parterres, we discover the centerpiece of the garden: the canal, cascades and grottos that have been hidden from view. Only at the last moment, when we are nearly at water's edge, do they appear. And they, too, are a distraction, for as we were looking down into the canal another slight of hand has taken place. Turning around for a glance of the château, we find that the view is suddenly very different; it isn't merely the reverse of what we would have expected, a château at the top of the hill, rather, reflected in the square basin we've just skirted, it now seems to float above the garden.

A stroll around the grounds of Vaux-le-Vicomte is garden entertainment, a 17th-century version of going to an exclusive country club. Which explains the club cars that may be rented to quicken the visit. Paddle boats in the form of swans, sea horses and tritons may also be rented to slow it down. Entering the gardens, we are pulled on and on from alley to ramp, along the arabesque embroidery of the parterres, the canals and cascades and fountains, the grottos, the finely pruned yews, the straight or staggered rows of plane trees, the basins and finally the fountains rising in a single jet or in a shower. The interplay of these elements turns the garden into a form of theater. It is of course intellectual theater—there is always an intellectual side to art and pleasure in France, therefore to the French garden. The more we explore the garden, the greater the effect of its geometry and the greater the surprise each time we find our way back to the central perspective. Finally, on the distant rise, we arrive at the statue of Hercules at powerful rest. And sit for a while before heading back to the château.

Practical Tips for Vaux-le-Vicomte

Getting there

Exploring the 17th-century glory of Vaux is highly rewarding—and part of the reward comes from managing to get there in the first place. Vaux-le-Vicomte is located three miles from the nearest town (Melun), making it the only major château in the Paris region not to be within easy walking distance of a train station. Melun, of little interest itself, is a 30-minute ride from Paris-Gare de Lyon station. From there it's possible to take a taxi to the château, though these are sometimes hard to come by. Bus tours also set out to visit the château from Paris. Private tours are possible in combination with Fontainebleau, 10 miles south of Melun (www.parisrevisited.com). Vaux is a 45-60-minute drive from Paris; return takes 60-90 minutes depending on traffic; avoid rush hour.

Opening times

Vaux-le-Vicomte is open daily from the last week in March to Nov. 11, 10am-6pm; open only for groups of 20+ with appointment the remainder of the year. A Carriage Museum located in the former stables presents a well-waxed collection of carriages and coaches. A self-service snack bar and a large gift shop round out the Vaux experience. If truly looking for château ambiance, consider a candlelight visit Saturday evenings 8pm-midnight, from early May to mid-October, when 2000 candles light the château and gardens and the sounds of period music transport visitors to the feast of Aug. 17, 1661, organized by Nicolas Fouquet in honor of Louis XIV. See www.vaux-le-vicomte.com for specific dates. Tel. 01 64 14 41 90.

VERSAILLES

Ever since the palace of Versailles was ransacked upon the fall of the monarchy in 1792, it has been a cliché to say that there are so many tourists here (now about 4 million per year) that you'll know what it was like for the nobles to come courting the king. Versailles is indeed too much—de trop—and that, of course, was the point. Both glorious and grotesque, Versailles continues to exert its power as one of France's most important historical sights, as one of its major tourist attractions, and as a glimpse of the marriage of power politics and artful splendor. The first-time visitor may be drawn here by some vague image of royal magnificence. The return traveler comes to more fully grasp the magnitude and complexity of France's palace of palaces.

Versailles is first and foremost the palace of Louis XIV, who transformed his father's hunting lodge into the center of the Western world, of Louis XV, who managed to keep up appearances, and finally of XVI, who eventually lost it all. The marble, woodwork, gilt, paintings, tapestries, chandeliers, vast halls and galleries, gardens and woods, and garden pavilions and palaces recall the height and decline of the absolute monarchy and the exceedingly public and occasionally private lives of those three kings and their queens and mistresses.

But Versailles did not then fade passively into history. It remains a powerful symbol, not just of the triumphs and excesses of the Old Regime (pre-1789), but of the role France has played and tries to replay in the world. It was here that the treaty ending the war for American independence was signed in 1783 and that a treaty officially ending WWI was signed in 1919. French democracy, too, holds a place within this monarchical luxury: the National Assembly was born near the palace gates, the two houses of Parliament, comprised of the National Assembly and the Senate, gathered here from 1875 to 1958 to elect the President of the Republic (since then the president is elected by direct popular vote), and joint

Practical Tips for Versailles

Getting there

Versailles is easily reached by train from Paris. Suburban train RER C, with several stops along the Left Bank, reaches the Versailles-Rive Gauche station, nine miles southwest of Paris, in about 20 minutes. The château is a 5-minute walk from the station: follow the crowds, i.e., turn right, then left at the wide boulevard leading to the château. A tourist office along the boulevard provides general information about the town and château of Versailles. An information booth by the front gate provides logistical information for visiting the château, gardens and park.

Opening times

The château is open daily except Mon., May-Sept. 9am-6:30pm, Oct.-April 9am-5:30pm. The Trianons are open April-Oct. noon-6:30pm and Nov.-March noon-5:30pm. Versailles is also closed certain French public holidays and for (rare) official ceremonies. The park and gardens are open daily except in bad weather, 7am-sunset in summer, 8am-sunset in winter. A show of the garden fountains accompanied by music takes place Sat. and Sun. May-Oct. Admission charges for a Versailles day depend on number and type of tours and sights, amounting to 15-25€ per person.

Visit www.chateauversailles.fr for further details and dates and times of seasonal events. Tickets for tours and shows can be reserved in advance by telephone: 33 1 30 83 77 89 from overseas, 01 30 83 77 89 from anywhere in France.

sessions are still held periodically and in great ceremony in the chamber of the south wing to debate constitutional amendments.

Touring tips

Trying to explore all of Versailles in a single day is too tiring, if not impossible. How and what you do visit largely depends on your own rhythms of fatigue and interest. You could certainly fill a whole day here or just come for a few hours to experience the luxury and expanse of the château and/or gardens. Return travelers, like those who live in the area, may just come for a stroll in the park or for the Fountain Show in summer.

The State Apartments, including the Hall of Mirrors and the King's and Queen's Apartments, can be visited on your own with an audioguide or with a N@vipass, using a color touch screen. A variety of guided tours lasting 1-1.5 hours cover other portions of the château, including the King's Bedchamber, the apartments of Louis XV and XVI, the royal chapel and the opera house. The schedule changes daily; you may not discover the exact schedule until you get to the front of the ticket line, however tours in English depart frequently.

In 1830 some of the apartments for the Court in the south wing of the château were demolished as King Louis-Philippe converted them to the Museum of the History of France. Among its displays are a large hall of paintings of victorious battles through France's history and another of statues of French monarchs. Though of interest to those with a solid base in French history, they come at the end of the visit of the State Apartments and mostly serve to further tire out visitors. The Parliamentary Chamber, created in the 19th century, where the two houses of French Parliament meet on extraordinary occasions, is the object of a separate tour that will be of interest only to those with a special curiosity about democracy à la française.

Early risers may consider arriving by 8am to begin with a quiet tour of the gardens. Otherwise, purchase a ticket for one of the guided palace tours upon arrival, so as to have a schedule to work around. A guided tour and an independent audio-guided tour can be done in succession or with a break in between. That break may involve a stroll through the park and gardens, either in the immediate area of the château or further down to the Grand and Petit Trianons and Marie-Antoinette's Hamlet or even further down the Grand Canal. For the hurried traveler, an electric train also goes from the château to the Trianons. A longer break or prolonged day can include a walk into the town of Versailles.

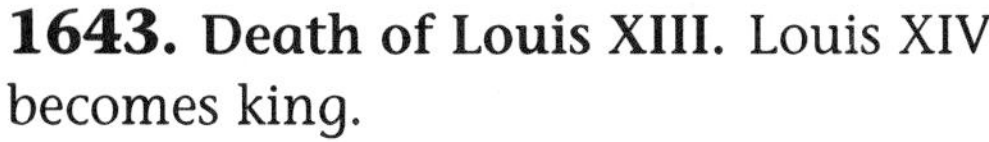

1638. Birth of Louis, son of Louis XIII and Anne of Austria.

1643. Death of Louis XIII. Louis XIV becomes king.

1643-1660. The Regency.

Louis XIV became king at the age of five and the regency was conducted by his mother, who appointed Cardinal Mazarin as principal minister. With Paris rocked by economic disaster and royal authority not fully anchored, an insurrection known as the Fonde (1648-1652), begun by attempts by the Parliament of Paris to limit royal prerogatives, forced the young king and his mother to flee the capital. In eventually putting down the Fronde, Mazarin affirmed his own authority and that of the monarchy. Under Mazarin's leadership, borders on all sides of the kingdom were secured by various treaties that greatly benefited France. The Treaties of Westphalia (1648) ended the Thirty Years' War in Europe and signaled the predominant role of French as the language of international diplomacy, which it would remain until well into the 20th century. (French remains an official language of diplomacy but the language of CNN is more common.) In 1659 the Treaty of the Pyrennees ended war against Spain, setting the groundwork for the marriage of Louis XIV to Maria-Teresa, daughter of King Philip IV of Spain, in 1660. French settlements in Canada marked the beginning of a colonial empire.

Symbols of royalty

A radiating gilt sun in full glory is the natural symbol of the Sun King. It welcomes visitors at the entrance gate to Versailles, decorates the façade of the Marble Court, and appears throughout portions of the château built by Louis

XIV. Its only rival as a decorative element at Versailles is the fleur-de-lis—the stylized iris, literally "lily flower"—that appears in gold on a blue background on the herald of the French kings and so reflects the presence of Louis XIV and his Louis successors here. The only exception is the furnishings in the Grand Trianon, redecorated under Napoleon, whose imperial heraldic elements include an eagle and bees.

1661. Beginning of construction of Versailles. Death of Mazarin. Louis XIV takes full power.

All was set for Louis XIV to take full control of his kingdom upon Mazarin's death. He ordered the arrest of Fouquet (see Vaux-le-Vicomte), designated Jean-Baptiste Colbert as Superintendent of Finance, and launched the construction of Versailles as his eventual seat of his power. Within months of Fouquet's arrest, the creators of Vaux-le-Vicomte—the architect Louis Le Vau, the painter-decorator Charles Le Brun and the landscape gardener André Le Nôtre—were at work on the development of Versailles and its gardens and park.

Versailles at the time was nothing more than a relatively small hunting château, built by his father, which the child-king had become fond of during his own hunting expeditions. By choosing this swampy wilderness, previously attractive mostly to wild boar, Louis XIV was able to start nearly from scratch as he set out to create a palace and gardens in his own image, that of the Sun King.

Through the 1660s, Colbert fully became the king's right-hand man. He oversaw moves to protect state industries, to develop commerce and to build empire in Canada, Senegal and the West Indies. La Salle claimed a portion of the New World for France, naming the enormous territory Louisiana after his king. Various wars confirmed or retook possessions at the edges of the kingdom. Meanwhile, the king continued to concentrate vast resources on Versailles.

The State Apartments

The original hunting château was restored by Le Vau and kept at the very heart of Versailles. Its entrance courtyard, laid with marble and with brick-and-stone walls, is still visible upon entering. But it is no longer visible from the back as Le Vau surrounded it on three sides, adding the State Apartments (*Grands Appartements*)—King's Apartment to the north, Queen's Apartment to the south. The rooms of these apartments were very much a part of the official lives of the royals. Select members of the Court were invited to witness and assist the king as he rose in the morning and retired in the evening. Royal births were witnessed by numerous official onlookers in the Queen's Bedchamber, now presented with decorative elements of the time of Marie-Antoinette, including a famous painting of Marie-Antoinette and her children. Unlike the King's Apartment, which has largely been maintained in Louis XIV style, the Queen's Apartment underwent changes from era to era and therefore now displays styles from the eras of Queens Maria Leszczynska (Louis XV) and Marie-Antoinette (Louis XVI).

Gobelins Tapestries

Address *42 avenue des Gobelins, 5th arr.* ***Metro*** *Gobelins.*
Tel*. 01 44 08 52 00.*

The Royal Manufacture of Tapestries of the Gobelins was created by Louis XIV under Colbert's impetus in 1662 in order to concentrate several workshops, including those created by Nicolas Fouquet near Vaux-le-Vicomte, into a single manufactory. The Manufacture des Gobelins still exists, creating tapestries ordered by the state or, rarely, by foreign monarchies. Its weaving workshops, largely employing 17th-century techniques, can be visited on 60-90-minutes guided tours in French. Tues.-Thurs. at 2 and 2:45pm, except holidays.

The Hall of Mirrors

The architect Le Vau died in 1670 and Jules Hardouin-Mansart, Le Vau's successor as the leading architect of the evolving style of Louis XIV's reign, further extended the château with the addition of the celebrated Hall of Mirrors. This is the centerpiece of Versailles, an 80-yard-long reception hall whose 17 garden-side windows are echoed by 17 window-size mirrors, embellished by busts of Roman emperors from the king's collection and by gilded bronze, all beneath a heavily ornate vaulted ceiling strung with chandeliers. This reception hall also served as the throne room for ambassadorial presentations. At its ends, the War Drawing Room leads to the

King's Apartment, while the Peace Drawing Room leads to the Queen's.

Charles Le Brun (1619-1690)

Le Brun, who worked with both Le Vau and Hardouin-Mansart, oversaw decoration throughout the château: tapestries, paintings, sculptural work, ceilings swarming with symbolic paintings and stucco-work, the use of gilded bronze, copper and various types of marble that combine to mark the Louis XIV style. Le Brun further provided the drawings for some of the garden sculptures. The King's Apartment as well as the sculptural elements in the garden frequently refer to Greek and Roman mythology, with the Throne Room honoring Apollo, god of the sun, the natural symbol for the Sun King.

1682. The Court moves to Versailles from Paris.

Long before the Court definitively moved to Versailles, they had been summoned to garden parties here, where they witnessed fountain shows, plays and regattas and partook in feasts. In 1682 Louis XIV and his government officially moved the seat of power to Versailles. The nobility were now obliged to follow, along with their valets and chambermaids, substantially slowing the construction boom that had been going on for several generations in the Marais. At Versailles the nobles lived in a strict hierarchy battling each other for position and advantage with the arms of intrigue, rumor, espionage and ridicule, all in the hopes of the slightest nod from the absolute king. The life of the Court and government at Versailles would then continue for another century, while the château, its park and the town developed into a vast political and entertainment complex.

Absolute King

Installed at Versailles with his submissive Court begging for attention, the Sun King achieved the absolute power that his predecessors had been aiming for two centuries. "One king, one law, one religion."

Installed at Versailles with his submissive Court begging for attention, the Sun King achieved the absolute power that his predecessors had been aiming for two centuries. "One king, one law, one religion," was his call to order. Catholicism had been gaining against tolerance of Protestantism for some time already when Louis XIV placed his seal on Catholic dominance with the **Revocation of the Edict of Nantes** (1685), making war against Protestants official again. At the same time, Louis XIV, as king by divine right, also bent the Catholic Church to his will, assuring that the Counterreformation fully worked in his favor.

Louis XIV had little interest in setting foot in Paris after Versailles became his seat of power. He nevertheless embellished the capital with a monumental front to the Louvre, the Invalides for his wounded soldiers, Place des Victoires, Place Vendôme and the Royal Observatory.

1683. Death of Queen Maria-Teresa and Colbert. Secret marriage of Louis XIV to the Marquise de Maintenon. The château expands.

Versailles was an endless project for Louis XIV and for his successors. Having completed the Hall of Mirrors, Hardouin-Mansart, the king's architect, designed **the Orangery** (a citrus greenhouse) and **the Royal Chapel**, where the king attended daily mass. He also built **the Grand Trianon**, a palace to the right of the canals, where the king would take a break from the public life of the château. Among post-Revolution rulers, Napoleon I, uncomfortable in the château itself or unwilling to assume its history, restored the Grand Trianon for his personal use. Against a backdrop of Louis XIV decorative elements, the palace is now largely furnished in Napoleon's Empire style. A wing of the Grand Trianon is still occasionally used for receptions for foreign heads of state.

> **THE SPANISH CONNECTION**
>
> **Louis XIV placed his grandson on the Spanish throne. Current King Juan Carlos is his direct descendant.**

Louis eventually abandoned the State Apartment; it then became an additional part of the Court's entertainment complex, which was one of Versailles's primary roles. A new bedchamber was then created for the king at the very center of the château, its balcony overlooking the Marble Court, on the axis of the path of the sun. **The King's Bedchamber** was created in the lighter Baroque style that marks the latter part of Louis XIV's reign. Louis XIV's day began here with a *petit lever*,

The Gardens

The entrance to Versailles is like the entry to a city rather than to a palace. A view of the huge extension of its arms is blocked by a mish mash of ministerial buildings. The more stunning view of the palace, with the Hall of Mirrors at the center, is from the back. Equally stunning is the view away from the palace and out into the gardens.

Fresh from the triumph of his gardens at Vaux-le-Vicomte, André Le Nôtre set to work on designing and executing the gardens of Versailles. Under Louis XIV's command, Le Nôtre transformed a swampy hunting ground into terraces and canals and fountains that only the Sun King could inspire and afford. Nowhere was the approach to landscaping so clearly military as at Versailles. As though to do Hercules himself one better, the king was prepared to turn the Eure River to feed his fountains and gardens. He finally had to agree with his engineers that the level of the river was too low, but he nevertheless ordered hydraulic engineering of mythological proportions.

While the English garden attempts to imitate nature, the French garden seeks to tame, even perfect, nature. It molds and channels water, earth, trees, flowerbeds, thickets, fountains, canals, alleys, tapis verts (lawns), sculpted bushes, gravel paths. Here, the bushes and lawns and waterways have become pieces of backyard architecture. Whereas the château and garden of Vaux-le-Vicomte echo a sense of splendor and self-confidence, those of Versailles speak of power and order; the geometry of the French garden was blown to enormous proportions. By the time of the king's death, the gardens comprised 4000 acres, while beyond it lay a forest nearly four times as large. But as the visitor soon discovers, the size of Versailles defeats its beauty. Like the minute etiquette of the Sun King's day, every line served the purpose of showing that unequaled power resided here. If all roads once led to Rome, all alleys now led to the French king. The very sun seems to have been positioned to honor his glory, made to rise on the entrance to the château and to set at the far end of the garden's great central perspective.

a little reception on his rise from bed. This led to the ceremonious *grand lever* and his entrance into the Hall of Mirrors, where the courtiers awaited him. Another formal procedure led him to retire each night. A gilded wood baluster separated the public space from the private space of the bedroom.

1701-1715. The setting years of the Sun King.

A confusion of skirmishes, battles and alliances with France's neighbors marked the Sun King's setting years, though these accomplished little more than a drain on the economy. The treasury was pillaged for luxury and war. In 1711, Louis XIV's son died, followed a year later by the king's grandson, then several weeks later his elder great-grandson.

In 1715 the court knew little more than luxury, privileges and intrigue, the Church was accustomed to intolerance and its own privileges, the economy was ruined by war, the people were heavily taxed, a system had been built around an absolute king who had outlived his son and grandson, and the king had died, leaving his 5-year-old great-grandson to deal with the future.

Louis XV, the Well-Loved

1710. Birth of Louis.

1715. Ascension of Louis XV.

The Court and government immediately left Versailles for Paris. The regency was conducted by Philippe d'Orléans, the king's uncle. The authority of the monarchy was weakened, but the system Louis XIV left behind made infighting at the Court less of a threat during the minority of Louis XV then it had for his great-grandfather. In 1720, speculation quickly bankrupted the banking system of John Law.

1723. The Court returns to Versailles.

Louis XV attained royal majority (13), yet a series of prime ministers, eventually Cardinal Fleury beginning in 1726, continued to run the kingdom.

1725. Marriage of Louis XV to Marie Leszczynska.

He was 16, she was 22, daughter of the deposed King of Poland. Typically, royal marriages were the fruit of lengthy negotiation, but one reason for their hurried marriage was that the young king was in poor health and an heir to the throne was needed as soon as possible. They eventually had 10 children, 7 of whom survived—6 princesses collectively called the Mesdames and 1 prince, father of Louis XVI.

Improved hygiene under Louis XV

Heavily powdered and perfumed, Louis XIV represented the height of luxurious fashion while being unaccustomed to bathing. He and the aristocrats of the 17th century were not known for their hygiene. Without a toilet or bathroom in sight, the thousands of visitors and occupants that roamed around Versailles on a given day (nobles, aristocrats, valets, servants, laborers, gardeners, etc.) were given to urinating in corners, defecating in stairwells, personally fertilizing the gardens. (Even now, you're hereby forewarned, toilets aren't so easy to come by.) The apartments and drawing rooms, however, were equipped with chamber pots and/or a seat called *la chaise percée*, a chair pierced with a hole below which there was a chamber pot. An increased, if modest, interest in hygiene came with the reign of Louis XV, who went so far as to install a bathtub in order to bathe upon return from the hunt. Actually, he installed twin bathtubs, to have a post-hunt chat with one of his fellow hunters.

Royal privacy

Louis XV was obliged to keep himself in public view and ceremony while seeking out more intimate, less public settings around the palace. He installed the **Petits Appartements**, new royal apartments that would also be used by Louis XVI. Though they were less public than those of Louis XIV, he was unable to escape royal protocol, specifically the ceremony created around his predecessor's rising and retiring. Ritual required him to publicly go to bed in the King's Bedchamber at the center of the château, even though he would then get up to go sleep in the new royal apartment, only to return in the morning to officially rise in public. One of Louis XV's pride possessions in his apartment was the high-tech astronomical clock by Passemant (1754), which he was fond of showing off to visitors. The clock still operates and is prepared to keep time, including the year and phases of the moon, until the year 9999. (To think that software makers knowingly failed to plan their clocks beyond 1999?!)

For further intimacy, Louis XV had a small complex of buildings set up just beyond the Grand Trianon, where he would meet with his mistress, confidante and primary advisor, Madame de Pompadour (1721-1764). In 1762, at her suggestion, he had royal architect Ange-Jacques Gabriel design a more substantial Classical palace called **the Petit Trianon** to be built there. Madame de Pompadour died in 1764, the king's only son died 1765, the queen died in 1768. The Petit Trianon then served as the backdrop of his relationship with the Comtesse de Barry, mistress of his late years. Gabriel also created the **Royal Opera.**

Economic developments

A scheme to colonize Louisiana failed, nevertheless trade continued to develop, agriculture improved and exchange with colonies and reduced military expenses contributed to a steady growth in the economy until the middle of the century. While Louis XV continued to rule from Versailles, he gave Paris enough of a glance to begin building the domed Church of St-Genevieve, later renamed the Pantheon, and Place de la Concorde. The middle class was developing steadily through the first half of Louis XV's reign, while pockets of the country were becoming wealthy. Bordeaux, for instance, had begun turning wine to gold. A triangle of trade enriched Europe's colonial powers as ships sailed from Europe to Africa, carried slaves to the West Indies and brought back to Europe the colonial commodities of sugar, coffee, tobacco, cotton and indigo.

But by the second half of the century the economy was in bad shape while social inequalities continued to exempt the clergy and nobility from taxes. The Age of Enlightenment was under way: Voltaire, Rousseau, Diderot and Montesquieu appealed to reason or to utopia, in either case to forms of justice that did not yet exist. But after a long reign Louis XV died without changing the basic inequalities.

1774. Death of Louis XV.

Louis XVI and the Approaching Revolution

1754. **Birth of Louis XVI.**

1755. **Birth of Marie-Antoinette.**

1774. **Ascension of Lousi XVI.**

Louis XVI, Louis XV's grandson, sought even more than his predecessor to withdraw from public etiquette and ceremony. While he made no major additions to Versailles, the delicate elegance of the decorative style of his era is visible in portions of the Queen's Apartments and the Petits Appartements, as well as in the Petit Trianon, which the king gave to Marie-Antoinette. She would go there to escape the weight and antagonism of the Court. Marie-Antoinette also sought refuge and amusement in **the Queen's Hamlet**, just beyond the Petit Trianon, where she and her ladies in waiting would play at being shepardesses and peasant farmers. The Hamlet wasn't merely a creation of queenly fantasy. It was inspired by a similar play village at Chantilly at a time when Jean-Jacques Rousseau, among the figures of the Enlightenment, was calling for a return to nature.

Marie-Antoinette never had an easy relationship with the Court. Attempts to vilify her had begun at her wedding to the future king. Fourteen years old, fresh from Austria, she was immediately accused of lacking refinement and an appreciation for French culture, therefore sealing both her reputation and that of the French upper classes. Her own extravagances combined with scandals contrived to discredit her (e.g. the affair of the queen's necklace, 1785), gave her an image of disregard for the needs of the state and its subjects.

The approaching storm

By the 1770s, the French economy was in need of shock treatment that neither the king nor the nobility nor the clergy, all greatly benefiting from the system of privilege in place, had the courage, willingness or even know-how to give it. Louis XVI called in his minister Necker to reform the economy in 1777 and Necker's presence in the government was a popular success, but when he began to attack the privileges of the Court the nobility resisted, and Necker was forced to resign in 1781.

On top of an agricultural system already in underproduction, several harsh winters brought famine, rising prices and civil unrest that a series of minor reforms failed to calm. Funds were found to keep the nobility and the clergy, known as the First and Second Estates, in fine robes. Also, money was provided to help the Americans fight for independence, a cause appealing to France because of its historical rivalry with the English.

"Let them eat croissants"

*Marie-Antoinette probably did not say "Let them eat cake (**brioche**)" during bread riots in 1789, though she may be credited with introducing the French to the crescent-shaped pastry **le croissant**, which originated in her native Austria. The croissant was first eaten as a celebratory pastry after the attacking Ottomans (Muslims, thus the crescent) were defeated at Vienna.*

1777. The Marquis de Lafayette began fighting for the American cause.

1778. Benjamin Franklin, a hit with the French Court due to his folksy wit and grandfatherly ways, negotiated an alliance with France.

1783. The American Revolution officially ended with the signing of the Treaty of Versailles.

1785-1789. Thomas Jefferson served as ambassador to France and witnessed America's friend stumble towards its own revolution.

Revolution

May 1789. Earlier, Louis XVI had called for a **meeting of the three orders of the Estates General**, comprising the clergy, nobility and the Third Estate (representatives of all others from throughout France), to take place at Versailles in 1792 to discuss necessary reforms. But continuing hostility caused the convention to be moved up to May 1789. Necker was called back to his post. A poor harvest, higher prices, bread riots and general unrest compounded the tense months leading up to the Estates General. Once arrived at Versailles, representatives of the Third Estate quickly demonstrated their opposition to the absolute monarchy.

June 17, 1789. The Third Estate declared itself the National Assembly and sought to meet independently of the First and Second Estates but its representatives were refused a meeting hall.

VERSAILLES . . . WASHINGTON, D.C.

Versailles never failed to impress foreign leaders and delegates who came to pay their respects to the French kings. Particularly, its garden would become a model throughout the Eurocentric world. Earlier, Le Blond, a disciple of Le Nôtre, had been commissioned by Peter the Great, having seen the splendor of Versailles, to design the gardens at Peterhof, the czar's summer palace near St. Petersburg. Toward the end of the 18th century, Washington, D.C. was designed by the Frenchman Pierre L'Enfant. L'Enfant gave the young American capital Versailles's royal sense of perspective while fitting it to the republic's ideals of a democracy, and so the Capitol became the centerpiece rather than the White House, while a long perspective flows toward the Potomac River.

June 20, 1789. The Third Estate gathered just beyond the palace gates in the Jeu de Paume (1686), an indoor court of a paddleball sport of the aristocracy that was an ancestor to modern tennis. There they swore, in what is known as the **Oath of the Jeu de Paume**, not to disband until they had given France a constitution. The result was the immediate erosion of the authority of the king and of what would come to be called the *Ancien Régime*.

July 9, 1789. The National Assembly became the National Constituent Assembly.

July 13, 1789. **A mob broke into government's arms depot at the Invalides in Paris.**

July 14, 1789. Storming of the Bastille.

Aug. 4, 1789. **The Constituent Assembly abolished feudal rights and privileges and adopted the Universal Declaration of the Rights of Man and Citizen** that had been put forth by Lafayette. Lafayette would later give Thomas Paine the key to the Bastille for him to present to George Washington. Paine, who didn't speak French, was elected to the National Convention. *Liberté, Egalité, Fraternité* became the motto of the Revolution.

Oct. 6, 1789. **The king and the royal family were forced to leave Versailles for the Tuileries Palace in Paris.**

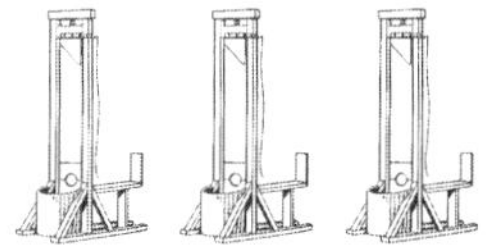

The Town of Versailles

Radiating from the front gate, a planned town developed alongside the château of Versailles. The town of Versailles would fill out over the 18th century, and visitors with time or desire to leave the luxury and crowds of the château will find many monuments from the eras of Louis XIV, XV and XVI while wandering the streets within 4-5 blocks of the château. Town maps are available at the tourist office and at the information booth in front of the château.

Directly in front of the château, to the left and right of the main avenue, are the former royal horse and carriage stables, one portion of which now contains a Carriage Museum. Open weekends only, April-Oct. 12:30pm-6:30pm, Nov.-March 12:30pm-5:30pm. The Jeu de Paume (see events of June 1789) is two blocks away. Open weekends only, April-Oct. 12:30pm-6:30pm.

***Other points of interest** include St. Louis Cathedral (mid-18th century); the royal vegetable garden, now a part of the National Landscaping School; portions of the home of Madame de Pompadour, prime mistress of Louis XV; Notre-Dame Church (late 17th century), parish church for the château, hence of the royal family; the home of the Comtesse du Barry, mistress to Louis XV several years after the death of "the Pompadour."*

***The Versailles appetite:** Versailles is still a posh town, as are many of Paris's western and southwestern suburbs, and the poshest place for lunch or dinner is Les Trois Marches in the luxury hotel Trianon Palace (1 bd. de la Reine; tel. 01 30 84 52 00; closed Sun., Mon. and Aug.). The Café Trianon (same address; tel. 01 30 84 52 10; open daily) offers simpler elegance with a beautiful terrace. You can harvest a picnic at the market square in town or have a seat at one of its surrounding cafés and restaurants, among them the notable Le Valmont (20 rue au Pain; tel. 01 39 51 39 00; closed Sun. dinner, Mon.) For the sweetest pastries in town visit the bakery Gaulupeau, 44 rue de la Paroisse.*

CHANTILLY

Chantilly is like a dream in which nothing quite belongs together. Outside it appears to be a different château from every angle, tending to raise more questions than cameras. Inside it's something like Wonderland, you're never quite sure what time and space you're in. The gardens seem to run off to the side, making it difficult to tell the front from the side from the back. It's a bizarre dream, but a rather enchanting one, exuding a mixed bag of late-19th century aristocratic luxuriance, like the mansions of American robber barons built in the same period. The presence of the palatial Great Stables and Living Horse Museum make this a special dream-come-true for visitors who find horses appearing in their reveries.

History of Chantilly

The aristocratic history of Chantilly begins in the 16th century when a medieval fortress on this site was rebuilt as a Renaissance château by Anne de Montmorency, a rich and powerful nobleman, friend of kings. An equestrian statue of Anne, a man, greets visitors at the top of the hill. Anne also built the château of Ecouen, now home to the worthwhile Museum of the Renaissance. At the time, the Montmorency clan owned Michelangelo's *Slaves*, two famous writhing figures now in the Louvre. After a Montmorency decendant found himself on the losing side in a power struggle with Cardinal Richelieu, Louis XIII's prime minister, he was forced to give the sculptures to Richelieu. That wasn't enough to keep the fellow from being beheaded for treason in 1632, so ending the Montmorency line. The copies of the *Slaves* standing seductive guard at the entrance to the château are reminders of their former owners.

By marriage, the Boubon-Condé family then inherited Chantilly, the most illustrious descendant being the Grand Condé, cousin and general to Louis XIV. Le Nôtre, the royal garden-landscaper, laid out for him the simple yet elegant gardens and fountains. The basins were large enough to accommodate colorful regattas, a favored diversion at 17th-century garden parties. Le Nôtre's strictly French garden with an exceeding long perspective along the canal was later complemented by an unruly English garden and a complex of rustic houses that form the Hamlet, which would inspire Marie-Antoinette to create a similar play village for Versailles.

The Great Stables at Chantilly were built in the 1720s on instructions for the Grand Condé's great-grandson, who, legend has it, believed that he would be reincarnated as a horse. More palatial than the château itself, the stable complex was once home to 240 horses and up to 500 dogs, at a time when hunting was the aristocratic sport par excellence. The majestic central alley of the stables was used for large receptions when royalty passed this way.

The French Revolution temporarily brought an end to the high life at Chantilly; the Grand Château was largely destroyed and the Petit Château left in ruin. The Restoration of 1815 and the return of the Condé family from exile brought Chantilly back to life, if not as a horse then as an equestrian center. Hunting in the forest of Chantilly was once again in fashion, but even more fashionable was horseracing, which became a passion of the elite by the middle of the 19th century. Nowhere in France was racing so associated with elegance as around the grass track at Chantilly, laid out beside the stables. Chantilly remains the French capital of thoroughbred racing.

Condé Museum in the Grand Château

In 1830, upon the death of the Duc de Bourbon-Condé, Chantilly was bequeathed to the Duc d'Aumale, young son of

King Louis-Philippe. The duke was also known as Henri d'Orléans; his initials HO appear throughout the château. Later in life, as an elderly man, with a sense of nobility in a time that had seen the last of the French kings and emperors, the duke had the main Renaissance château rebuilt (1875-1881). When the Renaissance château had been built 350 years earlier there were two distinct portions—the Grand and Petit Châteaux—separated by a moat. But the moat was now

Practical tips for Chantilly

Chantilly (pronounced Chan-tee-ee), 25 miles north of Paris, is reached by train from Paris's Gare du Nord station (27 minutes) or by suburban train RER D (45 minutes) departing from several stop in the center of Paris. A bus goes from the station to the château, a mile away, as do taxis. By car, take autoroute A1 past Roissy-Charles de Gaulle airport and follow the signs to Chantilly.

While a tour of the château and stables can fill a large part of the day, a daytrip to the area could include a stop at the Senlis, a charming historic town six miles east, or the Renaissance château and museum of Ecouen, between Chantilly and Paris. The town of Chantilly itself is of lesser interest.

Opening times: *The château is open daily except Tues., March-Oct. 10am-6pm, Nov.-Feb. 10:30am-12:45pm and 2-5pm. Also open Tues. in July and Aug. The Condé Museum in the Grand Château should be visited before the Petit Château. See www.chateaudechantilly.com for further details.*

The stables are open daily except Tues. April and Sept.-Oct. and including Tues. May-Aug., 10:30am-6:30pm; open daily except Tues. Nov.-March 2-6pm, weekends 10:30am-6:30pm. Ticket booth closes an hour earlier. Time your visit with a dressage presentation: 11:30am, 3:30pm, 5:30pm in summer and on weekends in winter, 3:30pm on winter weekdays. More extensive demonstrations and shows are given May-Sept., particularly on Sundays and holidays. See www.musee-vivant-du-cheval.fr for further details.

Chantilly hosts major races and shows in June, most importantly the Prix du Jockey Club early in the month and the Prix de Diane in the middle of the month. The track is also in use weekends in Sept.

filled in, making the neo-Renaissance Grand Château and the heavily renovated Petit Château appear as a single entity, albeit a hodgepodge.

Henri d'Orléans installed his rich and eclectic collection of paintings and drawings in the new portion. Placed according to the duke's whims, his collection comprises the Musée Condé. It includes works by Poussin, Watteau, Botticelli, Ingres and Raphaël, along with a collection of what is best described as other stuff. Since Chantilly once made a name for itself in the manufacture of black silk lace and porcelain, there is also a small display of those items. (That explains the term Chantilly lace. As to the term crème Chantilly, the sweetened whipped cream is said to have been invented here.)

The Petit Château

The Petit Château contains the apartments of the Princes of Condé along with a cozy library, coveted by this writer, containing 12,000 books and 700 manuscripts. The library's most famous work is *Les Très Riches Heures du Duc de Berry*, a 15th-century book of hours whose glossy illustrations present many of France's major castles of the time. Despite some fantasy elements in the illustrations, they allow us to imagine how those medieval castles might have looked in their heyday. A facsimile is on display here. A chapel lies beyond the marvelous staircase with a bright image of France overhead. The chapel, with its intricate woodwork, contains the mausoleum of the founder of the Condé clan. In the basement of the Petit Château, the old kitchen serves as a restaurant-tea room, providing an agreeable sit on a damp day.

The Great Stables

No visit to Chantilly is complete without touring its Great Stables, whether just for a quick view of palatial equestrian living or for a prolonged tour of the Living Horse Museum. All things related to horses are displayed inside: the stages of saddle fabrication, harnesses, riding outfits, merry-go-round horses, veterinary rooms, etc. Explanations are provided in English. Above all there are the horses themselves, several dozen pampered breeds. Dressage demonstrations are given in the ring at the center of the stables.

Dressage has held an important place at Chantilly since the 18th century, a time that saw a heightened interest in the elegance of the horse and in teaching it fancy steps, jumps and bows. When the presentation is given in French, you need only watch the riders' hands, feet and shifting buttocks to know what clues they are giving the horse. The trick is to make it all look effortless. Only when effort is evident does it become apparent that none of this is particularly natural for the horse, and then we begin to feel sorry for the beast.

ECOUEN

Far less famous than Chantilly yet far more pure in its Renaissance architecture and decor, the château of Ecouen is the kind of sight that rarely makes it onto the itinerary of even the most frequent return travelers. The reason is not its lack of interest – for this is a sweet little château with a major collection – but because it's so difficult to reach without a car, even though the château is closer to Paris than Chantilly.

While Chantilly is a puzzle and a maze of by-gone eras, Ecouen is clear and direct in its presentation of 16th-century art, decoration and architecture, collectively called the Museum of the Renaissance. The most fascinating of the château's exhibits is a series of 10 tapestries that tell the story of David and Bathsheba. Numerous painted chimneys further enliven the château. Another set of Michelangelo's Slaves stands on the portico, once graced by the originals.

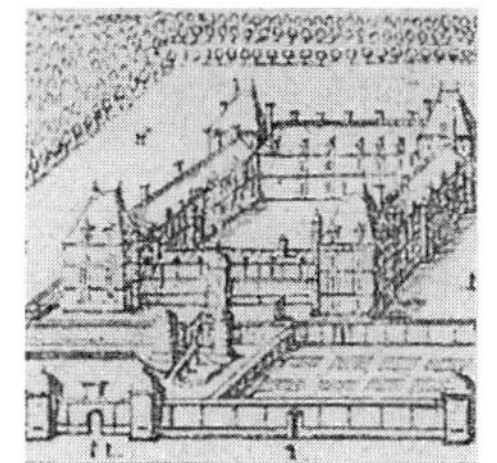

Ecouen has overlooked the plain of Ile-de-France, the capital region, for almost 350 years. It now also looks out to the planes taking off from Roissy-Charles-de-Gaulle airport; while here, you may see and hear the Concorde setting off for New York.

Open daily except Tues. 9:45am-12:30pm and 2-5:15pm. For directions and further details see www.musee-renaissance.fr.

TOWN OF SENLIS

Senlis (population 17,000) is one of the most pleasing towns in the Paris region, full of history and charm. An hour or two of wandering its medieval streets is not to be missed by those visiting Chantilly on a daytrip by car, while a taxi is also reasonable for the six mile trip. Senlis can also be included on a visit to Compiègne, which is 20 miles north.

As with many old towns, a brief history of Senlis can be read on the town map, where an inner ring traces the walls of the Gallo-Roman town that developed 2000 years ago and an outer ring follows the medieval ramparts. Walking around you'll find many pieces of the walls and towers from those two eras. But the centerpiece of the town is its cathedral.

Notre-Dame of Senlis

Medieval cathedrals should be approached as a gift from the ages, with a long look at the outside before opening the package. Consider the west and south entrances before entering. Senlis's Notre-Dame was begun in the 1150s, a decade before Paris's Notre-Dame, making this one of the earliest Gothic churches, designed in a period of transition from round-arched Romanesque architecture to pointed-arched Gothic architecture. Plain as the western entrance (across from the tourist office) may be, it clearly announces the transition to the new era. Its sculptural presentation of the Assumption of the Virgin, completed in 1170, would soon inspire similar scenes at Chartres and other Gothic greats. In 1230 the stone steeple reached its height of over a thousand feet. From the transitional Gothic western side go to the southern entrance, a celebration of the flamboyant design that preceded the extinction of the Gothic era and the development of the Renaissance in France in the early 16th century.

Inside, the narrow cathedral is relatively warm and intimate compared with France's Gothic monsters due to the absence of stained glass and the cleaned stone. The reason for the mix of transition and flamboyant Gothic at Senlis is a fire in 1504 that destroyed the roof. It was then rebuilt higher than before; the lower arch above the organ represents the original height. The northern and southern facades were rebuilt at the same time, hence the difference between them and the western facade. The reconstruction took place during the reign of

François I, whose symbol the salamander can be seen above the northern door.

The Royal Castle

François I took an interest in rebuilding the cathedral because this was a royal town that had played an important role in the early days of the kingdom. Scant ruins of the royal castle, built on the site of a Roman forum, are near the cathedral. Since the time of Clovis, in 511, the Frankish rules were frequent visitors to a fortress here while Paris had yet to become firmly established as the capital. In 987, Hugh Capet was elected king at Senlis, thus installing the Capetian dynasty. Tradition would have the kings stop here after being crowned at the cathedral of Reims. Later kings were also attracted to the area for hunting in the surrounding forests, which explains the presence of the **Musée de la Vénerie** (Museum of the Hunt) near the ruins.

Other than the cathedral, the true pleasure of Senlis is wandering its central streets with one eye on the look-out for medieval and Renaissance remnants and the other eye on the look-out for its bakeries and cafés.

COMPIEGNE

Heading north from Paris and beyond Charles de Gaulle Airport, the landscape soon becomes hilly and wooded and finally forested. The hunting in the area was the primary reason for Compiègne's attraction to French royalty, especially in the 18th and 19th centuries, from Louis XV to Napoleon III. And where there was royalty there was a château. The château at Compiègne is a major monument to the architectural style of Louis XV's reign and to decorative styles over the following 100 years.

Compiègne is 46 miles north of Paris. If arriving by train from Paris's Gare du Nord station, cross over the River Oise from the station and walk straight to the place de l'Hôtel de Ville. By car, park by the château.

Close to the river you'll come across the remains of the dungeon where Joan of Arc was possibly held prisoner. She was captured near Compiègne in 1430 when she came up this way to inspect and reinforce the French defenses in the area. A local Joan of Arc festival is held at Pentecost, in May.

The flamboyant façade of the **15th century Town Hall (Hôtel de Ville)** invites the eyes to detail—a great burst of Gothic flourish just before it went out of style. Louis XII (reigned 1498-1515) rides at the center. Town Hall's Bancloque, an ancient bell dating from 1303, still manages a dull thud and dong. The tourist office is here.

The château

Though a castle had existed at this address since the 9th century, the site was completely redesigned and rebuilt in the latter half of the 18th century by Louis XV's chief architect Ange-Jacques Gabriel. Here, in 1770, Louis XV's grandson and heir to the throne, the 16-year-old future Louis XVI, was first introduced to his fiancée Marie-Antoinette of Austria. It wasn't the kings Louis who got the most use from the palace, however (they continued to hold court at Versailles), rather the emperors Napoleon. In 1810, Napoleon I met his second wife, Marie-Antoinette's niece Marie-Louise, at Compiègne, but the first Napoleon generally preferred Fontainebleau.

Compiègne is primarily associated with Napoleon III (reigned 1852-1870). This was his preferred residence when he wasn't at the Tuileries Palace in Paris. In a sense this was his Versailles. He would gather the Court here during the autumn hunting season when he organized great feasts and weekend outings.

The 40-minute guided tour of the château in French (sometimes in English) gives a fine lesson in the decorative styles associated with Louis XV and XVI and Napoleon I and III. Note where the son of Napoleon III scratched into the table the date 1868 when his father wouldn't allow him to go on a hunting trip; for this he was made to write 100 times, "I will not write on the table." The sublime imperial theater is now a venue dedicated to works by French composers.

The château is open daily except Tues., 9:30am-4:30pm. Tel. 03 44 38 47 00. The ticket also gains entrance to the Musée de la Voiture, the Car and Carriage Museum, which displays 18th and 19th century carriages and later automobiles.

Clairière de l'Armistice

A replica of the railway car in which the armistice to end WWI was signed on Nov. 11, 1918, stands in a clearing (*clarière*) on the route de Soissons, four miles east of

Compiègne. In the same clearing, to Hitler's delight, the French surrendered to the Germans on June 22, 1940. The Germans later destroyed the original car. A small museum alongside the replica recounts those events. Open daily except Tues.

Pierrefonds

Nine miles east of Compiègne stands a feudal castle that was reconstructed by France's premier architect of medieval renovations under Napoleon III, Viollet-le-Duc. The castle, built in the 14th century but largely dismantled in the 17th, is therefore a monument to the era of Napoleon III. Too reconstructed with Viollet-le-Duc's fantasy elements to be deemed authentically medieval, it is nevertheless an imposing sight standing on a hill above a quaint little town and well worth a brief detour.

Castle of Vincennes

Vincennes contains elements of a 14th-century fortified castle and a 17th-century pleasure château, but its main attraction is its medieval portions, since this is the only fortified castle in the Paris region. To get there you need only take the metro to the end of the Château de Vincennes line to find the castle of the same name. Step out, cross the moat, and the dungeon appears.

As a fortified castle, it has defensive elements such as drawbridges, a moat, crenellations and battlement, guard towers and, rising above it all, a dungeon tower surrounded by its own moat. Dungeons now evoke lock-'em-up-and-throw-away-the-key prisons. But they only became that once feudal lords, or in this case kings, no longer needed them for their own safety. During the Middle Ages the kings moved frequently, taking furniture, tapestries and precious objects with them from castle to castle. Vincennes was one of a number of royal residences, attractive for the royal hunting grounds of the surrounding forest.

The 14th century dungeon is closed for restoration until 2007. In any case, the royal chapel, across the lawn from the dungeon, is the most impressive part of the castle complex. Built in the 14th-16th centuries, it's reminiscent of the Sainte-Chapelle, the royal chapel on the City Island. Since it was completed well after the 13th-century Sainte-Chapelle, it represents less of an architectural feat, nevertheless a visit here allows you to fully examine the (flamboyant) Gothic exterior, which isn't possible on the tight space surrounding the Sainte-Chapelle.

The King's and Queen's Pavilions were then added in the mid-17th century, giving Vincennes elements of a Classical château. By then, the dungeon had assumed its role as a prison. In 1804, shortly before declaring himself Emperor, Napoleon Bonaparte had the Duke of Enghien, Prince of Condé, kidnapped in Germany and brought to Vincennes, where he was quickly tried for plotting against Bonaparte and executed in the moat. The Duke was actually innocent of charges, and his murder raised the ire of the royalists, many of whom maintained their opposition to the emperor until his final abdication in 1815. After the fall of Napoleon the duke's body was exhumed from the moat and entombed in the chapel.

The Woods of Vincennes

Just beyond the castle walls the vast Floral Park is in blossom May-Oct (see *Gardens*). Even with the dungeon closed, the castle and the Floral Park can be combined for a stroll of 2-3 hours, best reserved for the oft-returning traveler. There are several cafés and bakeries across the street from castle.

The leisurely return traveler may wish to wander further in the area. The Woods of Vincennes also contain the unexceptional Paris Zoo (open daily) and the appealing Museum of African and Oceanic Arts (closed Tues.; metro Porte Dorée).

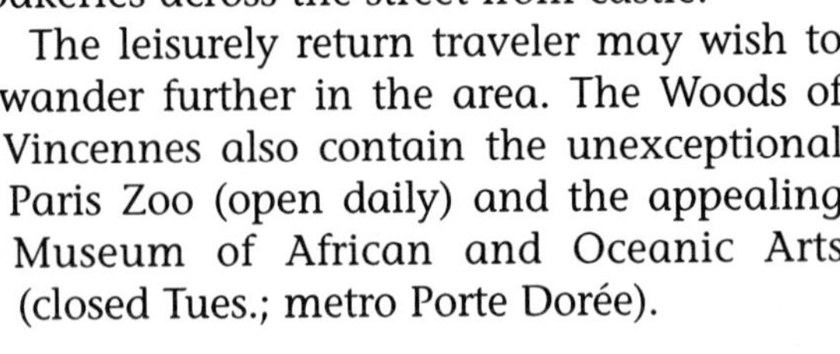

SHOP 'N' STROLL

...WITH FOOD AND DRINK ALONG THE WAY

There's nothing like shopping to know that you've been someplace and returned to tell about it. But shopping in Paris is about far more than merely buying stuff. It's also about the areas you shop in, the history and lifestyle of the surroundings, the pleasure of pauses along the way. Whether you're planning on filling an empty suitcase or in search of a specific designer or just wondering how prices compare with back home, window-shopping is every city stroller's pleasure. They call it *lèche-vitrines* in French, literally meaning window-licking, and enough window-licking is sure to raise a thirst or an appetite. That's why this chapter also notes food and drink stops that go to the heart of the quarter being visited.

You could live in Paris for a few days on these pages alone. And you could use this chapter to discover quarters you may not otherwise have encountered on your touring day, from chic shopping on the Right Bank to boutique bopping on the Left, and plenty of Parisian culture, character and charms in between.

The Bonjour Rule

Ever brush against a paranoid schizophrenic in the New York subway? That's what it's like when you don't say *Bonjour* to a salesperson in Paris. It may seem harmless enough, but you can then nearly read the thoughts of a non-bonjoured salesperson: "The bastard didn't even say *bonjour* and now he expects me to help him?, who does he think I am, his slave?, etc., etc." You don't want to know the rest.

As Americans we believe in the power of the smile; in France it's a courteous greeting that gets attention. Always say "*Bonjour*" as you enter a small shop or bakery or as you approach a vendor or anyone behind a counter. This equally holds true in situations where you're requesting information from someone on the street or on the phone. It's culturally incumbent upon the client or inquirer to begin with *bonjour* (*bonsoir* after sunset or 6pm, whichever comes first). Starting with *Bonjour* will not suddenly make salespeople warm and helpful, but failure to say it makes you rude and them self-righteous for providing shoddy service or information.

When the salesperson or information-giver is busy elsewhere or when you wish to stop someone on the street for information, interrupt with "*Excusez-moi*" before proceeding with the request—and it can't hurt to throw in a *bonjour* or *bonsoir* there either. Ever cut in front of guy driving an '89 Buick on the New Jersey Turnpike? Consider yourself warned.

Now let's go shopping!

CHIC SHOPPING

Haute couture and fine luxury goods: avenue Montaigne et al.

Metro *Franklin Roosevelt, George V, Alma Marceau.*

Avenue Montaigne is *the* Paris address for high fashion, a wide catwalk of haute couture, top-notch designers and stylists and luxury goods creators. Their major stores and showrooms are set back from the street so as to attract serious buyers and intimidate those who don't have the right stuff. A bit of name dropping: Céline, Chanel, Dior, Dolce et Gabbana, Escada Ferragamo, Lacroix, Mugler, Scherrer, Valentino. **Rue François I** (Courrèges, Versace), **avenue George V** (Balencaga, Givenchy, Zegna), and the southern sidewalk of the **Champs-Elysées** (Louis Vuitton, Lancel) complete the gilt frame of this quarter.

There are naturally many occasions for chic eats around here, with or without attitude. See *Bars* concerning the hotel bar of the Plaza-Athenée. For a coffee break or a meal, the **large brasseries by Pont de l'Alma**, at the end of avenue Montaigne, aren't as discreet or vogue as the offerings within the golden triangle south of the Champs-Elysées, but are nevertheless well-set for well-being. For chic eats with a view:

Restaurant: La Maison Banche

Address *15 av. Montaigne, 8th arr.*

Tel. *01 47 23 55 99.*

La Maison Blanche's wall of windows face rooftops, the gilt dome of the Invalides, and the Eiffel Tower—a stunning view deserving of stunning company. My own companions that evening were a vascular surgeon with the Legion of Honor on his lapel, his wife, who works for the Ministry of Justice, a renowned American vascular surgeon, and my date, J., an American novelist. I came as the interpreter, but the conversation got along fine without me, as did J. and the American surgeon. We ate well enough—that not being the point. A bit dear, but who's paying? The titanium gray waiters were as efficient as clones in a sex dream. One of those enjoyably bizarre evenings where you wonder how you ever got there.

Luxury and near-luxury: Saint-Honoré Quarter

Metro** Place de la Concorde, Madeleine, Tuileries.* ***See Late 19th-Century Paris *for a historical overview of this area.*

To feel in tune with avenue Montaigne you've got to be part of the right crowd, but the Saint-Honoré Quarter, though clearly high-end, is more inviting for general window shopping, whether you're buying or not. And a classy array of tearooms or hotels bars await you there.

The luxury brand names mentioned above are joined here by other top, bold or ambitious trademarks of top-end prêt-à-porter, jewelry and tableware, along with epicurean grocers.

Fashion boutiques line rue St-Honoré and its continuation rue du Faubourg St-Honoré.

Tableware, crystal and china shops stand out on rue Royale (between Place de la Concorde and the Madeleine)—Christofle, Lalique, Saint-Louis—while the crystal-maker Daum is on rue de la Paix. The department stores behind the Opera (see below) have more accessible objects of these top crystal and tableware houses.

The jewelry trade has its heart on place Vendôme and rue de la Paix.

Luxury food shops (Fauchon, Hédiard) attract window-lickers behind the Church of the Madeleine, while there's a pretty Maille mustard shop (6 pl. de la Madeleine) in front of the church.

Afternoon shopping in the Saint-Honoré Quarter naturally inspires a teatime break, which explains the presence of high-style tearooms in the area. If you prefer to call teatime cocktail hour also consider the bars of palatial hotels in this area described in the *Aperitif* chapter.

Pastry shop/Tearoom: Ladurée

***Address** 16 rue Royale.*

Home to one of the great names in Parisian pastry-making since the late 19th century. Light lunch also possible.

Tearoom: Angelina. ***Address** 226 rue de Rivoli.*

Grand tearoom from 1900, Paris's hot chocolate palace. Light lunch also possible. (See Late 19th-Century Paris *for full description).*

Restaurant/Tearoom: 1728

Address *8 rue d'Anjou, off rue du Faubourg St-Honoré;* ***tel.*** *01 40 17 04 77;* ***Open*** *Mon.-Fri. 8:30am-9:30pm, Sat. 3pm-9:30pm.*

Rue de Faubourg St-Honoré first made its name as a noble residential quarter during the 18th century, after the creation of Place Vendôme. Several palaces from that period are now embassies; one is the Elysée Presidential Palace (1718). The restaurant/art gallery/teahouse/music salon branded "1728" lacks the commercial history of the tearooms noted above but has haught history behind it nonetheless. Dressed in a classy Classical and Rococo décor, accessorized with Classical music and heavy chandeliers, this is a chic setting with chic eats, but for the quality of the pastries and the coziness of the surroundings consider it here as a teatime setting - unless the American ambassador across the street has already invited you for cocktails, in which case dinner might be appropriate.

SAINT GERMAIN BOUTIQUE BOPPING

Metro *Rue de Bac, Odéon, Sèvres-Babylone.*

Just as tearooms go so well with chic shopping on the Right Bank, cafés offer the perfect pause from boutique bopping in the Saint-Germain Quarter. Or, from the point of view of a less passionate shopper, window-shopping around Saint-Germain is the perfect way to stretch your legs between cafés.

Shop 'n' stroll on the Left Bank means bopping from boutique to boutique in the Saint-Germain Quarter. The main area is in the silver triangle bordered by the three metro stations mentioned above, particularly along **rues de Rennes, du Four, du Dragon, de Grenelle and de Sèvres**. Rue de Sèvres leads to the department store Le Bon Marché.

On the opposite side of boulevard Saint-Germain, a wide area near the river is largely devoted antiques and art galleries (see *Carré Rive Gauche* under *Antiques*), while rue Jacob has many shops for fabrics, prints and decorative hangings.

In addition to the quarter's many cafés, consider Au Sauvignon at aperitif time (see *Wine Bars*). Also see *Restaurants: Claude Colliot.*

Soldes=Sale

Soldes, *meaning sale, is a government-regulated term that applies to two periods of 4-5 weeks each—mid-January to mid-February and early July-early August—officially designated as the* soldes *period. Exact dates are determined by government agency just prior to the period, which may differ between Paris and elsewhere in France. At other times, a store can promote price reductions and specials but cannot use the term* soldes *to indicate that the merchandise is on sale. Between the American condition of the permanent sale and the French vision of state-regulated* soldes *lies a whole world of economic linguistics.*

TASTEFUL WANDERINGS

Galerie Vivienne, Place des Victoires, rue Montorgueil

From metro Palais Royal, cross the Garden of the Palais Royal (see Gardens*) to rue des Petits-Champs. Or from metro Bourse, walk south on Rue Vivienne to rue des Petits Champs. This tour can be taken in reverse starting at metro Sentier at the far end of the Montorgueil market street.*

For its combination of architectural, shopping, eating and wine-drinking charms (place the emphasis wherever you wish), this is enchanting shop 'n' stroll at its best—a must for the return traveler. The area from Palais Royal to Galerie Vivienne to Place des Victoires, then onto rue Montorgueil is especially rewarding for dawdling travelers ready to loosen their itinerary and leave the major monuments behind.

Galerie Vivienne. ***Address*** *4 rue des Petits Champs, 2nd arr.*

Galerie Vivienne is a shopping arcade circa 1820s, one of many that developed from 1800-1850, before the advent of the department store. These glass-roofed *passages*, as they're called, were early high-style city malls, complete with shops, eateries and entertainment. Many crowded between and within buildings from rue Etienne Marcel to the *Grands Boulevards*. Most disappeared with new constructions in the area in the late 19th century, and those that remained were more or less abandoned and deteriorated by the 1980s. Since then, a handful have been the object of loving restoration, if not to their former glory at least to a new quaintness.

Many of those that have been restored surround boulevard Montmartre; **Passage des Panorama**, 11 bd. Montmartre, which connects with several others, **Passage Jouffroy**, just across bd. Montmartre at #10 and its continuation **Passage Verdeau** (31 bis rue du Faubourg-Montmartre) are all worth seeking out. Another cute little cranny of a passage is just across the street from Galerie Vivienne, but Vivienne is the most charismatic of all, an elegant arcade with mosaic floors, glass ceiling, and a small wonderland of shops, as well as character-filled settings for lunch and/or wine.

The majority of the dozen shops are oriented toward decoration or fashion, including a Jean-Paul Gaultier shop. But the most appealing is L. Legrand Filles & Fils (closed Sun., Mon.) a delightful old-fashioned shop—grocer for preserves and jams, candy store for chocolates and sweets, wine and spirits merchant, purveyor of the accoutrements of wine—that has recently added a new-fangled wine bar.

Galerie Vivienne eateries: *There are only about a dozen shops here, so the incurious traveler can visit them all with a quick glance. But there are such of appealing lunch and wine possibilities that one is tempted to stay much longer. Legrand's wine bar is one of several in the area. Also see Willi's Wine Bar and Aux Bons Crus in* Wine Bars. *For a meal there's A Priori Thé, a quaint lunch/tearoom with "outside" tables under the glass canopy, Le Grand Colbert (see* Restaurants: Brasseries*), and Le Bouganvillier, a down-home old-fashioned café, where being grouchy is just their way of being friendly.*

Place des Victoires

Louis XIV wasn't a terribly handsome fellow, but back then a sun king didn't need to be particularly buff to convince people that he was the man in control. Nevertheless, Louis the Great cuts a handsome figure here on the equestrian statue at the center of this pretty little circle honoring his victories. The view of the Sun King facing the camera while the sky opens up behind him to the east is already worth the trip. Meanwhile, on or near the *place*, the king is surrounded by shops proposing smooth, feel-good fashion that goes so well with the right garden party: Apostrophe, Plein Sud, Esprit, Blanc Bleu, Cacharel, Henry Cotton's, Cerruti, along with a major Kenzo shop.

The fashion becomes more street and school as you proceed up rue Etienne Marcel, culminating at Le Shop, one block east at the corner of rue d'Argout. Le Shop offers everything a street-fashion child or teen could every dream of this season.

Rue Montorgueil

A few blocks beyond Place des Victoires along rue Etienne Marcel.

Rue Montorgueil is Paris's most appealing pedestrian market street. This is the final active remnant of the central food market of Les Halles that fed Paris for 800 years until 1969. Fruit and vegetable stands, food shops, bakeries and cafés still line the street, along with an array of 18th century buildings. Rue Montorgueil is at its most appealing in the morning when the food stands are all open, but it's got café appeal all day long.

VIADUCT OF THE ARTS

Metro *Gare de Lyon or Bastille. If exploring both the Viaduct of the Arts and the Aligre Market, begin with Aligre before noon, then either prepare your picnic or head over to the Viaduc Café for lunch. Then visit the shops and galleries along the viaduct.* ***Open*** *Their opening times are a bit haphazard; for optimal openings visit Tues.-Fri. afternoon.*

Everything appears stylish beneath the brick and stone arches of the old viaduct that once supported a train track between the Gare de Lyon station and the edge of the city at Porte Dorée. In 1986 the viaduct was converted by the City of Paris into a 2.5-mile planted walkway above and a shorter stretch of shops and galleries below, impressively occupying the tremendous arcades along avenue Daumesnil. The viaduct is reserved for high-quality and luxury craftwork, high-style furnishing, art galleries and clothing designers. An interior designer's delight. No need to wait until your fifth trip to Paris to take a (romantic) shop 'n' stroll here.

Le Viaduc Café: This café-restaurant offers a most comfortable seat for coffee or lunch midway along the viaduct.

Aligre Market

Metro *Ledru-Rollin, 12th arr. Along rue d'Aligre, two blocks north of the center of the Viaduct of the Arts.* ***Open*** *The outdoor and indoor markets are held mornings daily except Mon. The covered market alone is also open Tues.-Sat. 4-7:30pm.*

This is one of the most expressive food markets in Paris, a mix of French and North African traditions, culture and character, with a touch of Spain and Italy in the covered market. When the outdoor stalls along rue d'Aligre and the indoor market Marché Beauvau are closed the immediate surroundings look like a provincial square during a siesta. But come market hours the streets fill with such characters and performers that you'd think that the cacophony of the marketplace is about to give way to song and dance, as though this were the opening scene of a musical comedy. Actually, it already is song and dance!

CANAL SAINT-MARTIN AND THE "BOBO"

This walk begins at metro Place de la République. From there, take the Rue du Faubourg-de-Temple exit and walk up that street. The canal is two blocks up. Turn left. Quai de Valmy and quai de Jemmapes are the streets running alongside the canal.

Bobo is a term in much use in Paris these days to describe 30-40 something men and women who work in the more or less creative fields of film, fashion, advertising, etc., who seek both a bourgeois sense of comfort and a bohemian sense of lifestyle. Canal Saint-Martin invites a leisurely shop 'n' stroll, whether you feel more affinity with one *bo* or another, or no *bo* at all.

It's actually a misnomer to place Canal Saint-Martin in the shopping section of this book. But having lived in the area from 1998-2002 (call me what you will) and watched from my window (it's sometimes hard to concentrate on writing about Paris when Paris is right outside) as ambulances take the neighborhood's pensioners away and moving trucks deliver the belongings of newcomers to the bobohood, I can only imagine that more boutiques are on the way. The last of the many Oriental rug storerooms that once lined certain streets by the canal can't hold out much longer.

Canal Saint-Martin was dug in the 1820s, the final link connecting the Ourcq River with the Seine that had begun two decades earlier under Napoleon I. The series of canals was designed for the double purpose of providing drinking water for Paris and creating navigable waterways to bring wood, grain and stone to the capital. Formerly defined by the light industry and working classes that surrounded the canal, the neighborhood in the 10th arrondissement between rue du Faubourg-du-Temple and metro Jaurès has been undergoing gradual but significant gentrification since the 1980s. By the late 1990s it had attained a threshold of bobofication that began attracting cafés, restaurants, and, increasingly, boutiques, along with more visitors. (Coincidentally, by the elections of 2002, France's Communist Party headquarters, two blocks from the canal on Place Colonel Fabien, had lost much of its national political base.)

What shops are here currently gather along rue Beaurepaire and a small portion of Quai de Valmy north of Beaurepaire: **mod shops, avant-garde bookshops and**

Antoine & Lili lifestyle shops offer a combination of the coolest, latest thing you ever saw (if you didn't live through the 70s), stuff that would be junked if it weren't in the season's color, and clothes you'd love to be young or thin or famous or happy-go-lucky enough to wear.

But this isn't really a shopping quarter; it's a strolling quarter. The canal itself is the true draw, with working locks, turning bridges, arched footbridges and cobblestone paths alongside. On sunny days, warm evenings, and throughout late spring and summer, the canal teems with locals and visitors, picnickers and communicators, families and friends. On Sunday afternoon a half-mile portion of the streets running along the canal (above rue de Lancry/rue de la Grange au Belle) is closed to motorized traffic; small festivals and festivities are sometimes held then.

For history, head up avenue Richerand off quai de Jemmapes for a glimpse at **Hôpital Saint-Louis**, built under orders of Henri IV to accommodate victims of the plague of 1606. (Saint Louis, Louis IX, himself died of the plague in 1270.) The hospital is still known for its dermatological services, whose modern facilities are situated just behind the original buildings. The 17th-century courtyard, which may freely be visited on weekdays, echoes in a stark way its contemporary, Place des Vosges. Well before the hospital was built the land just north of it was notorious as the site of the gallows known as the Gibet de Montfaucon, which could accommodate dozens of condemned criminals at a time.

Continuing upstream you come upon the area's other historical landmark at 102 quai de Jemmapes, the **Hôtel du Nord**. Though known outside of France only to hardcore Francophiles and French movie buffs, Michel Carné's *Hôtel du Nord* (1938) is as famous (and famously French) in France as the *Wizard of Oz* (1939) is for us. And Arletty's well-remembered retort to Louis Jouvet, *"Atmosphère, atmosphere, est-ce que j'ai une gueule d'atmosphère?"* is as much a cultural icon as Judy Garland singing *Over the Rainbow*. The hotel and its surroundings were faithfully reconstructed in a studio for the film, nevertheless the actual hotel it was based on remains. The Hôtel du Nord is now a restaurant-cabaret, frequently presenting English-singing artist and therefore attracting an English-speaking and hardcore Anglophile crowd.

A stroll along the canal calls for frequent pauses. A minor

La Marine
Address *55 bis quai de Valmy.* ***Tel*** *01 42 39 69 81. ALC 30€.*
Tight seating and heavy smoking in this neighborhood fish bistro whose reputation extends well beyond the neighborhood.

Chez Prune ***Address*** *36 rue Beaurepaire.*
The area's defining bobo café.

Le Verre Volé ***Address*** *67 rue de Lancry.*
A nook of a wine bar to wile away an hour with a vinticultural chat, perhaps accompanied by a plate of cold cuts. Or pick up a bottle for your picnic—if without corkscrew, have it opened here.

picnic can be made from the sandwich, food and wine shops along rue de Lancry, to be unwrapped and uncorked along canal's edge. See three indoor possibilities of character above.

Continuing along the canal you eventually reach the Bassin de la Villette, the wide link connecting Canal Saint-Martin with the Canal de l'Ourcq. A full day can be made of dawdling along the canal if you continue to Parc de La Villette, bordered on one side by the **Cité de la Science et de l'Industrie** and on the other by the **Cité de la Musique**.

Canauxrama boats cruise the Canal departing from the pleasure port near by Bastille (across from 50 bd de la Bastille) or from the Bassin de la Villette (across from 13 quai de la Loire) are possible. With many locks to pass through, the going is very slow on this 2.5-hour trip (www.canauxrama.com; tel. 01 42 39 15 00). Better to visit on foot.

BERCY VILLAGE AND THE EVOLVING EAST

Metro *Saint-Emilion.*

Since the mid-1980s, an enormous sector on the eastern side of Paris, on either side of the Seine, has been undergoing transformation from industrial zones and warehouses to a new residential, cultural, entertainment and nightlife center.

Redevelopment of the Left and Right Banks on the eastern

edge of the city began with the construction of the Ministry of Finance and of Paris's major indoor sports and concert stadium across the street, both of which commonly go by the name Bercy, the name of the Right Bank quarter (metro Bercy).

In 1996, the opening of the National Library, the Bibliothèque Nationale de France François Mitterand, widened the scope of the development onto the Left Bank (metro Bibliothèque Fr. Mitterand). Much development—residential, commercial, cultural—accompanied its construction and continues to transform the area. While welcoming for an exploration of the oft-returned traveler, that Light Bank area's time has yet to come—except for researchers at the library and nightclubbers at the barge Batofar docked nearby.

The Right Bank, meanwhile, already hit its stride as a shopping, dining, nighttime entertainment zone with the creation of Bercy Village. This area was Paris's wine cellar for much of the 19th and 20th centuries, when vast storehouses received and redistributed kegs and cases that arrived by river and later by rail. The heart of the wine distribution network has since moved outside of the city and most of the zone formerly covered by storehouses has become a park. One remnant, though, a section called Cour Saint-Emilion, now forms the heart of Bercy Village. Old tracks still run down the cobbled streets, while its storehouses have been restored or reconstructed to shelter 25 (and growing) shops and restaurants. The anchor businesses of the area are the restaurant, nightclub and information center Club Med World (www.clubmedworld.com) and a multiplex cinema. In between there's a perfume shop, an adventurer's clothing shop, an olive oil shop, a flower and plant shop, a wine shop, several eateries, a toy shop, a computer and video game shop, and all the reassuring chains and names of lifestyle shopping in France. It's doubtful that you'd come across anything not available in your local mall, airport or mail-order catalog. But the area is so pleasant for a (brief) visit during the day that it shouldn't be missed on your fourth trip to Paris or on your second if you have a student ID.

See *Restaurants: L'Oulette*, for another reason to come out to these parts.

ANTIQUES SHOPS & FLEA MARKETS

Antique shops

Carré Rive Gauche. The umbrella association CRC covers 120 antique shops and art galleries, furniture galleries and curiosities shops that congregate along several streets on the Left Bank, just across the river from the Louvre. CRC is technically bordered by quai Voltaire and rues des Saint-Pères, de l'Université and du Bac, but for all intents and purposes extends further east past the National Beaux-Arts School to rue Bonaparte.

Louvre des Antiquaires. ***Metro*** *Palais Royal-Musée du Louvre.* A number of high-end antique shops under one roof across the street (rue de Rivoli) from the Louvre on the Right Bank, by Place du Palais-Royal.

Village Saint-Paul. ***Metro*** *Saint-Paul.* A courtyard between rue Saint-Paul and rue Charlemagne given over to shops selling knickknacky antiques. Can be visited during a tour of the Marais.

Flea markets

Paris's major flea markets (*puces*) are on the edge of the city: Saint-Ouen to the north, Vanves to the south, and Montreuil to the east. **Portions of these markets can be very crowded. Always beware of pickpockets!**

Puces de Saint-Ouen. ***Metro*** *Porte-de-Clignancourt then several hundred yards along avenue de la Porte de Clignancourt to just beyond the city's ring road. Otherwise come by taxi. When coming from the metro, you'll first pass though a series of downscale, sometimes downtrodden, stands and exchanges along avenue de la Porte de Clignancourt. Clothing stands are in one portion of the puces, however the true interest of this market is the vast complex of antique markets just beyond the ring road along rue des Rosiers.* ***Open*** *Sat.-Mon., rain or shine.*

The antiques section of Saint-Ouen occupies a variety of covered markets filled with a wide array of antique stands and other-peoples-junk dealers. The markets aren't strictly organized by theme, however certain rows are devoted to 18th-century French antiques or to up-market large pieces from châteaux or to pieces from the 1930s though 1960s, etc. As Paris's most appealing area for antiquing, the dealers at Saint-Ouen are accustomed to an American and international clientele, making communication easy and negotiation difficult. The markets along rue des Rosiers and neighboring streets are a charming setting for a morning stroll and aren't particularly crowded. The old-fashion cafés and bistros in the area add to the attraction of a visit here.

Puces de Vanves. ***Metro*** *Porte-de-Vanves then down avenue de la Porte de Vanves.* ***Open*** *Sat. and Sun.* Another popular market for international visitors, Vanves is mostly an outdoor flea market, with haphazard stands selling antique furnishings, knick-knacks and decorative items mixed in the old junk. Treasure hunters come early Saturday morning.

Puces de Montreuil. ***Metro*** *Porte-de-Montreuil then across the ring road.* ***Open*** *Sat.-Mon.* The Montreuil flea market has some low-end antiques and dusty, rusty, scruffy pieces calling out for restoration, but in order to find them you have to look through all anyone could hope to find or sell in a flea market, from third-hand clothing to pirate CDs. Montreuil is the most downscale of the city's main flea markets, yet this may be just the place for that 1930s door knocker or 1890s wine holder you've been looking for.

DEPARTMENT STORES

Department stores are generally open 9:30am-7pm Mon.-Sat. and until 9pm on Thursday. They may open some Sundays in December and January.

Five major department stores compete for attention in Paris, as they have been for over a century now. They have been centerpieces of shopping life in the city since the late 19th century (like Macy's in New York). They now have varying ambitions—local, national or international—yet these are their flagship stores, all at major crossroads in the city and fixtures in their respective quarters.

Galeries Lafayette and **Printemps.** ***Metro*** *Chaussée d'Antin and Havre-Caumartin, respectively.*

Galeries Lafayette and Printemps stand side by side along boulevard Haussmann forming an extensive department store complex offering so much store space and mid-upscale merchandise that they're a natural attraction to Parisians, suburbanites and tourists alike. Galeries Lafeyette's terrace and restaurant/tearoom, beneath a beautiful dome (1912), offer a stunning view of the back of the Garnier Opera. The French don't show the Christmas spirit and tinsel the way Americans do, but for Paris this is where store windows get paid the most attention in December.

Samaritaine. ***Metro*** *Pont Neuf.*

Talk about a store with a view! Samaritaine may have trouble competing with Galeries Lafayette and Printemps these days, but for a location with a view it wins hands down. Just coming up from the Pont Neuf metro station for the view by the Seine is spectacular enough. Across the street, the store offers its own unbeatable panorama over the river from its terrace and from its restaurant/tearoom.

BHV. ***Metro*** *Hôtel de Ville.*

A highly practical department store on the edge of the Marais. Less fashion oriented than the others, BHV covers all departments but is most useful for its hardware department in the basement, just in case you want to bring back a drill bit for that special someone back home.

Le Bon Marché. ***Metro*** *Sèvres-Babylone.*

The Left Bank's only flagship department store, this was also the city's first, founded in 1863. It occupies two buildings just beyond the square by the Sèvres-Babylone metro station, where the chic 6th arrondissement rubs shoulders with the stately 7th. The metal framework of the first building was designed by Gustave Eiffel in the 1870s. It's a warm, handsome place for fine shopping, the classiest of Paris's department stores, a place to go after you've gotten your hair done and are looking for clothes to go with the new you, including at the large lingerie department. The second store offers epicurean pan-European food shopping at La Grande Epicerie. An antique gallery is upstairs. There's a Conran Shop across rue de Babylone.

MALLS

The shopping centers of Paris are little different from your own neighborhood mall. **The Carrousel Mall** underground by the Louvre is attractive for its location and its museum store. **The Forum des Halles** (metro Châtelet-Les Halles) is noteworthy not for its vast underground shopping but for its surroundings. (See *Restaurants: Bistros: La Poule au Pot* for a description of this area).

HOTELS

A hotel in Paris is more than a place to sleep, it's your temporary home. You want to feel comfortable there – and more or less spoiled depending on your concept of the ideal Paris vacation. So make an informed choice.

CHOOSING YOUR HOME AWAY FROM HOME

The main criteria I consider in exploring hotels are character, quality, service, charm and location. In order to be selected here a hotel has to have something special to offer in at least three of those criteria, though an exceptional two sometimes gets the nod, and many are noteworthy in four or even all five categories.

French hotels are officially rated with 0 to 4 stars, with certain luxury hotels being officially designated 4★L (there is no actual 5★ category in France). The reviews in this book concern 3★ and 4★ hotels, i.e. mid- and upscale hotels. The number of stars shown beside each hotel in this chapter indicates its *official* category. I have a penchant for privately owned or small group hotels that are either central (Left and Right Banks) or that merit staying outside of the center. However, I do also consider hotels belonging to major groups if they have something more to offer than a US 1-800 number and advertisements in travel magazines.

You will use your own judgment in considering the price of these mid-upscale selections. While I speak of price in the reviews in this chapter, and while I know a good budget deal when I hear one, my goal is not to tell you how to travel as cheaply as possible. Furthermore, while I frequently advise upend travelers and business executives, I won't try to impress you with financial factoids such as the price of the Imperial suite at the Ritz (okay, it's $7000/night in high season).

My observations are largely based on my visits throughout the hotel, augmented or modified by the comments of the many travelers I meet throughout the year. Within this selection you'll find the hotel that's perfect for you to call home during your stay in Paris.

Prices

The prices given here are high-season rack rates provided directly by the hotel. The official rack rate (i.e. the highest price you could possibly pay) must be displayed outside the hotel, at the reception desk and in the rooms. Prcies naturally change over time, so be sure to inquire about most recent seasonal, standard or promotional prices when reserving.

High season in Paris generally runs March 1-June 30, Sept. 1-Nov. 15 and Dec. 29-Jan. 2, with occasional peaks in other periods during major fairs or events. Off-season prices may be lower, in many hotels to the tune of about 10%. Other special deals are sometimes announced on the hotel's website or by the hotel when contacted by e-mail or fax. Don't hesitate to send the hotel a fax or e-mail inquiring if there are any promotions going on at the time of your stay. Specifically use the term "promotions" or "promotional rates." (E-mail contact can be made by going through the hotel's website.) Large hotels have more leeway in their pricing than small hotels, and chain hotels have more leeway in their pricing and promotional offerings than non-chain hotels.

Other than price reductions, such promotions may include room upgrades, free breakfast, a bottle of champagne, a museum pass and/or other small but welcome giveaways. In winter, weekend deals also may be in the offering. Don't hesitate to mention that you saw the selection of hotels recommended here.

A credit card number will be requested in order to ensure a reservation. Cancellation times vary, generally between two and seven days of arrival, so you should request specific cancellation information if in doubt about your plans.

Breakfast

There are two types of hotel breakfast in France: continental and buffet.

A continental breakfast typically consists of a hot drink (tea, coffee, hot chocolate) with one or more breakfast pastries (croissant, pain au chocolat, pain aux raisins), bread, butter and jam, possibly yogurt.

A buffet breakfast, also sometimes called an American breakfast, will be more elaborate. There you'll additionally find hot and cold cereals, eggs, bacon, cold meats and more or less fresh fruit.

All 3- and 4-star hotels (i.e. those presented here) offer the possibility of breakfast in the room. In 3★ hotels that generally means the continental breakfast. In 4★ hotels the breakfast served in the room usually offers more. Some hotels offer both types of breakfast – yet the greater choice for a traveler is between breakfast at the hotel and breakfast at a café and/or bakery.

Hotel breakfast vs. café/bakery breakfast: You will not find $5.99 all-you-can-eat pancake-and-egg breakfasts anywhere in France, however some mornings you may prefer venturing outside of the hotel for breakfast. You're sure to find a cozy café in the neighborhood offering their own continental breakfast or a tempting bakery nearby. Some cafés frown upon clients entering with a pastry in hand and ordering coffee or tea when the café has its own (less fresh and/or less good) croissants to sell, but eating an "imported" pastry discreetly (i.e. not unwrapping it on the table as though you were having a picnic) is normally tolerated.

Price of Breakfast: The hotel breakfast generally costs 5-10% of the price of a standard room. In theory if you have not eaten breakfast at the hotel you may not be billed for it (except in the case of groups). If you have accepted a promotional price, however, it is difficult to say what one's obligations are. If a hotel proposes a price (not necessarily "promotional") in which breakfast is included and you are not always likely to have breakfast there, you may inquire how much is deducted from the price in case you do not eat breakfast at the hotel every day. Best to raise the question before check-out time. There's no surer way to spoil a stay than to dispute a bill as you leave – and (re)discover the aggravation of being confronted with the expressionless poise of the service industry in Paris.

Check-in/out

The official check-in time is generally 2pm, yet most flights from North America arrive in the morning. If you anticipate checking in before 2pm, then, you should let the hotel know so that they can do their best to have the room ready. Hotels will try to accommodate you, however, since check-out time isn't generally until noon, your room may not yet be available when you arrive. In that case, leave your baggage at the hotel, enjoy a bit of a walk and stop into a café for a bit before returning to a ready room.

Reservations are typically held until 6pm, so if you plan to be arriving after that time you should also be sure to notify the hotel in advance.

Tax

A city tax of about $1 per night will be added to your bill unless the hotel has already indicated that it is included in the price. All other taxes will be included in the price announced by a hotel.

Noise and air

With any visit to a major capital comes the noise of the big city. In most of the hotels selected here, double-glazed windows adequately isolate the rooms from the sounds of the street. Furthermore, air conditioning has now become standard offering in 3- and 4-star hotels. It may work more as a ventilation system than as a cooling system, nevertheless, with the movement of air provided by the system you typically won't need to open the window at night to let in a breeze and the accompanying noise.

Hotels located on major avenues may, however, endure a hum of traffic behind their double, sometimes triple, windows. This can be barely audible and of no bother to most sleepers. With the slight hum may also come a grand view, which will often enhance your appreciation of the room, so you'll need to consider the trade-off. Sufficient sound-proofing and the possibility of a view of the street or beyond leads me to prefer rooms facing the street in all of the hotels reviewed in this chapter. However, light sleepers may prefer a room on the courtyard or to the back of the hotel as those are usually sheltered from outside sounds. In large and palatial hotels the courtyard may be a spacious square or patio that may itself be pleasing to the eye. However, in small hotels the courtyard can be so narrow that from your window you could play handball against the opposite wall. When reserving, you should specify a room on the street or on the courtyard.

Honesty bar

An honesty bar is a small self-service bar counter in the lobby or lounge of some hotels where guests can serve themselves a variety of alcoholic and non-alcoholic drinks. Guests then note what they have served themselves on a form so that their drinks may be billed to the room. Several of the hotels reviewed here have such self-service bars.

Hotel Map

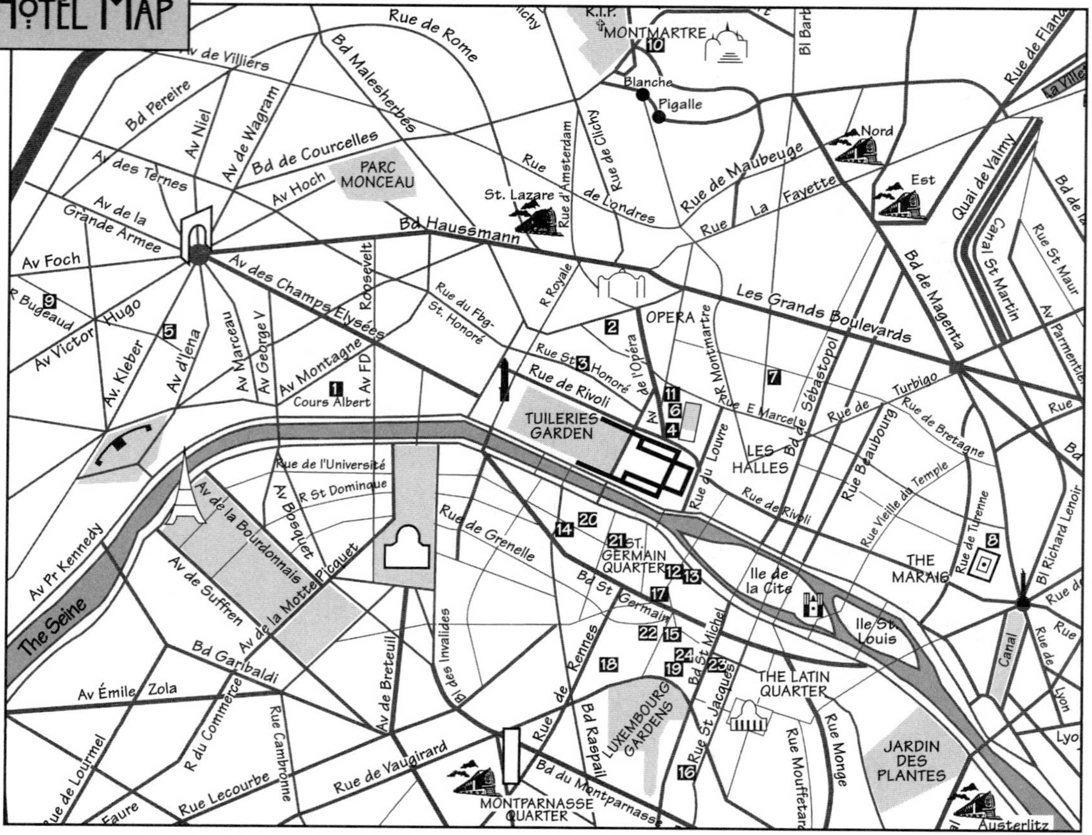

Right Bank Hotels

1 Hôtel Westminster
2 Hôtel de Vendôme
3 Hôtel du Louvre
4 Hôtel Raphael
5 Hôtel Washington Opéra
6 Hôtel Victoires Opéra
7 Pavillon de la Reine
8 Saint James Paris
9 Terrass Hôtel
10 Hôtel Thérèse

Left Bank Hotels

11 Hôtel D'Aubusson
12 Relais Christine
13 Hôtel Pont Royal
14 Relais Saint-Germain
15 Relais Saint-Jacques
16 Hôtel Buci Latin
17 Hôtel de l'Abbaye
18 Le Clos Médicis
19 Hôtel Verneuil
20 Hôtel du Danube
21 Hôtel de l'Odéon
22 Select Hôtel
23 Hôtel Saint-Paul

Right Bank Hotels

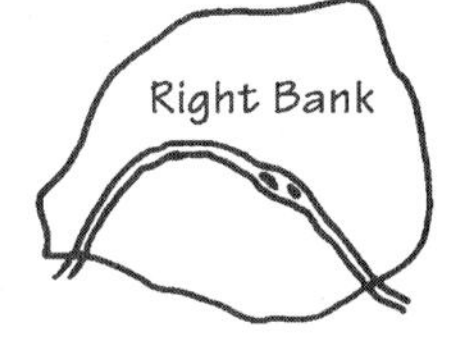

❶ Hôtel San Régis ★★★★

Address *12 rue Jean-Goujon, 75008 Paris*
Tel. *01 44 95 16 16 •* ***Fax*** *01 45 61 05 48*
Site *www.hotel-sanregis.fr.* ***Metro*** *Champs-Elysées Clemenceau, Alma-Marceau, Franklin D. Roosevelt.* ***Features*** *33 rooms, 11 suites. Small restaurant for clients or for their confidential meals with outsiders. AC.* ***Price*** *Single 300€, 335€, Double 395€, 455€, 540€, Junior Suite 590€, 650€, Suite 1025€.* ***Breakfast*** *22€ (continental) or à la carte.*

Discreet, intimate luxury

There are two types of luxury hotels, the palatial and monumental on the one hand, the discreet and intimate on the other. In the former you are meant to feel like a prince, in the latter you are meant to feel at home. The San Régis is one of the latter – discreet luxury at its finest, where "home" is an elegant 1857 townhouse (for the lower half of the building) in one of the city's most distinguished neighborhoods. The street itself is hushed and residential, yet just around the corner await the Champs-Elysées, the haute couture flagstores of Avenue Montaigne and the Seine. In short, the ideal place from which to explore Paris's Golden Triangle and all the other precious or common metals of the city.

Class – a word that fashion has long left behind – resides here with neither snobbery nor ceremony, rather with a courteous and attentive *je ne sais quoi.* The hospitality of the small reception area leads to a touch of quiet Victorian living in the form of the oak-paneled library/ dining/breakfast room and adjacent ornate lounge with a winter garden in one corner. Fine fabrics, deep rugs, optimistic curves and colors, and an appointment of 18th and 19th century period furnishings in the rooms help maintain a refined air of well-being throughout. Rooms were decorated by Pierre-Yves Rochon, currently one of the grandmasters of hotel interior design in Paris and beyond. Each room is unique: a touch of Pierre Frey here, a dash of Manuel Canovas there, Nina Ricci toiletries, a fireplace (rooms 44 and 34). Handsome marble bathrooms. Doubles on the street side are

There are two types of luxury hotels, the palatial and monumental on the one hand, the discreet and intimate on the other.

less spacious than those on the courtyard (hence the price difference), still sufficiently sized, and the street is extremely calm.

The private terraces off the three junior suites on the upper floor offer a view of the Eiffel Tower, the Grand Palais and a majestic private mansion across the street, with the grandest of "ah-Paris" views from suite #61. Small single rooms are well suited for business leaders looking to stay away from the who's who of the monumental hotels. Indeed, one doesn't come here to see and to be seen, rather to be well and to stay well, for the San Régis doesn't rhyme with ritzy, it rhymes with privilege.

❷Hôtel Westminster ★★★★

Address *13 rue de la Paix, 75002 Paris*
Tel. *01 42 61 57 46* • ***Fax*** *01 42 60 30 66*
Site *www.warwickhotels.com* ***Group*** *Warwick Hotels, US/Canada reservations: 800-203-3232.* ***Metro*** *Opéra.* ***Features*** *80 rooms, 22 suites. AC. Very fine gastronomic restaurant Le Céladon on weekdays (see Restaurants). Restaurant transforms into the nice but less ambitious Le Petit Céladon on weekends. Bar.* ***Price*** *Single or double 420€, 470€, 530€. Suites 680€, 950€, 1230€, 2000€.* ***Breakfast*** *23€ (continental), 28€ (buffet).*

Good old fashion grandeur

Don't get me wrong when I say that the style at the Westminster is old-fashioned, for this hotel on jeweler's row – the most expensive street on the French Monopoly board – is intentionally and successfully so. Its slightly bygone décor is in fact the fruit of thorough renovation and high maintenance. The easygoing grandeur of its style is sincere and unpretentious; you might well feel like a guest in the home of a tall duke and duchess. Commoners are very welcome, while non-commoners will find the suites well suited to their requirements.

The Duke of Westminster lent his name and arms to this former coaching inn in 1846. Those arms bear the motto Virtus Non Stemma – Virtue is not dependent upon pedigree. Pedigree is naturally accepted, but one needn't have a long chin to nod slightly to the doorman, stride down the hallway, and step graciously into a lobby that shows the duchess's touch: brownish pink faux columns with gilt Corinthian crowns, tremendous rug on the marble floor, centerpiece flower arrangement. Beyond velvet drapes, the neo-Gothic bar is solidly ducal: ornate chimney, coffered ceiling, wood paneling, green leather armchairs.

Professionals and business travelers and their spouses who

have seen a few too many Hiltons and Intercontinentals on previous trips (with all due respect to the nearby Intercontinentals and the new Hilton just a few yards down) should take note of this address when looking to stay within the business and shopping zones of the Opera quarter. Finally, bar-hopping lawyers can enjoy a few glasses of gin or whiskey at the Meurice, the Vendôme, the Ritz and/or Harry's bar without having to cross any major avenues on the way home, then stop for a nightcap in the Westminster's own cozy bar. After a day's – or night's – walking, you'll be happy to know that by leaving your shoes at a designated spot in your room you can receive a free shoeshine the following day.

The rooms are of decent size in the least expensive category and quite sizeable in all others. They're decorated with refinement – bygone, as I've said, but authentically Parisian at that – a subtle range of classically French edges with handsome fabrics of faint regal reds and blues and polished yellows (Pierre-Yves Rochon's handiwork, once again), with an antique bronze clock in certain rooms. Many rooms face the large inner courtyard.

❸Hôtel de Vendôme ★★★★

Address *1 place Vendôme, 75001 Paris.*
Tel. *01 55 04 55 00 •* ***Fax*** *01 49 27 97 89*
Site *www.hoteldevendome.com* ***Member*** *Small Luxury Hotels of the World, US/Canada reservations: 800-525-4800.* ***Metro*** *Concorde, Tuileries, Opera.* ***Features*** *19 rooms, 10 suites. AC. Two restaurants: Café de Vendôme open to the street, Lebanese restaurant upstairs. Bar.* ***Price*** *Singles 460-550€. Doubles 550-850€. Suites 835-1050+€.* ***Breakfast*** *25€.(continental), 35€ (buffet). Room prices vary with season. See website for promotions.*

An odd little palace

At the corner of Place Vendôme and rue du Faubourg St-Honoré, where luxury fashion meets opulent jewelry, the Mouawad family has appropriately, if perhaps unintentionally, opened their hotel to a breeze of kitsch. Rest assured, there's much luxuriance and no chintz to this kitsch. I refer here to the medley of ornate curves and drapes and fabrics by which the rooms tend toward an indefinite English/Louis XIV/Art Deco style yet manage quite comfortably to miss the mark. Call it character! The Vendôme is something of a little pleasure palace. For not only is kitsch fashionable, but how else to marry a smart café-restaurant, an English bar, a Lebanese restaurant, early 18th-century outer walls, and the fact that those walls once housed the Texan embassy – and do all that with great comfort and a certain opulence?

As a 4★L hotel with only 29 rooms and suites, the Vendôme calls itself Paris's smallest palace, yet mansion is more to the point. Service is gracious, if restrained, in the little lobby of polished wood and glistening marble. Upstairs, all rooms are different, and I would be happy to call any of them home for a few days – except perhaps for the top-floor suites which are spacious enough along the carpet but whose mansard roof and step-up windows leave them relatively viewless and cramped. Classic doubles are well sized at 270 sq. ft., deluxe doubles even more so at 320 sq. ft.

One flight up on the wonderfully rickety old elevator you'll find both the British-inspired bar and the handsome Lebanese restaurant. Hotel bar hoppers should keep the leather and mahogany bar in mind whether staying here or not. The fact that it's upstairs shouldn't dissuade you, though it does help keep out the, how do you say, riffraff.

The Texan Embassy

And you thought the Texan embassy was in the White House! Number One Vendôme, now address to the Hôtel de Vendôme, once housed the embassy of the short-lived Republic of Texas. The colonization of Texas territory, in the 1820s, then under Mexican control, produced growing differences between Mexico and the Anglo-American colonists. The Texas Revolution that began in 1835 resulted in the establishment – via the Battle of the Alamo – of the Republic of Texas in 1836 under the presidency of Sam Houston.

In the wake of the Franco-Texan treaty of September 29, 1839, France became the first nation to recognize Texas. The new republic opened its embassy here in 1842. It closed the following year. Unable to establish itself as a viable nation, Texas was willingly annexed to the United States in 1845. The subsequent war with Mexico led to the Rio Grande being set as the international boundary.

❹Hôtel du Louvre ★★★★

Address *1 place André Malraux, 75001 Paris.*
Tel. *01 44 58 38 38 •* ***Fax*** *01 44 58 38 01*
Site *www.hoteldulouvre.com* ***Group*** *Concorde Hotel, US/Canada reservations: 800-888-4747.* ***Metro*** *Palais Royal-Musée du Louvre.* ***Features*** *200 rooms and suites. AC. Bar. Brasserie.* ***Price*** *"Superior" 450€, "Deluxe" 500€, Junior suites 650€, 800€, Suite 1100€, Pissaro suite 1800€.* ***Buffet breakfast*** *21€. See website about seasonal promotions.*

A view from the heart

While many grand hotels pride themselves on the view going in, the Hôtel du Louvre can also boast a premium view going out: the grand bustling expanse of avenue leading to the gilt wings, green beret and devil-may-care elegance of the Garnier Opera. You can borrow this view without staying here, but you can only call it your own when you take a room.

> **There seems little point to staying in a grand hotel if you don't take advantage of the common areas.**

The Hôtel du Louvre was built upon order of Napoleon III to receive well-heeled travelers for the occasion of the World's Fair of 1855. It covers a square block in the city's right ventricular region where avenue de l'Opéra meets rue de Rivoli, surrounded by major monuments. The Louvre stands across the street on one side, the classical theater of the Comédie Française and the Palais Royal on the opposite side. All rooms facing the street therefore have a magnificent view: sculptural details of the Louvre, columns of the Comédie Française, the avenue and the opera and/or the rue de Rivoli.

With the Louvre across the street, the Orsay Museum across the bridge and the Garnier Opera and major department stores at the end of the avenue, you'll never have to worry about the weather spoiling your stay.

Completely renovated in the late 1990s, the 200 rooms and suites are all tastefully decorated in a classic burgundy (businessman's red) or in a fresher blue or yellow. Internet access is possible from all rooms. While the rooms are sizeable enough in the superior category, they're quite spacious in the deluxe and executive categories. Those on the 1st and 2nd lodging floors have 16-ft.-high ceilings to luxuriate beneath (the second floor is a non-smoking floor). The painter Camille Pissarro (1830-1903) lived here for a time and painted views of the Louvre from his apartment, now the Pissarro suite.

Behind excellent sound-proofing windows you may or may not sense the slight hum of the surrounding traffic. Indeed at times I may have merely imagined it upon looking out at the intersection as I went from room to decorous room and admired the view. This is intended as a warning only to ultra-light sleepers; others will pay scant notice as they enjoy the majesty of the setting. There are always rooms on the courtyard, yet the view from the heart of the city, traffic and all, is irresistible.

There seems little point to staying in a grand hotel if you don't take advantage of the common areas. The brasserie/breakfast room is one, while the centerpiece of this palace is its bar, The Defender. Surrounded by black and gold trompe l'oeil marble columns and a contemporary version of Napoleon III imperial red and green décor, The Defender calls for a long luxuriant sit in good company – a single malt, say, or a Cuban cigar, if no one else is game. The hotel is a part of the Concorde Hotel Group, which is within the Taittinger Group, hence the promotion of Taittinger champagne and Baccarat crystal in the bar.

Finally, I make special note of the attentive and trustworthy concierge service. Of course, having this book you won't need suggestions.

❺ Hôtel Raphael ★★★★

Address *17 avenue Kléber, 75116 Paris.*
Tel*. 01 53 64 32 00 •* ***Fax*** *01 53 64 32 01*
Site *www.raphael-hotel.com* ***Member*** *Small Luxury Hotels of the World, US/Canada reservations 800-525-4800.* ***Metro*** *Kléber.* ***RER*** *Charles-de-Gaulle-Etoile.* ***Features*** *85 rooms, including 32 suites and 9 apartments. AC. English bar. Louis XVI-style gastronomic restaurant La Salle à Manger.* ***Price*** *Rooms 435€, 520€. Junior suites 690€, 905€. Larger suites/apartments from 1085€.* ***Breakfast*** *27€ (continental), 33€ (buffet).*

A grand hotel of Old World charms

Relatively small as far as palaces go but with princely bearing nonetheless, the Raphael is a gracious setting of old world charms. While traffic gathers in halts and jerks around the Arc de Triomphe a block away, the Raphael, built in 1925, lounges in a rather discreet world of its own. Those in search of more showy and exuberant palaces should head elsewhere.

The Raphael offers 18th-century edges, 19th-century

majesty and 20th-century luxury for 21st century visitors. A path of Persian rugs over the black and white stone tiles in the wood-paneled gallery/lobby lead past the plush red velvet and wood-paneled bar to an old cage elevator that ushers you to your room. Adjectives everywhere! Along the way one passes (or enters) the plush red velvet and wood-paneled bar, a confidential, Bloody-Mary kind of setting for intimate or business conversation.

Upstairs, the lodgings provide a classically French bygone refinement whose furnishing, fabrics and pastel tones would have pleased the later Louies. The smallest rooms measure 270 square feet, so space is never a problem. In fact, a surprisingly high percentage of suites and apartments inhabit the building. Bathrooms are all spacious, each with a window.

In warm seasons, have breakfast, afternoon tea and/or evening cocktail with a panoramic view of Paris from the 7th-floor terrace. In other seasons, just pop up for the view, which General Eisenhower undoubtedly enjoyed when he used the hotel as his headquarters after WWII.

The Raphael is one of three similar-spirited 4★ hotels of the family-owned Regina Co. Its little sister the Hôtel Majestic (30 rooms), just around the corner, is a bit too nondescript for my taste. Its big sister the Hôtel Regina, by the Louvre, displays Art Nouveau touches on its ground floor and spacious comforts upstairs. The Regina is certainly noteworthy, but the Raphael has more cachet.

❻ Hôtel Washington Opéra ★★★★

Address *50 rue de Richelieu, 75001 Paris.*
Tel*. 01 42 96 68 06 •* ***Fax*** *01 40 15 01 12*
Site *www.hotelwashingtonopera.com.* ***Metro*** *Palais Royal-Musée du Louvre, Pyramides.* ***Features*** *36 rooms. AC. Trouser press.* ***Price*** *215-275€, suite 330€.* ***Breakfast*** *13€.*

Boutique hotel I: small but winning

We hear a lot these days about "boutique hotels," the term having been watered down to cover most any small hotels. But the true boutique hotel is defined not only by its size but by its other winning attributes. The common areas may be small but should always be cozy, the rooms should have either charm or style or elegance to make up for their lack of volume, while the staff, even when sparse, should always be helpful. Guests at a boutique hotel should be received as though they have an invitation to the presentation of a new collection.

The San Régis, noted earlier, is the finest of Paris's boutique hotels. Among the less luxurious 4★, the Washington Opéra (36 rooms) and its sister hotel the Victoires Opéra (24 rooms) also earn the appellation. They are proof in themselves that when it comes to fine comfort the central Right Bank isn't given over solely to palatial ambitions. It, too, has its pockets of charm.

Within its 18th-century walls, the Washington Opéra is attentively decorated in Gustavian and classic cozy-edged styles whose sky blues, sunny yellows and earthy reds give airiness to modestly sized rooms. Canopied beds add romance to the suites. Bathrooms are all pleasantly marbled. The cute little basement breakfast room with parquet flooring and the 6th-floor terrace overlooking the Théâtre du Palais Royal round out the offerings of this boutiqu'otel.

The location is excellent, for not only is monumental Paris (the Louvre, the Garnier Opera, the Palais Royal) close at hand, but so is a wonderful range of food and drink settings: high-gastromony at Le Grand Véfour, old-time brasserie at Le Grand Colbert, bistro fare at Mellière, sushi along rue Sainte-Anne, wine at Willi's Wine Bar and Aux Bons Crus, coffee at Le Nemours, cocktails at the Hôtel du Louvre. Major department stores are just a few blocks away.

❼Hôtel Victoires Opéra ★★★★

Address *56 rue Montorgueil, 75002 Paris.*
Tel. *01 42 36 41 08 •* ***Fax*** *01 45 08 08 79*
Site *www.hotelvictoiresopera.com.* ***Metro*** *Etienne-Marcel, Sentier.* ***Features*** *24 rooms. AC.* ***Price*** *215-275€, Suite 330€.* ***Breakfast*** *13€.*

Boutique hotel II: discovering another quarter

Rue Montorgueil is Paris's most appealing pedestrian street, an ancient and enduring market street that once led into the city's central market of Les Halles. Fruit and vegetable stands, food shops, bakeries and cafés still line the street, along with an array of 18th century buildings, including one occupied by this hotel. While most of the more worthwhile hotels on the Right Bank can boast locations within quick view of monumental Paris, this boutique hotel is ideally set for explorations of great charms of the Right Bank that are overlooked by first-time visitors. Return travelers intrigued by less familiar paths will be wise to consider basing their explorations at the Victoires Opéra.

The rooms were renovated in 2000 with peaceably classical style. As with its sister hotel above, size is always snug, which explains the modest price for a 4★. If claustrophobic, opt for the larger rooms, whether facing the small courtyard or the street.

The hotel is certainly pleasant but it's the area that offers the true attraction. Your explorations can begin among the pleasurable morning bustle of rue Montorgueil, a street sure to delight food lovers and picnic planners. Travelers who know how to take advantage of café life in the city will find the street particularly attractive as they move from seat to seat to follow the sun. There are many small restaurants in the area. Those on nearby rue Tiquetonne are upbeat and gay-friendly. An easy walk west takes you to the boutiques of Place des Victoires and Galerie Vivienne, while other covered shop-lined passages are found by wandering east and north. Having visited the major museums, the return traveler might now take advantage of the location to discover the great Musée des Arts et Métiers nearby (see *Museums*). A swimsuit (bathing briefs required for men) could come in handy should you choose to go for laps in the Olympic size pool down the street at Les Halles. The Louvre, Notre-Dame, the Pompidou Center and, beyond it, the Marais, are further on but within walking distance. A location that's sure to convince you to return to Paris more often.

❽ Pavillon de la Reine ★★★★

Address *28 place des Vosges, 75003.*
Tel*. 01 40 29 19 19* • ***Fax*** *01 40 29 19 20*
Site *www.pavillon-de-la-reine.com* ***Member*** *Small Luxury Hotels of the World, US/Canada reservations 800-525-4800.* ***Metro*** *Chemin Vert.* ***Features*** *55 rooms and suites. AC. Honesty bar in the lounge.* ***Price*** *Double 330€, "Deluxe" or duplex 395€/475€, Junior suite or "deluxe duplex" 590€, Suite 580€, Two-bedroom suite 720€.* ***Breakfast*** *20€ (continental), 25€ (buffet).*

The Marais by day... and by night

The Marais is often viewed as a quarter where a visitor can spend a good part of a day but not the night (except in the bars). But the savvy return visitor should know that the Marais is also a place to stay. And the best place for that is at the superb Pavillon de la Reine, the Queen's Pavilion, hidden behind Paris's most beautiful garden square, Place des Vosges.

The quaintness and prosperity that has led the Marais to be considered "the Left Bank of the Right Bank" (recently confirmed by real estate prices) is present in spades in this hotel. No rooms actually look out onto Place des Vosges. With windows facing a courtyard, a small garden or a quiet side street, the Pavillon de la Reine is a secluded and unpretentious country inn of high comfort in center city. The fact that this is the area's only luxury hotel makes it all the more special.

The rooms are decorated in a variety of soothing courtly styles with baroque touches: twisted iron here, stenciled headboards there, elegant pastel bedspreads, theatrical duplexes. From the courtyard entrance to the wood-paneled lounge (with honesty bar) to the vaulted basement breakfast room, the Pavillon hits the right tone at every turn. It manages to marry traditional and contemporary without falling into neo-something-or-other. The staff is neither obsequious nor aloof, just willing to help when they can.

The location is ideal for the return traveler intent not only on exploring every corner of the Marais but on exploring the larger soul of the central east side of the city. The food shops along rue de Bretagne and the open-air market along boulevard Richard Lenoir are both close by, the Bastille Opera is a few blocks away, the shops of the Viaduc des Arts are just beyond the Bastille, Ile Saint-Louis is within easy reach. Romance and discovery are sure to accompany you in an aimless stroll any direction.

The choice of restaurants in the area can keep you busy for several days in and of themselves: the quirky setting of Le Dôme du Marais, the good ol' time brasserie Bofinger, the hearty traditional fare at the Repaire de Cartouche and haute gastronomy at L'Ambroisie.

⑨Saint James Paris ★★★★

Address *43 avenue Bugeaud, 75116.*
Tel. *01 44 05 81 81* • ***Fax*** *01 44 05 81 82*
Site *www.saint-james-paris.com* ***Member*** *Small Luxury Hotels of the World, US/Canada reservations 800-525-4800.* ***Metro*** *Porte Dauphine. RER Avenue Foch.* ***Features*** *48 rooms and suites. AC. Library bar, fitness room, sauna, Jacuzzi, billiard room, restaurant.* ***Price*** *"Superior" 340€, "Deluxe" 430€, Junior suite 470€, 570€, Suite 730€.* ***Breakfast*** *20€ (continental), 25€ (buffet).*

A mansion-hotel in a gentlemanly world apart

Removed in both spirit and location from the frill and adornment of the city's other monumental hotels, the Saint James occupies a stately neo-classical mansion standing amidst two walled-in acres of ground in an upscale residential/office quarter on the western edge of the city.

The mansion dates from 1892 when it was built to house an academic foundation in memory of President Adolphe Thiers. In 1986 it was fittingly transformed into a traditional London gentleman's club, the Saint James Club. While the St. James still welcomes members, several years after becoming a club it became an actual hotel, so the doors are now open to all – all who savor a bit of elegant world-apartness in the big city.

There remains a distinctly clubby atmosphere here – not a stuffy clubbiness, but an admirably and graciously hushed clubbiness. Admittedly the entrance hall is rather stern and upright, in keeping with its origins, but beyond that the nicely spacious rooms (including many suites) are handsomely decorated in leathery beige, yellow, grey and brown stripes and tones. The view emphasized is the one inside rather than out. Rooms on the top floor open to their own patios, facing not the garden but inward, curtained off from one another under the sky roof.

There's very much a businessman's (or yachter's or big-city lawyer's) air to this mansion, but women, too, will find the pampering of fine service and discreet luxury much to their liking. And no one can resist a sit-back in the magnificent library-bar, but you can only get there if you're a member, guest or a guest of theirs. It's enough to make you wish for London weather so as to have a good excuse to stay inside.

⑩ Terrass Hôtel ★★★★

Address *12-14 rue Joseph-de-Maistre, 75018 Paris.*
Tel. *01 46 06 72 85 •* ***Fax*** *01 42 52 29 11*
Site *www.terrass-hotel.com.* ***Metro*** *Place de Clichy, Blanche, Abbesses.* ***Features*** *100 rooms and suites. AC. Non-smoking floor. Two restaurants including the namesake Terrace restaurant with a magnificent view. Bar with piano player three days per week, fire in fireplace in winter.* ***Price*** *Single/Double: "Comfort" 194€/232€, "Superior" 220€/256€, Suite 311€.* ***Buffet breakfast*** *12.50€.*

A special place in Montmartre for the repeat offender

While I've mostly selected very central Left and Right Bank hotels, I make a special detour uphill to Montmartre for this singular hotel of character. Its location will be a treat to repeat travelers looking to expand their horizons. For rooms facing front on the upper floors (5th and up), those horizons include a spectacular view over Paris. No crowds! No waiting in line! The view also includes sight of the Montmartre Cemetery at the foot of the hotel; I note this in case you might find such a view disturbing – though with Degas, Nijinski, Offenbach, Truffaut, Dalida and other celebrated names lying there, you'll be overlooking stellar tombs.

Even without the view the rooms are unwaveringly comfortable, with a bright, airy, contemporarily-tinged classic style, whether you choose the smaller "comfort" rooms, the ever-so-pleasant "superior" rooms, or opt for the small suite with terrace and grandest view of all. It takes a certain kind of savvy visitor to know how to appreciate a stay in Montmartre. Think not heavily-touristed Montmartre but village Montmartre, with its homey restaurants and local cafés and wide boulevards nearby. And lest you feel too off-center, know that from here one has easy access to the heart of the city by metro, bus or taxi and that the great bustle of the Paris boulevards is only 200 yards away. The price is very convincing for second or third honeymooners on a 3★ budget, in which case the Terrass Hotel makes for a very wise splurge. If you're considering other 4-stars, well, it's just simply wise. The Terrass has been owned and operated by the same family for 4 generations, which may explain the staff's amiability and attentiveness.

The hotel's ground-floor restaurant will be appreciated for a likable and moderately-priced dinner when you don't want to venture further than the front door. The 7th-floor roof garden restaurant, meanwhile, deserves special note: the fare is fine (at about 40€), the view sublime. Open May to September only, weather permitting. If you can score a table by the edge on an open-air evening, you'll not only be on top of the town but on top of the world.

⑪ Hôtel Thérèse ★ ★ ★

Address *5-7 rue Thérèse, 75001.*
Tel*. 01 42 96 10 01* • ***Fax*** *01 42 96 15 22*
Site *www.hoteltherese.com.* ***Metro*** *Pyramides.* ***Features*** *43 rooms. AC.*
Price *Single/Double (shower) 125€, Double 160€, "Deluxe" double 190€, Junior suite 250€.* ***Continental breakfas****t 12€.*

Two comfortable drawing rooms set the tone for the classic polish of the Thérèse, which opened in 2002 after complete renovation. This is Madame Sylvie de Lattre's Right Bank response to her popular little Left Bank Hôtel Verneuil. Like the Verneuil, the Thérèse is on a quiet side-street and well situated for exploring its part of the city, in this case near the Palais Royal, between the Garnier Opera and the Louvre. It is a location from which to take in the riches of the central Right Bank without devoting the budget associated with the upscale hotels for which the area is generally associated. Rooms vary in size from modest to moderate. See Hôtel Washington Opéra above for nearby eating and drinking establishments.

Left Bank Hotels

⓬Hôtel D'Aubusson ★★★★

Address *33 rue Dauphine, 75006.*
Tel*. 01 43 29 43 43* • ***Fax*** *01 43 29 12 62*
Site *www.hoteldaubusson.com.* ***Metro*** *Odéon.* ***Features*** *50 rooms. AC.* ***Price*** *Standard single or double 260€, "Superior" twin or double 340€, "Grand Luxe" and "Loft" 410€.* ***Buffet breakfast*** *20€. See website for promotions.*

High romance for honeymooners and other lovers

The Aubusson offers fine style, spacious luxury, and gracious service in a great Left Bank location, making it one very wise choice of a hotel. For those who would otherwise spend less, this is a great place for a splurge. For those who would otherwise spend more, take note. The top-tier rooms are ideal for a first or third or upteenth honeymoon setting – and they're spacious enough to hold a small wedding. The superior rooms are themselves large enough to hold an intimate cocktail party, while all of the rooms are elegantly styled with a handsome palette of fine, striped fabrics. The bathrooms, too, are worth an extra linger. The body of the Aubusson occupies a 17th century mansion set back from the street between the two other portions of the hotel, so the view may be limited, but calm is assured.

All the glowing terms for the location of the Relais Christine (see below) can also be credited to the Aubusson, which is just around the corner. I simply wonder why the hotel's coat of arms bears the motto Inter Spinas Floret ("they flourish among the thorns") for there aren't many thorns in the area. One wonderful aspect of its location, two blocks from the Seine, is that it's easy enough to return to the hotel in the middle of a day of touring. It isn't just your room that you'd happy to return to, though. The hotel's common areas are sweet settings to soothe travelers' soles.

The centerpiece of the hotel is the Louis XV-style living room where you can lounge by the fireplace beneath the enormous beams of the high ceiling. The mansion's other major room serves as the breakfast room, where an Aubusson tapestry has been hung to justify the hotel's name. The patio is another inviting and airy space to wile away an hour on a warm afternoon or early evening. Finally, there's the bar, Café Laurent. Nothing about the bar actually recalls the literary origins boasted in the hotel literature, nevertheless it remains a classy place to sit with a drink or a spot of tea and discuss the pleasures of international travel.

⑬Relais Christine ★★★★

Address *3 rue Christine, 75006.*
Tel. *01 40 51 60 80 •* ***Fax*** *01 40 51 60 81*
Site *www.relais-christine.com* ***Member*** *Small Luxury Hotels of the World, US/Canada reservations 800-525-4800.* ***Metro*** *Odéon.* ***Features*** *51 rooms and suites. AC. Honesty bar in the lounge.* ***Price*** *Single 325€, Double 375€, 425€, Junior suite or duplex 460-550€, 2-bedroom duplex 700€, Suite with terrace 715€.* ***Breakfast*** *20€ (cont.), 25€ (buffet).*

Warmth and character by the Seine

I highly recommend the Relais Christine for many of the same reasons that I recommend the Aubusson. There are more luxurious, obsequious, cater-to-every-whim hotels in the city, but these both hit high notes in the five criteria that matter in this selection: character, quality, service, charm, location. The Aubusson may have a bit more romantic charm, the Relais Christine a tad more heartwarming character, both are worthy of attention in their price range. But the two hotels have nothing in common as far as decoration; the Relais Christine is more traditionally laid out, with decorative printed fabrics or Empire stripes, quiet tones, solid wood antiques, and other hints of centuries past, yet put together in contemporary combinations.

> **Both the Aubusson and Relais Christine hit high notes in the five criteria that matter in this selection: character, quality, service, charm, location.**

Many of the 51 rooms (including 15 suites and duplexes) overlook the courtyard or a small garden out back. Ground floor rooms stepping out onto the garden are a wonderful place to relax after a hard day's touring or business… and to enjoy a romantic breakfast the following morning. Some wood-edge bathrooms give added warmth to otherwise irreproachable marble.

Entering from the narrow side street into the courtyard and into the vast former private residence dating to the 16th-century is as sweet as coming home to your dog. The original residence was built on the ruins of a portion of the Abbey of the Grands Augustins, and the high medieval vaulted basement, which may have originally been a kitchen, now serves as the breakfast room, watched over by a suit of armor.

The Seine and the Pont Neuf are two blocks away, and from there you're but minutes away on foot from Notre-Dame, the Louvre and the Orsay Museum. Stay here and you can't help but get intimate with the river, as you stroll the bridges and the riverbank or join the array of young lovers, friends, and solitary readers who gather at the western tip of the City Island.

Two great homes to fine dining are just around the block: Lapérouse and Relais Louis XIII (the latter is described in *Restaurants*).

⓮Hôtel Pont Royal ★★★★

Address *7 rue de Montalembert, 75007.*
Tel*. 01 42 84 70 00 •* ***Fax*** *01 42 84 71 00*
Site *www.hotel-pont-royal.com. Metro Rue du Bac.* ***Features*** *65 rooms, 10 suites. AC. Restaurant. Cute little bar. Small fitness room.* ***Price*** *"Classic" 370€, "Deluxe" 420€, Suite 570€, Suite with terrace and grand view 1000€.* ***Buffet breakfas****t 19€(continental), 26€ (buffet).*

Handsome and polished Saint-Germain style.

The Pont Royal plays it classic, cool and polished next door to the voguish Montalembert. Fully renovated in 1999, this hotel sports handsome rooms whose décor can make one forget that they aren't large. Silk and other soft fabrics in contemporary color schemes (a predominance of coral, plum and tobacco earth tones) are outlined in mahogany with occasional touches of wrought iron and a variety of discreetly hidden electronic accessories for the modern man and woman.

While the '90s saw the feminization of hotel decors, the turn of the century has brought about a mixed atmosphere more concerned with style than with the sex of the traveler. The new era of the Pont Royal has also coincided with an attempt in the Paris hotel industry to enliven what had become the traditional, monotonous marble-means-class bathroom. Hence the bathrooms have touches of dark wood and flashes of sparkling tile inlaid in the marble. I like it here.

It's nevertheless important to address the question of size. Despite their excellent use of available space, many of the classic rooms are best used as a single. The larger doubles are on the upper floors (5th to 8th), where they're scarcely affected by street noise and benefit from a view of the city extending to Sacré Coeur, with a glimpse of the Eiffel Tower from certain rooms – and a room with a view always appears more spacious. The one large suite with a terrace seems to embrace much of the city. On the lower floors, the occasional hum along the rue de Bac is muffled enough to be forgotten. However, if concerned with morning traffic, request one of the deluxe rooms on the upper floors facing the back.

The cozy wood-and-fabric bar/library/reading room is an invitation in its own right. In the bar and in the entrance hall photographs honor the memory of the 1950-1970 heydays of the Parisian intelligentsia, when this was a notable meeting place for the greats of French and Western literati who gathered in the St. Germain quarter. Calling itself a "literary hotel" on that basis may be a bit of a stretch, but the effort is appreciated.

This book goes to press just before the opening of the hotel's new restaurant under the supervision of Joël Robuchon, one of France's most famous chefs, who retired from his own top-rated restaurant in 1996. **L'Atelier de Joël Robuchon**, the new 40-seat restaurant, is being designed around a central kitchen, encouraging contact between diners and the restaurant's five chefs. It sets out to be chic and contemporary without aiming for the offerings or atmosphere of haute cuisine; average price is expected to be about 50€/person. With such an illustrious name attached to its restaurant, this worthy hotel is sure to garner added attention.

⑮Relais Saint-Germain ★★★★

Address *9 carrefour de l'Odéon, 75006.*
Tel. *01 43 29 12 05* • ***Fax*** *01 46 33 45 30*
Metro *Odéon.* ***Features*** *20 rooms, 2 suites. AC.* ***Price*** *Single 210€, Double (with or without kitchen corner) 280€, "Deluxe" 370€, "Deluxe" terrace 400€.* ***Breakfast*** *Included.*

Among Saint-Germain's top charmers

High charm awards for this most cozy and well-situated little hotel, which rivals with the Aubusson among the quarter's most romantic. With only 22 rooms and suites in this 17th-century townhouse, there is a warm sense of intimacy throughout – which is not in this case a euphemism for small rooms. Au contraire, the double rooms are comfortably sized. Each has its own alluring, classically winning style, with fabrics you want to touch and the original beams showing. The junior suite and the suite with a terrace have happy honeymoon memories written all over them. The marble bathrooms can be smallish but are attractive nonetheless. Carrefour de l'Odéon, a step off Boulevard St-Germain, is itself an appealing and central place to come home to. Double-glazed windows keep traffic at bay.

Add to the hotel's general sense of charming well-being its wine bar/café, Le Comptoir du Relais, which also serves as its breakfast room, and you may well find yourself tempted to be a hotel homebody. One of the sweetest little hotels around.

⑯Relais Saint-Jacques ★★★★

Address *3 rue de l'Abbé de l'Epeé, 75005 Paris.*
Tel. *01 53 73 26 00* • ***Fax*** *01 43 26 17 81*
Site *www.relais-saint-jacques.com.* ***RER*** *Luxembourg (direct train from Roissy Airport).* ***Features*** *23 rooms. AC.* ***Price*** *"Privilege" 195€, "Prestige" 230€.* ***Breakfast*** *13€. See site for off-season rates.*

Left Bank confidential.

The Relais Saint-Jacques is a Left Bank hideout for travelers looking for some umph to their 3★ considerations without digging too deep into 4★ pockets. Though a bit removed from the café-and-boutique charms of Saint-Germain, the hotel is within a few steps of such soothing Left Bank offerings such as the 17th-century Val de Grâce, rue Saint Jacques, the Luxembourg Garden, the Pantheon and a sprinkling of pleasing cafés and restaurants. Rooms on the upper floor offer an eyeful of the Pantheon. "Prestige" rooms have more light.

With only 23 rooms, the Relais Saint-Jacques exudes a sense of confidentiality. All are quite cozy. Of course, cozy is clearly a euphemism for small in the world of Left Bank hotels, but here it also well describes the 18th- and 19th-century curves and legs and prints of Louis XV, Louis XVI, Empire and Manuelian (Portuguese)-style furniture. The Louis XV lounge/library and the bar/breakfast area with handsome 1925 bar counter give the impression that you're staying in a private home. A quiet home, on a quiet street at night.

⑰Hôtel Buci Latin ★★★

Address *34 rue de Buci, 75006.*
Tel. *01 43 29 07 20* • ***Fax*** *01 43 29 67 44*
Site *www.bucilatin.com* ***Metro*** *Mabillon.* ***Features*** *27 rooms. AC. Honesty bar in lobby.* ***Price*** *Room with shower 190€, with bath 220€,*

"Superior" room with bath 235€, Duplex 300€, Junior suite 320€. ***Breakfast*** *Included.*

Spice of design, hint of hip, bouquet of character

When you've had your fill of Left Bank charm and want a whiff of something more original – the spice of design, a hint of hip, a bouquet of character – then this is the place to stay. The post-colonial, quasi-Africana design begins in the lobby with zebra printed armchairs and a wood-laid path leading to a friendly, laidback welcome at the reception desk. Here you won't find baroque and florid trinkets that otherwise signal "cozy décor" in this quarter. Oh, the hotel is cozy to be sure, even cute from certain angles, but on its own terms. A graffiti-decorated stairwell may lead to your artist-painted door; no need to know your room number, just remember your unique door. The rooms display a winning combination of off-white and woody-colored fabrics with the curves, posts and panels of light wood furnishings. The bathrooms are equally appealing.

The smaller rooms are best considered as singles. For more elbowroom choose "superior" or higher. Prices ever so slightly push the envelope, particularly off season, but distinctiveness does have its price.

The Buci Latin may pay homage to the African plains, but one doesn't step into the bush from here, rather out to the great communal watering hole of Saint-Germain café society. The hotel occupies a prime location from which to savor the quarter, with the added pleasure of having rue de Buci's picturesque food shops and the Saint-Germain Market close by.

There's a nice sense of intimacy at the Buci Latin along with enough nooks and crannies that you can get lost despite this being such a small hotel. One soon feels like an initiate here, for this isn't only a place to stay... but to return to.

⑱Hôtel de l'Abbaye ★★★

Address *10 rue Cassette, 75006 Paris.*
Tel. *01 45 44 38 11 •* ***Fax*** *01 45 48 07 86*
Site *www.hotel-abbaye.com.* ***Metro*** *Saint Sulpice.* ***Features*** *42 rooms, 4 duplex suites. AC.* ***Price*** *Standard rooms 185€, Larger rooms 260-276€, Slightly large still 345€, Duplex Suites 380-395€.* ***Breakfast*** *Included.*

The classic Parisian charmer

Withdrawn from the street and seemingly withdrawn from the city itself, L'Abbaye is a most friendly urban oasis. Not that there's any need for an oasis in this quarter, where the

Luxembourg Garden serves as an exquisite backyard and every café promises to be your livingroom. Friendly, of course, is always appreciated. Indeed, L'Abbaye wants nothing more than to soothe and reassure its guests. One reason why it attracts many Americans (the other reason being promotion).

Indeed, the sheer number of Americans in the hotel may make you feel at home – as will the chimney fire hissing away in the lobby-lounge in autumn/winter or the simple fountain murmuring beyond the veranda in spring/summer. The rooms display a downtone mix of colors and styles that might be called eclectic were it not for the fact that they remain squarely within the range of hushed charm. A fine, warm attention to detail is visible in both the standard and larger rooms. If size doesn't matter, then consider the standard rooms. However, the true pleasantness of this oasis hotel is found in the larger rooms, where the attention to detail is clearly reflected in the price. Several of those larger rooms and the duplex suites give out to a private terrace.

The breakfast room-veranda otherwise serves as a bar. It can't replace local café culture, which reaches its literary and bourgeois heights in these parts, but it's a fine place for not-yet-bedtime planning and conversation, amongst yourselves or with other guests. Single travelers take note.

⑲ Le Clos Médicis ★★★

Address *56 rue Monsieur-le-Prince, 75006 Paris.*
Tel. *01 43 29 10 80* • ***Fax*** *01 43 54 26 90*
Site *www.closmedicis.com.* ***Metro*** *Odéon –* ***RER*** *Luxembourg (direct train from Roissy Airport).* ***Features*** *38 rooms. AC.* ***Price*** *"Classic" (shower only) 135€ as single/165€ as double, "Superior" 180€, "Deluxe" 195€, Suite 400€.* ***Breakfast****: 11€.*

Pleasing situation, gentle welcome, refreshing style

The Clos Medicis is the kind of small hotel that you can easily get attached to. Like the nearby Luxembourg Garden, it is a setting for both seasons (Paris only has two). The spirit is there both in autumn/winter when a chimney fire is burning in the lobby-lounge, which also services as its bar, and in spring/summer when breakfast is served in the courtyard.

A block away, Boulevard Saint-Michel separates the Latin Quarter from the Saint-Germain Quarter, so this is an ideal location for exploring both. In style and warmth, though, it clearly leans toward Saint-Germain. The Luxembourg Garden and Palace (home of Marie de Médicis in the 17th century, hence the hotel's name) are around the corner, while rue Monsieur-le-Prince leads directly into the heart of Saint-Germain.

Like the nearby Luxembourg Garden, it is a setting for both seasons (Paris only has two).

The "classic" rooms are preferably reserved as singles, the "superior" average-sized for the quarter, while the "deluxe" buys more elbowroom and a queen-size bed or two singles. In all cases, the well-studied décor passes my test for what I want in this price range in a home away from home: a touch of class without false charm. The beige, olive, burgundy and mahogany tones, the duvet-covered beds, wood-framed mirrors and handsome furnishings provide solid comfort. The upbeat tile bathrooms are a pleasant change from the dull marble that defined hotel bathrooms for several decades in an attempt to signal class.

Overall, Le Clos Médicis displays attention to detail that's echoed in the helpful staff.

⑳ Hôtel Verneuil ★★★

Address *8 rue de Verneuil, 75007 Paris.*
Tel*. 01 42 60 82 14 •* ***Fax*** *01 42 61 40 38*
Site *www.hotelverneuil.com.* ***Metro*** *Rue du Bac, St-Germain-des-Prés.* ***Features*** *26 rooms. AC in some rooms (specify if desired).* ***Price*** *Single 120€, Double 140€, "Deluxe" double 185€.* ***Breakfast*** *12€ (quaint basement breakfast room).*

Sweet Left Bank tradition on a quiet street

From it's best angle, the Verneuil is exactly what we're looking for in a traditional little Left Bank 3★ retreat. That angle is its library-salon-bar, nestled between stone wall and wood beams, between the Seine and Saint-Germain, between the Louvre and the Orsay. Sitting there – studying the map and discussing plans in the morning, reading magazines and discussing travel in late afternoon, sniffing Cognac and discussing life in the evening – you might almost forget that this is a hotel and imagine that you're is visiting some cultured, heartwarming friend (not unlike the director Sylvie de Lattre herself) whose sense of elegance and tradition is now beginning to rub off. True, it's a simple little sink-down parlor, but you can feel so wonderfully relaxed and comfortable there that you may not want to go up to bed.

Admittedly, another reason you may be hesitant to go up

is that your room could be a bit cramped despite its traditional quaintness. Most hotels in 17th-century side-street buildings in Paris share the same limited room space, so I don't mean to single out the Verneuil. Indeed, all is pleasant enough and the price of the standard singles and doubles isn't excessive, but don't expect much square footage either in the standard rooms or in the beige marble bathrooms. If you require push-up and make-up space opt for the "deluxe" rooms. Or just linger longer in the parlor. Parlor, from the French *parler*, to talk.

Benjamin Franklin in Paris

On September 3, 1783, at the former Hôtel York (56 rue Jacob), next to the Hôtel du Danube, David Hartley, in the name of the King George III of England, and Benjamin Franklin, John Jay and John Adams, in the name of the United States of America, signed the definitive peace treaty recognizing the independence of the United States.

Benjamin Franklin (1706-1790) was one of America's first international stars, after the native Americans who had been brought over as curiosities to the Courts of Saint James and Versailles. His colonial bestseller Poor Richard's Almanac *was also a hit in Europe, and his discoveries of electricity with lightning, of the lightning rod and of the slow-convection Franklin stove, gained him fame in the Old World. Preceded by his reputation as a country philosopher, an inventor and a man who stood up to the British, he arrived in Paris in 1776 to a hero's welcome. Following the signing of the* Declaration of Independence, *he came as the head of a commission seeking help from France in the American Revolutionary War. He appealed to and was at ease with both the common people and the Court of Louis XVI, and the French adored him. An alliance with France was signed Feb. 6, 1777, and Franklin then obtained financing. With help from the Marquis de Lafayette he obtained the services of the French army (1780), then a battle fleet (1781). He lived in Passy, now in the 17th arrondissement, until 1783. After Franklin's departure, Thomas Jefferson served as ambassador to France, a position from which he witnessed America's friend stumble towards its own, very different revolution.*

㉑Hôtel du Danube ★★★

Address *58 rue Jacob, 75006 Paris.*
Tel. *01 42 60 34 70 •* ***Fax*** *01 42 60 81 18*
Site *www.hoteldanube.fr.* ***Metro*** *St-Germain-des-Prés.* ***Features*** *40 rooms. Internet access from lobby computer.* ***Price*** *"Standard" single/double 105€, "Superior" on street 140€, on courtyard 155€.* ***Breakfast*** *9€.*

Price-wise with character and location

There are a few things you should know about French bathrooms before being an overnight guest in a French home:

1. One does not ask for the bathroom when what one wants is the toilet, for the *toilettes* are not necessarily in the same room as the bath, rather they are likely to have their very own closet.

2. Men should learn to recognize the difference between the bidet and the toilet; the easiest way to tell the difference is to remember that French toilet seats look strikingly similar to our own, whereas the bidet is the low rectangular sink.

3. The showerhead in a typical French home is not fixed to the wall, rather it is at the end of a flexible hose that may or may not be hooked onto the wall, the idea being that a hand-held showerhead that can reach everywhere is preferable to washing only by stream from the top down.

A stay at the Danube is your chance to practice bathroom rule #3. You see, in certain rooms the owners are averse to piercing the marble bathroom walls to provide a hook for the showerhead. Hence the occasion to learn how to soap and lather while holding the showerhead. Using a third hand is cheating, but you're on vacation, so what the hell!

There is more reason than a brief lesson in cross-cultural differences to stay at the Hôtel du Danube:

1. Location: The Danube is ideally situated for Left Bank promenades and is only several blocks from the Orsay Museum and the Seine.

2. Room size: Relative to other hotels in its price range in central Paris, the rooms here are rather roomy, especially the "superior" rooms (the standard rooms are small but so is the price). Many of the larger rooms have two single beds rather than one queen, so be sure to specify your preference. Most of those larger rooms are on the street side where one can hear some street traffic, however they are in fact the nicer rooms, and quite acceptable, though perhaps less so in summer when one might want to sleep with the window open (no AC). Rooms

on the courtyard are quiet, except for the occasional creak of parquet beneath the carpet.

3. Character: The décor is a bit odd and worn at times, nevertheless suitably tradition-minded in a late-19th-century fashion to give the place character. The rooms display a potpourri of chintz, colonial, Chinese and Victorian styles, so stay elsewhere if you have an aversion to profuse fabric motifs since chances are your room will have one, most likely in red. There's a pretty little inner courtyard for a spring/summer pause.

Altogether a good and quirky choice for the price.

㉒ Hôtel de l'Odéon ★ ★ ★

Address *13 rue Saint-Sulpice, 75006 Paris.*
Tel. *01 43 25 70 11* • ***Fax*** *01 43 29 97 34*
Site *www.hoteldelodeon.com.* ***Metro*** *Odéon.* ***Features*** *29 rooms. AC.*
Price *Single 142€. Most doubles 209-232€.* ***Breakfast*** *11€.*

Old World comforts and character

I've long enjoyed the antiquated airs of this hotel, its style lolling between late Middle Age gloom and upright Regency, its wooden beams, its collection of bed frames – tester beds, brass beds, beds 3 feet off the ground, beds with ornate woodwork – its granny lace bedcovers, the woodsy little lobby and sitting room, the receptionist standing behind a counter beneath the stairwell looking up from the reservation sheet with that wary-friendly half-smile with which the French greet unknown visitors. Those antiquated airs appeared more worn on my last tour, giving the hotel a bit more homespun character. But while Left Bank hotels shun old-world character in favor of Eurocharm, the Hôtel de l'Odéon deserves consideration as one that has managed to stick to its point of view. The old-fashioned slumber inside still allows visitors to waken to all the Saint-Germain quarter has to offer, as an astounding array of cafés and boutiques are close by and the Luxembourg Garden is just two blocks away. Rooms in the front of the building, on the street, are larger than those on the tiny courtyard. The street is fairly calm, while quiet is absolute on the courtyard.

㉓Select Hôtel ★★★

Address *1 place de la Sorbonne, 75005 Paris.*
Tel*. 01 46 34 14 80 •* ***Fax*** *01 46 34 51 79*
Site *www.selecthotel.fr.* ***Metro*** *Cluny-La Sorbonne.* ***RER*** *Luxembourg (direct train from Roissy Airport).* ***Features*** *68 rooms. AC.* ***Price*** *Smaller rooms 132€, otherwise 149-163€.* ***Breakfast*** *Included.*

Good location, comfort and price by the Sorbonne

Call me a snob, but I've no affection for standardized chains when traveling in Europe. If a hotel (or restaurant) can't provide character or charm or luxury, it should at least offer a little atmosphere. Snob that I am I nearly didn't visit the Select because I suspected the worst: something about the forced smile of the lovely receptionist in the pink-edged brochure, not to mention the name of the hotel itself. But I was attracted by the budget-wise price at a wonderful location overlooking Place de la Sorbonne in the Latin Quarter. And so I came… and I liked what I saw: a recommendable combination of location, amenities and price.

The Select manages to avoid the been-there-done-that nature of contemporary standardization. In its own modest way it actually offers a bit of character, charm and atmosphere. There's something quirky about the place. The contemporary design makes good use of the space in the rooms, and each has a real exposed beam and/or old stone walls as a reminder that the Latin Quarter is steeped in history. The common areas have

The Sorbonne

In 1257 Robert de Sorbon, chaplain to Louis IX, founded a college in this area both to teach theology students and to house poor students and teachers. Its significance as one of Europe's first universities and its involvement ever since its inception in the currents and countercurrents of history have made it, for centuries now, France's most well known though not its most elite university. The Sorbonne's chapel was rebuilt at the impetus of Cardinal Richelieu (1585-1642), who had studied at the Sorbonne and became its headmaster – as well as principle advisor to Louis XIII. The view of the façade from the square outside the school is monumental, but the grander view is inside the college's main quadrangle, which can be entered at 17 rue de la Sorbonne. The chapel itself, with Richelieu's tomb inside, is rarely open for visits.

enough nooks and ambiance that you may actually wish to sit downstairs on a rainy afternoon or evening and read this entire book. If you sometimes long for your youth-hosteling days yet can now afford midscale pleasures, the Select is right up your alley. It has a great location from which to explore both the youthful Latin Quarter and the middle-aged St-Germain Quarter.

Some of the rooms give out to a small courtyard/winter garden, but it's far more interesting to have the view overlooking Place de la Sorbonne and facing the chapel of the university of the Sorbonne. Request an upper floor. Place de la Sorbonne is an animated but not noisy pedestrian square during the day when students and employees of local businesses take to the brasserie-cafés or sit along the fountains.

㉔ Hôtel Saint-Paul ★ ★ ★

Address *43 rue Monsieur le Prince, 75006 Paris.*
Tel*. 01 43 26 98 64 •* ***Fax*** *01 46 34 58 60*
Site *www.hotelsaintpaulparis.com.* ***Metro*** *Odéon.* ***RER*** *Luxembourg (direct train from Roissy Airport).* ***Features*** *31 rooms. AC on 4th and 5th floors.* ***Price*** *Single 112-128€, Double 128-158€.* ***Breakfast*** *10€ (Continental), 13€ (American).*

A modest manor in a noteworthy location

Enter the Saint-Paul and you find yourself in the sitting room of an English manor with wooden beams, stone walls, plaid-covered armchairs, dusky rugs, dark heavy curtains, touches of kitsch (e.g. the upright piano). The style carries over partially into the 31 rooms, helped along by the exposed ceiling beams of this 17th-century building. The rooms are of modest size, some quite small, though those on floors 1 to 3 have high ceilings to offset the somber wall fabrics and carpets. In exchange for lower ceilings, floors 4 and 5 are brighter and fresher and air-conditioned. All have basic marble bathrooms, most with bath. A vaulted basement with remnants of an old well serves as the breakfast room, which is the practical fashion in many Left Bank hotels whose foundations are centuries old. Despite a promising entrance and certain similarities, the Saint-Paul has less character than the Hôtel de l'Odéon, albeit at a lesser price. The hotel is well-situated, on a street that straddles the Latin Quarter and the Saint-Germain Quarter.

THE APERITIF

Sometime between 5:30 and 8:30pm, l'heure de l'apéritif, aperitif time, arrives. This is a nearly sacred time of day in France, when lovers, friends, colleagues and individuals mark the end of the afternoon and/or the start of the evening. As travelers, we then rest our weary feet, reflect on the discoveries of the day and the promise of the evening, and luxuriate in the pleasures of foreign travel as the aperitif begins to stir our appetite.

We call this cocktail hour, of course, or happy hour. Increasingly, happy hour is also used in Franglais-speaking Paris, though it has yet to be employed by the more discerning bars. But think of it as aperitif time to better set the mood for that special moment of romance, companionship or solitary ease.

While any café on your path may do for a late afternoon-early evening pause, this chapter explores drinking establishments more specifically catering to this time of day. Wine bars, also appropriate for aperitif time, are covered in the Wine chapter.

France, as café territory, has far less of a saloon/bar/pub tradition than the U.S., Canada, U.K. or Ireland – though many Irish pubs can now be found in Paris. Joints calling themselves "American bars"may also have a good selection of whiskey, but there you are often expected to choose for two, yourself and one of the very friendly women sitting on the velvet stool next to you.

Aperitif time can further be divided into two periods, 5:30-7:00pm and 7:00-8:30pm:

5:30-7:00pm It's late afternoon and your touring legs are beginning to drag. This is especially true Oct.-March, when there's no late-setting sun to keep you touring into the evening. But you're not ready to return to your room where you'll only turn on CNN and wind up wasting the evening watching the world spin. No, you want to be someplace where you can just sit and relax and be in Paris, and so your day drifts smoothly into *l'heure de l'apéritif*. The hotel bars noted here favor varying degrees of formality, so if your touring clothes are too casual you will be considered underdressed.

7:00-8:30pm: Eventually you've returned to your room, had a brief rest and washed up or changed for dinner. Evening has begun. What kind of evening will it be: a short evening to further rest up for tomorrow's tour or a long evening of encountering the pleasures of Paris by night? If the latter, then your evening may well begin with one of these drinking establishments or in a wine bar, your exact choice often depending on where you'll be dining afterwards.

If you plan to drink and walk, look both ways before crossing the street.

Santé

Glasses are most commonly clinked to a toast of *santé*, meaning health, or *à la tienne* (singular, informal) or *à la vôtre* (plural or formal), indicating "to your health." In bars, as in restaurants, the first toast is typically left to the person paying the bill.

Luxury Hotel Bars

There's something deeply satisfying about reclining in a hotel bar in a foreign country. Dressed up or handsomely casual, one steps into the bar with a possessive air and orders, not some local drink but a hometown favorite. The French and the English have taught us much about colonialism and imperialism, but as Americans we know how to strut, swag, swank, stroll or stride in with the best of them.

In Paris the café is king, but that doesn't mean you can't step out of café culture for the evening and into a hotel bar before heading off to a good meal. You needn't be staying at these hotels. In my opinion being a bar patron at any of the hotels mentioned here also gives you permission to take advantage of the hotel's concierge service, though the hotel may not fully agree. No need to apologize for not spending the night before requesting that they suggest a restaurant or call to push back your reservation. Furthermore, while Paris isn't known as a place where you go to a have a drink in a hotel bar, doing so is just shy of fashionable these days.

Hôtel Meurice

Address *228 rue de Rivoli, 1st arr.* ***Metro*** *Tuileries.*

The bar at the Meurice is a damn nice place to end an afternoon or start an evening. Its natural grace and charm and openness make it the most even-keeled of the major hotel bars, in touch with both its masculine and feminine sides. A facelift several years ago restored all of the Meurice's trappings of exclusiveness, yet the bar remains approachable, even if you aren't quite dressed for success. The clientele is no less affluent than at the city's other palatial hotels and the price of a drink no less stiff, yet the lobby/winter garden/bar area appears to wear its elegance with more ease. Get lost on the way to the rest rooms for a peek at other portions of the ground floor. The staff appears more naturally inclined to excellence than at some the Meurice's top-tier competitors.

Hôtel du Louvre

Address*1 place André Malraux, 1st arr.* ***Metro*** *Palais Royal.*

A cozy mix of contemporary vogue and mid-19th century schmaltz, The Defender, as the hotel's bar is known, calls for a long luxuriant sit, followed by a world-is-my-oyster view of the avenue de l'Opéra on the way out. Napoleon III ordered the construction of the hotel to receive well-heeled travelers for the occasion of the World Fair of 1855, making it one of Paris's earliest lavish hotels. It now stands on the second tier of grand hotels, yet the décor of black and gold trompe l'oeil marble columns and a contemporary version of imperial red and green holds its own with the best of the lot. The Hôtel du Louvre is part of the Concorde Hotel Group, which is within the Taittinger Group, which explains the promotion of Taittinger champagne and Baccarat crystal in the bar, its one lack of discretion.

Hôtel de Vendôme

Address *1 place Vendôme, 1st arr.* ***Metro*** *Tuileries.*

Take the rickety old elevator from just beyond the lobby of this quirky little luxury hotel one flight up and you'll find yourself in a British-inspired bar with Chesterfield armchairs, mahogany paneling and a piano being jazzed in the early evening. Suitable for a refined yet relaxed moment before or after dinner. The fact that it's upstairs shouldn't dissuade you from entering, though it does help keep out the, how do you say, riffraff.

The Four Seasons George-V

Address *31 av. George V, 8th arr.* ***Metro*** *George V.*

The bar and lounge at the FSG-V have modern/classy/international hotel-bar written all over them. The living-room of a bar and the gallery lounge near the piano are rather subdued, edging on dull despite a dozen shades of marble, with only kitsch chandeliers to remind you that this palace from the 1930s has recently come out from extensive renovation. It's a backdrop against which everything else seems to sparkle: teeth, shoes, earrings, ice – everything. Even the conversation, in a hundred shades of English, seems to sparkle as men raise their voice when talking of boats and golf. And women's eyes sparkle, too, as they do their best to show that they have both inner peace and outer breasts.

You've got to love the high professionalism of the service staff here, the way they slip around you like pickpockets, stealing away dirty ashtrays and empty canapé dishes with one hand as they light cigarettes with the other. You'll feel so well-heeled, whatever the size of your heel, boat or breasts, that you'll barely notice of the prices at the gastronomic restaurant you'll be going to next.

Martini or martini

Getting your martini fix in France is simple enough at international and fashionable upscale bars, but elsewhere the term Martini more immediately calls to French minds the famous 19th-century trademark for vermouth made by Martini & Rossi. Understood as a trademark, a Martini is a dry, white, rose or caramel-color herbed vermouth that is served alone as an aperitif or used in a variety of cocktails, including the classic dry Martini cocktail, a.k.a. the gin martini. Better to entrust your martini to a bartender who understands your accent well enough to know that your drink of choice has a small m.

Hôtel Ritz

Address *15 place Vendôme, 1st arr.* ***Metro*** *Opéra.*

Bar Vendôme. Entering the Ritz when you aren't staying there can be intimidating if you approach it wrong. It isn't the opulence of the lobby that intimidates, for that's too subdued and unexpressive to truly impress. Rather the intimidation comes from the staff, for they, too, are subdued and unexpressive. They are the perfect mirror for your view of yourself. The moment you let on that you are unduly impressed by the hotel's reputation and may not belong, they'll sense it and let you know that you don't. But arrive sufficiently well dressed and lift your sense of self-worth a notch or two and they'll be offering you some of the purist French service around. And that's just getting to the table.

From there, the Bar Vendôme serves up a classically soothing setting that is one part cocktail, one part martini, one part single malt, and where every detail aims to create a sense of heightened and cordial well-being: gracious service, spacious seating, subtle lighting, the sweet sound of the grand piano, the view out to the patio, the gentle buzz of conversation, the glass of water dotted with a raspberry and a blueberry, the crab canapés. What's not to belong to?!

Bar Hemingway. Open Tues.-Sat. 6:30pm-2am. A second bar is named for the Ritz's favorite son, Ernest Hemingway, who was introduced to it by F. Scott Fitzgerald. Harry's Bar, around the corner (see below), has its own Hemingway nostalgia, but suffice it to say there are enough Hemingway drinking stories to go around. He did indeed have a special affection for this bar and enthusiastically followed the advancing Allies into the city on August 25, 1944, in order to take part in the liberation of ... the Ritz. The Hemingway is at the opposite end of the hotel from the Bar Vendôme, reached at the end of a long corridor of boutique displays where you risk sinking into the carpet if you don't keep walking. The small bar is now a hushed, confidential place for a man and his journal (*Wall Street*), a woman and her bartender, or vice versa – or for a couple in placid harmony.

Hôtel Lutetia

Address *45 bd. Raspail, 6th arr.* ***Metro*** *Sèvres-Babylone.*

Many of the other hotels in the nearby Saint-Germain quarter have their own cozy bars that are easy to get attached to when you're staying there, e.g. the little bar at the Pont-Royal (see *Hotels*), but when you want to bathe in the abundance of an expansive grand hotel, the Lutetia is your place for an aperitif. This is the Left Bank's most palatial hotel, with a plush red lobby bar whose couches and armchairs are such comfortable seats for a drink that you may have to push your dinner reservations back an hour.

Plaza-Athénée

Address *25 av. Montaigne, 8th arr.* ***Metro*** *Alma-Marceau or Franklin D. Roosevelt.*

I'm beginning to understand why the Plaza-Athénée declined my request to visit their rooms: they must have thought my readers weren't mod or celeb enough to appreciate the place. But I came to the bar anyway. And they were right, because I didn't get it. I mean, I got the fact that since avenue Montaigne is Paris's high fashion avenue, the bar of this top-flight hotel would naturally lean in that direction. What I didn't get is why it would lean so far over as to fall flat. But I accept that that's my problem; I just didn't fit in. Or I wasn't wearing the right clothes to go with the black lights, or I didn't come with the right woman in black (sorry, dear), or with the right couple of guys with cell phones on their hips.

This bar is a cool, mod, high-concept place, a large joint that does indeed have style, panache, cigar smoke. It's got stools around high tables with little chandeliers suspended just above head level. It's got highly comfortable leather armchairs. It's got ceaseless rhythms. It's got waiters in skin-fitting collarless suits and comfortable shoes; they may not have the same kind of polish as the other hotel bars on this list, but they grow on you with their sophomore smiles, and always a *Thank you, sir, madam.* It's got very nice glassware. This is indeed a place to unwind, though perhaps not truly to relax, where a tie is not only optional but too old-fashioned to get you any added respect. Which might also have been my problem. I am ashamed to admit it but I was wearing a tie; I'd just come from the Ritz. Had I stopped in the classically luxurious gallery (hallway) lounge that leads to the bar, out of woofer distance of the bar, I might have written a glowing report.

I nevertheless suspect very good things about the rooms upstairs, for nothing tells more about a hotel's luxury than the lobby restrooms, and here in the gallery at the Plaza-Athénée they've got ultra-soothing urinals. The water starts running as you enter and then keeps on dripping so that you stand there without even having to whistle. Now that's style as it should be, effortless; all you've got to do is act supremely contented and pose. So why does everyone in the bar seem to be trying so hard?

Other Bars of Character

Harry's Bar

Address *5 rue Daunou, 2nd arr.* ***Metro*** *Opéra.*

Harry's Bar went out of fashion with the zoot suit or with that day in July 1962 when Hemingway closed his own book forever. Which makes it great place to be a regular – or to be a visitor who wants a drink rather than an aperitif. Enough of this French frou-frou. Sometimes you just want a place where you can saddle up to the bar or lean against the wall and have a few belly laughs with friends. The smell of its 1923 origins, of Hemingway himself, of the original Bloody Mary, of international business circa 1950s, and of the defunct Anglo-American community still linger. Fashion may come and go but Harry's is still Harry's, a mix of hard edges and romanticism – in other words perfect for a drink with the guys or with a woman with an accent. Well-measured machismo goes well here as does toughened femininity, but ladies never come alone.

We – a toughened lady and I – mistakenly thought that we were being ignored at the bar. Then we realized that we had it all wrong. Harry's Bar has its own way of serving customers, of making cocktails. It's got its own kind of humor. Harry's is an institution – they can do whatever they want, and you can stay and enjoy it or leave and regret. To be served you've got to stand up to the bar and call out your poison. Of course, first you have to know what you want.

Traveler writers are known for taking the slow approach. We like to have a look around first, get a feel for the place, try to figure out what the bartender is making as he crushes mint and pours in a heavy dose of rum (a mojito), or casts sour mix into a shaker, or throws together spice and tomato juice and vodka (Bloody Mary, we're not stupid). None of that studious "I prefer single malt" crap – save it for Ritz. And don't bore them with your what-beer-you-got-on-tap? Harry's clients may like to wear pants when they go out, but this is still cocktail territory. Beyond the saloon doors here they fancy the Texan approach, but between you and me it's a tender little woodsy after-work, before-dinner bar at heart. The dames who come here know that. People come for a strong cocktail or two (three gets ugly, and expensive) before staggering off to eat – which may explain why the block is now crowded with eateries.

Like everyone else, Harry's Bar has an image to protect. In 1996 they got crabby when a comparatively wimpy '90s resto-bar opened bearing the name Barfly, a name that Harry's claimed ownership to in the form of a trademark, as in International Bar Flies, or "Home of IBF." A generational thing perhaps: Harry's had flapping saloon doors, Barfly had a velvet rope. Apparently there wasn't room in this town for both of them, so Harry's sued, and largely won (despite losing some rights to the trademark in the appeal). Barfly then changed its name to B*fly.

B*fly

Address *49/51 avenue George V, 8th arr.* ***Metro*** *George V.*

Been there, too. Ordered sushi, then they turned up the music (CD sold at the bar). Enough to make anyone over 40 want to protest, unless you're entertaining a date under 30, in which case you just light a cigar and pretend you belong. Whatever makes her happy.

Buddah Bar

***Address** 8/12 rue Boissy d'Anglas, 8th arr.* **Metro** *Concorde.*

Barrio Latino

Address** 46/48 rue du Faubourg St-Antoine, 12th arr.* ***Metro *Bastille.*

Next of kin to B*fly, each with its own music compilations. I nearly hesitate to call these bars as they are clearly intended to be scenes. These are bar-restaurants-nightclubs where, little by little after 8pm, the bouncers show their talent for distinguishing between gottabes and gonnabes and it becomes increasingly important to be accompanied by the right woman. Once inside, the upbeat atmosphere, the expansive décor, the youthfulness (whatever your age), and the music make one feel alternately grand and cheesy. Buddah Bar is across the street from the residence of the American ambassador and seems to be having no problem maintaining its own image. Barrio Latino, down the street from the Bastille, is a seductive Latino lover but could use a good dose of Viagra some evenings. In either case, if you aren't coming to party into the night, these are preferable as bars for an early evening drink, on weekdays.

Sir Winston

Address** 5 rue de Presbourg, 16th arr. Intersection with avenue d'Iéna, by the Arc de Triomphe.* ***Metro *Charles de Gaulle-Etoile. Serves a Sunday afternoon "Gospel brunch."*

With leather armchairs and padded leather bar stools, Sir Winston could well be a gentleman's bar, a British answer to Harry's. But it is too uptempo for that, too under-middle-aged and goldenboyish, above all too post-Hong Kong. By 6:30pm the ties are already off, jackets have been exchanged for sweaters, and the codes of flirtation, posturing and cell-phone use are far too obvious. Nevertheless, Sir Winston is well worth considering in the late afternoon when you've finally made it to the top of the Champs Elysées or down from the Arc de Triomphe or want to unwind after a day of business in the area.

While open most of the day and night, I recommend SW as a snappy after-work or after-tour bar. For business travelers, it lends itself to relaxed professional conversations or a solitary tour of the paper (the *Times of London* or the *Herald Tribune*) before they've turned the lights down and the music up and evening fully falls. For intimacy (or backgammon) head for a cozy booth in the back or to the bar downstairs. Otherwise just come around 5 and relax.

Sir Winston appropriately calls itself a café-salon/bar-club/restaurant because it manages to avoid being any one of them; for there is no greater sin in the contemporary bar scene than to be categorized as anything but *in*. It is therefore too vibrant for a café, too sophisticated for a pub, too conservative for a vogue bar, too accessible for a club, too animated for a restaurant; it's a mixed bag that's clearly reflected in the (less than pricey) drink list: white russians, black russians, orgasms, sex bombs, suitable whiskeys, sours, an unambitious if satisfying selection of beers. In other words, this is a nicely busy neutral place where you can't go wrong. Sir Winston would be rolling in his grave.

Beer, Kir and Pastis

In addition to the usual spirits, here are a few classic French selections for aperitif time:

Un demi(-pression), a draft beer (*pression* meaning draft, *demi* meaning half). A *demi* originally referred to a half-liter, but the beer glass actually holds a quarter-liter, which is a little more than half a pint. Bottled beer is *bière en bouteille.*

Une (bière) panache, the original light beer, a mix of beer and lemonade, a.k.a. a shandy.

Une coupe de Champagne, a glass of Champagne, often simply called *une coupe,* referring to the glass.

Un kir, a dry white wine with blackcurrant liqueur (*crème de cassis*).

Un kir royale, a kir in which the liqueur is mixed with Champagne. The house aperitif proposed in many restaurants is frequently a variation on the theme of the royal kir, e.g. peach liqueur with sparkling wine.

Un pastis, an aniseed-flavored liqueur served with ice and a pitcher of water, which you then dose in at about 4 or 5 to 1 as the mixture changes from liquid gold to murky white. As a Mediterranean drink, pastis has connotations of sunny café terraces and unhurried living. It is therefore largely considered a summertime drink in Paris. Pastis has a strong licorise after-taste, so it isn't recommended as an aperitif immediately prior to a gastronomic experience or a meal with fine wine.

Rue Oberkampf Hangouts

Address *Between avenue Parmentier (Metro Parmentier) and boulevard de Ménilmontant (Metro Ménilmontant), 11th arr. Continuing east, the Oberkampf quarter seques into the Ménilmontant quarter, 20th arr.*

The development of the Oberkampf quarter from a working class residential area to a string of eating and drinking establishments filled by 20 & 30 somethings reflects the gentrification of a wide swath of the eastern side of Paris over the past 10-15 years. There is still a large mix of populations in the neighborhoods between the high-rent Marais and the immigrant/working class neighborhoods further east, but middle-class money has now fully taken root, as realtors are happy to explain.

That doesn't detract from the fun, the hip, the hop, the funk and the brass of an evening on rue Oberkampf, but it does explain why it's increasingly cool to call Oberkamph passé, like last year's college graduates scorning a keg party. Café Charbon, Café Mercerie, Mecano and other café-restaurant-bars that line the street are now a part of the lexicon of eastern Parisians in the way that La Coupole and Le Select immediately call to mind life in Montparnasse. These smoky eastside joints may not have the same staying power, but they're icons in their own right.

These café-restaurant-bars are all cut from much the same ambient mold, yet each has a mild distinctiveness arising from the hard-edged "décor"of the former working class shop or café that once occupied the space. Being 40something myself, I personally appreciate them more during the day hours, when they come across as funky Paris cafés, than during their evening hours, when they look more like safe East Village, New York bars. Nevertheless, Oberkampf deservedly remains an evening attraction when on a laid-back search of a crowd, when the photo on your passport says "entertain me."

In addition to being drinking spots, the places noted below also serve basic comfort food. You might also consider them for an acceptable Sunday brunch (generally served noon-3pm, about 15€), keeping in mind that a French café brunch is far less extensive than an American brunch.

Following rue Oberkampf east from metro Parmentier, with a brief detour along the cross-street rue St-Maur, you'll come upon to the following hot spots:

Mecano, 99 rue Oberkampf. A former tool and machine shop.

Blue Billard Club, 111 rue St-Maur. A billiard palace beyond the bar area.

La Bague de Kenza, 106 rue St-Maur. One of the city's most noteworthy Algerian bakeries. Continuing north along rue St-Maur one finds a good deal of local character in the mix of hip and North African spots.

Café Charbon, 109 rue Oberkampf. Linchpin of the quarter and the street's most popular drinking hole.

Chez Justin, 96 rue Oberkampf.

Café Mercerie, 98 rue Oberkampf. A former hardware store.

L'Estimet, 116 rue Oberkampf.

...And so on up the avenue to the Café Ménilmontant, at the corner of Oberkampf and boulevard Ménilmontant. Rue Ménilmontant, the continuation of rue Oberkampf, shows the more day-to-day bazaar of commerce in the area, with an array of ethnic restaurants (Indian, Kurd, West Indian, North African and others) reflecting the diversity of the neighboring area.

WINE, WINE BARS & WINE RESTAURANTS

Consider two clichéd images of good times: in the first, a few Ameican guys are standing outside a gas station in Nowheresville, USA, having a soda pop; in the second, a few French guys are outside Trouperdu, France, pouring wine in someone's cellar. I place these images for you side by side to show that wine consumption is as common an expression of life in France as gasoline (not to mention soda) consumption is in the United States. They go to the very heart of their nation's sense of heritage, territory, culture and place.

Wine is more than a cultural heritage in France, it is an agricultural heritage as well. The regions where the Romans planted grapes following their conquest of Gaul in 52 B.C. remain the famous wine regions of France. The French don't think of serving or ordering cabernet or merlot or pinot noir or chardonnay, they think of ordering a wine from Burgundy, Bordeaux, Champagne, Rhone, Alsace, Loire, Chablis, St-Emilion, etc. And therefore the wine calls to mind not only a grape but the land on which it is grown, a land a Frenchman can not only find on a map but with which he may well have some intimate connection. When he pours you a glass of wine and says "Did I ever tell you about that *charmante* girl I knew from Burgundy" his relationship with the wine is far more evocative that of the man who says, "Did I tell about that full-bodied 20-year-old cab I had last month?"

This isn't to say that everyone in France is a connoisseur, nor that the French drink wine all the time, but wine consumption is such a normal and casual activity that it needs no explanation, no special occasion. The quality of wine people drink naturally varies with their budget, but wine knows no class boundaries in France. Everyone knows what a vineyard looks like, everyone even seems to know someone who has a friend in the business. Most people actually have a wine cellar, even if their cellar is just a couple of bottles lying on a kitchen shelf.

The selections in this chapter are accessible and central wine-oriented places: bars, restaurants, and shops where an easy-going traveler, connoisseur or not, can enjoy and explore wine culture. They will appeal to veteran wine people, special occasion drinkers, and novices alike. You needn't know winespeak (or even French) to feel welcome.

...

TIP: For the anxious host

As every good host knows, if you've got a bottle of champagne in the fridge (for the aperitif) and a bottle or two of red on the shelf (for the meal) you can always improvise the rest.

...

㊶ La Robe et Le Palais

Address *13 rue des Lavandières-Ste-Opportune, 1st arr. A block north of the Seine, a block west of Place du Châtelet.* ***Metro*** *Châtelet.*
Tel. *01 45 08 07 41.* ***Starters*** *10 €,* ***Main courses*** *15 €,* ***Desserts*** *9 €.* ***Most wines*** *10-40 €.*

Best wine restaurant

Olivier Schvirtz and his hearty staff are like regular guys from New Jersey, except that they're French and know all there is to know about wine instead of beer. Actually, Olivier Schvirtz knows a lot about beer, too, as he has a hand in the crafting of the beer served here. But leave the beer to the regulars, we've come for the wine... and the food... and the laid-back atmosphere... and the price.

Le Robe et Le Palais has a no nonsense non-décor consisting of yellow-green walls with stenciled grape bunches and the usual wine and vineyard trimmings that were probably just easy things to put up in 1995 while Mr. Schvirtz and his staff were busy stocking the cellar.

You needn't be a wine person to enjoy this wine restaurant, which is one reason why I consider it the best of the lot. In fact, you needn't have any wine sense at all, for you're in trustworthy hands if you just let yourself be guided. We – a fellow writer and I – didn't even look at a wine list corresponding to the 6000 bottles in house. This is the perfect occasion to let down your guard and go with the flow. When Mr. Schvirtz or one of his men makes a suggestion just nod.

"How about a cool red wine from the Loire?" he said. It was summer.

We nodded.

You needn't be on a liquid diet at La Robe et Le Palais either. Decent, well grounded, earthy fare is also served: an arugula and parmesan salad sprinkled with olive oil, a compact tomato tart, avocado and goat cheese warmed in an earthenware cassoulette, a nice bass or sea bream.

We were too full to test desserts (a sin for restaurant testers, but by then there was no doubt we'd be back), so Mr. Schvitz recommended a sweet wine from south of Saumur to end the meal.

We nodded.

He said that the growers are friends. He explained how they work their land and their grapes. He brought over a map to point out the village. He told us of his dream of owning some vines in the area; in the meantime he's got friends there. He left the bottle at the table. You've got to like the guy.

The thought then crossed our minds that we were being set up for a horrendous bill. After all we hadn't seen any of the wine prices, and when someone leaves a bottle on your table what do you do when the wine is good? At as it turned out, our red Loire was billed at €15, the sweet Layon at €10. Easy

WORDPLAY

The name La Robe et Le Palais is wordplay referring to both wine and the presence of the Paris Law Courts just across the river: *la robe* refers to a wine's color and as well as to the legal profession (which wears a robe in court), *le palais* means both palate and law courts (or palace).

prices to digest.

How can he tell the acceptable price range when giving suggestions? Mr. Schvirtz said he just knows, and for more expensive wines he always announces the prices or inquires about one's range. The French are sometimes shocked by money talk, he says, but not Americans. In any case, all wines are less than expensive, mostly maxing out at 60€. So don't come here seeking that old Bordeaux that you read about in *The Wine Spectator*. Come for friendly advice. Come for friendly atmosphere. Come with friends.

㊷Willi's Wine Bar

Address *13 rue des Petits Champs, 1st arr.* ***Metro*** *Palais Royal or Bourse. Behind the Palais Royal and across the street from the old National Library.* • ***Tel*** *01 42 61 05 09* • ***Fax*** *01 47 03 36 93.*
Site *www.williswinebar.com (displays menu).* ***Menu*** *25€ (L), 32€.*
Wine list *Extensive. Most 28-110€.*

Aux Bons Crus

Address *7 rue des Petits Champs, 1st arr.* ***Metro*** *Palais Royal or Bourse. Two doors down from Willi's.* • ***Tel.*** *01 42 60 06 45.* ***Main courses*** *12-14.50€.* ***ALC*** *25€.* ***Wine list*** *Elementary, most under 25€.*

A polished British-owned wine and dine vs. a traditional local wine bistro

Willi's Wine Bar and Aux Bons Crus both give a prominent place to wine and both are undeniably Parisian and well integrated in the same alluring quarter. But the similarities end there. They are so much the antithesis of one another that together they have all the makings of a prime time sitcom: two neighboring businesses, the one impersonal, polished, and sophisticated, the other folksy, drab and talky.

There's nothing exceptional about the young wines brought up from the cellar to the counter at Aux Bons Crus except that they go down perfectly well with the country-style dishes brought out from the kitchen: ribsteak served with potatoes baked in cream (*entrecôte pommes dauphines*), beef with carrots, salmon, filet of lamb, cured ham, ripe cheese. And they go well with the rustic décor: the zinc bar, the massive pulley of the goods lift, dark wine barrels along the walls.

This local bistro is so unpretentious that you've got to wonder whether its homey plainness, in this well-heeled banking and boutiquing quarter, is in fact some ultra-sophisticated joke that you don't quite get. Its very simplicity may make it a bit intimidating for non-French-speaking travelers; you get the feeling that everyone's a regular here. But it's also the kind of place where, if you're willing to venture in for a glass at the bar or literally duck into a seat in the back (without complaining about the smoke), you'll soon feel like a regular yourself. There's an actual complicity between the staff and the familiar patrons, as there is amongst the personnel themselves – a rarity in Paris, where one typically suspects that the staff dislikes each other as much as they do their clients. Aux Bons Crus is the kind of place where nothing's more important than entering with a resounding "Bonjour" ("Bonsoir" in the evening).

The menu at Willi's is seasonal, while at Aux Bons Crus the only thing that's seasonal is the conversation about the weather.

Willi's, on the other hand, is the kind of place where nothing's more important than entering with a reservation. In order to appreciate this wine bar/restaurant you needn't be a wine connoisseur but should nonetheless feel comfortable with a stem glass in your hand, for Willi's may be moderately priced but nevertheless has a sophisticated edge and a Parisian coolness to it, despite its British ownership. English, however, is the language of choice, making it that much more accessible.

Willi's has a small counter with a half-dozen stools and a variety of appetizing by-the-glass selections of wines and sherries (*xérès*): e.g. a wonderful Châteauneuf-de-Pape white, an Irouléguy white worth discovering, a sweet Jurançon. A solitary wine man looking for a viticultural conversation with a barman can feel quite at ease on a corner stool in the early evening, though he may find the dining area too snug to dine alone. Willi's counter is a reputable place to start the evening even if you'll be dining elsewhere. There are, however, reasons to head back into the nook of a dining area. Happily, the greasy potato and zucchini crisps we were served at the bar did not reflect the overall quality of our meal.

At table the varied selection of 250 wine references is enticing reading material (including some wise Italian, Spanish, and Portuguese selections along with the French). Wine advice and service is generally informative, if impatient. The dinner menu is commendable for its classic modern fare. The lunch menu is equally promising. No fireworks but a fine backdrop for the right bottle and the right company, business colleagues or wine-leaning friends or what was once called "ladies night out."

The menu at Willi's is seasonal, while at Aux Bons Crus the only thing that's seasonal is the conversation about the weather. From Willi's October menu, my tuna tartare, followed by roast duckling, followed by mango and vanilla fondant icing held up well to criticism. My dinner companion was more blasé about his pumpkin soup, but the tuna was nice (if slightly overgrilled), followed by a decent soft walnut cake with roast peaches and figs. My companion this evening was an American writer who now wonders whether having three children under the age of three has dulled his appetite, which answers the question as to why a man of 40 would order pumpkin soup at a wine bar in the first place. Half the battle is knowing what to order.

Lunch vs. Dinner vs. Drink: Aux Bons Crus need only be considered as a lunch choice or for a pre-dinner glass, while Willi's is more appropriate for a late-afternoon/pre-dinner glass or dinner.

Wine-bar-hopping winefellows might begin at Aux Bons Crus, followed by another at Willi's and/or at nearby L. Legrand (see *Wine Shops* below). With all due respect to Willi's kitchen, your good cheer could then prepare you for dinner just around the corner at Le Grand Colbert (see *Restaurants: Brasseries*). A chance to discover an admirable range of Paris offerings within a few unsteady steps.

㊸Vins des Pyrénées

***Address** 25 rue Beautreillis, 4th arr. Just off rue de Rivoli in the Marais. **Metro** Saint-Paul or Bastille. **Tel** 01 42 72 64 94. **Open** Daily for dinner, daily except Sat. for lunch. **ALC** 24-31€. **Most wines** 20-30€.*

Trendy wine bistro for hip traditionalists

Vin des Pyrénées strikes a warm and pleasing note between cool and traditional, though it's owners clearly tend to the former – because only places striving for hip play Latino music in Paris. Nevertheless, you needn't be a 30something hipster with a comfortable income, like most of the clients, to enjoy a meal here. Vin des Pyrénées has a good deal of simpatico, beginning with the casual welcome and the decorative marriage of Paris circa 1900 and kitsch circa 1950.

Whatever your age or style you should be casual enough to be not too critical of the food. Actually, I found the general bistro fare more heartwarming than did my dinner companions, who mistakenly ordered fish dishes weighed down by heavy cream sauces. Lesson learned: Beware of cream sauces in a wine-oriented restaurant. All dishes are served in sizeable portions, so in order to maintain an adequate balance between quality and quantity keep it simple: opt for grilled fish or for other dishes where the sauce does not get equal billing with the meat or poultry. No complaints about the honorable selection of the wine.

Bar du Caveau

Address *17 place Dauphine, 1st arr. Adjacent to the restaurant Caveau du Palais.* ***Metro*** *Pont-Neuf.*

The wine bar version of an afternoon nap

With the massive backside of the courthouse running along one side, the Paris Bar Association at one corner, and the Paris police headquarters down the street, the half dozen deceptively casual bistros and restaurants along the triangular place on the Cité Island naturally cater to the judicial/law enforcement crowd. At midday you'll have to fight with the law if you hope to find a seat for lunch.

But by mid-afternoon the square has nearly emptied, turning this 17th century triangle into a provincial square, complete with *boule* players tossing metal balls on the sandy ground. Such calm in the heart of the city is a treat in itself. At 4-5:30pm on a lazy traveling day or after a few heady hours in the Louvre across the river, there are two honorable things to do in Place Dauphine, lie on a bench beneath the trees for a nap or take a seat in this hushed little wine bar/café.

By mid/late-afternoon a few straggling law folk may be in the Bar du Caveau reviewing briefs or sharing scant conversation, so come either with peaceable companions or alone with documents to shuffle (otherwise there are newspapers available). Tea and pastry go well with this warm old setting of stone walls and wooden beams. But the Bar du Caveau is better suited for a glass of wine and an afternoon tartine (a light open-faced sandwich) or plate of *charcuterie* (cold cuts) or cheese before heading outside for a nap on a bench.

Wine From Paris

A thousand years ago the hills surrounding Paris were spotted with vineyards, and those vineyards continued to be extended through the Middle Ages. Well into the 18th century 100,000 acres of the surrounding countryside were covered with vines. The expanding city and finally the phylloxera epidemic of 1928 brought about the demise of the Paris vineyards.

In 1932, a half-acre plot on the northern slope of Montmartre was replanted in the name of tradition. Since then, vines have been planted in several other parks in the capital. The Montmartre vineyard remains the most celebrated of these, not for quality but for maintaining the spirit of "village" Montmartre. Its gamay and pinot noir grape vines, bordered by peach trees, receive relatively little light because their situation on the northern slope of this northern hill, therefore the harvest doesn't take place until several weeks later than in the Champagne region, 100 miles east of Paris. But when the harvest finally does arrive – early/mid-October – it is an occasion for celebration. The grapes are then pressed and placed in vats in the basement of the district hall of the 18th arrondissement, downhill from the vineyard. More celebration follows as the 500 bottles of Montmartre wine are then sold at auction to the benefit of local charities.

Au Sauvignon

***Address** 80 rue des Saints-Peres, 7th arr. Cattycorner to the Hôtel Lutetia, where the 6th arr. nestles against the 7th. **Metro** Sèvres-Babylone.*

A Left Bank wine café for a 5-7 pause

Au Sauvignon makes for a welcome stop when on the late afternoon shopping tour of this upmarket corner of the Left Bank. In many ways it's just a plain old café to rest your weary feet, so feel free to order any café beverage. However, the talky buzz inside Au Sauvignon comes from the fact that it's served as a local watering hole since 1957. Consider it for a 5-7pm pause over a glass of a classic young white (Sancerre, Chablis, Quincy, Loupiac) or red (Sancerre, Chinon, Pinot Noir Burgundy, St-Emilion), by the glass or by the bottle. The above go well with the choice of open-faced sandwiches on sourdough bread or of foie gras, cheese, or smoked salmon on toast. Share one for an hors d'oeuvre, then order another if what you really wanted was a snack.

WINE SHOPS

Fantasies aside, most French wines bought in wine shops are relatively inexpensive compared with prices in the United States. A $20-$30 bottle for a picnic can make you feel like a king, while a light red for $5 is nothing to be ashamed of.

If planning on returning home with wine for yourself or as a gift, note that an individual may bring back into the United States one liter of alcoholic beverage without paying duty. You are allowed to bring home more, however duty may be charged – though typically easy-to-carry quantities will be ignored. Other than the amount at which duty is charged, Federal regulations do not specify a limit on the amount of alcohol you may bring back for personal use. However, unusual quantities are liable to raise suspicions that you are importing the bottle for resale, which would require a permit. Actually, the main limitation on carrying back alcohol is that the bottles are heavy.

L. Legrand Filles & Fils

Address *12 Galerie Vivienne (or 1 rue de la Banque), 2nd arr. The entrance to Galerie Vivienne, a charm-filled shopping arcade circa 1820s, is across the street from Aux Bons Crus, noted above. For more on Galerie Vivienne see Shop 'n' Stroll.* ***Metro*** *Palais Royal or Bourse.*
Tel. *01 42 60 07 12* ***Shop and wine bar open*** *Tues.-Fri. 9am-7:30pm, Sat. 9am-1pm and 3-7pm.*

Grocer, candy store, wine and spirits merchant, Legrand is an old-fashioned hodgepodge shop with something for all tradition-minded travelers: chocolate and sweets, canned goods and preserves, wine and accessories. The selection of these various goods isn't exclusive so much as wise. The emphasis is above all on the wine end, and the little shop has recently expanded to include a wine bar and to more fully display its viticultural know-how: wines, cork screws, carafes and other trimmings of fine living. Wine producers conduct free tastings some evenings.

Augé

Address *116 bd. Haussmann.* ***Metro*** *Saint-Augustin.* ***Closed*** *Sun., Mon. morning.*

Augé is to wine and spirit connoisseurs what a dusty old bookstore with a couple of cats is too book lovers: a place to linger and to dream, whether you intend to buy or not. Augé has that collector's air to it. Like an independent bookstore, better prices may be found elsewhere, yet the selection here is wide-ranging and the advice forthcoming and reliable. Extensive selection of brandies: cognac, armagnac, bas-armagnac, calvados (apple brandy).

Nicolas (Madeleine)

Address *Place de la Madeleine.* ***Metro*** *Madeleine.*

Nicolas, a moderate-to-upscale wine and spirits chain with outlets throughout France, has a showcase shop behind the church of the Madeleine, in the company of Paris's most famous luxury grocer and caterers (Fauchon, Hédiard, Ladurée). Feel free to go inside and wander around the wine shop to get some ideas for your cellar back home. If planning your dream cellar, be sure to go down into the basement to admire the selection of rare and top vintages: Mouton Rothschild 1928, Margaux 1900, etc.

THE RESTAURANT WINE EXPERIENCE

ORDERING WINE

You'll notice that the majority of people in French restaurants order a bottle of wine with dinner, but you certainly needn't feel obliged to do the same. Wine is now less frequent at lunchtime than a generation ago due to shorter lunch breaks, but having a glass or two is still acceptable behavior then.

If you have questions or would like assistance ordering wine in a restaurant don't hesitate to ask. Any waiter will be capable of giving basic advice or suggestions, naturally more so in restaurants with more pronounced wine leanings or extensive wine lists. Gastronomic restaurants have a sommelier, or wine steward, whose job it is to help. He (the sommelier is usually a man) can be trusted, as long as you beware of superlatives and understand that the final choice is yours. Most sommeliers do a very good job at advising without pushing their point of view too hard.

If you prefer not to speak directly of price with a sommelier, especially when inviting others to dinner, a discreet way of letting him know your acceptable range is to tactfully point to or inquire about something in that price range as you ask his help. The sommelier's job is not only to know wine but to pick up your clues. When you leave your fate entirely in his hand he will point it out to you on the wine list so that you can see the price.

You should feel free to order whatever you like with any course, so you needn't be insulted if the sommelier or waiter attempts to point out a more culturally acceptable direction. He may only be trying to keep you from making a "mistake" that would confuse the palate. He may also be called upon to help you come up with the balanced compromise that is often necessary in order to find a single wine to satisfy the entire table throughout the entire meal.

Here are certain standard notions that can be used in choosing or serving wine to enhance a meal:

❧ To marry a wine with your chosen meal, introduce light wines to light dishes, young wines to rustic dishes, and wiser, more mature wines to sophisticated dishes. Salads, vinegary appetizers, creamy cheeses, and chocolate are just as happy when accompanied by a flat young H2O.

❧ Dry white wines (chilled 50°-54°F) sit well with oysters and other seafood, grilled and fried fish, snails and goat cheese.

❧ Richer, sweeter white wines (53°-57°) may serve as escorts with fish and crustaceans in sauce, crawfish, refined cold cuts, foie gras, fowl and white meats.

❧ Chilled rosé can be placed at a convivial table of hors-d'oeuvres, cold cuts, omelets and many light summery dishes.

❧ Light red wines (50°-56°) may dance with roast meats, white meats, grilled meats, fowl, pasta and light cheeses.

❧ Heavy and older red wines (60°-63°) live happily ever after with meat in sauce and all but very strong cheeses.

❧ Champagne and its sparkling cousins from other regions, mousseux and crément, (served at 43°-46°) may start the party as an aperitif or flirt with dessert.

❧ When having one wine with the appetizer and another with the main course, light and delicate wines typically come before older and more forthright wines, generally meaning white before red and young before old.

French wines naturally represent most of what you'll find on any wine list in Paris, except for the foreign (non-French) restaurants representing other wine-growing countries. At equal price you may find a satisfying Italian or Spanish wine, but other foreign wines on all but the most extensive lists are unlikely to compare favorably for the price. The French do know wine – but the wine they know is primarily French. The average restaurateur knows or cares as little about American wines as American voters know or care about French politics.

Tasting Wine

Unless you've ordered a carafe of wine, the waiter or the sommelier will present the unopened bottle to you at the table. Examine the label as long as you wish. *Appellation d'origine contrôlée* is a legal declaration that the wine is made from specific varieties of grapes grown in a specific area. *Mise en bouteille au château* is an encouraging sign that the wine was bottled where it was produced. Be sure that it is indeed the wine you ordered, particularly that the year is correct. The temperature may also be off – the red too cool, the white too warm. If you have doubts feel the bottle. Within a few degrees this isn't a problem because the bottle will be warmed by room temperature or it can be chilled on ice. However, if you find the temperature unacceptable then you should signal that as a problem before the bottle is opened. If the label and temperature are as expected then you will nod in approval.

The bottle will then be opened, discretely, without effort or pop. The waiter or wine steward may look at and sniff the cork, examining it for mold or crumbling, signs of poor storage or poor corking. He may place the cork on the table for you to examine for yourself. A red wine may then be set aside to breathe, a white may be placed in a bucket to chill. An older, generally red, wine may be decanted by being poured into a decanter or a ewer, thereby aerating the wine and leaving behind the sediment, undisturbed. Sometimes decanting is performed merely to add elegance to the proceedings. The entire process from the bottle being brought to the table to the wine being served is more or less the same in all restaurants, great and small. It is carried out with more care in direct proportion to the price of the bottle, and the process naturally appears more formal in a more formal setting.

A large gulp's worth of wine will be poured into the glass of the person who has ordered the wine, unless that person volunteers someone else. Then, if that person is you, it's your chance to shine.

The three features of dégustation or wine tasting are:

❧ **The eye:** Hold the glass up to the light to examine its robe, swirl it to air the wine and to bring out its bouquet, examine whether its has legs, the trails it leaves inside the glass.

❧ **The nose:** Smell the wine to take in its fragrance, aroma, and bouquet, collectively called its nose. This is the most important step: the nose knows.

❧ **The mouth:** Eventually, you take a good amount in your mouth, feel it against all areas of your tongue then swallow, then reflect on the aftertaste.

You may make your examination of the wine as formal and studious as you like – or you can take the glass in hand

and do the old sniff and gulp. Then, finding the wine acceptable, nod or say *oui* to the waiter, who will then serve the others, women first, before returning to fill your glass.

Sending Back Wine

Chances are that your wine, outside of price considerations, will be acceptable, though perhaps unexpected if you are unfamiliar with the specific vineyard or vintage. But wine is sometimes, if rarely, off. Poor production, excessive aging, and more likely poor corking or poor storage can give a moldy, corky or vinegary taste. But unless the wine you've ordered is truly off it will be difficult to send it back at this point.

You should feel free to question the bottle's integrity. However, if you have ordered a cheap wine, or merely an overpriced wine, declaring the wine "not very good" is not generally considered an acceptable argument. Claiming that the wine isn't what you expected is another argument without legs. Stating that the sommelier steered you wrong requires a very good argument to back it up, especially considering that you've just insulted the guy's professional skills.

French businesses and service people are not guided by the principle that the customer is always right. Nevertheless, your doubts will get a hearing. Eventually, the sommelier will pour himself a taste then give his professional opinion, and, if doubt persists, he will call over the maitre d' to have him taste it. (If there is no sommelier, the waiter will just call over his boss.) At any point in your complaint the sommelier or maitre d' or owner may agree with your assessment of the wine or seek to appease you anyway. Perhaps not. They may try to convince you that the wine you've ordered is not truly off and refuse to take it back. If they fail to convince you and/or if you refuse to be humbled before your table companions, you may have no choice but to make the proverbial scene. After that you're on your own.

THE PARIS RESTAURANT ADVENTURE

FROM MY CHOICE TO YOUR CHOICE

Restaurants are a traveler's most accessible entrance to foreign culture. They rouse and satisfy both your appetite and your curiosity. Whether you're a foodie or just a hungry traveler, a gastronome on a mission or a hearty eater looking for something simple yet delicious, eating out will be one of your most memorable adventures in Paris.

The restaurants I've selected here explore a wide range of French, regional and foreign traditions, along with creative variations on traditional themes. In making these selections, I seek neither to sell the star system nor to tell you how to eat on slim budget, and I prefer to leave the merely trendy to the merely trendy. Value is important in any price range. Along with some fabulous and upstanding gastronomic restaurants, I've chosen many wonderful yet relaxed restaurants that I nevertheless consider among the best in the city: the best bistros, brasseries or regional restaurants, the best place of oyster ice cream, onion soup or southwestern savors.

Sometimes, "the best" simply means that my table companion(s) and I had "the best" time there. As I hope you will.

I have tested, and in many cases retested, these restaurants personally. The personal nature of these choices will be clear to you as you read them. You will encounter some of my co-testers on these pages: a smorgasbord of food-friendly French and American professional, from my faithful friend L. to my cat's veterinarian. Much of my personal appreciation of these restaurants has come from sharing the experience with them. I hope you don't imagine that that takes way from my critical eye. Indeed, a decade of writing about Paris restaurants has taught me much about the restaurant experience in the culinary capital of the world, but the most important lesson I've learned is the value of good company. Wherever you eat, it's the people at your table who make or break a meal. Good company will save a bad meal, but a good meal rarely makes up for bad company – though good wine helps.

As a visitor, you won't have the luxury of trading in your dinner companions to suit the restaurant or your mood, as I do living in Paris, suddenly exchanging, say, your wife for your golf partner because you'd rather go to a wine bar than a polished restaurant, or your husband for your best friend because, well, just because. Presumably you have chosen well to start.

I am especially grateful to my co-testers for their company and their comments and for joining me to try these restaurants when sometimes all they really wanted was to go for pizza. During your stay in Paris you will find at times that all you want is to go for pizza, too, or some place "easy." Well, you won't find pizza on any of the menus I've selected here, but you will find enough information to help you choose the right place to fit your mood or culinary ambitions on a given day.

> **There are no "must eats" on the Paris restaurant scene, only wise selections.**

There are no "must eats" on the Paris restaurant scene, only wise selections. The wise traveler knows that there's a time to spend more for quality and a time to spend less for character, a time when you want to luxuriate in the view from the high road and a time to sit down to hearty tradition, a time to go regional and a time to go foreign, a time for a brasserie and a time for a café, a time to make reservations and a time to just wing it or to carry bread and cheese to the park. More than any specific restaurants, it's variety that I recommend. It isn't where you *should* be eating in Paris that counts, but where you will find your personal blend of enjoyment, gratification, learning and discovery while best enjoying your companions.

If you want what are generally considered the elite of French restaurants you need only head for the stars in the Michelin Red Guides, a major influence of the reputation of restaurants of haute cuisine in France. However, you're setting yourself up for disappointment if you choose a restaurant by anyone's ratings alone. I love haute cuisine with the right company, on the right expense account. I highly recommend the experience, the romance, the luxuriance. Yet I've chosen not to consider the most famous of them in this edition (occasionally reviewing them on www.parisrevisited.com), preferring to examine restaurants that are lesser known.

A sophisticated palate is a nice arm to have in your traveling arsenal, but eating out in Paris shouldn't be approached as an intellectual exercise or some form of X-Game in which only the strongest stomachs survive.

A sophisticated palate is a nice arm to have in your traveling arsenal, but eating out in Paris shouldn't be approached as an intellectual exercise or some form of X-Game in which only the strongest stomachs survive. Instead, this adventure calls for exploring the rich variety of eating experiences available in the French capital: outdoor markets, cafés, bistros, brasseries, cuisine bourgeoise (serving polished classics), regional cuisine, gastronomic restaurants, foreign restaurants, wine restaurants (see the *Wine* chapter). You'll find that variety – and variety within that variety – described here.

I am a hopeful, optimistic critic. I hope that every restaurant I test will be a hit, that I can recommend it as a perfect place for romance, small groups, new business, old friends, onion soup, duck, fish, apple pie, etc. So I enter each restaurant wanting to believe the promise that led me there in the first place – its situation, its menu, its décor, an advertisement, my own previous meals there, suggestions of friends, strangers, travelers met on tours, chefs, restaurateurs or fellow restaurant critics. By the time I leave I want to feel that I've discovered (or rediscovered) something, even if what I've just (re)discovered has been known and written about for years.

I may be a hopeful critic, but I'm not an easy one, so I won't hesitate to point out a weakness, to mock a restaurant's very success or to offer a cautionary tale. However, all of the selections in this book have something specific and worthwhile to recommend them, and I do in fact recommend them all.

I now leave it to you to make your own wise choice. Add to these reviews the company you've chosen and to a lesser degree the neighbors you haven't, and factor in your own mood for the evening, and you come away with your own Paris restaurant adventure. My hope is that the information provided here will guide you to the table of those adventures as you set out on a daily quest to be indulged or surprised, comforted or seduced, entertained or warmed. Bon appetit – and enjoy!

Reservations

Just say the magic words – "I'd like to reserve a table for..." – and you're on your way!

If there's a particular restaurant of any type where you'd like to eat then it's recommendable to reserve a week or more in advance. If you're not a planner don't force yourself. But for the selections in this book you should at least call before showing up, unless you just happen to be in the neighborhood already. If you pass by the restaurant during a touring day you might stop by and reserve then. Most of the bistros and brasseries and regional restaurants noted here will be able to accommodate you if you call a day or two in advance, or in many cases the very day or evening. You may be more comfortable having the concierge or receptionist at the hotel call for you.

Lunch is typically served noon to 2pm, though you may stay seated later. Aside from brasseries and some bistros and very touristy or fast food places, restaurants rarely open for dinner before 7:30, and typically not until 8pm. If you are invited to a Parisian's home for dinner, the invitation will typically be for 8-8:30. Dinner is served after the aperitif, and only a nervous host rushes the aperitif.

The time of the last order in a restaurant, meaning the latest you can arrive, varies from place to place and often depends on the type of restaurant. Most restaurants will accept reservations until at least 10pm and some beyond that. You can then generally stay seated well past midnight. There is a natural tendency for thriving non-gastronomic restaurants to funnel reservations into two dinner seatings, one beginning 8-8:30pm, the other 10-10:30pm.

If you'd like to experience a top or very popular restaurant, it's advisable to reserve several weeks or more in advance. Having said that, one way to snag an elusive table is to call the day you wish to go there or the day before. Many top restaurants require confirmation, at the latest either the day before or by noon for an evening reservation, so you may luck into a recently cancelled or unconfirmed reservation. There's no harm in trying. Lunch reservations in such restaurants are normally easier to come by than dinner reservations.

Travelers on tours with the author receive personalized assistance in selecting and reserving restaurants.

Making your way through the meal

SERVICE

Back home we demand friendly service with a smile, we promise tips and we want to be treated as though we, as customers, are always right, so we have allowed our waiters and waitresses to act as flirts, buddies and mothers. The French, meanwhile, demand efficient service, maintain a clear distance between client and staff and believe that the customer may well be wrong, so they've wound up with service people who don't want complications: cordial career waiters, disinterested servers, not a buxom waitress in sight. A culture often gets what it asks for. (As to the happy medium, see review of L'Oulette.)

Hollywood sitcom writer's handbooks instructs writers that one sure way to show your character to be an ordinary, fun-loving guy is to place him and his girlfriend, wife or in-laws in a French restaurant, direct the waiter to look down his nose at the guy, have someone say "Grey Poupon," then turn up the laugh track. Yuck, yuck. Everyone loves to make fun of French waiters, but some travelers seem to get special pleasure from returning home with stories about rude maitre d's, pompous waiters, hoity-toity restaurants and chain smoking at the next table, stories that they hold up as certified proof that the French hate the Americans.

Bad or snooty service is indeed the most common complaint from overseas travelers in Paris. I've got my own horror stories. But travelers who repeatedly find themselves in such situations have to share the blame: either they haven't figured out that they're not in Kansas anymore or they've been buying the wrong guide.

This is no apology for surly service, just a warning that American and French notions of good service are not exactly the same. Understanding the fundamentals of French, more particularly Parisian, service – efficiency, discretion, professionalism – is the best way to benefit from rather than clash with it.

Efficiency. Efficiency means nothing more nor less than this: Dishes are served and cleared properly and if you want something the waiter will get it for you, without undue hesitation.

As a foreigner you will naturally have more questions about dishes than the average French person would, besides which you may be asking them in English. Answering questions is naturally a part of a waiter's job, and many waiters are accustomed to responding in English. But from the point of view of a waiter striving for efficiency you may come across as a slow and demanding client, even when you're simply a client in need of assistance. Your waiter may further be frustrated if he believes that you're asking him French cuisine's equivalent of "What's in the beef with broccoli?" And since French waiters are not good at faking a smile, yours may not have the facial reflex to hide his impatience.

As a general rule, if you need a waiter he will come, if you don't need him he will not come, and if you need him too often he will ignore you.

An efficient waiter has nothing against you taking your time when ordering, he just doesn't like you taking *his* time, and so he may be quick to leave you to think about your choice. An efficient waiter isn't necessarily a friendly, charming or cheery waiter, nor one who will stop by occasionally to see if everything is alright. As a general rule, if you need a waiter he will come, if you don't need him he will not come, and if you need him too often he will ignore you.

Discretion. Some travelers start off on the wrong foot by trying to get a waiter to laugh at their jokes. Big mistake!

Unlike the tight-bunned flight attendants in business class who will open their mouth in delight to every dull-witted comment an upgraded client may make, Parisian waiters do not laugh. They don't laugh in French and they don't laugh in English. Kind and amiable French waiters do exist, but in no case will one appear overjoyed to see you or attempt to impress you with his outgoingness.

One might say this is a result of their livelihood not being dependant on the financial reward for a client's gratitude since the gratuity in France is always included. But give or take 3%, tipping is practically as obligatory in the U.S. So it isn't exactly the tip that makes French waiters appear or act cold or aloof to us. Their distant approach is more culturally innate than that.

Discretion is a guiding force in French business and service and neighborly relations. This discretion comes from a combination of reserve, detachment, disinterest and politeness. In a restaurant, a respectful distance is expected between the staff and the clientele. The French, as many other Europeans, are accustomed to and often demand that. The waiter is not expected to be a part of the entertainment. A discreet waiter keeps his distance, speaks minimally, stands before you attentively and awaits your order. When he approaches the table he does so in the least obtrusive way, so that you may continue your conversation as he clears or delivers plates. Naturally, relaxed dining has more relaxed service, but even there discretion is emphasized. One naturally expects and receives greater attention from waiters as price and space between tables increase, but that attention generally leads to glasses that never empty rather than increased dialogue with the staff. Actually, in finer restaurants you will encounter someone interested in an engaging conversation with the table: the sommelier or wine steward. That's because the more he understands where you're coming from the more appropriate wine he can recommend.

Otherwise, forget any preconceived notion that good service means service with a smile. Do not feel snubbed by his lack of expression. Au contraire, good French service means gracious dispassion.

Professionalism. In France, waiters are not hopeful actors, part-time students, nurses with a second job, men and women who haven't yet found something better to do. French waiters are professionals in the restaurant business whose career ambitions are more likely to involve owning or managing their own restaurant or café. Furthermore, they get employee health coverage. Sometimes their very professionalism leads them to approach the table like a surgeon with no bedside manner; you need some veal kidneys you'll get veal kidneys.

As a service professional, your waiter expects to serve, but he also expects to be treated like a professional. A request for a waiter's attention should begin with *"S'il vous plaît."* If you wish to address him by title you would call him *"monsieur"* –

Cuisson? or How would you like that done?

Meat is customarily served more rare in France than in the United States, so it's important to answer appropriately when the waiter asks "Cuisson?" *meaning* "How would you like that done?"

The French often choose either ***rosé*** *and* ***à point****, which are typically translated as medium rare or medium, but are closer to what we would consider as rare and medium rare. You may therefore wish to say* ***bien cuit****, literally well done, to have meat served to the American notion of medium or medium well. In order to assure that it's well done specify* ***très bien cuit****.*

It is also not unusual for a Frenchman to order beef ***saignant****, literally meaning bloody and thus truly rare, or even* ***bleu****, which gives it no more than a quick flip on the grill. Beyond that there's* ***steak tartare****, uncooked lean ground beef mixed with raw egg yolk, to which capers, chopped onions and parsley are added to make it appear less Neanderthal. Duck and game are frequently served medium rare to rare, so you must specify if you prefer them otherwise.*

Finally, Americans are accustomed to eating grilled meats that are easily taken back and thrown on the grill for an extra minute or two. But French sauces, not to mention French waiters, make doing so a more awkward proposition.

You may have to suffer through a learning curve on this one.

"madame" for a woman.

A professional waiter, efficient and discreet, believes that he knows what is expected of him. He would like to believe that he is very much in tune with the rhythms of your meal, and so you should barely have to instruct him at all once you've ordered. As the meal proceeds you may then find that your professional (perhaps stubborn) waiter is so accustomed to French rhythms (e.g. coffee served after dessert rather than with dessert) that he may unintentionally (I'm giving him the benefit of the doubt) ignore a request that goes against the cultural grain.

Do not take this personally. If you do, and if you approach the French, particularly French service people, with the attitude "If not for us they'd be speaking German," you may be setting yourself up for a bit more confrontation than is called for.

The Stages of the Meal

You needn't order something from every page of the menu, but if you did your meal would proceed as follows:

L'apéritif: A drink – and a moment – before the meal to stimulate the appetite as well as companionship. May be ordered at the table, but may well be taken in a café, bar or wine bar prior to going to a restaurant. May be served with *les hors-d'oeuvres*, small appetizers before the meal.

L'amuse-gueule: Served largely in gastronomic restaurants, this is a little treat to tickle the appetite while waiting for your first course to arrive. It isn't ordered, and so it does not appear on the menu, it's just set in front of you.

L'entrée: The appetizer or starter. Though we use the word *"entrée"* in English to designate the main course, the French word actually means "entry" and therefore refers to the first course.

Le plat principale: The main course or dish.

Le plateau de fromages: The cheese board or tray. Taken before dessert or instead of dessert. In meals in a French home the cheese is often served at the same time as a lettuce salad.

Le dessert: Dessert.

Le café/décaféiné:

Coffee/Decaf. Not traditionally served with dessert, even if waiters sometimes take the coffee order at the same time. If you do want coffee with dessert you will have to insist and perhaps remind the waiter again when he returns to the table without it. In finer restaurants the coffee is served with chocolates and other small delicacies such as the sweet arched almond-flavored biscuits called *tuiles*.

Le digestif: Digestive; after-dinner spirits such as cognac, armagnac, and other *eaux-de-vie* (brandies).

WATER

It is safe to drink the tap water in Paris. In fact, one of France's domestic security responses to 9/11 was to increase the chlorine level to guard against attempts to poison the water system. At times you can taste it. But asking for tap water in a restaurant is less likely to upset your stomach than to upset your waiter, who would prefer adding some mineral water to your bill. If you prefer tap water you need only ask for *une carafe d'eau* (a carafe of water). The waiter may or may not then start suggesting name-brand waters. Just insist on *une carafe* if that's what you want. In a café you should feel free to ask for *un verre d'eau* (a glass of water) along with your cup of coffee or whatever else you've ordered.

It may partially be an illusion, but bottled water does seem to go better with more refined cuisine. Evian and Vittel are the main brands of bottled plain water; Badoit, Perrier and, more recently, San Pellegrino, are the major brands of mineral water with bubbles, better understood as "with gas." In restaurants they are served in liter or half-liter bottles. Smaller bottles may be served in cafés.

Some public fountains have signs indicating that the water is not drinkable (*nonpotable*).

RESTROOMS

The restroom, the bathroom, the john, the WC, *les toilettes*, however you think of it it's important. But if you want to ask for it – rather *them* since *toilettes* are plural even if there's just one – better to remember the latter two:

- **WC**, pronounced *dou-ble-vay-say*, and
- **les toilettes**, pronounced *lay twa-lette*.

• **Où sont les toilettes, s'il vous plaît?** gets you pointed in the right direction.

• To find them on your own you usually need only **search for the stairs** and go down, sometimes up.

• The door may be indicated by WC (water closet) or the letters **H for hommes (men)** and **F for femmes (women)**. Unisex restrooms are not uncommon in small restaurants and cafés.

Keep sanitary expectations low and tissues and spare coins handy

As a return traveler you may have been to enough cafés in the past to know that the restrooms in Paris are small and cramped and are paid scant attention by the staff during service hours. Generally, the more expensive the restaurant the more restful the rest room, but the quality of that rest varies greatly. Seatless Turkish toilets are still found in some cafés.

If you haven't been to Paris in many years you'll find that installations have indeed become more user-friendly, though it still helps to keep sanitary expectations low and tissues and spare coins handy.

PRICES

Unless otherwise indicated, the prices noted here are for 3-course meals – starter + main course + cheese or dessert – and do not include drinks. Your choice of drinks and wine will naturally greatly affect the final bill.

• **Menu**. The French call the fixed-price menu *le menu*. At the top of the reviews in this book, the word "Menu" refers to the cost of fixed-price meal or meals. Two-course menus (starter + main course or main course + dessert) are often available at lunch and sometimes at dinner. The "menu" price is sometimes followed here by an L or a D to indicate that it is only available for lunch or for dinner.

• **A la carte**. The bill of fare that we call the menu in English is called *la carte* in French, therefore *à la carte*, or the abbreviation "ALC," is used here to indicate the average range of prices for three courses selected from that bill of fare. Exceptionally higher or lower priced dishes have been excluded in that average range. When ordering *à la carte* you may naturally order however many courses you wish.

• **Menu/Carte**. The term "Menu/Carte" indicates that the

restaurant's bill of fare comes to a fixed price whatever you choose for three courses; i.e., all of the starters are the same price, all of the main courses are the same price, all of the desserts are the same price, though some selections may be indicated as having a small supplement.

GETTING THE BILL

Sometimes the most difficult task in a restaurant is getting the waiter to give you the bill. Relax. This is often a good sign, it means that you can sit as long as you wish. Restaurants, by tradition that still holds but may be fraying at the edges, do not actively seek to turn over tables. In most restaurants you won't be given the bill until you actually ask for it. In theory, then, you can stay seated as long as you want. The French dinner can extend well beyond the moment that the last plates have been cleared. Good conversation is considered the best digestive, whether or not this is accompanied by a liquid *digestif.* If you ask for the bill as the dessert plate is being cleared you may actually be told, "There's no rush," which could make it difficult if you actually *are* in a rush.

• *"L'addition, s'il vous plaît,"* with or without air writing, means "The bill, please."

TIPPING

Tax and tip are always included in the price in restaurants in France. By paying the bill you are therefore "leaving" a 15% tip. No more is expected. However, if you've appreciated the service you may leave an additional 1€ (about $1) per person in modestly and moderately-priced restaurants, or 1.50-2€ per person in more polished settings. In a café you might merely leave small change behind as an extra tip. Overtipping makes you look naïve rather than appreciative, which wouldn't be so bad if not for the fact that it makes the rest of us look bad.

LUNCH

While the restaurants reviewed here will certainly be welcoming for lunch, particularly when situated along your touring path for the day, you may not want to be tied to a midday reservation, preferring instead to play it by your appetite. Fast food chain outlets have made great headway in France since the early 1980s, but you might as well leave the chains to the locals and to less adventurous travelers. Head instead to the café, the bakery, the market or the *traiteur* (delicatessen) when hunger strikes.

The bakery lunch

Bakeries propose a variety of sandwiches along with small quiches, meat- or cheese-filled puff pastries, and other savory picnic possibilities, which you can ask them to warm in the microwave if necessary. *Traiteurs* additionaly propose handsome arrays of prepared dishes that can be warmed up before taken to the nearest bench.

Side-street bakeries may have a very limited sandwich list that goes no further than the classic ham and butter (*jambon-beurre*) or ham, cheese and butter (*jambon-gruyère-beurre*), often heavy on the butter and light on the ham. Otherwise you'll also find sandwiches with chicken (*poulet*), tuna (*thon*), *pâté*, camembert or other cheeses, sliced sausage (*saucisson*) or egg-lettuce-tomato (*crudités*). Butter is the traditional condiment of choice on ham and sliced sausage sandwiches, mayonnaise on chicken and tuna.

The café lunch

Cafés typically serve meal-size salads as well as simple hot dishes such as pork, beef or chicken with sautéed potatoes or fries, including the classic *steak-frites* and *poulet-frites*. The choice of steak for the steak-frites often includes sirloin (*faux-filet*) or ribsteak (*entrecôte*). Be sure to understand the tips on doneness indicated earlier before ordering. The *croque monsieur* (a grilled ham and cheese sandwich) and the *croque madame* (same with an egg on top) are other café standards. Basic baguette sandwiches are also served.

Cafés typically begin serving lunch at or shortly before noon and will serve until about 2/2:30pm. Larger cafés and café-brasseries may serve to 3pm or beyond, and it may be possible to have a *croque* or a sandwich at any time. Between 1 and 2 pm the crowds and the pace of waiters can make entering a café intimidating. Be bold. In the crush you'll be thrown a menu and expected to decipher by yourself the name of the dish of the day (*le plat du jour*). (Actually, cafés in well-traveled quarters often have English translations on the menu.) When the rush hits, waiters, low on patience to begin with, are likely to ignore hesitant clients. A firm *s'il vous plaît* is required to get their attention.

The Culinary Aphorisms of Brillat-Savarin

Anthelme Brillat-Savarin (1755-1826) is one of the great names in French gastronomy. Though he managed to make a full political career in an era of revolution and counterrevolution – lawyer, judge, politician, expatriate (lived in New York during the Terror, from 1794-1796), then military and governmental official – literary and gastronomic fame came with the publication of his Physiology of Taste *(1825), the culmination of lifelong epicurean interests. Today Brillat-Savarin is known for his culinary aphorisms and for a creamy cheese from Normandy that takes his name. Here are some of his aphorisms:*

La destinée des nations dépend de la manière dont elles se nourrissent.
The destiny of nations depends on the way they feed themselves.

Ceux qui s'indigèrent ou qui s'enivrent ne savent ni boire ni manger.
Those who get indigestion or who get drunk don't know how to drink or eat.

Un dessert sans fromage est une belle à qui il manque un oeil.
Dessert without cheese is a beauty missing one eye.

Attendre trop longtemps un convive retardataire est un manque d'égards pour tous ceux qui sont présents.
To wait too long for a late table guest is a lack of respect for all those already present.

CAFÉS

There's a café for every mood and many moods for every café, depending on the weather, the time of day, the clientele, the view, the news and whether you want to watch the world go by or ignore the world completely.

You enter and sit where you wish. Sooner or later the waiter will come by to take your order. Efficiency is what it's all about for the café waiter; he doesn't like hesitation. If he senses you aren't ready he may say that he'll give you a minute, but he may just walk away. When he stops by again he will hear your order and possibly turn away again without a word. Parisians are accustomed to this and don't consider it poor service.

The bill, a cash register receipt, will be brought with your order. Sometimes you may be asked to pay immediately, particularly if the waiter is going off duty, but more often he will walk away after setting the bill under the ashtray, and you will pay him (rather than the person at the counter) when you are ready – sometimes when he's ready.

There is one price for standing at the counter and another price, 30-40% higher, for a seat inside or outside on the terrace. Therefore you may not order at the counter and then take your drink to a table. Prices are posted at the entrance, so there should be no surprises. Prices in popular cafés may also go up 50 cents or so after 10pm, which will also be indicated. Do verify the bill and count your change. Despite their impersonal service, Parisian waiters are not known for dishonesty, but the fact remains that foreigners are easy targets in every country.

You can order bottled fruit juices, freshly squeezed juices, wine by the glass, mineral water, tea, hot chocolate, alcohol, liquors and much else in a café. Yet the most common beverages are coffee and beer.

• Coffee: Straight espresso coffee, though not as strong as Italian or Turkish coffee, can seem harsh if you're not accustomed to it. Order *café allongé* (pronounced allo[n]-jai) to have the shot of espresso stretched out with hot water. *Café noisette* (pronounced nwa-zette) adds a nip of milk to an espresso, often served on the side. *Café au lait* or *café crème*, which Americans have come to call latte, will add a large volume of steamed milk.

• Beer: Beer – *bière* – is another major staple of café life.

Draught beer is *une bière pression*, typically sized as *un demi*, representing a quarter liter or about half a pint. When a tourist simply requests *une bière*, calculating waiters in central cafés sometime reply, "Large or small?" or merely "Large?" in the hopes that you will supersize the bill in a single order. Germans and Brits rarely blink an eye when the oversized beer glass arrives at the table, but since there isn't much savings with a "large" when compared with a couple of *demis*, and since one or two small cool (never frosted) beers are preferable to one large lukewarm beer, you might as well specify *un demi pression* from the start. Two other common draught beer beverages are *une panaché*, the true light beer or shandy, in which a light lemonade is freshly added to the beer, and *un monaco*, which is a *panaché* sweetened with a dash of grenadine. Bottled beer is *bière en bouteille*.

See *Hotels/Breakfast* concerning a café breakfast.

Everyone's a critic

Returning home from Paris without good food stories shows a lack of appetite, imagination or interesting company. You may not rave about every place you eat, but when the trip is over and Paris's art and architecture have been left far behind, everyone goes home a restaurant critic. So welcome to the club! I'd enjoy hearing your comments on any of the restaurants suggested in this book. Feel free to send your own review detailing your restaurant experience(s). Please be as specific as possible: dates, times, what ordered, how served, where seated, how you appreciated or couldn't stand your dinner companions. Good food stories – don't go home without them!

Send your comments to reviews@parisrevisited.com.

Your Restaurant Itinerary

Date	Restaurant	Dress Code	Time

Pages are reserved at the back of this book for you to write your own reviews.

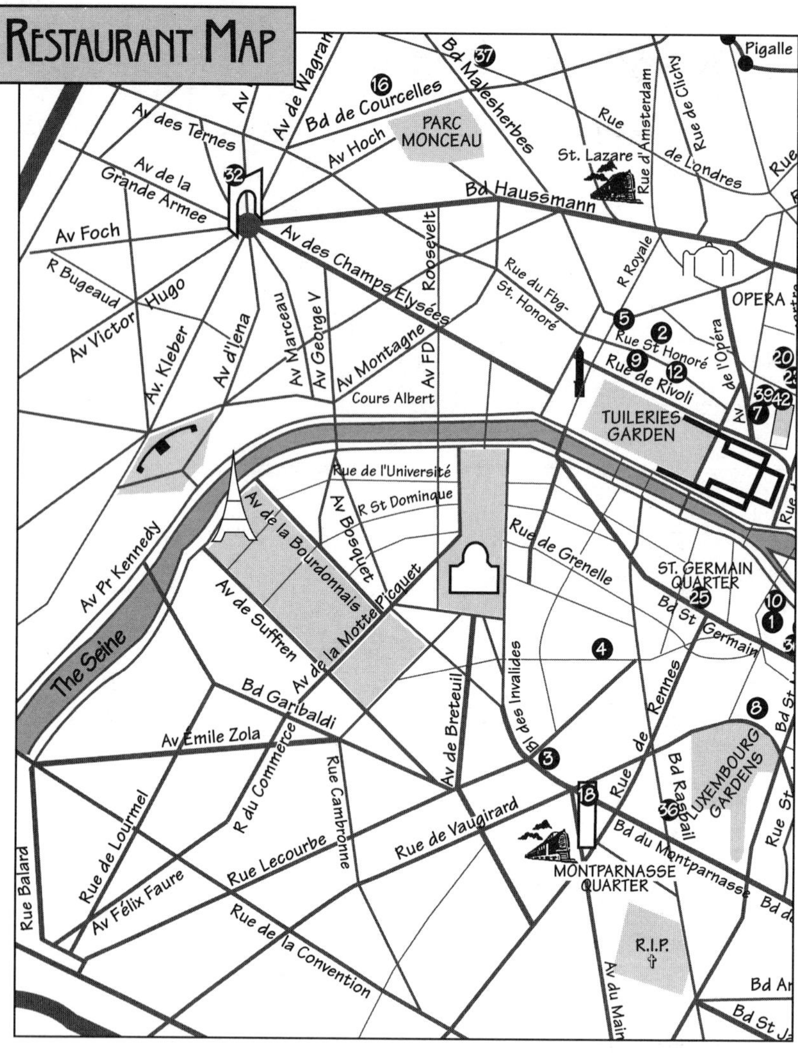

Gastronomical
1 Relais Louis XIII
2 Le Céladon
3 Le Maxence
4 Le Bamboche
5 Goumard
6 L'Aiguière

Central and Polished
7 Le Poquelin
8 La Bastide Odéon
9 L'Ardoise, Le Soufflé
10 Les Bookinistes, Ze Kitchen Galerie
11 Le Dôme du Marais
12 Marché Saint-Honoré

Wider Horizons
13 Le Villaret
14 Le Repaire de Cartouche
15 L'Oulette
16 Les Messugues
17 La Boulangerie
18 Le Ciel de Paris

Bistros
19 La Poule au Pot
20 Mellifère
21 Allard

Brasseries
22 Bofinger
23 Le Grand Colbert
24 Julien, Brasserie Flo
25 Le Petit Zinc

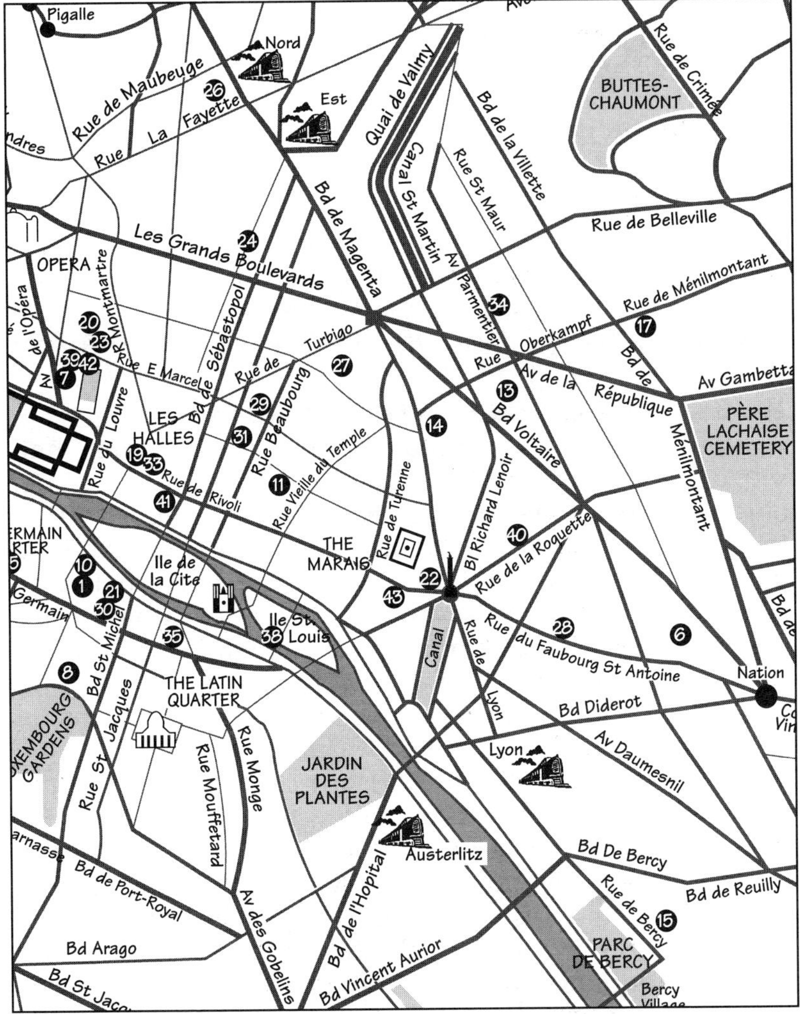

Regional Restaurants
26 Chez Michel
27 Au Bascou
28 Paris-Main d'Or
29 Ambassade d'Auvergne
30 Maison de la Lozère

Foreign Restaurants
31 A la Mexicaine
32 Graindorge
33 Saudade
34 Kasaphani
35 Fogón St-Julien
36 Dominique
37 L'Epicerie Russe
38 Isami
39 Baan Boran
40 Blue Elephant

Wine Restaurants
41 Le Robe et Le Palais
42 Willi's Wine Bar, Aux Bons Crus
43 Vins des Pyrénées

RESTAURANTS

GASTRONOMICAL

❶ Relais Louis XIII

Address *8 rue des Grands-Augustins, 6th arr.* ***Metro*** *Odéon or St-Michel.* ***Tel*** *01 43 26 75 96 •* ***Fax*** *01 44 07 07 80* ***Site*** *www.relaislouis13.com* ***Menu*** *45€(L), 69€ (D, except Sat.), tasting menu 89€ (D).* ***ALC*** *85-98€* ***Wine list*** *First-rate Closed Sun., Mon., 3 weeks in Aug.* ***Dress code*** *Dress up.*

Traditional French gastronomic heaven

Where better to begin our restaurant exploration than with a traditional view of French gastronomic heaven – a culinary paradise in the Saint Germain quarter. Though Relais Louis XIII ranks up there with the best of them, this is far from the most talked about of fine restaurants in Paris, not having the necessary chic or gloss for that. It is instead home to the kind of classic high gastronomic dining that institutions are made of. It's no surprise that prior to opening here in 1996 Manual Martinez was head chef at Paris's most famous restaurant institution, La Tour d'Argent.

As a restaurant, Relais Louis XIII certainly doesn't have the history or renown of La Tour d'Argent, yet it, too, gives the impression of having been here for centuries. The setting has much to do with that: the vaulted cellar, remnant of the convent of the Grands Augustins that occupied this entire quarter in the Middle Ages (see the male and female chastity belts displayed beneath one of the arches); the wood-beamed, stone-walled main room where, in 1610, the 9-year-old dauphin was proclaimed King Louis XIII following the assassination of his father Henri IV; the high-ceilinged upstairs dining room with a painting of Louis XIII on horseback at one end.

The likeable dining-room staff, beginning with Véronique Martinez, has a warm presence that is sometimes absent in other restaurants of this category where service tends to keep the professional distance preferred by European aristocrats but not by American dentists.

Having tasted Chef Martinez's preparations as part of a celebratory party of 10 and as part of a well-traveled party of 5 and having sent other happy guinea pigs here, I've never heard praise of the restaurant toned down by criticism. For some that may suggest a lack of risk-taking, but it seems to me to be moreover a reflection of this restaurant's even-keeled integrity, without prices going into the stratosphere.

There's richness to the appetizers, e.g. flaky pastry of asparagus and Dublin bay prawns and raviolis of lobster, foie gras and a juice of creamed cèpe mushrooms. There are subtleties to the highly classic main courses, e.g. wild turbot steak, rack and saddle of lamb, breast of duck with confite leg. There is a delicate flourish to the vanilla *mille-feuille* with whiskey cream and the pear and cream-of-almond soufflé.

By the end of the meal you nearly want to congratulate yourself for having ordered so well, just as my friend L. congratulated me for having chosen her as my dinner companion to the aforementioned celebration. I congratulated myself – for then she owed me one.

❷Le Céladon

Address *15 rue Danou, 2nd arr. Entrance also via the Hôtel Westminster, 13 rue de la Paix.* **Metro** *Opéra*
Tel *01 47 03 40 42* • **Fax** *01 42 61 33 78* **Site** *www.leceladon.com*
Open *Mon.-Fri. On Sat. and Sun. the setting changes names and menus to become Le Petit Céladon, a hotel restaurant serving less gastronomic fare. This review, therefore, concerns only the weekday ambiance and fare.*
Menu *45€, including wine and coffee (L), 59€ (D), tasting menu 100€ (D).* **ALC** *75-100€.* **Dress code** *Dress up.* **Cocktail hour** *The English bar at the Hôtel Westminster, Harry's Bar, The Ritz, Hôtel de Vendôme.*

A drawing room for grace, subtlety, texture

In lesser restaurants, dishes with lengthy titles are merely intended to impress, but in a restaurant of outstanding gastronomy such as this the full titles offer both a challenge to our own imagination and a dare to the chef himself: Can he pull it off? The mere fact of trying to decipher *la caille de Dombes supreme confisée et poêlée à la truffe d'été, cuisse en gelée de Xérès* or *les encornet braises et farcis à la compote de poivrons, coulis de tomates, rouelle d'oignons frits* is among the preliminary pleasures of the dining experience as we try first to understand the words, then to fathom their savory promise. Those terms that are somewhat easier to comprehend — e.g. *saint Pierre piqué et marine au romarin, brochette de legumes, jus gras* — can nearly be tasted on the page.

Given the mix of promise, challenge and dare that is essential to a fine restaurant adventure, having the right company is of utmost importance. My companion this evening, then, is L., a French trademark lawyer specializing in fashion and perfume, whom no one can accuse of being unprepared to weigh in on the struggle between good taste and bad. To fortify ourselves for the task ahead we've arrive after a healthy drink at Harry's Bar a block away (see *Bars*). We are led to the second of Le Céladon's succession of three quietly ornate drawing rooms that are done up in the ashen yellow-green tone of Celadon vases. Showcase windows between the rooms open up the space and display the restaurant's collection of namesake ceramic glazed vases.

L. finds the temperature in the restaurant a bit cold this summer evening, which I attribute to the sudden change in weather rather than to true failure on the part of the restaurant. Then I realize that she has confused my invitation to test a classy restaurant with going on a date, for what L. really wants is for me to sit closer. Instead, seating is spacious here, with only three or four tables in each drawing room, for a total seating of 40. That makes Le Céladon an ever-so-pleasant venue for dinner among two or three couples. But if, as L. eventually confesses, "a truly romantic restaurant should make you want to ravish your date on the table," then either she has watched "Pretty Woman" one too many times or this restaurant (or at least L. and I) cannot be considered romantic. Probably both — if not all three.

> **"A truly romantic restaurant should make you want to ravish your date on the table."**

The unaffected staff is so kindly, attentive and informative, the head waiter so precise in his explanations (for one eventually gives up on deciphering the menu and asks questions) and the sommelier so clear in his advice, that L. is beginning to wonder if I'm famous. I'm not. They are merely good at their jobs. And we can taste immediately from the appetizers that chef Christophe Moisand is, too: the quail (*caille*) is both delicate and pronounced; the ginger-tinged crab (*tourteau au parfum de gingembre*), presented as a handsome spring roll, is both tangy and refined.

Yet it is with the main course the M. Moisand truly takes up the gauntlet. In person and in preparations, M. Moissand, a young chef who came to lead Le Céladon's gastronomic challenges after 9 years at the Meurice, presents the reserved confidence that is so attractive in a stellar chef. His preparations are noteworthy for their grace and subtlety and texture. When the ingredients are of highest quality and the timing is perfect, as here, the lobes of warm foie gras served with young turnips and braised girolle mushrooms melt in the mouth. The lamb accompanied by a hint of smoked mozzarella — otherwise known this evening as *noisette farcie à la mozzarella fumée, feuilleté à l'oignon et à la tomate* — is a mix of savors in which, like romance, you can approach as a collection of distinct sensations or pursue as a whole. One effect of a successful dish with a long title is that you want to have another look at the menu to see what, precisely, you've just eaten... and to imagine what you haven't.

Desserts, such as roast peach with nectar of blackcurrant or panful of strawberries with warm chocolate-covered blinis and mint-leaf ice cream, are less subtle, yet as appealing as they sound.

Coffee and sweets, brandy and good laughs, so ends another successful battle for the right restaurant for the right occasion with the right company. As for romance, once outside L. feigns a shiver in the cool summer night and says, "The least you could do is hold me close," to which I take her arm and reply, "The least you could do is thank me for getting you out of the house," the two of us already bantering like a good couple.

❸Le Maxence

Address *9 bis boulevard du Montparnasse, 6th arr.* ***Metro*** *Duroc.*
Tel *01 45 67 24 88* • ***Fax*** *01 45 67 10 22.*

Open *Daily.* ***Menu*** *35€ (L),* ***Tasting menu*** *60€ (D).* ***ALC*** *60-70€.* ***Wines*** *Mostly 40-60€, along with a choice selection of pricier Burgundy and Bordeaux; reasonably-priced Champagne list.* ***Dress code*** *Sophisticated casual or business attire.*

Northern France deliciously revisited

David Van Laer knows that in order to revisit tradition you must have one foot firmly planted somewhere, in this case in the traditions of northern France. M. Van Laer is from Roubaix, near the Belgian border. From there he uses the other foot to step in many directions for a touch of whimsy, a dash of an unexpected herb or oil, a splash of beer, a marriage of bitter and sweet, sweet and sour. His is a restrained revisitation, as would befit this exceedingly cultivated quarter, yet a delicious revisitation it is.

My dinner companion this midwinter evening is less satisfied. I should say before going further that JM is wary of anyplace where they hold your seat out for you. There are people who have a difficult time enjoying a meal beyond the price of a decent bistro, and JM is one such person. He likes and knows good food and good wine when served at someone's home or in a restaurant in the provinces, but he is constantly focused on Paris prices. It's as though he were obliged to use his credit card as a spoon and then finds that everything tastes like plastic. We all know people like this. Don't go to gastronomic restaurants with them.

I recognize my mistake in bringing him here immediately, by the wary way in which he gives up his coat at the entrance. I know I'm in trouble when he responds to my appreciation of the décor of saffron yellow and autumn leaves by saying "Very '90s."

The 50-seat restaurant (opened in '99) is divided into three distinct sections: the entrance section with a large round table for group dining; the central, main central dining room which is also a wide hallway that requires the waiters to wind through a tight passage between two rows of tables; a back room that is preferable for romantic dining. The atmosphere is subdued but not hushed, suitable for normal conversation, though men's voices tend to carry when talking about food and wine, which is the French way of talking about money.

JM is a thorough critic, so his natural negativity does deserve a hearing. I respect his comment as to the mildness of his snail and frog appetizer, though some of the mildness was in fact a touch of refinement to what is otherwise sauce-heavy country fare. He would have been better off ordering the grilled prawns or the northern dish *presskopf,* in which lobster joins the traditional veal headcheese with a balsamic vinaigrette. My own duck foie gras served on spice bread and a light Chinese radish called *daïkon*, was an exquisite mix of sweet and savory, and even JM agreed.

Oftentimes in gastronomic restaurants, appetizers reflect the chef's sense of teamwork, while the main course demonstrates both his talent and passion. And so, M. Van Laer shows his abilities above all in the main course, as with the pigeon. When it doesn't live in the city, pigeon is a noble and refined bird with a delicate dark red flesh. It is one of the few dishes you needn't hesitate to pick up with your hands in an upscale

Tradition Revisited

The battle lines of the Parisian gastronomic wars have once again been drawn, with the camp of traditional French fare on the one side and the coalition of world cuisine on the other. At their worst the world restaurants will do anything to try to keep up with a trend (e.g. Y2K sushimania) and the traditionalists will find any excuse not to change. But at their best each it camp has something important to say—something delicious to offer.

This is the classic battle between the ancients and the moderns, and no other country fights that type of battle with more passion than France. That's one reason we love to revisit France. One of the pleasures of foreign travel is naturally to experience the traditions of a foreign country. I therefore give a clear edge in the selection of restaurants in this book to the ancients and traditionalist—not because I think they are always better than the moderns but because world food is easy enough to find back at home.

Being in touch with local, regional, or national traditions does not mean that such chefs or restaurants are stuck in a prior age. Within the camp of the ancients is a visible yet varied group called "tradition revisited" who proclaim that traditionalists are not necessarily retrograde and can in fact be downright progressive. Tradition revisited is currently one of the most widely used terms in French cooking. It is a rampart against world food yet open to winds of change. The term is overused in that some chefs apply it to their preparations though they merely replace a lemon by a lime or simply add a dash of curry to the leaks. Yet there are chefs, several of which are mentioned here, who keep one foot firmly rooted in regional French traditions while using the other foot to step—shyly or boldly—out of their grandmothers' clogs.

restaurant—a pleasure in itself. Served here with a woodcock sauce and accompanied by foie gras fritters called *cromesquis* (themselves a wonderful discovery), the dish is nothing short of finger-lickin' great.

Sometimes M. Van Laer lets tradition speak for itself, as with the enormous, hearty pork chop but—poor JM—the result here is perhaps too rustic and without heightened succulence to rave about. Again, I've no doubt that JM would have done better to consider one of the fish dishes, such as the grilled John Dory (*St. Pierre*) scented with vanilla and green pepper or the brill (*barbu*) herbed with smoked tea or the cod sauced with beer. But you can't tell a Frenchman how to order.

Desserts could use a bit more fantasy, but you can't go wrong with the warm soufflé with Grand Marnier or the chocolat passion or the cheese tray itself.

When JM tests a restaurant with me I offer a guarantee: if he isn't satisfied I'll pay. Tonight I paid. But since I was nearly fully satisfied I didn't mind. My feeling is that the prices are in keeping with M. Van Laer's current ambitions for Le Maxence, which are notable but not excessive. He is one step short of playing ball with the big boys, so this is a place to watch. With a bit more revisiting—and a less awkward layout—he may indeed head to the max.

❹Le Bamboche (Claude Colliot)

Address *15 rue de Babylone, 7th arr. Behind the Bon Marché department store.* ***Metro*** *Sèvres-Babylone.* ***Tel*** *01 45 49 14 40*
Fax *01 45 49 14 44.* ***E-mail*** *claudecolliot@wanadoo.fr* ***Open*** *Mon.-Fri.*
Tasting menu *57€* ***Lunch menu*** *26€ (2 courses), 32€ (3 courses)*
ALC *50-55€* ***Wine*** *27€ and up* ***Cocktail hour*** *In the red plush armchairs and couches of the lobby bar at the Hôtel Lutetia (45 bd. Raspail) or at the wine bar/café Au Sauvignon (80 rue des Saints-Pères).*

Delightful discovery for the palate

Claude Colliot's oyster ice cream (*glace d'huître*) appetizer is no longer confidential information, but it—along with nearly everything else served in this tiny Left Bank gastronomic treasure chest—is still a discovery. The oyster ice cream is a creamy mix of about a dozen heady appellation oysters of Isigny, Normandy, surrounded by an emulsion of verbena, delivering the potency of an aphrodisiac from Atlantis. It's no wonder that my dinner companion, L., insisted that I order it, for not only is it an oyster-lover's dream come true but, she hoped, hers, too. Her own raw prawns with a lemony thyme cream offered flat-spoonfuls of sensuality. It wasn't long before we were dipping into each other's dish as though it were some form of foreplay.

What appears at first to be a cold modern restaurant with an oddly intimate edge soon proves itself to be one of the most enchanting places in the capital. The quartet of businessmen at the next table—two Scandinavians, an American and a

Frenchman—appeared equally enchanted as they delighted in their own iodized ice cream and raw prawns and what must have been some warm and creamy foie gras, to judge by the expression of one of the Scandinavians. Businessmen do not particularly appreciate being seen as "delighted," much less "enchanted," so I tried not to notice, but they were seated just behind L. and she was in such ecstasy over the appetizers that I had trouble looking her in the eye.

M. and Mme. Colliot, meanwhile, have got their own harmony working. While Claude Colliot articulates his self-taught savoir-faire in the kitchen, Chantal Colliot lays the groundwork for gastronomic adventures with expressive and attentive service in the two miniscule dining rooms of their 32-seat restaurant. To begin with, her sage wine advice steered us within the selection of wines from the Loire Valley to a well-priced Sancerre Château de Tauvenay that amiably accompanied the varied savors of our meal.

What appears at first to be a cold modern restaurant with an oddly intimate edge soon proves itself to be one of the most enchanting places in the capital.

You needn't be an oyster-eating swashbuckler to enjoy Claude Colliot's preparation of first-rate ingredients. It doesn't take bravado to eat here, just an open mind, or palate. For our autumn test I chose the Discovery Menu, which offered a tasting of two familiar main courses—roast cod and panned veal, both cooked simply to perfection and served with choice, delicate vegetables—along with less familiar starters and finishers—a light cream of nestle soup, the oyster ice cream and for dessert a delicious napoleon (*mille-feuille*) of candied tomato with basil and mascarpone. After the prawns, L. regaled herself with center rib chops of lamb served with girolle mushrooms and bits of apricot, before offering me half of her roast fig dessert. Afterwards, we dipped spoons into the amusingly romantic chocolate and cream post-dessert served in egg shells on a portion of an egg box.

By then the four businessmen were also on dessert. There seemed to be no sharing going on as far as I could politely see. But who knows how their evening ended!

❺Goumard

Address *9 rue Duphot, 1st arr.* ***Metro*** *Madeleine*
Tel. *01 42 60 36 07 •* ***Fax*** *01 42 60 04 54.****Open*** *Daily.* ***ALC*** *65-135€.*

Quality fish restaurant excelling in simplicity

Simplicity in a fish and seafood restaurant, however subtle, studied or deceptive it may be, begins with the quality of the catch. At Goumard that quality itself can be tasted. Their buyers have impeccable taste when it comes to selecting rod-caught bass, scallops, oysters, red mullet, sea bass, Dover sole, turbot, frog legs, prawns—which pretty much sums up the menu. The addition of truffles, lobster or caviar accounts for the upper edges of the price range noted above, as in the appetizer of carpaccio of scallops with caviar or the main course of sea bass with black truffles.

The quality of the fish and seafood is underscored by the minimalism of the preparations, from the light fry of the tempura prawns to the gentle grilling of the bass or monkfish lain gently on a futon of vegetables, and onto the rhubarb dessert. Those diners who seek crafty surprises in this price range might read such minimalism as a caution. What can be delightfully subtle to some will seem overly restrained to others. There's always the cheese tray to more fully rouse the senses.The delicious stewed sole in a veal sauce served with spatzle seems to hit just the right note.

I appreciate a good laugh in a gastronomic restaurant; people do tend to be a bit morose in such settings, so it's nice to know people are enjoying themselves and not just taking notes. But...

The clean-cut 1920s dining rooms reinforce the impression of pure waterways and create a classy setting for an evening among friends or business companions. Our party of five was of the former sort, a gathering of dear friends freshly arrived in Paris and staying in one of the area's many luxury hotels. We had the misfortune of being seated beside an oversized gathering of the latter sort, a group of a dozen international businessmen communicating in what the Americans and Germans apparently believed to be the international language of such dinners, hearty laughter, though their Japanese colleagues, despite profuse nodding, may not have agreed.

I appreciate a good laugh in a gastronomic restaurant; people do tend to be a bit morose in such settings, so it's nice to know people are enjoying themselves and not just taking notes. But the noise level of the business table grew beyond the range of what one might expect in a restaurant otherwise dedicated to tidy harmony. The business table didn't actually lessen the companionability of our happy reunion, however, the size of their group and their frequent habit of raising a finger to the waiter led the staff, which had been attentive and serene when we first arrived, to become harried and impatient... with us. Nevertheless, I'm willing to give Goumard the benefit of the doubt on accounts of both the noise and the frustrated service, though next time I will either ask to be seated in the smaller dining room or come with a larger group myself.

Actually, I forgive the disturbance thanks to the sommelier. Other than knowing wine, the greatest task of the sommelier is to be alert to clients' needs and desires, and here we found a most alert sommelier to guide us to the right vineyard, twice.

❻L'Aiguière

Address *37 bis rue de Montreuil, 11th arr.* ***Metro*** *Faidherbe-Chaligny.* ***Tel*** *01 43 72 42 32 •* ***Fax*** *01 43 72 96 30* ***E-mail*** *patrick.masbatin1@libertysurf.fr* ***Closed*** *Sat. lunch, Sun.* ***Menu*** *23€ (L), 29€, 48€, 58€.* ***ALC*** *47-63€.* ***Dress code*** *Sophisticated casual to dress up, depending on your mood.*

Cozy, elegant dining at a sensible price

L'Aiguière awaits on a street beyond the Bastille that's otherwise known for nothing much at all. The fact that the restaurant stands in front of the remnants of the 17th-century barracks built for Louis XIII's Black Musketeers (black being the color of their horses) is nothing but a factoid. The evening quiet of the street and the inconspicuous façade of L'Aiguière may well make you wonder if you've come to the right address. But push open the door and you'll be immediately reassured by the grace of the décor—yellow and blue Gustavian style reminiscent of Scandinavian seaside luxury—and of the welcome.

Patrick Masbatin commands his young staff in the dining room with a firm hand that weakens only when he must call upon them to assist him with English-speaking diners. Meanwhile, chef Pascale Viallet keeps up his end of this enduring restaurant team along with his assistants in the kitchen. While high gastronomy requires more studied dishes prepared with more delicacy and complexity (hence a larger staff), M. Viallet performs valiant feats of most honorable fine cuisine. His passion for the art will be further evident should you ask to speak with him after the meal, something he is often happy to do, in English.

L'Aiguière proposes classic gastronomy with an edge of chef's passion. Service is gentle, with some charming awkwardness. The setting is romantic enough for 2, relaxed enough for 3-5; it lends itself to a wine-and-dine lovefest for a table of 6-8 leisure or business travelers; there's a handsome private room for a celebratory gathering of 10-14.

The 48€ menu known as the "*menu accord des mets et des vins*," meaning it marries each course with a different glass of wine, offers an excellent selection of food and drink at a sensible price. That menu is served only for the entire table. At 58€ the same menu further includes a good whiff of the cheese cart and its companion wine. With or without cheese, the marriage menu is in such fine tune with the surroundings and service that there may well be no need to read on.

One reason to venture à la carte is the quality of the foie gras dishes, such as the foie gras duo appetizer or the main course tournados Yella. The latter is a classic dish of late-19th-century luxury, in which a thick tenderloin is topped with a melting slab of foie gras. (Tournados Rossini, which is not served here, adds truffles to that dish.)

One reason to venture à la carte is the quality of the foie gras dishes

There's also a 4-course *formule gustavienne* which is so economical for the setting that you may feel you should be spending more just because you bothered to get dress up and come out this way. In that case you can always add drinks and wine, for M. Masbatin is a master sommelier who knows how to find quality (and profit margin) in wine. Order a bottle and it may be served in an *aiguière*, a stylish pitcher with nice lips, a ewer—as in ewer gonna like it here.

Food People

Epicures: *Epicures are exceptional connoisseurs of pleasure, luxury and/or sensuality, generally relative to food and drink. Their storehouse of knowledge and experience give them sensitive and discriminating tastes. For instance, an epicure knows how to stick his nose deep into a glass of red wine, but he sometimes does it in a way that makes a non-epicure want to rub his face in it.*

Gourmets: *Gourmets may be less refined than epicures but have educated palates nonetheless. A gourmet certainly knows food and fully grasps the meaning of words like "braised" and "Conran." Though a gourmet need not know how to cook, the word gourmet is frequently used to qualify someone's cooking skills, as a gourmet chef.*

Foodies: *Foodies can be more faddish than gourmets, but they can also be more joyous and passionate. They're the Trekkies of the food chain, and when they congregate, as they tend to do, they have a fondness for citing their favorite recipes from* Bon Appetit *and for making inside jokes such as: "They say you shouldn't watch the Food Network within two hours of going to sleep." Foodies visit foreign food markets the way others visit museums, checking out the name of the legume on the price card then stepping back to comment: "Arugala, I thought so."*

Gastronomes: *Gastronomes are close to epicures in that they have a wealth of food knowledge and dining experience that give them discerning tastes. They are enthusiasts, fond of judging and comparing, and can thus be name-droppers when it comes to fine restaurants. Though not necessarily snobs, gastronomes have been known to miss out on the social sensuality and pleasure of the dining experience.*

Connoisseurs: *From the French word literally meaning "one who knows." When a connoisseur knows how to keep his abundance of knowledge in check, he's a welcome guest. His ability to appreciate subtleties in his field can make for informative and entertaining company. Some connoisseurs, however, make sure that the conversation is dominated by their expertise, which then also makes them bores. A wine connoisseur, for example, can come in handy when it comes to choosing wine, as long as he doesn't make wine the sole topic of conversation for the evening.*

Mavens: *Mavens are generally highly educated people with a specific expertise, which makes them excellent company... for a book. Unfortunately, in public they seem to believe that because*

they are an expert in one thing they are an expert in everything, including everything on the menu and every topic of conversation.
Gluttons: *Gluttons, given to immoderate consumption, are voracious and wolfish eaters and drinkers. Some gourmets and connoisseurs are actually closet gluttons, using their intellectual interest in good food and wine as a cover for a greedy appetite.*
Gourmands: *A gourmand has a good appetite and may also have discerning tastes, but since the strength of his appetite is greater than his need to discern he won't turn his nose up at anything. Not gluttonous but occasionally given to excess, he can make for entertaining company and may well be married to a gourmet.*
Bons vivants: *Literally "ones who live well," the term refers to those with a healthy, lively appetite for the finer things in life, particularly food and drink. They sometimes calm down after their first heart attack.*

CENTRAL AND POLISHED

❼Le Poquelin

Address *17 rue Molière, 1st arr.* **Metro** *Palais Royal or Pyramides.* **Tel** *01 42 96 22 10* • **Fax** *01 42 96 05 72* **Open** *Lunch Mon.-Fri., dinner Mon.-Sat.* **Menu** *25€ (L), 32€.* **ALC** *40-48€. Wines Modestly priced.* **Dress code** *Nice casual or business.*

When you've got a taste for the classics

The work of the actor and playwright Molière (1622-1673), alias of Jean-Baptiste Poquelin, is the cornerstone of the Comédie Française, France's premier national theater, which is down the street from this gracious little restaurant. A sculpture of the great Classical playwright sits nearby at the fork in the road. Le Poquelin pays homage to the man and to the classics in general through the modest elegance of its décor, its sketches of actors and theatrical drapes, and its ageless cuisine.

Michel and Maggy Guuillaumin's kind welcome has its own longevity, undimmed after nearly a quarter century of service. With an edge of refinement to some dishes and a rustic flair to others, all is reliable, prepared and served with a steady hand. The fixed-price menus are well grounded (and well priced) from start to finish: blue cheese in a puff pastry, potato pâté, duck terrine with foie gras, steamed ray fish, roast cod, duckling, leg of lamb, chocolate mouse, thin warm apple tart. For a bit more sparkle to the classics, however, you might venture à la carte to starters of salmon and tuna marinade or various foie gras specialties, followed by sole, turbot, tuna, veal kidneys, or beef tenderloin.

L. works nearby and comes here with clients whom she doesn't have to overly impress and as a treat to her staff in lieu of a raise. I occasionally join the latter because L. believes that if her expense account is good enough for her secretaries then it's good enough for me. She only invites me here for lunch, when the atmosphere is business proper, but seating is cozy without being tight, so romance is not out of the question. In fact, L. is sure, she tells me, that those who come for dinner are making passionate love afterwards. Her way of saying that I pay for our next meal.

❽ La Bastide Odéon

Address *7 rue Corneille, 6th arr.* ***Metro*** *Odéon.*
Tel *01 43 26 03 65 •* ***Fax*** *01 44 07 28 93.* ***Open*** *Tues.-Sat.* ***Menu/ALC*** *36€ (3 courses), 30€ (2 courses).* ***Wines*** *Mostly 25-30€.* ***Dress*** *Casual.*

Smoothly Provençal

I could just declare La Bastide Odéon a most reliable and highly pleasing choice of a restaurant with strong Provençal biases, an easy walk from many Left Bank hotels, and leave it at that.

But I can't.

M., a visiting conductor, and I have come as spies, come not only to test the food but to see how they respond to people from New Jersey. As good American spies we pretend that we only speak our native tongue. I hold up two fingers to indicate that we've come in peace and have reserved for two. But then the waiter takes all the fun out of it and asks us in English to wait a moment, and then a moment later another waiter comes over and invites us, again in the language of CNN, to follow him to our table. It's as though someone had tipped them off that Americans might be coming to the Saint Germain Quarter!

We're led to comfortable armchairs at a roomy table and given menus in English, albeit with just enough spelling mistakes to make it authentic (though there's always the possibility that those are British spellings). We don't even get to feel annoyed by being relegated to the lesser dining rooms, because both the ground floor room and the larger upstairs room are equally desirable. This is too easy, we decide. And wondering if perhaps our New Jersey accents are too pure and easy to understand, we conspire to weaken our tongues and undermine our speech.

We order a drink that way, but are fully understood.

So we order another.

We slur further as we order our meal, but except for a slight leaning forward on the part of the waiter to be sure that he has indeed understood he doesn't let on that we are anything but intelligible.

We plot then to send back the wine just to see how they respond to the proverbial scene. Then we remember that we've already had two drinks (and one in a café beforehand, there being no sense in meeting a friend in the St. Germain Quarter if not at a café) and haven't ordered wine in the first place.

As it turns out, there is nothing to send back because everything is well prepared and well presented. To start, an artichoke heart topped with goat cheese and a warm *millefeuille* of grilled eggplant. To show its southeastern leanings, La Bastide Odéon also offers pasta and gnocchi as appetizers and main courses. The grilled tuna with sweet peppers is then admirable, though the red snapper swam in a tad too much cream sauce—thereby creating a slight regret that one of us didn't order the squid and chorizo with hot peppers.

Snapper sauce aside, one might even say Bravo!, these people know how to treat a traveler from New Jersey. One might even applaud the fact that everyone who takes a reservation these days speaks English. Sometimes, though, we miss the days when you'd think you were ordering chicken and get veal kidneys instead. The closest we come to that this evening is having a baked apple topped with rhubarb arrive at the table and momentarily wonder whether we've been served another artichoke heart topped with goat cheese because both dishes appear to come from the same mold. But it was indeed dessert, and rather good at that.

Bravo!, these people know how to treat a traveler from New Jersey.

Lest you think that the ease of speaking English here means that this is an American or tourist restaurant, I note that there is plenty of French around to drown out the more familiar accents. It just so happens that there are a zillion hotels in the area. In any case, the distance between tables allows for private conversation.

Nowadays the only linguistic discovery left for Americans in the St. Germain quarter is one of nuance. So we linger at the table trying to name the reddish color that underlies the parchment yellow of the décor. What is that red of the menu, the red of the waiters' vests, the red of the seat fabric, the red of the carpet upstairs, the red of the pastilles in the urinals? Blushing orange, Roland Garros red, old-Bordeaux-held-up-to-candlelight, Burlington brick, burnt cinnamon, tomato sauce mixed with virgin olive oil, late-October-leaves-at-the-Delaware-Water-Gap auburn?

Count on the waiter to spoil all the fun, for he has the perfect answer: "Red Provençal, sir," — adding "The red of Provence" to avoid any misunderstanding.

❾ L'Ardoise

Address *28 Mont-Thabor, 1st arr.* ***Metro*** *Tuileries or Concorde.*
Tel *01 42 96 28 18* ***Closed*** *Mon.-Tues.* ***Menu/Carte*** *29€.* ***Dress code*** *Casual.*

Le Soufflé

Address *36 rue du Mont-Thabor, 1st arr.* ***Metro*** *Tuileries or Concorde.*
Tel *01 42 60 27 19* ***Closed*** *Sun. Menu 29€, 36€.* ***Dress code*** *Casual or nice casual.*

Ask the concierge at any of the upend hotels congregating between the Opera and the Tuileries to suggest "a relaxed restaurant in the area where we can get a nice French dinner without to much fanfare" and chances are that his short list will include L'Ardoise. Especially on Sunday when many other restaurants are closed.

The menu/carte on the *ardoise* (slate, i.e. blackboard) proposes an extensive list of French classics, especially those from its Mediterranean edges, with much fish and seafood. The price is right and the fare is fine and the wine is modestly priced, so you can't go wrong. A wise choice for your first supper in Paris when staying in the area.

On Monday or Tuesday, when L'Ardoise is closed, the concierge may well suggest Le Soufflé. Le Soufflé has a cool, clean-cut atmosphere that is less casual than that of L'Ardoise, but it is enlivened by the amusement of so many soufflés being poked into around the room. Here you can enjoy three courses of soufflé or mix and match with other French classics.

Southeastern and Provencal Cuisine

While each of Europe's Mediterranean countries has its own references in matters of the kitchen, geographical commonalities naturally exist. This leads to extensive use of garlic, tomatoes, olive oil, peppers, Mediterranean fishes, zucchini and the range of herbs that, in France, get bottled with the label Herbes de Provence *(rosemary, thyme, bayleaf, basil, summery sages and occasionally other herbs). Fruity young red and rose wines regularly join the feast for moderate consumption.*

Rounding the Mediterranean you'll find steamed semolina for couscous (North Africa), rice for paella (Spain) or for risotto (Italy), not to mention pasta, yet the starch of choice in southern France remains the potato. The potato became a prime staple of French cuisine in the 18th century, after its cultivation and use was popularized by the economist and chemist Augustin Parmentier (1737-1813), and various spud dishes (along with a metro station) now bear his name.

Here are several other items that a traveler to France's southern shores or to Paris's southeastern/Provencal restaurants is sure to come upon:

Pastis · *France's version of the Mediterranean aniseed aperitif. Served in a tall glass to which one adds water, it is especially associated with sunny afternoons in a village square or overlooking a port or, in Paris, on a café terrace.*

Anchoyade · *An anchovy purée with garlic and olive oil, used as a bread spread. Also a sauce of the same ingredients.*

Tapanade · *A purée of black olives, capers and anchovies, served as an appetizer to be spread on bread.*

Aïoli · *A "mayonnaise"/sauce of olive oil and garlic. Also the name of a cold dish of boiled fish, potatoes and other vegetables served with that sauce.*

Brandade de morue · *A salted cod and garlic purée mixed with dashes of olive oil and cream.*

Salade niçoise · *Salad with tuna, lettuce, olives, onions, peppers, anchovies, and egg. Its sandwich version is the* pan-bagnat*, a tuna salad sandwich in a thick roll.*

⑩Les Bookinistes

Address *53 quai des Grands Augustins, 6th arr.* ***Metro*** *Odéon or St-Michel or Pont Neuf.* ***Tel*** *01 43 25 45 94 •* ***Fax*** *01 43 25 23 07.*
E-mail *bookinistes@guysavoy.com* ***Closed*** *Sun.* ***ALC*** *40€.*
Dress *Casual+.*

Ze Kitchen Galerie

Address *4 rue des Grands Augustins, 6th arr.* ***Metro*** *Odéon or St-Michel or Pont Neuf.* ***Tel*** *01 44 32 00 32 •* ***Fax 01 44 32 00 33. Closed*** *Sat. lunch, Sun.* ***ALC*** *40-43€.* ***Wines*** *20-40€.* ***Dress*** *Casual+.*

Left Bank contemporary

Les Bookinistes and Ze Kitchen Galerie—trendsetting Seine-side tourist-drawing restaurants par excellence—sit elbow to elbow on the Left Bank. Situated across the street from the august, antique restaurant Lapérouse, they are case studies in the evolution of the Paris restaurant scene in well-heeled, well-traveled quarters such as Saint-Germain.

Les Bookinistes got here first, its millennium reputation assured by glowing reports in U.S. publications, confident recommendations by Paris concierges and its association with stellar chef Guy Savoy. M. Savoy powers one of France's most reputable homes of high gastronomy at his eponymous restaurant near the Arc de Triomphe. When a chef so accomplished and enduring as Mr. Savoy opens a spin-off and places his name and reputation clearly in view, like a hand on the shoulder of the on-site chef, one naturally looks forward to mouthfuls of savvy and savor. Even factoring in the important element that a meal here will cost about a quarter of the price of his "real" restaurant, one naturally comes with expectations.

Expectation, of course, is a double-edged knife, one side to spread the sweet butter of trip-planning, the other side to cut yourself. Had B. and I been first-time travelers who just stumbled upon Les Bookinistes that rainy night during a stroll along the Seine, we might have felt soothed by the staff's professional welcome, comforted by the English menu, happy to be fed at 10pm. But it wasn't romantic spontaneity that brought it here, it was all the press.

Like many big-chef spin-offs, Les Bookinistes sets out to revisit tradition. It does so with a certain intelligence, nevertheless the recipes we tasted were a bit tired of the road. The sauces were well conceived and the presentation quite pretty. But a smart hand with sauce and herbs failed to cover the mere adequateness of the bass marinade or the duo of raw and smoked salmon, nor the ordinariness of the hogfish and the dryness of the guinea fowl. While the cheese course does no more than cover the lactate group, the chocolate tart did have the virtue of being served warm on this cool, rainy night.

Without expectations we might have found the food quite fair instead of merely safe. And the wait staff does a nice job at being present and English-friendly. Perhaps we were the only ones not fully enchanted. After all, the atmosphere was rather cheery, or so it seemed because of the high noise level.

Opening an attention-grabbing restaurant that can attract both tourists in this hotel-rich quarter and the trend-conscious Parisians who live or work in the neighborhood naturally involves a good deal of conceptual work. I doubt that such projects can begin to take form without the "right" name and I hear their choice—Les Bookinistes, Ze Kitchen Galerie—as a sophisticated form of self-mockery (your self, their selves) and a non-apology for being the trend-and-tourist places they are.

Expectation, however, is the breeding ground of disappointment.

Les Bookinistes refers to what the French call *les bouquinistes*, the second-hand book sellers visible across the street who work out of stalls along the Seine, *bouqin* being an informal word for book. The name is re-anglophied here, perhaps as a subliminal message to book early.

The kitchen at Ze Kitchen Galerie is visible behind a window in the back wall, where the white-clad staff appears like a multimedia work presented on a wide flat screen. Contemporary gallery-type works decorate the walls. As to the "Ze," it may be intended to remind us that although this restaurant follows in the footsteps of the New-Yorking of Paris and the globalization of trendy restaurants, it—and we—are indeed in France.

It was summer when L. and I tested Ze Kitchen Galerie, having waited for the spring hype of this new restaurant to calm down and for her boyfriend to be on vacation. On the way there we dawdled along the Pont Neuf, Paris's most romantic bridge, and were prepared to like anything by the time we arrived.

You should count on all the warmth coming from your own table (party of two to four) because, while some will come from the pleasant staff, none will come from the décor. It is the kind of décor the French call "*clean*": cool lighting, straight lines, office-style horizontal blinds, an absence of frou-frou. The plastic double placemats that decorate the brown tables are apparently an important details here, for why else would a restaurant put something on the table that is so obviously annoying to clean, annoying both for the staff, who must rub and rub to rid them of crumbs, and for us, who can't help but notice the rubbing process as though it were a neighbor's dog with fleas?

Having fully taken in the décor and the gracious vogue of the staff, we turned to the menu of Franco-world cuisine. It is apparently a point of honor for the creators here to include one unfamiliar term in each dish: nori seaweed, casareccia, "green-zebra" tomatoes, piperade, galango, wood of mara. We welcomed the surprise, but no sooner had we set to talking about being relatively single in summer than our first course emerged from ze kitchen, quickly followed by the second. The un-French-like speed was too fast for my taste, though those accustomed to quick dining or in less appealing company will find this in the restaurant's favor. (Dishes came out at a less hurried pace on a subsequent visit.)

Lest you think that my intent is to ridicule a trend, here's the kicker: without exception, each dish was tasty, interesting, satisfying: cold soup of Berlutti beans, calamari salad with "green-zebra" and "pineapple" tomatoes; tuna with grapefruit-ginger-kumquat, marinated duckling; nectarines with ginger and verbena-mango sorbet, white-chocolate-passion-coconut soup with wild strawberries and wood of mara. Whatever some of those ingredients were, ours was a smooth, well-balanced meal from start to finish. The culinary concept here may involve more chopping and mixing than baking and cooking (which would explain the speed), nonetheless a welcome addition to the Paris tablescape. Not a word of dissent from L., who'd been in the mood to agree with my every comment ever since she turned off her cell phone.

Exiting Ze Kitchen Galerie and walking past Les Bookinistes next door, we spotted none other than Chef Guy Savoy at a front corner table by the window, which is the gastronomist's equivalent of glimpsing Bruce Willis at Planet Hollywood: you want to apologize for having preferred the Schwartenegger film, even though you like him so much more.

These two restaurants are noteworthy above all for being up-to-date, Les Bookinistes looking to modernize traditional leisure, Ze Kitchen Galerie aiming to expand horizons, both convenient enough to satisfy travelers on their first evening in Paris when staying the Saint-Germain Quarter. Afterwards, a stroll along the Seine or across the Pont Neuf. The beauty of riverside Paris is never disillusioning.

⑪Le Dôme du Marais

Address *53 bis rue des Franc-Bourgeois, 4th arr.* ***Metro*** *Rambuteau or Hôtel de Ville.* ***Tel*** *01 42 74 54 17 •* ***Fax*** *01 42 77 78 17.* ***Closed*** *Sun., Mon., two weeks in Aug.* ***Menu*** *23€ (L) 28€, 38.50€.*

An architectural pleasure

Along with its many charms, the Marais is also known for the unexceptional quality of its food and service. For its moderate price range, Le Dôme is one of the more worthwhile restaurant experiences in the area. Were it only for the architectural pleasure of eating in the circular neo-Classical dining room beneath the grand dome, built in the late 18th century to house the official Pawnshop of Paris, I might recommend a moderately priced lunch or dinner here. As it turns out, the food is quite decent, the atmosphere relaxed and cheerful, and the service affable if sometimes harried, making this an attractive locale for an easygoing meal among friends.

Be sure to specifically request a table in the main room (i.e. beneath the dome). Several other tables occupy the glass-canopied entrance courtyard, which is pleasing enough, but there you're likely to feel left out.

The cuisine, while not gastronomic, does have a nicely thought out World-leaning French twist to reflect the originality of the architecture. For appetizers, chicory salad with dried fruit and Serrano ham, or avocado and salmon, or lemon-glazed scallops. For a main course, a tasty rabbit, duck fillet, or pollack (*lieu*). The range of desserts fill any remaining appetite well: grapefruit baked with chestnut honey, crispy banana rolls with ginger and banana sherbert, a dark chocolate trio. As a digestive, choose the stroll through the Marais.

⑫ Place du Marché Saint-Honoré for Lunch

Address *A pedestrian square around the block from Place Vendôme, 1st arr.* ***Metro*** *Tuileries or Concorde.*

You're sure to find yourself one touring day within the quadrangle formed by the Garnier Opera, the Madeleine, Place de la Concorde, the Palais Royal, the Louvre and the Tuileries Garden. Though these major sights and their neighboring shops and thoroughfares are close by, Place du Marché St-Honoré is frequently bypassed by travelers. Indeed, there's nothing here to see—but much to eat, served in a half-dozen bistros, cafés, and restaurants, and a pastry shop. As with L'Ardoise and Le Soufflé, described previously, these can be kept in mind for relaxed dining for those staying at hotels in the area. For others, I mention them as a lunch stop during your tour of the central Right Bank.

Sunny days bring the city business folk out to the café and restaurant terraces, while rainy days and winter bring with them a small-town atmosphere whereby one gladly lingers at the table. L'Absinthe and Bistrot St-Honoré are quite popular with the local business and shopping crowd, so reservations are recommended there at lunchtime, though no harm in just stopping by.

L'Absinthe ***Address*** *24 place du Marché St-Honoré.* ***Tel*** *01 49 26 90 04 •* ***Fax*** *01 49 26 08 64* ***Site*** *www.michelrostang.com* ***Closed*** *Sat. lunch, Sun.* ***Menu*** *25€ (2 courses), 30€ (3 courses).* Chef Michel Rostang's baby bistro is deservedly the most respected of the square's eateries. The preparations are polished by intelligent use of fresh produce, fish (roasted cod or pollock), meat (grilled veal or sirloin), olive oil, balsamic vinegar, and the right herbs. Pleasing desserts. A reasonable and readable wine list. Honorable service.

Bistro St-Honoré ***Address*** *10 rue Gomboust, at the northeast corner of the square. •* ***Tel*** *01 42 61 77 78 •* ***Fax*** *01 42 61 77 78.* ***Closed*** *Sat. dinner and Sun.* ***Menu*** *25€.* A relaxed downhome restaurant where the traditional cuisine and wines of Burgundy are served with kindness.

Flo Prestige ***Address*** *42 pl. du Marché St-Honoré*

The local outlet of this upscale caterer/pastry shop can set you up with a picnic lunch to be unwrapped in the Tuileries Garden, two blocks away.

⓭Le Villaret

Address *13 rue Ternaux, 11th arr.* ***Metro*** *Parmentier or Oberkampf.* ***Tel*** *01 43 57 89 76 or 01 43 57 75 56.* ***Closed*** *Sat. lunch, Sun., most of Aug.* ***Tasting menu*** *46€.* ***Lunch menu*** *25€.* ***ALC*** *33-42€.* ***Wine list*** *Extensive.* ***Dress*** *casual.*

Where gourmands gather in happy anticipation

Le Villaret's got buzz—and it has for 10 years now. Not the buzz of hype but the buzz of gourmandise, the promise and enjoyment of good food and drink. We sense it in the way we and our fellow dinners—young or old, out with friends or family or colleagues—discuss the menu. On any given evening, the 48 seats of this side-street restaurant east of center are likely to be filled with gourmands sharing the pleasure of relaxed yet enticing dining.

J-F Quinton, son of the late distinguished chef George Quinton whose restaurant in Brittany earned its Michelin star in the 1960s, is an ideal companion for a restaurant test during the autumn game-and-seafood season. Not only did he once work in his father's restaurant, but he is now a successful veterinarian, meaning that he knows a thing or two about both seafood and animal parts. Furthermore, he had been lauding Le Villaret for some time already, and the wise travelers knows which friends to trust with restaurant recommendations.

The wise travelers knows which friends to trust with restaurant recommendations.

This is a moderately-priced restaurant, but at dinnertime the menu nevertheless forecasts a bill whose range calls for greater than moderate expectations—largely fulfilled. For starters, my (overly?) rich creamy cèpe mushroom soup stirred into a buttery scoop of foie gras and J-F's upstanding mussels-and-artichoke lasagna exhibited chef Olivier Gaslain's way of mixing and matching fresh ingredients. The main courses then displayed his (self-taught) skill in revisiting tradition: a delicious cut of fresh cod served with creamy potatoes and sprinkled with herring eggs, a delicate and earnest young partridge (*perdreau*) seasoned with rosemary and served with garlic potatoes.

Desserts included a sensual *fricassee de muscat au porto,*

where the muscat grapes of early autumn are warmed in port wine and served with spice-bread ice cream, and a voluptuous Grand Marnier sponge cake (*baba*) served with roast figs and yogurt ice cream. The homemade ice cream was pitch perfect on both accounts.

Service is well-paced though the staff doesn't have much time for individual pampering. A bit more spacious seating and more patient service would certainly better reflect the cuisine, but would also hike prices another notch. Wine assistance is sound and informed, whether you're considering the list of "medications" (25-40€), as the frequently changing list of lower priced wines is called, or the heftier list of 200 references that largely focus on prescriptions from Burgundy and the Côte du Rhône. From the latter list you're welcome to pamper yourself enough to add an extra 0 to the bill.

⓮Le Repaire de Cartouche

Address *8 boulevard des Filles-du-Calvaire, 11th arr. The boulevard entrance is beside the metro, the bandits' entrance is around the block at 99 rue Amelot.* ***Metro*** *St. Sébastien Foissart.*
Tel *01 47 00 25 86.* ***Closed*** *Sun., Mon., late July-early Aug.* ***ALC*** *30-40€.* ***Wine list*** *Unpretentious, mostly 20-37€.*

Traditional, rustic cuisine worth writing home about

The inside cover of the menu at Le Repaire de Cartouche (Cartouche's Lair) tells us that in the early 18th century a band of outlaws led by the infamous Cartouche, a bandit and a lady's man (therefore someone of whom the French will pardon anything), once gathered here outside the old city walls and...

Who the hell cares!

My own band of restaurant testers and I lost interest in the story of Cartouche as soon as we saw a steaming slab of veal and golden brown potatoes arriving at the next table. So we quickly turned the page to the better script, the one promising the adventure of French cuisine. The tale it tells is largely traditional, with occasional leaps into unfamiliar territory, and the

> **TID-BIT:**
>
> **French cuisine has been heavily inspired by the produce and preparations of this southwestern zone, and many restaurants in Paris consider themselves as ambassadors of southwestern cooking.**

characters are close to the earth or direct from the farm, sincere without being sentimental.

Our story thus began with a cumin-scented lamb terrine self-served from the terrine mold (a hint of portions to come), an eel and leek terrine (a twist of tradition) and a most appetizing eggplant, served like a gaping baked potato, smothered in thick cream mixed with herring eggs (to tempt us down the road of the unknown). In keeping with the general atmosphere of this countrified lair, the service is relaxed and distracted enough to give the impression that no one here takes himself very seriously—except for the chef, Rodolphe Paquin.

The plot thickens with the main course as we cut into our own tasty slab of veal, a chunk of monkfish (*lotte*), a bone-picking plate of young pigeon (*pigeonneau*) and a sweet gathering of lamb cutlets. My companions this evening are two brothers from a village near Toulouse and the aforementioned vet, guys who know how to order and how to eat, none of them about to be fooled by the mask of a sauce. Indeed, in many restaurants the sauce conspires to hide a lack of freshness, effort, or talent. Not so here, where the slab of veal, the chunk of fish, and the bone-picked pigeon speak well for themselves. Such adjectives may offend the finer sensibilities of designer foodies, but we didn't come here to eat pretty—we came to eat well! And to drink heartily from the judicious selection of unpretentious wines.

We didn't come here to eat pretty—we came to eat well!

The price of a meal at Le Repaire fully reflects the quality of the goods, for one cannot imagine the décor being factored in, though it does indeed recall a rustic haunt of yesteryear.

The sizeable portions mean that you won't go hungry by opting for two courses instead of three. But do read on to the denouement, where you may find that while the traditional fruit-pie *clafoutis* is a misstep, the *sablé* (a sweet crumbly shortbread pastry) with strawberries is a fine finish. Above all, the *profiteroles*, fresh pastry balls filled with homemade ice cream and served with hot melted chocolate, is the kind of happy ending that that makes you want to read the menu all over again.

⑮ L'Oulette

Address *15 place Lachambeaudie, 12th arr.* ***Metro*** *Cour St-Emilion or Dugommier.* ***Tel*** *01 40 02 02* • ***Fax*** *01 40 02 04 77.*
Site *www.l-oulette.com* ***Closed*** *Sat., Sun.* ***Menu*** *45€ (includes wine), 28€ (L).* ***ALC*** *46-54€. Wine list Extensive.* ***Dress*** *Polished casual.*

Relaxed, southwestern gastronomy, ideal service

My personal quest for the happy medium between distant French service and buddy-buddy American service has ended. I have finally come across friendly, efficient servers who neither prostitute themselves nor treat me as a necessary evil but who always seem to make the right approach at the right time. As Alain Fontaine, the dining room half of L'Oulette's team, puts it, the wait staff here is expected to speak with clients without being too enterprising—a simply policy that goes a long way and that is apparently far more difficult to pull off than one would imagine. Given what one experiences elsewhere in Paris, the servers at L'Oulette do indeed seem so naturally inclined to be amiably present when needed and to anticipate our needs without much notice that they could well serve as an example to restaurants of a higher brow.

Meanwhile, Marcel Baudis is busy in the kitchen keeping up his end of L'Oulette's partnership—and doing an equally fine job of it. He prepares ambitious yet accessible versions of southwestern dishes. A mastery of traditional regional dishes such as *foie gras, cassoulet* and *confit de canard* is to be expected. Also successful in their not-quite-simplicity are starters such as *millefeuille de sardines* (a sardine high-rise), *escabèche de calamars* (squid in an olive oil, aniseed, and curry marinade, served with warm potatoes) and cream of artichoke soup flavored with truffle extract. These may be followed by rich southern classics such as *aioli* (monkfish, codfish and snails garnished with vegetables and served with the garlic and olive oil "mayonnaise" of the same name), braised ox-tail (*queue de boeuf*) wrapped in green cabbage and served with pan-fried *foie gras*, or a grilled *lisette* (a small mackerel) lightly lemoned and gingered and served on an eggplant compote. For dessert, try the armagnac-brushed apple *tourtière*, the homey rich *pain d'épices perdu "à la coque"* or roast nectarines with honey and lavender served

L'Oulette is well off the beaten track, proof that it isn't all happening in the center of the city.

Southwestern Cuisine

L'Oulette may sound like it was named after your 10th grade French teacher, but in fact refers to a cooking pot in langue d'oc, *the medieval language of southern France where yes was pronounced* oc, *as opposed to* langue d'oïl *of northern France, where yes was pronounce* oïl.

Southwest France, a vast, heavily rural zone abutting the Pyrenees, is among France's most eye-catching regions. The region's main city is Toulouse, the queen of southern France, known as la Ville Rose, the Pink city, because of its brick that glows bright in the southern sun. Within a radius of 100 miles of Toulouse lies a stunning array of sights and towns and history: the fortified cathedral of Albi, the tremendous fortifications of Carcassone, and a rural cortege of market towns, goose farms, castle ruins, Romanesque churches and hilltop and valley villages built along meandering rivers.

French cuisine has been heavily inspired by the produce and preparations of this southwestern zone, and many restaurants in Paris consider themselves as ambassadors of southwestern cooking. (The area is therefore too vast and varied to be included in the regional section of this chapter.)

North and west of Toulouse, the palate is especially rich in the historic regions of Gascony, Quercy and Dordogne, each bringing its own traditional twist to game, goose, duck, turkey, lamb and river fish. Throughout the Middle Ages, those regions were caught alternately between and within the reaches of the counts of Toulouse (followed by the kings of France) and the dukes of Aquitaine (followed by the kings of England). Nowadays they are united by nothing less than their production of foie gras, liver with a college education, taken from specially fattened geese and ducks.

*Southwestern France is indeed prime goose (*oie*) and duck (*canard*) territory. While the region is southern enough to know the pleasures of olive oil, the oil may be set aside here in favor of duck and goose fat.* Confit *means that the breast of goose or duck has been preserved in the bird's fat. Sliced thin and with little fat, duck becomes* magret, *which is generally served medium rare. Come winter, cassoulet is king around Toulouse; it's a hearty everyman's stew of tomatoes, white haricot beans and pork or goose or lamb (or all three), depending on the local variation.*

At the northwest corner of the region, beginning in the Lot Valley, Quercy offers specialties of galantine or truffled turkey, jugged hare, leg of lamb and trout from nearby lakes. Roquefort, the strong blue cheese, comes from cellars near the town of Roquefort-sur-Soulzon, between Albi and Montpellier. Flat round goat cheese produced in these areas goes by the name cabacou. Further southwest, Pau is the capital of Béarn, which gave the world Béarnaise sauce, a warm sauce of white wine, vinegar, shallots, spices, egg yolk and butter that is served with a variety of dishes.

In the higher reaches of gastronomy, any of the dishes mentioned above may be scented with traces of the pungent mushrooms called truffles, a.k.a. "black diamonds," that are harvested in the wild in this region from November to March.

with lavender ice cream, if the season warrants. All courses are prettily presented while also being sizably portioned.

The price of such a feast is quite reasonable, though beyond the prices noted above, the final size of your bill depends on your willingness to be tempted by the list of aperitifs (especially whiskeys), coffees and digestives (particularly armagnacs). You may need an aperitif because it can take a while to decipher the menu; explanations are sure to be required—and forthcoming. The extensive wine list of 200 appellations, at a price for everyone, thoroughly covers the French countryside, but this is your chance to get to know southwestern wines outside of the usual Bordeaux and Saint-Emilions, e.g. a Madiran. The southwestern spirit is especially visible once the dessert plates have been cleared and digestifs are proposed. Among the offerings, the possibility to end one's meal with coffee and 3 armagnacs or 3 cognacs of different ages. Armagnac brandy comes from an area between Bordeaux and Toulouse, while its more famous cousin, cognac, comes from a zone north of Bordeaux.

Start to finish, L'Oulette is intelligent without being sophisticated and refined without high gastronomic pretensions. The décor is neat and cheery, with sunny yellow walls and hardwood floors, well-spaced tables and a large centerpiece bouquet. A terrace is open in the warm seasons. Not a bad seat in the house. Altogether welcoming for a romantic dinner, while also ideal for a larger table—2-3 couples or a group of friends looking for a relaxed fine dining experience. But you've got to want it, because L'Oulette is well off the beaten track, proof that it isn't all happening in the center of the city

⑯Les Messugues

***Address** 8 rue Léon Jost, 17th arr. **Metro** Courcelles.*
***Tel** 01 47 63 26 65. **Closed** St., Sun., holidays. **Menu** 22€ (L), 29€ (D, includes drinks). **Dress** Casual or business attire.*

When nice is just right

Travelers have been taught to look for high-end adjectives from reviews, and many restaurant reviewers like to spoon them out: the best... the hottest... the up-and-coming, etc. As though your only interest in coming to Paris were to impress your friends back home or your third wife.

Meanwhile, there are admirable restaurants run by nice people serving nice meals at nice prices and that are largely known only to those who live or work in the quarter. Les Messugues is one such place: nice, downright nice. I recommend it for nothing more (or less) than a nice meal, nice service, a nice evening—you supply the nice company. Alain Lafôret in the dining room and Gérard Fontaine in the kitchen have been maintaining an admirable quality-price ratio since 1984. The fixed-price menu is full of sincerity, pared down to the basic niceties of bourgeois cuisine: terrine, salad of warm duck foie gras, baked shellfish and crayfish gratin; a duo of salmon and scallops, a nice cut of beef, leg of duck confite.

There are 20 seats on the ground floor and 20 seats upstairs, both rooms presenting an unassuming, sober décor, leading to a serene ambiance that lends itself to both business and leisure. When considering a restaurant for a detour, Les Messugues has stiff competition from others in the chapter but nonetheless holds its own. And should you find yourself in this quarter, perhaps after a spring or summer evening stroll in Parc Monceau (see *Gardens*), and/or if you enjoy places that quietly carry on through the years, this restaurant is worthy of attention. If, on the other hand, you've just whisked your third wife off to Paris for the weekend, pack platinum and head elsewhere.

CUISINE BOURGEOISE

Several years ago I recommended Les Messugues to a couple of well-heeled travelers who claimed to be looking for "someplace nice but not too dress-up." They seemed quite interested as I described the restaurant—until I told them that it served bourgeois cuisine, at which point that got huffy and asked for a better recommendation.

Since then, I've been wary about using the term. Yet "bourgeois" aptly describes conventionally polished French cuisine, the kind of dishes that lie between country-style fare, creative cookery and sophisticated gastronomy.

In the Middle Ages, the old bourg lay near the marketplace, somewhere between the castle and the domains of the landed gentry—medieval suburbia with a good grocery store. The bourgeois were the people who lived there. The term later came to apply to enterprising capitalists and town leaders, then merely to the contented middle class. Bourgeois now also connotes attitudes and behaviors that conform to middle-class conventions. Naturally, no one truly wants to consider himself as subscribing to safe mediocrity.

But bourgeois isn't a slur when it comes to food. Enjoying bourgeois cuisine doesn't make a traveler bourgeois any more than eating Italian cuisines makes a person Italian. Considering it as cuisine bourgeoise *can take the edge off.*

Cuisine bourgeoise *covers many modern French cookbook classics in which good seasonal produce and fresh meat and fish are prepared with somewhat studied sauces and/or herbs and are well presented without excessive pretensions: e.g. goat cheese in a puff pastry on an endive salad, mullet tart, beef tenderloin, duck fillet, scallops, John Dory fish, sole, handsome dessert tarts and napoleons.*

The restaurants that serve this cuisine often strike the perfect balance a traveler looks for in a place that is "nice but not too dress-up." Representatives of the genre cover a wide range of territory; Les Messugues, Le Poquelin, Les Bookinistes, La Bastide Odéon, L'Absinthe and others in this chapter are steeped in bourgeois traditions, but that doesn't mean that they're stuck there. Bourgeois cuisine is something to be wary of only when the restaurant would have you believe that it serves highly refined fare meriting truly bourgeois prices.

⑯La Boulangerie

Address *15 rue des Panoyaux, 20th arr.* ***Metro*** *Ménilmontant.*
Tel *01 43 58 45 45 •* ***Fax*** *01 43 58 45 46.* ***ALC*** *26€.*
Cocktail hour *Across the square at Lou Pascalou (same owner) or anyplace that suits your fancy along rue Oberkampf (see Bars).*

A local favorite in the hip Ménilmontant quarter

La Boulangerie is a neighborhood restaurant that stands out in an area known for its basic French and ethnic comfort foods. Situated just east of the Oberkampf/Ménilmontant junction (see *The Aperitif*), it is one of the better lunch or dinner choices in the area, therefore one of the most popular. Success has meant that prices keep inching up, nevertheless the preparations are surprisingly attentive for the yet reasonable price. Classic French cuisine is revisited and lightened here with a bit of curry, a touch of saffron and other touches of culinary whimsy. The atmosphere is relaxed and pleasing, and the rather unadorned décor of this former bakery (*boulangerie*) is enlivened by its old mosaic floor.

At a table of three we were soothed by enhanced bistro dishes such as guinea fowl terrine, shredded celery rémoulade with fried brick of St-Marcellin cheese, grilled bass, lamb stew and several heartwarming desserts: apple crumble, French toast, soft chocolate tart. Even JM, so hard to please at the gastronomic Le Maxence, gave it the nod.

Some brownie points may be lost on the wait staff. I've found them calmer and more attentive on a subsequent visit but this evening they were so overstimulated by each other's presence that we wondered if they'd been sniffing too much saffron in the kitchen. Or maybe they know that they can do whatever they want and the crowds will still come for well-turned dishes at a decent price.

⑲Le Ciel de Paris

Address *56th floor, Montparnasse Tower, 33 av. du Maine, 15th arr.* ***Metro*** *Montparnasse.* ***Tel*** *01 40 64 77 64.* ***Open*** *Daily for lunch and dinner. Also daily for continental breakfast (11€), 8:30-11am, and for teatime, 2:45-5:45pm.* ***Menu*** *32€ (L, except Sun., holidays), 52€.* ***ALC*** *60-75€.* ***Dress*** *Generally business attire, though polished casual is fine for lunch.* ***Elevators*** *The elevator to the restaurant is reached by way of the building's main entrance.*

For the view... and the meal

One of Paris's best kept breakfast secrets is Le Ciel de Paris, not for the quality of the pastries but for the expansiveness of the view. The 56th-floor restaurant of the Montparnasse Tower offers the grand view over the western half of Paris. (The 59th-floor observation deck, reached from a separate entrance to the building, offers the full frontal view of the capital.) While the tower's major architectural legacy is to have taught the powers that be that skyscrapers don't belong in the center of the city, it has the merit of offering a spectacular view: cityscape, Louvre, Sacré Coeur, Garnier Opera and above all the Eiffel Tower. Tea with cake in the afternoon offers the same view. Reservations aren't necessary for breakfast or teatime.

One of Paris's best kept breakfast secrets is Le Ciel de Paris, not for the quality of the pastries but for the expansiveness of the view.

But for lunch or dinner, reserve a window seat, though even without one the view is full and wide. Le Ciel de Paris, meaning the Parisian Sky, offers a mixed bag of decent-to-refined Franco-European fare, with more borders being crossed à la carte than on the fixed-price menu. I particularly recommend Le Ciel de Paris for either a lingering lunch at any time of year or for a sunset dinner during the long evenings of May-July. After nightfall, though, the late-70s/early-80s decor gives the restaurant a pleathery late-disco feel.

The 31€ lunch menu may be a call price but it is decent and priceworthy and goes down well with the view. In it you may find the classic good-natured savors of gaspacho, terrines, duck breast, trout, pollock and other dishes that vary with the seasons. Choicer cuts and fillets of fish, fowl and beef are kindly treated in the 49€ lunch or dinner menu and more studied dishes are available à la carte.

BISTROS

What is a bistro?

No one opens a restaurant anymore in Paris, they open a bistro. That's because a bistro sounds more relaxed and local and cool than a restaurant. But it's a vague term. The French themselves are so unclear as to what exactly constitutes a bistro that they can't even agree how to spell it—bistro or bistrot!

One definition of a bistro is a neighborhood restaurant or café offering traditional dishes using farm-fresh ingredients served along with inexpensive and moderately-priced wines. In short, the kind of place you'd return to often if you lived nearby. That covers everything from a greasy spoon near a market square to the French version of an English neighborhood pub to a tight-tabled eatery for country-style cooking to a so-called "baby bistro," a trend of the mid-late '90s by which well-known chefs of high gastronomy lent their names and consulting skills to the genre.

What they all have in common is a relaxed atmosphere and an emphasis on earthy preparations that leave you loosening your belt while trying to decide whether to have dessert (do!). No self-respecting bistro would present a menu without tripe sausages, salt pork and lentils (French soul food) and other dishes using lesser cuts of meat. You'll also find a wide range of recipes from grand-mère's kitchen: terrines, rustic soups, boeuf bourgignon, coq au vin, duck steak, duck cooked in fat, veal chops, pork chops, finer cuts of beef, salmon, monkfish, crème brulée, apple pie, blueberry tart. Several waves of beef scares have made the menus less adventuresome than before as many of the organ meats have vanished. They have been replaced by a greater variety of fish dishes. As for drink, while the café traditionally places the accent on coffee and the brasserie on beer, the bistro's drink of choice is wine, rather cheering table wine in most cases, though more complex choices are available in pricier bistros.

Conviviality

But nothing describes a bistro more than the French word *convivial*. It's impossible to understand the difference between a bistro and other types of restaurant—as well as the difference between the ways French and Americans socialize—without understanding how the French use the term.

Convivial is an English word as well; the American Heritage Dictionary defines it as "1. Fond of feasting, drinking, and good company; sociable. 2. Merry, festive." But few Americans other than Francophiles and, not surprisingly, restaurant writers, would dare use the word. Americans tend to prefer the word fun to describe their feasting.

In French, however, *convivial* is commonly used when describing a congenial place or situation for social interaction where food and drink are present: a talky lunch, a loose-tie cocktail party, easy conversation at a bar counter, a relaxed supper... a bistro. What distinguishes a convivial place or situation is that the guests aren't as guarded as usual.

Nothing describes a bistro more than the French word *convivial*.

For a Parisian that means that in a convivial restaurant—a bistro—he will feel so relaxed that he won't hesitate to ask you if he can borrow the jar of mustard three inches away on your table. In less convivial restaurants he will first address the waiter. Conviviality is therefore a base state of slightly unguarded social interaction... and not necessarily much more than that.

Convivial is now also employed to mean "user-friendly" relative to computers. That, in fact, may be the best way of defining a convivial bistro: a user-friendly place for food and drink.

A cheap bistro is something you just stumble upon when visiting a food market, an expensive bistro is a concept I don't understand. Consider here three of the best and most authentic of those that lie somewhere inbetween.

⑲La Poule au Pot

Address *9 rue Vauvilliers, 1st arr. Across the park from St. Eustache Church.* ***Metro*** *Les Halles or Louvre.* ***Tel*** *01 42 36 32 96.* ***Menu*** *29€.* ***ALC*** *37-45€.* ***Open*** *Tues.-Sun., 7pm-dawn.*

Character and tradition—and best onion soup

For 800 years, the area beside this fabulous little bistro served as the city's central food market, *les halles*. The streets were filled with the sights and sounds and smells of wholesalers, retailers, peasants, greengrocers, truck farmers, fishmongers, carts and stands, pig, ox and horse carcasses, rotting fruit and vegetables, fish and seafood. In 1969, "the belly of Paris" was moved south of Paris, to Rungis (near Orly airport), leaving the Les Halles Quarter to be developed into the linchpin of transportation to and from the suburbs, feeding directly into an underground mall and entertainment complex. That complex is of scant interest to more distant travelers, unless you're in search of an Olympic-size swimming pool.

While the central market has moved elsewhere, remnants of the time when the quarter bustled day and night with the food trade can still be found. Rue Montorgeuil (see *Shop 'n' Stroll*), leading into Les Halles from the north, remains a vibrant market street. The monstrous church of Saint-Eustache, nearly the size of Notre-Dame, is also a reminder of the density of population and the importance of Les Halles in the 16th century. In one of the side chapels of the church, a cartoonish sculpture illustrates "The departure of fruits and vegetables from the heart of Paris, Feb. 28, 1969."

Le Pied de Cochon, beside the church, maintains the old market tradition by staying open 24/7 and by specializing in pig's trotters (*pieds de cochon*), chitterling sausages, and tripes, along with more recognizable cuts of beef or duck, tuna steak or salmon, also snails and seafood platters. It is now a large brassy brasserie with heavy tourist leanings.

What we call French onion soup, is the traditional late-night/early-morning meal or snack of night-combers... if you were to choose but one place for French onion soup in Paris, La Poule qu Pot should be it.

La Poule au Pot, by contrast, stays contemporary yet remains a warm 1935 bistro at heart. I can well image the departing souls in the sculpture at St-Eustache stopping here for a mug of onion soup before moving on. *Soupe gratinée (au vin blanc)*, what we call French onion soup, is the traditional late-night/early-morning meal or snack of night-combers. On market day, it would serve to warm and fortify a traveler before or after a 4-hour ride to/from the country. Nowadays it fortifies diners and suppers before or after several hours of dancing or partying... or exploring Paris. For the sake of both tradition and quality, then, if you were to choose but one place for French onion soup in Paris, La Poule au Pot should be it.

The soup may suffice as a meal in itself; not only is it substantial but it includes all of the basic French food groups: cheese, wine, bread. It is well accompanied by a glass of dry white or fruity red wine, then perhaps followed by a blueberry tart or a caramelized upside-down apple pie (*tarte Tatin*) or a *crème brulée*. But while you're here you might as well unbuckle your belt a notch and order a main course as well.

Henri IV, who reigned 1589-1610, declared that every family should have a chicken in a pot (*un poule au pot*) on Sunday. Henri IV's peasanty *poule au pot* stew is naturally on the menu. As to Henri, he was assassinated on rue de la Ferronerie, 300 yards east of here. (Note: the onion soup and the chicken stew are both broth-based, so they don't go well together.)

You'll also find some of the best country-style food around: a hefty morsel of leg of lamb (*souris d'agneau*), fattened hen with morel mushrooms (*poulard aux morilles*), veal chops, veal kidneys (*rognons de veau*), beef tenderloin and several fish choices.

La Poule au Pot is wonderful not just for a meal but as a place to linger, partly because the food will be long in coming from the kitchen (take that as a good sign), partly because there's something about the place that lends itself to enjoyable conversation, whether it's just the two of you or the whole gang. The room itself is a delightful mix of glitz and convention: copper bar, 30s fixtures, bistro benches, an old radio, plates on the wall, etc. (The dining space in the basement is better suited only for groups of 8 or more.) The friendly, willing and attentive waiters further give the place character.

Between midnight and 2am, La Poule au Pot often fills as the post-concert/theater/movie crowd crosses paths with the pre-nightclub crowd. A group of actors or musicians will occasionally enter with their entourage—notice the odd mix of French and international celebrities whose names appear on small plaques along the benches, and ask to see the guest book. On and off through the evening and night the restaurant may also be nearly empty. That's the other great thing about this place, it's got ambiance even when yours is the only table occupied.

⑳Mellifère

Address *8 rue de Monsigny, 2nd arr.* ***Metro*** *Quatre-Septembre.* ***Tel*** *01 42 61 21 71 •* ***Fax*** *01 42 61 31 71.* ***Open*** *Mon.-Sat. Seating possible as early as 7pm.* ***Menu/Carte*** *26€.* ***Wine*** *A wise selection.*

Satisfying, warm, a toast to the simpler things in life

After a decade of finding famous chefs as trademarks on a bistro menu but absent from the kitchen, it's a pleasure to find a bistro with an actual owner-chef. In this case, a chef whose sole pretension seems to be to satisfy clients at prices that are simple to understand. If satisfaction, simplicity, and an actual chef in the kitchen don't come across as a strong enough recommendation, think again.

As Mellifère's Alain Atibard puts it, "Life is complicated enough; it's good to simplify things." That may not be a very original quote, but originality isn't the question here. The question is: Where to find well-prepared, quality bistro fare that is kindly served?

First we had to navigate away from the non-smoking section because, though nonsmokers, we found ourselves being directed to a space beneath the stairwell, a space that might otherwise have served as the cloak room. Faced with the choice between living in a less smoke-tinted environment and joining the world—those often being your options in France—I recommend opting for the latter. Mellifère's layout places tables close enough to encourage conviviality yet provides enough nooks and sideways tables and separation that you won't have to worry about a miscut sautéed potato flying onto your neighbor's lap. There are also tables on the terrace, weather permitting, and a small room upstairs. In fact, the space seems to adapt to the individual rather than the other way around; therefore Mellifère is enjoyable for a table for two, a 4-head, a we-are-the-party of 6, or, in our case, a round table for three.

The lack of a menu in English is a good sign. This doesn't mean that Mellifère is some unknown hideaway (it's located in a banking and business quarter, several doors down from the 1863 theater of the Bouffes-Parisiens, devoted to comic opera and theater), rather that Véronique Atibard believes that having the staff assist with questions helps create a link with the clientele. Anyway, the menu is anything but complicated; there are no lengthy explanations. Just the facts, ma'am.

Don't dis the unfamiliar meat and organ dishes without considering that fresh ingredients make this the occasion to try the *assiette de charcuterie* (assortment of cold slice meats) or even the *boudin poêlé* (pan-fried blood sausage) that hark back to the chef's Basque origins. And when was the last time you had an honest-to-goodness steak tartare? A place that otherwise prides itself on dishes such as *cochon rôti* (roast pig), leg of rabbit, and other grilled or roasted meats is nevertheless obliged to have a significant offering of fish dishes these days, hence a rather rustic feel to the mixed fish dish *panache de poisons au basilic* and to the lemon butter sauce served with the grilled salmon. Desserts are simple and rich enough to write home about, particularly the house classic t*ourtière aux pommes* (apple tart) and the French classic *profiteroles* (puff pastries and vanilla ice cream with chocolate melted on top).

Throughout the evening the service was efficient and kind, with the occasional gentle interruption of the generous smile of Mme. Atibard checking in to see if all was well. All was.

㉑ Allard

Address *41 rue Saint-André-des-Arts, 6th arr.* ***Metro*** *Odéon.*
Tel *01 43 26 48 23 •* ***Fax*** *01 46 33 04 02.* ***Open*** *Mon.-Sat.* ***Menu*** *23€ (2-course L), 31€.* ***ALC*** *40-63€ for 3 courses, though 2 may suffice, or just a main course at lunch 18-32€.*

Hearty, belly-rub tradition in the St. Germain quarter

Allard is firmly rooted in a major vessel of the tourist heart of the 6th arrondissement, rue St-André-des-Arts. But the entrance to this exemplary belly-rub of a Paris bistro is actually around the corner on rue de l'Eperon, where the door opens not to the tight-tabled dining rooms but to the mouth of the kitchen. Upon entering, then, one risks bumping into a waiter carrying a dozen escargots or a slab of duck foie gras or, more dangerously, a veal cutlet with sautéed potatoes or guinea fowl with lentils. *Chaud devant!*, this is the occasion to learn, means "Hot coming through!"

Since Allard is located within walking distance of many hotels in the St. Germain and St. Michel Quarters, the accent at the next table may or may not be French, but the accent elsewhere is steeped, sauced and herbed in the good ol' traditions that I'd call cliché if they weren't so tasty. In a sense this is the old-fashioned Paris bistro that we come looking for on every trip: faded yellow walls, retro prints and lighting, impersonal, competent waiters, filling dishes that prompt us to wonder how the French manage to stay so thin. Prices have some buoyancy to them, but you'll leave so jovial and satisfied that it won't matter.

The menu is easy enough to understand with a basic French restaurant vocabulary—*escargot, poulet, boeuf, canard, sole, turbot, sorbet, tarte*—so it isn't a dictionary that you'll want to bring but a map of France. The menu is a perfect example of quality food labeling from the country that brought you *appellations contrôlées*: the *escargots* are naturally from Burgundy, the *poulet* from Bresse (center east), the *canard* from Challans (center west), the *boeuf* from Salers (center south), the *cassoulet* a tradition from Toulouse (southwest). The most classic of traditional bistro dishes are proposed as the *plats du jour*: *veau à la berrichonne* (veal garnished with braised cabbage and bacon), *petit salé aux lentilles* (salt pork and lentils), *coq au vin, boeuf aux carrots.*

Dishes are served home-style, heaped on large plates, which explains why several of the main courses are portioned for two, even three. While fish dishes earn their place on the menu, this is more of a meat and fowl and red wine place. Thus, Allard is most fitting for a cool or grey day or evening, party of four—*chaud devant*!

BRASSERIES: THE PARISIAN DINER

Visiting Paris without eating at a brasserie would be like driving through Pennsylvania without stopping at a diner—a missed opportunity. In fact, brasseries—with their lengthy menus, long serving hours and bright decors—*are* the diners of Paris. Brasserie food is typically uncomplicated and predictable, making it right for a thousand occasions, planned in advance or not. And so families gather at a brasserie for Sunday lunch, co-workers celebrate finished projects there, friends dine there after the theater, everyone goes there to satisfy an urge for oysters, couples go there when they need someplace big and brassy to contain their emotions, etc.

A brasserie, which also means brewery, was originally a beer bar introduced to Paris in the 1860s by beer merchants and tavern keepers from Alsace, France's northeastern region. Traditional Alsatian dishes were also served, such as various smoked and salted sausages. By the turn of the century, while Alsace was annexed to Germany (1870-1919), the brasserie was developing into a distinctly Parisian institution, less defined by the drink than by the menu, and then less by the menu then by the chatter and mirth in a spacious setting with a showy décor.

Visiting Paris without eating at a brasserie would be like driving through Pennsylvania without stopping at a diner. In fact, brasseries are the diners of Paris.

Part of the pleasure of going to a brasserie is taking part in that grand old brasserie ambiance. The most famous brasseries are now landmarks (official or not) with a touch of Main Street Disney to them, therefore many, including those explored here, are in the hands of two major groups, Flo and Les Frères Blancs, or their offspring.

Brasseries are appropriate for any time of year, yet they're especially appealing as a place to take the chill out of fall and winter. That's when the variety of eastern sausages and pork are placed on a heaping of sauerkraut and boiled potatoes, creating *choucroute*, the heartiest of Alsatian cool weather dishes. And by October, seafood stands are overflowing with oysters, mussels, spider and tourteau crabs, prawns and crawfish, whelk and other marine snails, as aproned men go about shucking oysters and creating seafood platters. Beer goes well with choucroute, but it has stiff competition from the Alsatian gewürztraminer, pinot noir and pinot gris.

In order to aspire to the brotherhood of authentic Parisian brasseries in the Alsatian tradition, a menu should call special attention to either the seafood or the choucroute, or both. Meanwhile, another branch of the brasserie tree follows in the traditions brought from northern France and Belgium, in which case the choucroute is replaced by mussels and fries and the gewurzt plays second fiddle to Belgian beer. Many large and showy cafes that combine both traditions are also considered as brasseries. And whatever the tradition it follows, or doesn't, a brasserie menu may also include onion soup, escargot, calf's liver, steak tartare, roast chicken with a heaping of thick fries, various cuts of beef and freshwater water fish. The list may go on, the main aim being to keep it simple.

Brasseries open earlier and stay open later than other restaurants, they also open on Sunday, and some are open 24/7, which not only makes them convenient but removes any excuse you may have of missing out on the experience.

㉒Bofinger

Address *5-7 rue de la Bastille, 5th arr.* ***Metro*** *Bastille. Tel 01 42 72 87 82.* ***Open*** *Daily noon-3pm, 6:30pm-1am, continuous service weekends and holidays.* ***Menu*** *20€ (weekday 2-course L), 31€ (includes wine).* ***ALC*** *34-44€.*

Classic Alsatian-cum-Parisian brasserie

The only surprise in place de la Bastille's famous old-time brasserie is that there's no surprise at all. Which is why one comes here. Opened in 1864, and therefore ancient enough to call itself the oldest brasserie in Paris, Bofinger exemplifies the Alsatian-cum-Parisian brasserie tradition. Staples on the menu include oysters galore, onion soup, veal, steak, salmon, bass, guinea fowl, chitterling sausage and choucroute. For any season or appetite, keep Bofinger in mind before or after a tour of the Marais.

The waiters here are consistently pleasant and efficient, while the décor (1919) is consistently soothing, whether you're seated beneath the floral design of the glass cupola on the ground floor or beside the Alsatian woodwork upstairs. Most people ask to be seated beneath the cupola, but I've never felt second-class in the woody space upstairs, which is in fact more laid-back. In either case, the toilets of choice are those in the basement—a pleasing period piece in a city otherwise not known for the appeal of its restrooms.

㉓Le Grand Colbert

Address *2-4 rue Vivienne, 2nd arr.* ***Metro*** *Bourse.*
Tel *01 42 86 87 88 •* ***Fax*** *01 42 86 82 65.*
E-mail *le.grand.colbert@wanadoo.fr.* ***Open*** *Daily until 1am.* ***Menu*** *25€.* ***ALC*** *30-35€.*

Tradition and atmosphere

I like to admire a restaurant from the outside before going in, wander around the block, get a feel for the surroundings. Especially here, since Le Grand Colbert is situated in one of Paris's most likable historic quarters; a tour of the immediate neighborhood is part of the experience of this 19th-century grand brasserie. Having rounded the block, revisiting the charming Galerie Vivienne and Place des Victoires, I stand across the narrow street for a minute before entering—leaning against the old National Library (Bibliothèque Nationale) or huddling with dinner companions beneath an umbrella—and admire the curves of the 1900 entrance to the restaurant, while the doorman/valet approaches to know whether I've reserved or not. Sometimes I have, sometimes not.

Le Grand Colbert is listed as an historical monument. The décor is an authentic mix of its 1830s origins and 1900 restyling: 20-foot high ceilings, decorative trim, frescoes, kentia fronds greening the long wall, horribly passé lamps sprouting like Christmas balls around the columns. Service is busy and gentle. Le Grande Colbert has the feel of the first-class dining car on the Orient Express and an edge of Agatha Chistie. (Despite the grand air there's no use in attempting snobbery here, though some do try.) One can well imagine intriguing plots being played out at the surrounding tables and amongst the waiters, characters one and all. We nearly regret arriving as the couple at the next table approaches the end of their meal—a buxom diner finishing an *île flottant* (caramel-coated egg white floating in thin custard) while her date whispers sweet nothings in her ear. Like all foreigners, we're slightly paranoid and wonder whether in fact they're talking about us, as we are about them.

Like all foreigners, we're slightly paranoid and wonder whether in fact they're talking about us, as we are about them.

From the kitchen, meanwhile, comes tasty brasserie basics, neither pricey nor class conscious: tomato and mozzarella with a crushed basil sauce and anchovies, salad with goat cheese fried in a crispy pastry, onion soup, fresh oysters, tasty leg and breast of chicken with *frites*, well grilled steak, classic desserts. This isn't the stuff that gastronomic raves are made of, but with the right company—a partner or partners to intrigue—or even alone, Le Grand Colbert offers a most enjoyable and historic ride.

This brasserie is especially recommendable as a lunch stop while touring the area or as a dinner setting when staying in the Opera quarter. See *Shop'n'Stroll: Galerie Vivienne* for more on this quarter.

㉔ Julien

Address *16 rue du Faubourg-St-Denis, 10th arr.* ***Metro*** *Strasbourg-St-Denis.* ***Tel*** *01 47 79 12 06 •* ***Fax*** *01 42 47 00 65.* ***Open*** *Daily noon-3pm, 7pm-1am.* ***Menu*** *30.50€, includes wine.* ***ALC*** *30-35€.*

Brasserie Flo

Address *7 cour des Petits-Ecuries (in alleyway entered through 63 rue du Fbg-St-Denis), 10th arr.* ***Metro*** *Strasbourg-St-Denis.*
Tel *01 • Fax 01 47 70 13 59.* ***Open*** *Daily noon-3:30pm, 7pm-1am.*
Menu *30.50€, includes wine.* ***ALC*** *30-35€.*

Ambiance and character

Julien and Brasserie Flo are two distinct brasseries of character belonging to the Flo chain.They lie just beyond Porte St-Denis, a triumphal arch celebrating the military victories of Louis (XIV) the Great along the Rhine. Two blocks east along the boulevard St-Denis stands another, smaller arch, the Porte St-Martin, honoring other victories of the Sun King. These served as majestic entrances to the 17th-century city. North of them you leave the monuments of the old city and, with them, the tourist quarters of the central Right Bank.

Arriving by metro in the evening, you may wonder if you've landed in the right district, for once you've admired the triumphal arch you find yourself on a street that is otherwise given over to North African and Central Asian shops and eateries. So it's surprising to venture 50 yards on and find a liveried valet standing by the door, nodding to you to indicate, yes, this is indeed the place: Julien. Of course you can always arrive and depart by taxi. In either case, the life of the street is quickly forgotten in favor of the exuberance of the restaurant's Art Nouveau décor.

Julien and Brasserie Flo may share ownership, location, even clientele, but they invite two very different restaurant experiences. While both satisfy the appetite, only Julien is a feast for the eyes. In the late 19th century, the the terrain of the former ramparts of the city developed into what became known as the Grands Boulevards. Cafés, restaurants, theaters and then cinemas cropped up, turning the boulevards into one of the city's main hot spots. Julien was created in 1900 as part of that movement. Here, the Art Nouveau style flourished in all its dreamy passion: curves and countercurves, floral motifs, paintings in the fashion of Symbolism, tremendous mirrors leading the eye to a glass ceiling. Though the area itself is no longer as grand as it was a century ago, this remains Paris's main theater district, and after-theater/cinema diners still flock to Julien as well as to Brasserie Flo.

Julien's décor is nearly reason itself to come for a meal. The art nouveau lushness undoubtedly explains the showy air of success or chic that is sometimes displayed by the clientele once the room has filled (by 9:15pm), for such attitudes aren't called for in the rather moderate price. You may notice some diners, particularly those with cigarette in hand, striking a pose that would have been considered daring or elegant if the old-fashioned hats that adorn the hat hooks were theirs.

The pleasure is in the plate as well. Fresh ingredients are used to offer an appetizing range of starters, from salads to foie gras, followed by solid classic meat and fish dishes or a hearty goose cassoulet. Desserts are a bit bland, and in such a determinedly French chain anything with a foreign name (e.g. tiramisu) should be ignored. But you may feel so contented in this impressive dining hall that you'll want to stay seated for the length of a few more courses. Because of its size, Julien is ideal for a meal for a large group of 4-8, though also appealing for any number, even for a traveler lunching alone.

In Art Nouveau lushness of Julien's décor is nearly reason itself to come for a meal.

The marked absences on Julien's menu are seafood and choucroute, undoubtedly because Brasserie Flo, the elder member of the restaurant group, is so close by and those are among its specialties. To reach Brasserie Flo you need to venture further up the street away from Porte St-Denis then down a well-lit alley before entering this dark, smoky, wood-paneled and invariably crowded hideaway. While it draws much the same neatly dressed clientele as Julien, Brasserie Flo gives the impression of being a clandestine speak-easy. In addition to seafood and choucroute, you'll also find this a warm setting for onion soup, a warm slice of foie gras and rustic preparations of fish or beef. Brasserie Flo is therefore recommendable for grayer seasons and racier conversations.

㉕Le Petit Zinc

Address *11 rue Saint-Benoît, 6th arr.* ***Metro*** *Saint-Germain-des-Prés.* ***Tel*** *01 42 86 61 00 •* ***Fax*** *01 42 86 61 09.* ***Site*** *www.petitzinc.com* ***Open*** *Daily, noon-3pm and 7pm-midnight.* ***Menu*** *22€ (2 courses), 27€ (3 courses). ALC 38-53€.*

The Flo group's main competitor in the brasserie arena is the Les Frères Blancs group, which operates many of Paris's other celebrated brasseries—Au Pied de Cochon, L'Alsace, Charlot—along with flashy restaurants such as Le Procope, La Fermette Marbeuf and Le Grand Café. These are generally bright, handsome, up-edged places with a certain amount of historical attraction (e.g. Le Procope, founded in 1686). In the case of the brasseries, the seafood platter holds the place of honor, followed by the full range of brasserie comfort food. I am less enamored of these restaurants than the others mentioned in this section because, while alluringly gaudy, they seem to lack character, though not quality. They can also be rather pricey. Nevertheless, when one is conveniently available or when reservations elsewhere are hard to come by, I would certain consider them. L'Alsace (open 7/24) for Alsatian cuisine on the Champs-Elysées, for example, or Au Pied de Cochon (also 7/24) for marketplace history (for more see *Bistros: La Poule au Pot*), and most certainly Le Petit Zinc in the heart of the St. Germain Quarter.

Le Petit Zinc specializes in seafood and calf's liver (*foie de veau*), while also serving duck steak, lamb, hearty chickens and a good variety of fish. This is a sizable restaurant with a variety of alcoves and booths along with round and square tables, all surrounded by an attractive Art Nouveau-style décor, making the setting as fitting for a tête-à-tête as for a large gathering. Because of its location, décor, reliable cuisine and honorable service, this is a good place to keep in mind when you're staying in the area and don't want to venture too far for a feast. But since you won't be alone in that, it's advisable to reserve during prime time. In late spring and summer, Le Petit Zinc's sidewalk tables are among the most sought-after in the quarter.

REGIONAL RESTAURANTS

The renown of French cuisine doesn't merely come from its gastronomy but from the diversity of its regional cuisine. In fact, French gastronomy is above all a graceful and imaginative rendition of what the various regions and localities have brought to the table. France is a true culinary melting pot, comprised of 22 regions and within them 95 departments on its European territory (a department is comparable to a county), each with its own cheeses, wines, livestock, fish, fruits, vegetables and herbs that are its cultural and agricultural birthright. These ingredients are combined in regional, departmental and local preparations that manage, even today, to resist being submerged beneath wider influences.

The culinary traveler driving north to south through France for a week or two will witness daily changes in cuisine. The Loire River, for instance, not only splits the national weather map in two (clouds to the north, sun to the south) but also vaguely serves as the butter/oil dividing line, with butter being the grease of choice to the north and oil to the south, along with goose and duck fat in the southwest. Driving south you'll also find that goat and ewe cheeses increasingly compete with cow cheese, until cow cheese all but disappears along the Mediterranean. These and so much else distinguish the regions and departments of France.

The renown of French cuisine doesn't merely come from its gastronomy but from the diversity of its regional cuisine.

Some restaurants recommended in the previous section also have a regional bent (e.g. southwestern cuisine at L'Oulette, Provençal cuisine at Bastide de l'Odéon). They have not been placed here because they are less intimately attached to their territory than those explored below. The placement of these five restaurants in the regional section doesn't mean they are lesser restaurants. Chez Michel, for example, is a noteworthy restaurant in its own right, as well as being an excellent introduction to the tastes of Brittany. They're mentioned here because of their particular efforts to display the time-honored products and culture of their source. In many cases they set out unapologetically to present all of the clichés of local fare and to serve as veritable ambassadors from their region.

Brittany, France's West Wing

Made of stone, water, wind and tide, built of legend, tradition, faith and superstition, at once armor *(sea) and* argoat *(forest), Brittany is one of the most distinctive regions of France. Traveling through Brittany, France's west wing, one comes upon lighthouses, belfries, menhirs, dolmen, ossuaries, fortresses, roadside crosses, stone houses holding fast against the wind, boats setting out from craggy inlets and returning with the day's catch. Train tracks and highways have brought the coast back from centuries of relative isolation. Still Brittany's special Franco-Celtic culture exist, its traditions felt mostly to the west and center of the region, where the flag of Brittany—black and white with black symbols of ermines—is often displayed.*

26 Brittany: Chez Michel

Address *10 rue de Belzunce, 10th arr.* ***Metro*** *Poissonnière or Gare du Nord.* ***Tel*** *01 44 53 06 20.* ***Open*** *Tues.-Sat.* ***Menu/Carte*** *30€.*

A detour full of discover and seduction

Other than crêpes and galettes, the culinary traditions of Brittany aren't normally the stuff of French cookbooks. Brittany is reputed for its catch of fish and harvest of seafood and for bringing to market hearty vegetables such as artichokes, cauliflower, potatoes, onions, carrots and endives. But its recipes are generally considered to be practical and earnest. Thanks to Thierry Breton, however, and to his warm, upbeat Chez Michel, one is tempted to add another chapter. (As well as being the chef's name, Breton is the adjective for people and things from Brittany.)

It's unlikely that you would venture by Chez Michel without prompting given its situation behind a generic, if imposing, church in a nameless neighborhood where the only landmarks are the North and East Train Stations. In fact, neither the quarter nor the thought of Breton cooking sparked much interest from my usual co-testers. This led to two decisions: 1. I would write about Chez Michel only if it was worth the detour, 2. Better call L.

L. is a versatile dinner companion who is equally at home

in the lap of elegant gastronomy, in the seat of regional adventure and on the stool of a local hangout. Furthermore, she recently bought a blue and purple cotton and wool ensemble that she had the genius of making appear both chic and funky, depending on her earrings and hair color. It was well suited for the upstanding stellar restaurant we'd tried in December and it was equally appropriate for this unadorned, convivial restaurant in January. Nothing prepares a traveler better for Paris restaurant explorations than a versatile wardrobe.

Despite appearances, Chez Michel is far more than a neighborhood joint. Nor should it be considered merely a regional restaurant. M. Breton, who trained at the Ritz and other smart restaurants, clearly aspires here to offering excellent, unfamiliar cuisine while keeping prices moderate and the ambiance earthy. He succeeds on all accounts. Actually, the ambiance isn't so much earthy as seafaring; Chez Michel resembles an old cargo ship, with the pillar of the bar standing like a crow's nest in the middle of the room. Downstairs, the hold of this ship serves not only as its wine cellar but as a wonderful setting for a *table d'hôte*, where you and your traveling companion(s) can join up to 30 unacquainted diners gathered around long tables for a set 4-course meal of soup, fish, meat, and dessert (beverages chosen individually).

Nothing prepares a traveler better for Paris restaurant explorations than a versatile wardrobe.

While M. Breton prides himself on the quality and provenance of the fish and seafood he prepares, his culinary interests also include a range of inland dishes. For appetizers, the menu on our visit promised the saltwater scents of scallop tartare with an oyster sauce, herring-style marinated salmon, and fish soup, along with land-oriented dishes such as minced pork, foie gras with sweet prune cream sauce, and a tasty salad with crispy basil goat cheese biscuits (*craquelins*). L. declared her own warmed oysters "seductive." The menu changes frequently, so yours may propose other seductions.

The cool-weather Breton dish *far ha farz* is a succulent stew of pig's cheek, veal knuckles and grilled breast of pork served with the Breton pudding cake called *far*. L. had a taste of mine and declared it "very seductive." As for her scallops, they were so well prepared country-style that she almost forgot to share. And our neighbors' grilled duck cutlets and lamb sweetbreads appeared to be giving them so much pleasure that we nearly asked for a bite. The joint is easy-going enough that we probably could have; this is a great sharing restaurant. We also found a certain romance to the place, but the occasional peaks in noise level mean that it's well adapted for a party of 3 or more. Any number can reserve for the *table d'hôte*.

A table for 4 might share all of the heartwarming selectsions of traditional Breton desserts (Paris-Brest, *farz forn, kouign-amman, blanc manger*), though I found M. Breton's version of the region's signature warm, buttery milkbread kouing-amman rather ordinary. L. made the more interesting choice, crisp candied chestnuts served with a light spiced cream. "Try it," she said with a nod, "extremely seductive, don't you think?" I could only agree.

Basque Country

Basque country (Euzkadi in Basque) comprises a zone of conflicting ambitions within and around the western Pyrenees. Of the seven traditional Basque provinces, three are in France and four are in Spain. South of the border, Bilboa has received an inordinate amount of press and visitors in recent years due to Frank Gerhy's architecture for the Guggenheim Museum. The Spanish side is also notorious for terrorist attacks and political killings carried out by militant Basque separatists, ETA. France's Basque region is best known to travelers for the resort town of Biarritz, whose stretch of beach signals the start of the beautifully tormented shores of the Bay of Biscay. Saint-Jean-de-Luz is a popular, lower key bayside town near which the Pyrenees step into the sea. Aside from the occasional tuna or ttoro festival along the sea and in festivals in the regional capital Bayonne, Basque traditions and accents are most pronounced inland, particularly up in the hills. Sare, Aïnhoa and St-Jean-Pied-de-Port are among the most picturesque French Basque villages.

㉗ Basque Country: Au Bascou

Address *38 rue Réaumur, 3rd arr.* ***Metro*** *Arts et Métiers.*
Tel *01 42 72 69 25.* ***Closed*** *Sat. lunch, Sun., Mon. lunch.* ***ALC*** *30€.*
Wines *Extensive list of Basque and southwestern wines, mostly 22-30€.*

Simple and winning

If you lived in this neighborhood on the northern edge of the Marais, you would be proud to call yourself a regular in this winning Basque restaurant. You'd bring your American visitors here, pointing out the wonderfully brainy national museum of technical innovation (Arts et Métiers), a block to the west, and the site where, in 1792, Louis XVI and Marie-Antoinette were held prisoner after attempting to flee France (square du Temple), a block to the east. You'd show them your local food shops and market on rue de Bretagne and tell them about some deliciously rotting cheese you'd bought there the other day. By the time you arrived at the unassuming entrance to Au Bascou your friends would be telling you that you could pass for a real Parisian (as though a real Parisian would ever go to the museum of technologies or know where the royal family was held prisoner), only to be further impressed to see you receive a jovial welcome from Jean-Guy Loustau, the owner, who will never let on to your friends that your French is anything less than impeccable.

> **... J-G Loustau, the owner, who will never let on to your friends that your French is anything less than impeccable.**

It happened to be wood pigeon (*palombe*) hunting season in Basque country, October, when I first tested Au Bascou, and Madame Loustau was overseeing the restaurant for the week while her husband was out in the woods—during palombe-hunting season no woman would try to hold back a southwestern man with a rifle. His absence was a sign of authenticity; it not only meant that the pigeon was fresh but that the couple's regionally-minded restaurant had its heart in the region. A further sign was the wide selection of Irougéluy white and red wines from the Pyrenean slopes; M. Loustau may well know every winegrower in the appellation.

On a subsequent visit, in May, Madame was handling the accounts while Monsieur was extending a welcoming hand and, extroverted in both French and English, paying generous attention to diners with questions. To my own question, "How was the hunting last October?," he confessed that wood-pigeon season was above all a chance to hunt down old friends.

He is equally forthcoming in offering help with the menu and in discussing wine. For starters, consider *piperade* basquaise, a scrambled egg concoction containing tomatoes, onion, and garlic and served with warm cured ham, *pimiento del piquillo farcis*, peppers stuffed with seafood puree, the salty pleasures of Basque ham, or a cold mussel soup. For a main course, regional classics include *ttoro*, a Basque bouillabaisse, the most tasty Espelette-style *axoa de veau*, in which the veal is simmered along with onions and mild chili peppers for 5 hours, or the Spanish-leaning dish of small fresh calamari called *chiperons*, served with bits of chorizo on a bed of rice, perhaps a wild boar stew or roast wood pigeon in season. For dessert try the chocolate-lover's *beret basque* or a duo of basque pies.

It is perhaps because M. Loustau spent the first half of his career working in halls of elevated gastronomy, as sommelier then as director, that the décor of his own restaurant is so nondescript: a bunch of tables and chairs and yellow-brown walls. I note that favorably, for I highly recommend Au Bascou for a heartwarming introduction to the earnestness of preparations from France's far southwestern corner.

Corsica, the Isle of Beauty

Corsica is striking for both its natural beauty and its clannish protection for territory and privileges, but for the foreign traveler it is the former that shines through. The Isle of Beauty, as it's called, is a sun-drenched mountain rising from the Mediterranean, 113 miles long and 51 miles wide, with hundreds of miles of jagged, rocky inlets sheltering sand beaches. The rugged interior holds pastoral villages surrounded by a scrubby herb-scented underbrush called maquis. Corsican seasons are much like those along the Riviera, 80s in summer, 50s in winter. For the proper mix of warmth and crowds, it's ideal for a visit May-June or Sept.-Oct.

㉘Corsica: Paris-Main d'Or

Address *133 rue du Faubourg-St-Martin, 11th arr.* ***Metro*** *Ledru Rollin.* ***Tel*** *01 44 68 04 68.* ***Open*** *Mon.-Sat.* ***ALC*** *25-30€.*

Like a warm embrace

Peek in through the inconspicuous windows of Paris-Main d'Or and you may wonder why you've been summoned here. The sight of several men standing at the bar, the barman slowly wiping the countertop and a handful of clients sitting at bare tables can intimidate by its seeming confidentiality or lead you to wonder, given Corsica's quasi-Sicilian reputation, whether this is a racketeer storefront that you dare not enter. But do—past the few bistro tables, past the bar, down the gloomy hallway and into the dining area where, squeezed between brick and clay-painted walls, Main d'Or takes you in like a warm embrace.

Main d'Or manages to maintain an air of speakeasy confidentiality while being nothing of the sort. It is Paris's premier home of Corsican cuisine, with an authentic attachment to the earth, traditions, accent and nonchalance of the Isle of Beauty. The waiters come across less as French service people than as a group of accommodating Corsicans intent on offering a glimpse of their island culture.

Olive oil, tomatoes, peppers, pasta and herbs otherwise associated with Italian or Provencal cooking are naturally present in the island's cuisine. But make random choices from the menu and you're sure to come up with at least one course containing *brocciu*, Corsica's favorite (you might think only) cheese. Made of ewe's or goat's milk and used fresh or slightly aged, it finds its way into or alongside sardines, artichokes, ravioli, pastries and more. In fact, *brocciu* or no *brocciu*, you can't go wrong with making random choices from the sizable menu, which is written in French and in Corsican, an Italian derivative.

For an appetizer, you may be lucky enough to let your finger land on *charcuterie corse* to enjoy the pronounced tastes of Corsican cold cut meats, or on baked eggplant, a reminder that Corsica is indeed close to Italy. For a main course, you may again have to rely on chance to choose between the variety of offerings, each worthy of a healthy appetite: a good cod, a homey meat stew in red wine (*daube*), a well-herbed baked tianu of lamb, roast goat (*cabri rôti*) or game in season. Fruity yet earthy young red wines from Calvi, Patrimonio and other island appellations make for amiable company whatever dishes you select.

Substantial portions for the first two courses leave scarce room for dessert, but they are well worth a share or more. Especially since that's where the *brocciu* is best: as a stuffing for crepes or in the island's celebrated pie called *fiadone*.

㉙ Auvergne: Ambassade d'Auvergne

Address *22 rue du Grenier-Saint-Lazare, 3rd arr.* ***Metro*** *Rambuteau.* ***Tel*** *01 42 72 31 22 •* ***Fax*** *01 42 78 85 47.*
Site *www.ambassade-auvergne-com.* ***Open*** *Daily.* ***Menu*** *27€.* ***ALC*** *30-39€.*

The best provincial ambassadors around

If all embassies (*ambassades*) were as appealing and friendly representatives of their territory as the Embassy of Auvergne, there would be peace on earth and brotherly love and joy throughout the world.

Just kidding. If nothing else, people would eat heartily while waiting in line for their visas.

As with any unfamiliar region in France, Auvergne is best approached by way of its cheese, namely the pressed cow-milk laguiole and the blue ewe-milk roquefort. The laguiole is found in the baked vegetable appetizer *clafoutis de legumes*, or combined with sliced potatoes, garlic and bacon in the robust *truffade*, or thickening the garlicky potato puree called aligot. The aligot is stretched like taffy in the dining room before

Auvergne

Auvergne is France's mid-southern region, where extinct volcanoes dominate the landscape and major rivers take their source. For a visitor, it is a region for hiking, eco-tourism, mountain-top panoramas (Puy de Dôme), stone villages, and for dipping into the spa waters of La Bourboule or Châtel-Guyon or for hiding out in the darkly alluring spa town of Mont-Dore, with or without a brief stop in the regional capital Clermont-Ferrand to visit its old town built of black lava. Even for frequent return American travelers this is among the country's least explored regions. The Ambassade d'Auvergne, created and operated by the Petrucci family since 1967, may be more well known.

being served from a copper pan along with a country sausage. The roquefort makes for a rustic starter when mixed in with cabbage soup or a fine finisher from the handsome selection of regional cheeses (since desserts are less interesting). Other tasteworthy regional dishes include pork stewed with braised cabbage, panned trout and roasted lamb with rosemary.

This is the kind of fare to reward yourself with after a long hike around a crater lake… or along the streets of Paris. More adventuresome travelers may be tempted by other regional specialties such as blood sausage, mutton tripe and veal intestines. Unpretentious table wines and regional brandies complete the meal.

The ground-floor dining room, known here as *l'auberge* (the inn), is preferable for its more countrified ambiance. Yet the classically provincial room upstairs, with peach walls, heavy wood furnishings and paintings of villages in Auvergne, enjoys the same pleasing service from some of the best cultural attachés around.

Despite this restaurant's popularity, it may be possible to find room at the inn if you arrive without a reservation. That is if you don't mind joining (or if you ask to join) the *table d'hôte,* a large table for an assortment of 10 unexpected guests. The dining experience is especially homey and conversational there. Don't count on your tablemates shifting to English on your behalf, but if you're the least bit Francophone you'll find this the next best thing to being invited to someone's country home.

㉚Lozère: Maison de la Lozère

Address *4 rue Hautefeuille, 6th arr.* ***Metro*** *Saint-Michel or Cluny.*
Tel *01 43 54 26 64.* ***Open*** *Tues.-Sat.* ***Menu*** *15€ (L), 21€, 25€.*
ALC *21-27€.*

Rustic and homey traditions

Though the tourist office for the department of Lozère is next door, a meal at the Maison de la Lozère may be sufficient promotion on its own. They are no foreigners to animal intestines in Lozère, but here you can also find a decent rib steak, a fine cèpe mushroom omelet, a filet of smoked trout, a salmon trout served with cured ham, a delicious garlicky saddle of lamb and lamb chops. Quarters of rounds of country-style bread are set at each table to be cut and distributed companionably—bread, by the way, that goes very well with the roquefort salad or with the generous cheese tray.

Along with the food, the tile floor and massive wood furnishings give this small restaurant the feel of a clean country cottage, which may set you renewing dreams of renting a house in the French countryside some summer.

Lozère

Lozère is a rural, backwoodsy department northwest of Provence that is so little known to American travelers that this may well be the closest you'll ever get. With only 73,000 inhabitants, a 50% decrease since 1910, Lozère is a case study in the depletion of the back-road villages of France and the resulting effort to promote itself as a back-to-nature zone. Roving Francophiles should stop into the department's tourist bureau next door to the restaurant. It may well tempt you to plan, or at least imagine, a breathtaking drive along the gorges of the Tarn and the corniche roads of the Cévennes.

Foreign Restaurants

As a multiethnic capital, Paris offers not only the best of France but also the best of other communities that have carved out a place for themselves in the city. This section presents detours to foreign cuisines in Paris, a selection for travelers ready to expand their culinary and cultural horizons as seen from overseas. Sometimes you just get tired of French food, however diverse it may be. Or you suddenly feel nostalgic for a previous vacation in Portugal or Cyprus. Or you want to seize the occasion to taste the forbidden fruit (and leaves) of Cuba. Or you have some Spanish or Russian blood in you and need a fix. Maybe you just like sushi or Thai. The restaurants selected below are not necessarily the top-rated representatives of their country. I have chosen them rather for their combination of character, quality and authenticity.

㉛Mexican: A la Mexicaine

Address *68 rue Quincampoix (intersection with 66 rue Rambuteau), 3rd arr.* ***Metro*** *Rambuteau.* ***Tel*** *01 48 87 99 34 •* ***Fax*** *01 42 77 66 21.* ***Closed*** *Mon. lunch, Tues.* ***Menu*** *15€ (L), 23€, 45€.* ***ALC*** *29-43€.*

When the French think of American cuisine they imagine us feasting on nothing but Bic Macs because they never had a fresh, juicy 4th of July hamburger hot off the grill. Similarly, our own thoughts of Mexican food tends to have a distinctly flatulent Tex-Mex air to them. The late '90s brought a strong whiff of Tex-Mex to Paris, but it's generally as ordinary in Paris as it is north of New Mexico.

Well, wake up and smell the salsa! Rather studied Mexican cuisine does exist. If it takes Paris to introduce you to it then so be it. If fine Mexican dishes are no revelation to you, then you can already sense the savors to be found in this laid-back, spacious, popular restaurant near the Pompidou Center. In either case, after several days of trying to use your high school Spanish on French waiters, this is your chance to shine.

Well, wake up and smell the salsa! Rather studied Mexican cuisine does exist.

The menu at A la Mexicaine is a scribble of details, but do try to decipher it, because once a dish has been set before you you'll find that the flavors and fragrances promised on the menu are all present. The menu is also worth a read in order to learn such culinary nuggets as the origin of the word avocado as found in the word guacamole—from the Aztec expression for "testicles of the gods." With all due respect to the scholar behind the menu, I'm not quite convinced this is true, but it deserves mention anyway in case anyone might want to use it as a pick-up line.

To start, consider the soft-boiled eggs *à la poblanita*, the *chalupitas* or the assortment of three *antojitos*. The *pozole* soup can make for a meal in itself—if you don't mind that some of the flavor comes from the presence of pig's snout and ear. The *taquedas, enchiladas* and *tamales* are each more refined versions than those most of us are accustomed to, while the beef is from Argentina. For something less familiar, try the spicy monkfish or the peppers stuffed with zucchini and cheese. And save room for dessert, a tough choice between a bittersweet chocolate Moctezuma, a creamy guanabana pie, a soothing plate of 7 ice creams and sherberts, and a *capirotada.*

Gastronomy is too strong a word to describe this cuisine, for it lacks the refinement associated with the term in Paris. Furthermore, the occasional chipped tableware doesn't earn gastronomy points. Nevertheless, A la Mexicaine offers a discovery of savor and is well worth the return to the Americas. And the staff is so gentle and amiable (if occasionally wary of questions) that you'll know they didn't develop their public relations skills in Paris.

㉜ Belgian: Graindorge

Address *15 rue de l'Arc de Triomphe, 17th arr.* ***Metro*** *Etoile or Ternes.* ***Tel/Fax*** *01 47 54 00 28.* ***Closed*** *Sat. lunch, Sun.* ***Menu*** *28€ (L), 32€ (D).* ***ALC*** *40-45€.*

France's northern neighbor is forever associated with mussels and fries (*moules-frites*), the Belgian equivalent of the French *steak-frites* or of our own burger and fries. Graindorge presents a more sophisticated side of Belgian cuisine, particularly preparations from Flanders, the western, Dutch-speaking part of the country. There are *moules* on the menu, of course, but they're served here in a tasty soup of mussels and shrimp from Ostende and in mussel-and-shrimp-stuffed tomatoes. For a less coastal starter try *potjevleesch*, an appetizing terrine of slowly simmered veal, pork, fowl and rabbit en *gelée.*

While chef Bernard Broux revisits and updates classic Belgian recipes and then some in the kitchen, Sophie Broux and her young staff provide gentle service in the Art Deco-style dining room. Seating is intimate enough for private conversation, yet one can't help but be aware of the characters around the room: the two men who have placed their cell phones across from each other on the table as if some kind of challenge, a lap dog being passed back and forth between a couple nearby.

One of the giddy pleasures of ordering in a foreign restaurant is trying to pronounced the names of the dishes. I dare you to order the potjevleesch without pointing to the word.

One of the giddy pleasures of ordering in a foreign restaurant is trying to pronounce the names of the dishes. I dare you to order the *potjevleesch* without pointing to the word. With a little practice, though, *waterzooï* will easily roll of your lips—

and, once in front of you, easily roll back in. *Waterzooï* is a flavorsome stew which, this evening, takes its polished seafood form, with prawns and scallops along with herbs and light vegetables. Chicken and fish-and-eel versions also exist in Flanders.

Diners needn't choose only from among the classics of Belgium cuisine and drink, as we did. M. Broux also intelligently prepares several attractive and less regional meat (lamb) and fish (red mullet, cod) dishes. Still, as venturesome travelers, there would be something unreasonable about going to a Belgian restaurant in Paris and not having a northern feast. My co-tester, Joan, therefore dutifully ordered the *civet de lièvre*, a hare stew in which the beast has been steeped in a batter of beer with a hint of cocoa. The result was a delicious sauce, yet the meat itself was rather tough. Neither of us being expert in the dish, we could only conclude that we didn't much care for hare stew. Unless it was just a bad hare night! That joke itself made the dish well worth ordering. Good company and a good laugh is often all it takes for curious travelers to enjoy a restaurant.

That and the right beverage.

Grain d'orge means barleycorn, meaning you'll find here a wide selection of traditionally-made beers from both French and Belgian Flanders. The wine list may well be ignored. Most of the 20-some variety of beers are served in 75cl (wine-size) bottles to be shared—or not. France is not generally known for the quality of its beer, nevertheless some evocative brews are created on this side of the Belgian border: low-fermented Ch'ti, high-fermented Angélus, bitter Rouge Flamande. Belgium's brewing traditions are better known: cherry-flavored Kriek, hearty Gueuze, sweet Far, potent coffee-laced Kastel bier. A Trappist Chimay accompanied us smoothly through the meal, Joan being thoughtful enough to prefer something dark.

㉝ Portuguese: Saudade

Address *34 rue des Bourdonnais, 1st arr.* ***Metro*** *Pont-Neuf or Châtelet.* ***Tel*** *01 42 36 30 71.* ***Open*** *Mon.-Sat.* ***ALC*** *27-38€.*

Saudade, we're told on the menu cover of this engaging restaurant, is an untranslatable word that speaks of nostalgia for the past, melancholy of the present, tenderness of memory, romanticism of Portugal. For a traveler to Portugal *saudade* is at once a depth of bittersweetness and a cliché that we imagine we have found in the dull blue of old Azulejo glazed tile, on the slopes of the Alfama, in the Bairro Alto, in the view of a tugboat on the River Tagus, in the fog at Sintra, in the songs of fado on the Amalia Rodrigues album we brought home—for you have to leave someplace and return (or not) in order to feel the sad joy and hopeful sadness of *saudade*.

If you've been to Portugal then you might consider this Saudade at the center of Paris as a bit of a return. If you've never been, then let this restaurant serve as your introduction. It's unpretentious and earnest, with provincial chairs, Azulejo tiles images on the wall, and songs of fado over the speakers (or live the first Tuesday of the month). The service is at once virile and obsequious, a rare combination in Paris, contributing to a subdued atmosphere that fully lends itself to focusing on the pleasure at your own table—food, drink, companion(s).

If you've been to Portugal then you might consider this Saudade at the center of Paris as a bit of a return. If you've never been, then let this restaurant serve as your introduction.

I found that a delicious way to start dinner was the aromatic *sopa alentejana*, a soup with coriander, garlic, onion, egg and olive oil. For a main course, while there are meat dishes on the menu, Portuguese cuisine is above all a celebration of fresh cod (*bacalhau*), and Saudade does a great job of demonstrating the variety of possible cod dishes. Among the highlights, the copious *cataplana de bacalhau* (for two)—in which shellfish and chorizo accompany the cod in a sauce of garlic, onion, tomato and white wine—is a feast in itself. After that, you needn't order much further (desserts aren't the strong point here) unless to enjoy some sheep's milk cheese along with the last glass of Madeira.

34 Greek-Cypriot: Kasaphani

Address *122 avenue Parmentier, 11th arr.* ***Metro*** *Parmentier or Goncourt.* ***Tel*** *01 48 07 20 19.* ***Closed*** *Sat. lunch, Mon.* ***Menu*** *26€.* ***ALC*** *24-34€.*

When the Latin Quarter's narrow streets rue de la Huchette (behind place St-Michel) and rue Mouffetard (behind the Pantheon) are visited in the morning, they exude the joys and mysteries of an old and enduring city. But as the day wears on they become increasingly defined by their congregation of inferior Greek restaurants, the stuff of youthful backpacking adventures of the 20th century and of the security-in-English-speaking-numbers approach to budget travel today. Do include those streets in a stroll through the Latin Quarter, but when it comes to a meal, beware of Greeks bearing gifts, i.e., a dark-haired man with a wide smile promising a free house aperitif if you'll enter his restaurant.

Not far from rue Mouffetard, by the Censier-Daubenton metro stop, Mavrommatis is a far more trustworthy Greek restaurant, but it is a trademark that lacks character and is more notable as a caterer than as a restaurateur.

If you're going to do it, do it right. That means heading well off the tourist trails to Pavlos's Kasaphani. (Admittedly, Kasaphani, the owner's birthplace in Cyprus, is Greek-Cypriot rather than Greek-Greek.) Part of the restaurant's natural warmth comes from the fact that Pavlos is accompanied on and off by several of his brothers and a sister. While Kasaphani is always easy-going and folksy, the ambiance varies from downbeat to party-like depending on the time, the day and the number of Greeks and Cypriots present. Later is better, after 9 or even 10, when the sense of well-being emanating from the visible kitchen and from the bar counter have fully permeated the room.

But don't come looking for the ambiance alone because it may be a slow night. Come rather for the pleasures at your own table. Good company to start. Then perhaps a glass of ouzo. Followed by the large variety of Cypriot hors d'oeuvres—calamari, octopus, tahini, tsatsiki, tarama, etc.—which, like the restaurant itself, lends itself to both an intimate share and to a gathering of friends. The most familiar Balkan dish, *moussaka*, is naturally on the menu as a main course, as is *yemista* (vegetables stuffed with rice and beef) and *sheftalia* (a pork sausage). However, Kasaphani's true specialties are its grilled lamb and fish, dusted with a peppery oregano from Cyprus. Greek-Cypriot desserts and/or a variety of liquored coffees may follow. After which one does not necessarily ask for the check. Even on a slow evening, when the atmosphere is merely hospitable, one wants to linger at table. Late some evenings, particularly on weekends, Kasaphani becomes a veritable party, either due to the evident enjoyment of the clientele or thanks to the surprise visit of a Greek or Cypriot musician, a rembetico player perhaps, prolonging the evening with his sultry, seductive folk sounds.

No less a knowing diner than L. introduced me to Kasaphani, for she has been coming here since her friend Pavlos opened the restaurant in 1983. You could consider their friendship—and now mine—as a disclaimer of self-interest, but after a meal or two here you'll find your own self-interest in the warmth of Kasaphani.

㉟Spanish: Fogón St-Julien

Address *10 rue St-Julien-le-Pauvre, 5th arr.* ***Metro*** *Saint-Michel.* ***Tel*** *01 43 54 31 33 •* ***Fax*** *01 43 54 07 00.* ***Open*** *Daily for dinner, also Sat. and Sun. for lunch.* ***Menu*** *28€ (3 courses of tapas), 37€ (tapas + paella + dessert).* ***ALC*** *33-48€.* ***Historical note:*** *Paris's oldest living tree stands on a crutch in the square out front of the restaurant, a black locust (Robinier false acacia) planted in 1601 by the royal botanist Jean Robin.*

Fogón means fire, *tapas* are an assortment of small appetizers, *chorizo* is a pork sausage spiced with paprika and garlic, *paella* is the shallow pan the famous rice dish is made in, *postres* are desserts, *vino* means… Oh, you know all that already! Well put on something colorful, admire the old tree out front and Notre-Dame across the river and come on in.

Fogón doesn't set out to fulfill fantasies of southern Spanish flamboyance. This is a relatively restrained restaurant with a sober décor. But don't let that fool you. The ambiance in the two compact dining rooms comes from a vibrant, well-groomed crowd and, more importantly, from the aforementioned Spanish words above translated on your plate.

The menu is limited to what chef Alberto Herraiz apparently knows best: Spanish cold cuts, tapas, and paella, along with a short selection of emphatic Spanish wines (served in curious glasses typically reserved for drinking fermented cider in Galicia) and an excellent basket of (French) bread.

The fresh quality of the appetizer tapas (e.g. sardine rolls, deep-fried minced ham, John Dory fish, octopus) and the assortment of dessert tapas nearly tempt me to recommend the tapas menu, but Fogón is above all an *arroceria*, so it succeeds or fails on the merits of its rice dishes. Señor Herraiz prepares a refined paella without the oiliness that is found in more ordinary versions. Five different paellas are on the menu: a vegetable paella, three fish and seafood paellas and a chicken-rabbit-snail-vegetable paella, each made with a different kind of rice. All paella dishes are for a minimum of two people,

Cuban food, drink, smokes

Cigars: La Casa del Habano

***Address** 169 blvd. Saint-Germain, 6th arr. Near rue des Saints-Pères. **Metro** St-Germain-des-Prés. **Tel** 01 45 49 24 30 • **Fax** 01 45 44 65 64. **Open** Mon.-Sat.*

Restaurant/Bar: Little Havana

***Address** 5 rue de Sévigné, 4th arr. **Metro** Saint-Paul. Tel 01 42 74 75 90. **Open** Daily.*

Restaurant/Bar/Club: La Bodeguita de Medio (a.k.a. La B del M)

***Address** 10 rue des Lombards, 4th arr. **Metro** Châtelet. **Tel** 01 44 59 66 90 • **Fax** 01 44 59 91. **Open** Daily 11am-2am.*

Nothing in Paris excites some American doctors, lawyers and businessmen more than the possibility of partaking of the forbidden leaf: Cuban cigars. They're easy enough to come by in tobacco stores (tabac) throughout the city center. The mojito—the classic Cuban cocktail of white rum, lime, sugar, tonic, fresh mint leaves and ice—is also now a staple of upscale and popular bars alike. But to feel even closer to the origins of Cuban smoke and drink (and rice) here are a few suggestions to help you do your part to end the embargo:

***La Casa de Habano**, befitting the St. Germain quarter, is a well-dressed, modish restaurant and bar for guys who look good with a cigar and dolls who look good with a guy with a cigar. The joint downstairs is classy enough to have a couple of ladies out for lunch together and cheeky enough that they can light up, too, after dinner. But for our purposes it's just a place to buy Cubans. Cigars, that is. Day or night, just head upstairs to the smokes counter by the humidor room for one of the widest selections of cigars around.*

*In the Marais, **Little Havana** is a small restaurant/bar where the ambiance is alternately uptempo and melancholic but always sweet and friendly. Come here for Havana Club rum, moderately priced Cuban fare and cohibas. Like love, I've been told here, they're open every day.*

*On a narrow nightlife street of the Châtelet quarter, **La B del M**, a simulation of the celebrated bar in Havana, serves the same rum and robusto cohiba but here there's frequently an air of fiesta, a fiesta that's either about to begin, on-going or winding down. A long bar, a Cuban band, a smoking room, Che iconography and many mojitos complete the picture.*

making for a sweet table-for-two share. But due to the high level of chatter bouncing off the walls by 9pm, Fogón is better suited for a party of four. I only lament that the fixed-price menu comes with the strict stipulation that only one type of paella may be chosen per table. You'll all just have to enjoy the same dish.

㊱Russian 1: Dominque

***Address** 19 rue Bréa, 6th arr.* ***Metro** Vavin.* ***Tel** 01 43 27 08 80.*
***Open** Tues.-Sat., 7:30pm-1am, take-out counter and tasting bar open 11am-1am.* ***Menu** 40€, 55€.* ***ALC** 40-75€.* ***Caviar** 42-99€/30 grams.*

In 1928, George Gershwin wrote *An American in Paris* during a stay in the City of Light. It's a piece so airy, optimistic, and contemporary (still) as to make us want to saunter down the boulevard, fall in love, buy roses for strangers and cozy up to the crowds in the grand cafés along boulevard du Montparnasse.

In 1928, Sergey Prokofiev, who spent much time in Paris through the 1920s, was reworking a flagging opera as his *Third Symphony*. It's a piece that's heavy, haunting and grim enough to make you want to plod down the boulevard in obsessive reverie, fall in love, give coins to vagrants and seek warmth among the crowds in the grand cafés along boulevard du Montparnasse.

In 1928, the Russian restaurant Dominique opened its doors a block away from those grand cafés (La Coupole, Le Dôme, La Rotonde, Le Sélect), where émigrés, artists, students, celebrants, tourists, the bourgeoisie and aristocrats alike gathered day and night. Among them were a great number of Russians: Prokofiev, Eisenstein, Maiakovsky and Ehrenburg, to name several 30-something artists on the rise.

So you're nearly obliged by tradition, as well as by location, to have a drink along the boulevard before passing behind Rodin's cloaked Balzac to dine at Dominique.

Beyond the take-out counter (herring, salmon, caviar, etc.) and a quick-dining/vodka bar lies a red-tinged interior that will be considered warm if you've got any Russian blood and moody if you don't, or vice versa. With Russian music playing discreetly in the background but with few of the decorative clichés of the old country, Dominique reaches some essential yearning in the life of a Russian émigré or artist or thwarted (or now-successful) heir, as well as for Franco-Russian pacts of yore.

The waiters take the undertaker approach to honorable service, leaning with a stiff bow to set before you a dish of Gien porcelain containing an assortment of herring preparations that would have made your great-grandmother think she'd been invited to dine with the czar. The evocative tastes of deliciously smoked eel and salmon eggs, the assortment of herring, the *zakousa* (or *zakouski*, hors d'oeuvres), the sturgeon on a skewer and the *charchlik kasky* of roast lamb are all the more noteworthy in that they are so uncommon in Paris. Vodka, meanwhile, the Russian drink of choice since the 14th century, goes with any course but dessert, unless it is dessert.

The waiters take the undertaker approach to honorable service.

Dominique offers a wistful dining experience that can be enjoyed by anyone in the spirit of adventure. The price of such wistfulness may limit its appeal to those with Russian blood, Russophiles and travelers who still plan to (re)read *The Brothers Karamozov*. For others the finely smoked tastes of distant foods may be worth a splurge, yet at about 75€/person (without caviar but with a couple of glasses of Stoly) you could already have one foot in the glossy reaches of French cuisine—and a glimpse of Gene Kelly dancing by.

㊲ Russian 2: L'Epicerie Russe

Address *13 rue de la Terrasse, 17th arr.* ***Metro*** *Villiers.*
Tel *01 40 54 04 05.* ***Open*** *Mon.-Sat. 10am-midnight.* ***Zakouski menu*** *30€ for two.*

The vodka may have the same color, otherwise this tiny Russian take-out/eat-in shop has nothing in common with Dominique. This is a homey place with a pronounced accent, where you can pick yourself up a zakouski picnic of herring, cold pureed eggplant, smoked salmon, tarama and stuffed grape leaves. Or take a seat at one of the few tables to share a mix of those Russian hors d'oeuvres for lunch or for a teatime snack of *watrouchka* (egg and cheese baked in a dough roll), *koulibiac* (fish baked in a dough roll) or *pirojki* (fruit-filled dessert). Or add borscht and strogonoff to that for a complete dinner.

㊳Japanese: Isami

***Address** 4 quai d'Orléans, 4th arr. On the southern side of Ile Saint-Louis. **Metro** Pont-Marie. **Tel** 01 40 46 06 97. **Closed** Sun. lunch, Mon. and August **ALC** 24€.*

Sushi and other rice rolls are now a frequent sight in Paris, a fad whose rise can be situated sometime around the decline of tex-mex a few years ago. You'll find sushi at French caterers, in supermarkets, at "Chinese" food stands, at hip bars.

Where does that leave a sushi-sashimi master the likes of Katsuo Nakamura? Concentrated on the task at hand in Isami, his little restaurant on Ile Saint-Louis. Yes, Ile Saint-Louis, otherwise known as home to the quaintest of Parisian charms, to Bertillon ice and to aristocrats and foreign wealth.

Isami is far removed from Paris's little Japan, whose sushi bars and various Asian restaurants gather along rue Sainte-Anne (between Palais Royal and avenue de l'Opéra, Metro Pyramides). Elsewhere, upscale Japanese and Franco-Japanese restaurants are found in the business/ palatial hotel/high fashion quarters surrounding the Champs-Elysées.

You come to Isami for raw fish and seafood and rice or you don't come at all.

But I prefer Isami for its simple purity. Isami consists of a half-dozen stools at the counter and a half-dozen tables nearby. Dirty dishes disappear into the dumbwaiter. The basement restrooms are themselves wise use of limited space. Isami is so sweet and clean and kindly and unassuming that it is at once an oddly romantic setting and welcoming for a solitary lunch. It may be possible to arrive unannounced between 1:30 and 2pm after the initial lunch crowd has left, otherwise reservations are advised.

Mr. Nakamura serves sushi, sashimi and maki. Period. Oh, you get your light miso soup to start, your Sapporo beer or sake to accompany, dessert if you like (through you might as well skip it, what with Bertillon sherberts available just around the corner). But you come to Isami for raw fish and seafood and rice or you don't come at all.

Mr. Nakamura has been fondling sushi for 40 years, and that's that. His wife tells me this as she and I watch him pick up a slice of tuna, mold a palmful of rice, dip a finger in wasabi, rub it on the fish, twist it all together—and voilà, lunch. "My husband is a traditionalist," she says, tapping a finger to her temple to indicate either that he is very wise or very stubborn.

Mrs. Nakamura herself is very kind, with a surprisingly generous laugh that she offers when I tell her that I'm writing for Americans. "Tell them the *wasabi* is inside," she says, referring to the pungent green horseradish-like root."We only put it on the side for children. We are Japanese.""

"California rolls," she laughs, as though it were a zen punch line.

㊴Thai 1: Baan Boran

Address *43 rue Montpensier, 1st arr.* ***Metro*** *Palais Royal or Pyramides.* ***Tel*** *01 40 15 90 45.* ***Open*** *Mon.-Sat.* ***ALC*** *26-30€.*

㊵Thai 2: Blue Elephant

Address *43-45 rue de la Roquette, 11th arr.* ***Metro*** *Bastille or Voltaire.* ***Tel*** *01 47 00 42 00* • ***Fax*** *01 47 00 45 44.*
Site *www.blueelephant.com.* ***Closed*** *Sat. lunch.* ***Menu*** *44€, 48€.* ***ALC*** *40-45€.*

While generic coconut-milk-based Thai dishes are found on the menus of Paris's numerous Chinese and Vietnamese restaurants, a truer taste for the savors and mild heat (or more) of Thai cuisine may lead you to one of these two uptone restaurants.

Baan Boran is more accessible in all respects: central (on a narrow street alongside the Palais Royal), moderately priced, a cheerful orderly décor, a staff of efficient kindness. It is especially recommendable for a change from French cuisine when staying in one of the hotels in the area or, as L. would say, when you want to be on a diet without tempting the devil: green papaya salad, *tom khaa kai* (slightly spiced chicken-and-coconut-milk soup), *gaeng som* (sour shrimp-and-vegetable soup); fish with coconut milk, duck, beef curry with coconut milk; mango soup, various coconut-milk desserts.

While Baan Boran offers emblematic Thai food, Blue Elephant invites more of a Thai adventure. From the smiling welcome to the leafy, exotic décor to the beef curry served in a freshly opened coconut shell, Blue Elephant transports travelers to some far-off Hilton or Intercontinental. The most ambient way of getting here is by walking from the Bastille along rue de la Roquette, with a detour along rue de Lappe, to witness the mix of hip, funky, salsa-laced, sexual and passé venues that crowd along those streets. However, Blue Elephant tends to be the kind of place business travelers take a taxi to while gazing out the window. This would be a great sharing restaurant if the portions were bigger. But don't let that stop you from begging a bit of your companion's spicy green papaya and dried shrimp appetizer (*som tam*) or fish fritters with curry and citronella (*tod man pla*). Blue Elephant is famous for its spicy dishes (e.g. *homok talay*, a seafood stew, or the Siamese duck curry) yet one can choose to eat mild.

North African cuisine

The latest official census reports that there are 308,266 foreigners in Paris, comprising 14.5% of the city's population. Of those, there were more than 33,500 Algerians, 23,000 Moroccans and 18,000 Tunisians, not including the many more French of North African descent in and around the capital. Cafés, shops and restaurants in pockets of the northern and eastern arrondissements most clearly indicate the presence of North African cultures in Paris, however a good and relatively inexpensive couscous or tagine can be found in any quarter. Every Parisian has got his favorite couscous restaurant, the way we might have our favorite pizza or Chinese place at home. Asking around for a good North African restaurant is therefore one of the best ways to make contact with native or foreign-born Parisians. So I leave it to you to find your own. Here are a few definitions to get you on your way:

Couscous: *Steamed semolina served with a vegetable stew and your choice of one or more of the following: mutton, chicken, lamb, beef, merguez, occasionally fish.*

Tagine: *A tender stew generally of beef, lamb or chicken, long-cooked in an earthenware dish with a cone-shaped cover.*

Merguez: *A spicy reddish sausage containing no pork (the Muslim religion forbids eating pork). Served as a hot dog at street fares and demonstrations.*

Harissa: *A thick and very spicy paste containing pimento, cayenne pepper, garlic and oil. Served on a small saucer to be mixed in (or not) with the couscous broth or with other dishes or spread on bread.*

Food Markets

You can't help but be a food tourist in Paris, but the Paris food experience isn't limited to restaurants. There are bakeries, of course, and deli/caterers, and as with everywhere you travel, a cultural experience is available in the grocery store. But there's nothing like an outdoor or covered food market or a traditional market street to discover the life, people and language of a destination.

The supermarket may have taken over from specialty stores in many parts of Paris, yet traditional covered or outdoor food markets continue to thrive. Five thousand stalls in the city's 68 markets are available for merchants in Paris to sell their produce, meats, cheese, bread, fish, seafood, ethnic dishes, etc. Outside certain banking, business, up-end sections of the Right Bank, every quarter of the city has one or more markets within easy walking distance, creating a small-town or even village atmosphere there, where the traveler can feel the beat of a season, the pulse of a neighborhood.

Here are a few notable markets (*marchés*) to aim for:

Marché St-Germain

Metro *Mabillon, 6th arr.* ***Open*** *Tues.-Sat. 8:30am-1pm, 4-7:30pm, Sun. 8:30am-1pm.* The covered market on rue Lobineau is a must for anyone staying in the Saint-Germain quarter. Rue de Buci, across bd. St-Germain, is the other market street in the area.

Rue Montorgueil

Metro *Les Halles or Etienne Marcel, 2nd arr.* One of the city's most charming market streets, rue Montorgueil is the final active remnant of the central food market of Les Halles that fed Paris for 800 years until 1969. A pedestrian street of much appeal for café lovers.

Rue Cler

Metro *Ecole Militaire, 7th arr.* Another sweet little market street with appealing lunchtime cafés, a few blocks from the Invalides. Many Americans live in this area.

Marché Richard-Lenoir

Metro *Bastille or Bréguet-Sabin, 11th arr.* ***Open*** *Thurs & Sun. mornings* Bastille's market is one of the largest in the city, spreading along bd. Richard Lenoir from Place de la Bastille to rue Saint-Sabin.

Marché Beauvau/Marché d'Aligre

Metro *Ledru-Rollin, 12th arr.* ***Open*** *daily 8:30 am - 1 pm* ***Closed*** *Mon* Great atmosphere and local flavor at this exuberant traditional outdoor/indoor market combination. The covered market alone is also open Tues.-Sat. 4-7:30pm.

Marché Mouffetard

Metro *Censier-Daubenton, 5th arr.* The morning market at the bottom of rue Mouffetard near the architectural hodgepodge of the Church of Saint-Médard is another charmer. A picturesque grouping of food stalls and people spill out onto this narrow old street, which covers over the old course of a stream. An outdoor market fills nearby Place Monge *(Metro Place Monge)* on Wed., Fri. and Sun. mornings.

Marché de Belleville

Metro *Belleville, 11th/20th arr.* ***Open*** *Tues. & Fri. mornings* The Belleville market stretches like a magic carpet along the boulevard de Belleville, offering glimpses and tastes of the rich ethnic mix of the neighborhood.

Marché Bio Raspail

Metro *Rennes, 6th arr.* ***Open*** *Sun. morning* Reflecting an interest in organic produce that outgrew the specialty store in the 1990s, the Raspail market is given over to organic foods on Sun. morning. A standard market occupies the space Tues. and Fri. mornings.

PRACTICAL INFORMATION TO REFRESH YOUR MEMORY

PASSPORT

U.S. citizens need only a valid passport to enter France. No other document is necessary for those remaining in France for less than 90 days. Those planning to stay longer, such as students on study programs, require special visas. Consult the Consular Section of the French Embassy in the United States for visa information: www.france-consulat.org.

If you are an American citizen and lose your passport, you should immediately contact the U.S. Consulate in France. The American Consulate in Paris is located at 2 rue St-Florentin, near Place de la Concorde, tel. 01 43 12 48 40. There are also U.S. consulates in Bordeaux, Lyon, Marseille and Strasbourg.

When traveling with children, parents should hold onto all passports themselves. Nevertheless, it's wise to put a photocopy of a child's passport in his or her pocket, along with the address and phone number of the hotel, in case you get separated.

MONEY MATTERS €

Currency

France's sole valid currency is the euro, whose symbol is €. One hundred cents or *centimes* make a euro. Euro bills come in seven denominations: 5, 10, 20, 50, 100, 200, 500. For practical purposes, it's preferable when exchanging money to request that denominations be no larger than €50. Coins come in amounts of 1, 2, 5, 10, 20 and 50 cents as well as in 1 and 2 euros.

At press time, the euro and the dollar are of nearly equal value, give or take several percent, so to simplify your calculations you might just as well consider the euro as a dollar. If you have francs from a previous trip, you can still (but only) change them at France's central bank, Banque de France, which will exchange coins until 2005 and bills until 2012.

In prices as in other measurements, the French use a comma where we would use a period and vice versa. Therefore 2,500.95 euros will be written as €2.500,95. The € symbol is sometimes placed after the amount, e.g. €2 or 2€.

The euro is also the official currency of Austria, Belgium, Finland, Germany, Greece, Ireland, Italy, Luxembourg, the Netherlands, Portugal and Spain. Bills are the same in each country. Coins have a European side shared by all and a national side that was different in each country when originally distributed. Over time, coins originating in one country naturally intermingle with those of those of other countries. While in France, therefore, you will notice that some of your change bears symbols from other Euroland countries.

For ease of payment, ask for bills of €100 or less, preferably €50 or less, when exchanging money; €200 and €500 bills are rarely used in France.

You cannot pay directly in dollars, though most hotels and some stores in heavily touristed quarters will be willing exchange money on the spot. If a hotel or store is exchanging or accepting dollars you can be sure that it is doing so at a highly unfavorable exchange rate for you.

Arriving with euros in pocket

It can be reassuring to arrive in France with some local currency—say, €100—so as to be sure to be able to make it from the airport to the hotel and perhaps to get something to eat in case you don't immediately have the opportunity to change money at the airport. Your local bank, perhaps even your travel agent, can order a few euros through banks dealing in currency exchange.

But you needn't go out of your way to obtain euros at home since you'll have the possibility to exchange dollars for euros as soon as you arrive. There are ATMs and change bureaus at Paris's airports and train stations. With a valid credit or debit card (with a PIN for use in ATMs) and a few hundred dollars in cash (more or less depending on your comfort level of carrying cash) you'll have no problem changing money at the airport, train station, or elsewhere in Paris.

Be sure that before leaving home you've verified your maximum credit or debit level so that the card or cards you plan to use overseas can be used throughout your entire trip.

Traveler's checks are reassuring for some travelers but if you have a suitable credit or debit card and are willing and able to use it for most of your hotel and shopping purchases then traveler's checks won't be necessary. Furthermore, it's easier to withdraw funds from an ATM than to cash a traveler's check. Purchase traveler's checks only if you don't want to be using your card all the time or if you prefer not to carry any cash and will be traveling on to a country where credit cards are less common means of payment.

Exchanging money

The rate of exchange between the dollar and the euro fluctuates on the international market. You can find the current exchange rate by looking in the business section of major daily newspapers or on the Internet, e.g. most banking sites, CNN's money site money.cnn.com/markets/currencies, or the site of the European Central Bank www.ecb.int/home/eurofxref.htm. The ECB's site www.ecb.int shows pictures of the euro and provides other information about the European currency.

The exchange rate noted in the press represents the interbank or wholesale rate, but when exchanging money for the purposes of your travels you will get a retail rate of 2-10% less.

At press time the dollar is about equal to the euro, give or take several percentage points, so unless you're purchasing diamonds or property, you could just consider a euro as a dollar and leave it at that. Nevertheless, it isn't uncommon for exchange rates between the euro and the dollar to fluctuate 5-10% in either direction in a given year.

Keeping a budget when you travel may be important, but counting pennies is a waste of time. It would be a shame to waste much time on the money trail and drive yourself silly with thoughts of a few cents lost or gained. Rather than the exact figure, it's more important to know where and how to exchange money as you travel.

Finding a place to exchange dollars for euros in Paris will require very little searching. You can exchange money at banks, change bureaus, post offices, hotels and some stores or by withdrawing euros directly at an ATM. When you use a credit or debit card to make direct purchases, the amount is automatically exchanged into dollars on your statement.

Only exchange money where you can see the rate posted as well as notice of any commission (flat amount or percentage). The posted rate will announce 1) the rate at which the exchanger will buy your dollars in exchange for euros and often 2) the rate at which the exchanger will sell you dollars (and other currencies) in exchange for euros. In some cases there are two buy rates, one for changing bills, the other for cashing traveler's checks. The "true" wholesale exchange rate of the moment is about halfway between the buy and sell rates. Therefore, where there is no commission, the smaller the difference between the buy and sell rates the more "honest" the deal, while the greater the difference the more the exchange is costing you.

Typically, you get the best rates with direct purchase on a credit card, followed by withdrawal at an ATM or cash exchange in an international bank. Some change bureaus have rates that are about as good as an exchange at the bank, but rates vary greatly. Hotels and stores offer the least attractive exchange.

Banks The exchange rate available in banks in Paris will be about 1-3% lower than the wholesale rate as seen in the paper. There may then be an additional commission of about 2% or a flat rate. Similar exchange rates will be available in the post office since post offices in France also have banking services. Banks in Paris are usually open weekdays 9am to 4:30pm, though some open Saturday and close Monday. Banks may also close at noon the day before a holiday.

Change Bureaus The rate available at change bureaus

may be about the same as in a bank or up to several points less. While one change bureau may post a more favorable exchange rate than another nearby, there may also be a commission at the former. The commission may take the form of a percentage or a fixed amount. When it is a fixed amount be sure that you're exchanging enough to make it worthwhile; I needn't tell you that paying a $4 commission to change $10 is a bad financing. Be sure to understand the commissions, fixed percentages and rates before exchanging money so as to avoid bad surprises. In the absence of a commission, the posted rate could be 4-6% less than the wholesale rate. Change bureaus are easy to come by in the areas where most of the hotels in this book are found, i.e. around Saint-Germain and Saint-Michel on the Left Bank and around rue de Rivoli and the Champs-Elysées on the Right Bank. They stay open until about 7pm and are often open on Saturday. There are also change bureaus at the airport.

Credit cards often have the most favorable exchange rate, one that is at least as good as what you would receive in an international bank. In that respect you should use your credit card for hotels and restaurants and major shopping purchases.

ATMs provide exchange rates that are as good as or better than those of a bank or change bureau. There may be a surcharge at an ATM, therefore you may wish to avoid withdrawing small amounts such as €10 or €20. ATM instructions are typically available in English on the screen, either directly or by pushing the language button. As at home, be vigilant when using ATMs. Avoid ATMS in isolated, unlit areas or when loiterers are in the vicinity. Be aware of anyone standing close enough to see the PIN being entered into the machine. If the card becomes stuck, be wary of strangers offering to help. No legitimate bank employee will ever ask for your PIN to get the card back.

Your hotel will undoubtedly be willing to make the exchange, though at a rate 3-5% lower than what you might receive in any of the above. Exchange money at the hotel as your last—or most convenient—resort.

Credit cards

Credit cards are accepted in most hotels, restaurants and stores, and they offer the most favorable exchange rate. Businesses typically require a minimum purchase of €15 to use a credit card, though metro and train ticket machines will accept lower amounts.

Visa and Mastercard are the most commonly accepted cards. American Express is not accepted by some businesses, so if you are traveling only with American Express be sure to inquire in advance or to see if the American Express sticker is at the entrance.

French credit cards are chip cards requiring a PIN in payment machines, so the French do not sign their receipts. If your card does not have a chip then you will sign the receipt. There is no space on the credit card receipt to add a tip, as you might in a restaurant at home. (See *Restaurants* for restaurant and café tipping customs.)

If your credit card is lost of stolen, immediately call the credit card company to report it. You will reach an English-speaking operators at these numbers:

MasterCard	0800-90-13-87
Visa	0892-70-57-05
American Express	01-47-77-72-00
Diner's Club	0810-31-41-59

Tax refunds

Tax is almost always included in the posted price in stores. A sales tax known as the value-added tax or VAT (TVA in French) is 19.6% on most articles. If you are not a resident of the European Union and are staying in the European Union for less than six months, you can obtain a refund of some of that, 13% on most items. To be eligible for a refund you need your purchases to total more than €183 in any one stores. Your purchases need not all be made at the same time in that store; you can accumulate them over a 6-month period. The refund doesn't apply to food and drink, tobacco, medicine, firearms, non-mounted precious stones and metals, and some art objects.

When making purchases that may eventually add up to €183 in a single store, ask the store to fill out a VAT refund form. Just because a store doesn't advertise this refund doesn't mean that it is not possible to go through the refund process there.

You will initially pay the tax at the store. The form is then given to Customs (*la Douane*) when leaving France or, if France is not your final destination in Europe, the last country of the European Union that you visit. Count on 15 extra minutes at the airport or train station when leaving the European Union if you will have to stop at the customs desk.

Before checking your luggage in which you've placed the purchased articles, go to the customs desk, where you will show the items and receive a stamp on the form. The form must then be mailed to the store which will refund the tax by crediting the amount to your credit card, presuming that you've made at least a portion of the original purchase on a credit card. The refund process can take 2-3 months.

Though all taxes are assumed to be included in most articles, large items (e.g. automobiles) as well as service fees may not include the tax directly. In that case, HT will be indicated beside the price. HT is *hors taxe*, meaning the tax has not yet been added on. (The HT rate is important for B2B transactions since the sales tax is refunded for purchases made by French businesses.) When the price does not indicate HT, it will indicate TTC or *toutes taxes comprises*, meaning all taxes included. In restaurants it will indicate SC or *service compris*, meaning service (i.e. tip) included.

U.S. Customs

A VAT refund may make the price particularly attractive, but keep in mind that you may be required to pay a U.S. custom's tax when returning home with your purchase or with gifts received overseas. Items purchased in duty-free shops may also be dutiable upon your return home.

You are required to make a custom's declaration when you return, indicating on a form that will be handed out in the plane the nature and value of items purchased or received as gift. When bringing back articles for personal use (including gifts), you have a personal exemption up to a value of $800, meaning you can return with $800 worth of goods from overseas without having to pay duty. The $800 does not apply if you have not already used your exemption in the past 30 days. This exemption covers only items in your possession. Items that you may have sent from overseas cannot be counted.

Family members who live in the same household and return to the U.S. together may combine their personal exemptions and make a joint declaration upon returning. Therefore a couple living under the same roof would have an exemption of $1600, no matter which individual owns a given item. Children and infants are also included in this exemption, except concerning alcoholic beverages or tobacco.

Beyond the $800 exemption, the next $1000 in value will be taxed at a flat duty rate of 3%. Beyond that, various duty rates apply, depending on the nature of the goods. If any duty is due, you will be asked to pay it immediately at U.S. Customs.

The cost of any alcoholic beverages are to be included in your declaration and exemption. Nevertheless, you are only allowed to bring home one liter (33.8 fl. oz.) duty-free, even if your total declaration is less than $800. If you are at least 21 years old, you may bring in for your personal use as many bottles as you're willing to carry (without raising suspicion that you intend to resell it), but beyond one liter the total will be dutiable at 4% plus any IRS tax. In practice, it would be rare to be asked to pay duty on two or three bottles. Note: Certain states have additional restrictions on bringing in alcohol.

Antiques that are at least 100 years old and fine art may enter duty-free and so are not included in the $800 exemption, though you must nevertheless declare them.

Your exemption can include up to 200 cigarettes and 100 cigars.

Cuban cigars are available in France but returning home with them is illegal. If caught, the likely sanction is seizure.

In theory, items that you already own but were made abroad and that you take with you overseas, such as jewelry or a lap top or a Louis Vuitton handbag, could be subject to duty if the custom's inspector believes that you actually obtained them during your trip. The U.S. Customs Service suggests carrying some form of proof that you brought these items from home, e.g. sales receipts or jeweler's appraisals. Such items can also be registered at a U.S. Customs office. In practice, you shouldn't be bringing expensive jewelry overseas anyway. And custom's officers typically have enough to keep busy without worrying about your laptop.

For more information visit the U.S. Customs website at www.customs.gov.

HEALTH MATTERS

The prepared traveler: insurance, medication, glasses

Most major insurance companies extend coverage to European travel but it's a good idea to check before leaving. Your insurer may have a list of approved medical facilities overseas. If your policy does not cover foreign travel, temporary coverage is available. Always carry your insurance card and any medical ID tags that may be necessary. Keep all receipts for medical treatment abroad as you will need them for claims when you return.

No special inoculations are required for travel in France.

If you're on medication, you'll want to be sure you have enough prescription medicine with you, but also have your doctor note the generic name of the drug in case you need some overseas. You may also wish to pack limited quantities of the brand of any basic medications (e.g. aspirin or antacid) you may prefer.

If you have an extra pair of glasses, you may want to bring them along as an emergency pair, no matter how unfashionable they may now be.

Pharmacies

You will find toothpaste, shampoo, shaving cream and some other health and beauty products in the grocery store. However, medications and most pharmaceutical products are sold exclusively in the *pharmacie*. Pharmacies are indicated by a green cross. They are numerous and easy to find. There is likely to be one within a block or two of your hotel. When a pharmacy is closed, the locations of nearby open pharmacies will be posted on the door.

All medications are behind the counter, whether you need a prescription for them or not. Center-city pharmacies will undoubtedly have a pharmacists who speaks sufficient English to get what you need. Furthermore, pharmacists are among the better service (and sales) people in France.

The French pharmacist plays a more active role than his North American counterpart and is more likely to intervene in the case of an accident and to offer a diagnosis of problems for which over-the-counter medication may be advised. You will not be dealing with a simple cashier.

While you should consult a doctor if you think it's necessary, do not hesitate to describe to the trained pharmacist the exact nature of your aches and pains. When you are given medication, be sure to have the pharmacist note the exact dosage and frequency since the indications may only be in French.

Contact lens solutions are available in pharmacies or in optician's shops.

Doctors

If you wish to consult a doctor there are several possibilities for finding one. You can ask directly at the hotel; they certainly know how to reach an English-speaking doctor. You can ask at the pharmacy for a list of generalists or specialists in your area—and perhaps have the pharmacy or your hotel call ahead to see if he speaks English. If you feel that you need a doctor in the middle of the night or are bedridden but don't necessarily require ambulance assistance, you can ask the hotel to call S.O.S. Médicins, a public service which sends doctors over for a house call.

The S.O.S. Médicins number is 01 47 07 77 77.

If the problem is an emergency and/or requires an ambulance, the phone number for medical emergencies is 15.

Due to France's socialized medicine, the cost of medical care at pubic facilities and from non-private doctors is relatively low compared with American-style medicine. A house call will cost $40-50. A visit to a generalist will cost $20-30. In the center of Paris, your chances are good of coming upon an English-speaking doctor at a public facility.

Private doctors and private hospitals do exist in France. The American Hospital in Paris is one such hospital. The doctors there, though not necessarily American, will speak English and the hospital is experienced in dealing with American insurance claims. The hospital's rates are naturally higher than those of public hospitals and you will have to pay a certain amount up front.

The American Hospital is on the edge of the city at 63 boulevard Victor-Hugo in Neuilly; tel. 01 46 41 25 25.

SOS help

An English-language crisis line is manned 3-11pm daily at 01 47 23 80 80.

Second-hand smoke

There's no escaping second-hand smoke in cafés and restaurants. Ever since the 1994 anti-smoking laws went into effect, businesses have been required to designate non-smoking sections, but typically the room is too small for it to make much of a difference, or the café or restaurant doesn't make any effort to set aside or enforce a non-smoking section. Sometimes, if you ask for the non-smoking section you will notice that the waiter or maitre d' will then scan the room for an isolated table then seat you there—but 5 minutes later a group of smokers will be seated next to you.

Smokers will find this one of the perks of travel to France, while non-smokers will be frustrated to find that smokers still have an edge in terms of who should be tolerant of whom. The tide has been turning, if slowly, but the edge still goes to smokers in café and restaurants and businesses operated by a smoker. Cultural rules of acceptable public behavior and legal regulations have been undergoing revision, gradually heading France in the direction of a smoke-free environment that Americans are now accustomed to, but there's still a long way to go.

Ask a smoker at the next table in a restaurant to kindly refrain from smoking and he will either switch his smoking hand or merely turn to his tablemates and sigh, "Americans." Do not try to engage your smoking neighbor in a conversation about the criminality of second-hand smoke unless you're prepared to have him redirect the debate to the merits of American gun laws and the death penalty. (They learn how to do that in school.) Come to think of it, that's not a bad way of getting to know a few Parisians while in Paris.

CONNECTIONS

Post offices

Post offices, called La Poste, are open 8am-7pm weekdays and 8am-noon Saturday. Most post offices are also able to exchange money. Stamps for post cards and light letters to the United States currently cost €0.67. Stamps can also be purchased at *tabacs*, which are cafés and stands selling tobacco. However, a *tabac* will not weigh your letter and may not have stamps of the exact amount for mail overseas. Your hotel is also likely to have stamps. Yellow mailboxes are attached to walls or to posts in public places.

Public telephones

Most public telephones in Paris use only phone cards, though some cafés and restaurants have pricey coin phones. Phone cards are called *télécartes.* They are sold at post offices and *tabacs* and often at metro ticket counters. They come in amounts of €7.50 and €14.80, corresponding to 50 and 120 units of phoning time.

Though cards with access numbers exist in France, those that use chips are more common and easier to use. You insert the card into the slot of the public telephone and simply dial the phone number. The amount of units remaining on the card will be displayed on the screen.

A local call in Paris costs 9 euro cents for the first minute and 2 or 3 cents per minute thereafter (depending on time of day or night), or 1 unit of a *télécarte* for about three minutes. A call to the United States from Paris costs 11 euro cents for the first 15 seconds then 23 cents per minute from 1-7pm Mon.-Fri or 12 cents per minute at other time. You therefore get a lot of conversation out of a 120-unit *télécarte.*

Hefty surcharges are added when you call from your hotel, so lengthy calls from the hotel should be avoided.

Phoning

French telephone numbers have ten digits starting with 0. Phone and fax numbers provided throughout this book are given in their 10-digit format as called from within France. Numbers for Paris and the surrounding region begin with 01. The exceptions are toll-free or toll-supplement numbers, which begin with 08, and cell phones, which begin with 06.

When calling France from the U.S., begin by dialing 011 (the international access code from the U.S.), followed by 33 (the country code for France). Of the 10-digit number, the initial 0 is then dropped. Therefore, Paris number 01-23-45-67-89 would be dialed from the U.S. as 011-33-1-23-45-67-89.

It's customary in France to separate numbers by pairs, and they are also read that way, e.g. zero one, twenty-three, forty-five, sixty-seven, eighty-nine—or better yet, *zéro un, vingt-trois, quarante-cinq, soixante-sept, quatre-vingt-neuf.*

To call the United States from France, dial 00 (the international access code from France) then 1 (the country code for the U.S. and Canada), followed by the area code and phone number.

Emergency phone numbers

Presumably you will ask for assistance at your hotel or wherever you may be when in need of emergency assistance, but it can't hurt to know the French equivalent of our 911. These numbers can be called directly from a public telephone without inserting a telephone card.

Medical emergencies	15
Police	17
Fire Department	18

E-mail

Your hotel may offer Internet access. If not, you might inquire at the hotel as to the nearest cybercafé. There are many around. Otherwise, disconnecting is one of the pleasures and rewards of travel.

Language

There's a common misconception that the Frenchman you ask directions from on the street actually does speak English but is being a snob and won't use it. According to this theory, French isn't the really the official language, but the official attitude. But French is indeed the official language. As for the Frenchman you ask for directions, if he doesn't actually speak English it's to his own shame; otherwise, he would be all too willing to use it... unless he's utterly put off by your approach.

On the whole, it's a mix of politeness and firmness that gets attention in Paris (this is also true of matters of romance). Always begin a question to a stranger by *Exusez-moi* (Excuse me) or *S'il vous plaît* (Please). Adding *Bonjour* also helps (*See Shop 'n Stroll: The Bonjour Rule*). Beginning an encounter by asking a question in English without gracious foreplay is the surest way to put someone off.

If you come upon someone who does not speak English, chances are you can make yourself understood. Speak slowly and distinctly, not loudly. Don't repeat the same word 20 times in the same way; you may think you're clearly asking for directions to the Eiffel Tower, but to the foreigner it may sound like "Wawa Tupple Upple" each time.

Posing your question in French may get you a certain amount of sympathy, but you may be disappointed to find that the person you're speaking with prefers his or her English to your French.

TRANSPORTATION

The Metro

Paris is to be discovered on foot! Then, between long promenades, the subway system can allow you to go far and wide, practically and simply. Getting around on the metro is easy—unless there's a strike. The metro is also relatively safe, but always keep a hand on your valuable to guard against pickpockets (see comment below on Pickpockets and Thieves).

There are 15 metro lines which are distinguished on the official map by color, number and terminal direction. The name of the metro stop is indicated along with addresses throughout this book to help you situate them on the map. In addition to using the metro map in this book, you may wish to ask for a small metro map when purchasing your ticket: *un plan, s'il vous plait*. Maps are also available in all hotels. Larger maps are posted at the mouth of the station, underground in the ticket area, and on the platform. The route of the particular line you are on will be shown above the doors inside each subway car.

Terminal direction is the best indicator of the appropriate line to take. Look on the map past your destination to the station name at the end of the line; that is the direction in which you will head. The direction and line number will be indicated overhead in the middle of the platform. Parisians do not speak of colors when they refer to the lines and many are not even familiar with line numbers.

The metro runs from about 5:30am to 1am. If you wish to avoid the discofort of heavy metro crowds, avoid the rush hours of 8:30-9:30am and 5:30-7:30pm.

A single ticket is valid for the length of your trip, even with several changes. Hold onto the ticket until you have left the metro, as a transit inspector may asked to see it at any time. The ticket will also be needed to exit the turnstiles of some stations. If caught without a validated ticket, you will have to pay a fine on the spot.

The RER

The RER is the suburban train network, indicated by thicker lines on the metro map and by the letters A through E. Its 5 lines split off into sub-lines as they lead out from Paris, so when you take the RER be sure that you are on the right train. A full list of stops will be lit overhead on the platform. The RER is most frequently used by foreign travelers going to/from the airports, Versailles and Disneyland Paris.

The RER can also be used within the city limits in the same way and with the same ticket as the metro, with which it connects. A single metro ticket is valid when you are using the RER solely within the city limit; you may use that same ticket to transfer between the RER and the metro. Metro passes are also valid for RER stops within Paris.

When taking the RER outside of the city limits (e.g. Versailles, the airports, Disneyland), a different ticket is required that must be purchased at the entrance to the RER stations. As with the metro ticket, be sure to hold on to your ticket until you exit the system. You will not be able to exit the turnstile without it.

Tickets for Public Transportation

Metro, bus and RER (within the city limit) all use the same ticket. A single ticket is valid even if you are changing between metros or between the metro and the RER. An individual ticket costs €1.30. Children 4-9 ride with half-price tickets, but such tickets are not sold individually, rather only as passes or in packs of 10 tickets. Children three and under ride free.

10-pack A packet of 10 tickets, called *un carnet*, costs €9.60, a savings of more than 25% over the price of 10 individual tickets that also relieves you of repeatedly buying individual tickets.

Daily passes Paris Visite cards are valid for 1, 2, 3 and 5 consecutive days, with the prices depending on the number of days and zones. They can be practical but are not likely to be a savings over purchase of a carnet. I do not recommend them.

Weekly pass The weekly pass, called *une carte hebdomadaire*, is more worthwhile than Paris Visite passes provided the timing is right. This pass is valid for one week beginning Monday of the week in which you've purchased it; you can purchase it Tuesday or Wednesday, for example, but it will be valid only through Sunday.

Montly pass The *carte orange* is valid for one month from the first. Again, you need not buy it on the first.

When you purchase these passes, you'll indicate that it is for Paris alone (considered zones 1 and 2). When you take the RER out of the city you will then purchase a separate ticket.

When purchasing a weekly or a monthly pass, ask for the free plastic jacket, called *une pochette*, in which you must place a passport-size photo. Most metro stations have photo booths for this purpose. You must also write the number that's on your ticket on the appropriate space in the jacket.

The metro ticket is also valid in buses. Individual tickets are validated in the bus by placing them in a small box by the driver. Do not, however, validate a pass in the box. Instead, hold up the pass (in its plastic jacket) for the driver to see; he may or may not acknowledge it, in either case keep walking.

Taxis

Taxis are far less romanticized in Paris than in New York or London due to the quality and coverage of Paris's public transportation system and to the fact that taxis come in all models and colors. Nevertheless, 149,000 of them ply Paris and the surrounding region. You'll find taxi stands on major squares and thoroughfares and near sights and museums throughout the city. Taxis can also be hailed on the street (but not within 50 yards of a taxi stand) and you can have your hotel or restaurant call one.

The taxi is available when the sign at the top is lit. It is unavailable when only one of the three colored bulbs at the top is lit. The bulbs correspond to rate indicators, which are signs to the police that the driver is charging the appropriate fare corresponding to the place and time.

The rates are the same no matter what type of car is used. In addition to accepting cash (euros), many taxis are also equipped to accept credit cards for amounts over €15. If you wish to pay by credit card, verify before getting in that the cab is equipped to take your card.

After a starting charge of €2, taxis charge €0.60 per kilometer (.62 miles) from 7am to 7pm and €1 per km from 7pm to 7am. Higher rates apply for rides into the suburbs (e.g. Versailles or other sights in the Paris region). Paris's day rates are among the lowest among capitals in Western Europe.

There is a minimum charge of €5. When a cab is called for, the meter will start running at the taxi stand from which it's been called, so there may already be €4.50-8 on the meter when the taxi arrives.

Many taxis will only take up to three passengers, so if there are four people in your party you should mention that when requesting the taxi. A few taxis will take five passengers. Supplements are added for pick-ups at train stations and airports, for a fourth or fifth passenger if taken (€2.45 each), and for bulky items, typically meaning each piece of luggage (€0.90). That could explain why you may be asked to pay a bit more than is shown on the meter. You can round up to add on a tip of 5-10% tip. However, when supplements have been added you are not out of line in considering them as a part of the tip.

Ask for *un reçu* to have a receipt.

Airports and airport transportation

Paris has two international airports, Roissy-Charles-de-Gaulle, 15 miles northeast of the city and Orly, 9 miles south of the city. For automated arrival and departure information when in Paris call 0892-68-15-15. The website covering both airports is www.adp.fr.

Taxis from Orly Airport to the center take 25-40 minutes and cost about $22-30. Taxis from Roissy-Charles-de-Gaulle Airport take 40-60 minutes and cost about $35-$45.

There's good public transportation by bus or RER between Paris and the airports. Air France buses leave Charles-de-Gaulle Airport frequently 6am-1am, with stops at Porte Maillot (Metro Porte Maillot) and the Arc de Triomphe (Metro Charles-de-Gaulle-Etoile). Another bus stops at the Garnier Opera (Metro Opéra).

Charles-de-Gaulle Airport is also connected with the RER B3 train line, either directly from terminal 2 or via a quick shuttle bus from terminal 1. See the metro map for center-city stops on the RER. Also see "Pickpockets and Thieves" below.

From Orly Airport, Air France buses stop at the Montparnasse train station and the Invalides Air Terminal, while the Orly bus goes from the airport to Denfert-Rochereau. Also, a shuttle from Orly connects the airport with RER line C2 (see metro map), which then has a number of stops along the Seine's left bank.

HOLIDAYS AND EVENTS

France has 11 national holidays during which banks, post offices and many stores will be closed. Bank holidays are indicated with an asterisk (*) below. Many (but not all) restaurants and museums close May 1 and Christmas and New Year's Day. Most remain open for other holidays. And you'll never have to wander far to find an open bakery in the morning. Museums generally follow a Sunday schedule on holidays.

Tourists alone don't fill hotels, which is why July and August are generally the easy months to find a room at the last minute. However, a combination of tourists and business travelers does fill hotels. That's why you should make reservations several months in advance if you plan to be in Paris during such major events as the Paris Air Show in June, the Car Show in October, or the fashion shows in March and October. Ready-to-wear fashion shows in late January and early July also hike occupancy rates. For specific dates of upcoming fashion events, visit the official site of the Fédération Française de la Couture at www.modeaparis.com.

Holidays, major trade shows and other notable events are listed here.

***January 1. New Year's Day.**
Winter Sales. Mid-January to mid-February.
Fashion Week, proceeded by Fabric Trade Show. Early-mid March.
***Easter Monday. March 31, 2003; April 19, 2004; April 4, 2005.**
***May 1. May Day/Labor Day.** In addition to union parades, May Day tradition includes offering loved ones a spray of lily of the valley (*muguet*).
***May 8. V.E. Day, commemorating Victory in Europe 1945.** The president lays a wreath at the Tomb of the Unknown Soldier beneath the Arc de Triomphe in the morning.
***Ascension Thursday. May 8, 2003; May 27, 2004; May 12, 2005.**
***Pentecost Monday. May 19, 2003; June 7, 2004; May 22, 2005.**
Roland Garros, the French Open. Last week in May and first week in June. The Roland Garros tennis center is located just outside the western edge of the city and is accessible by

metro (Porte d'Auteuil). For ticket information, see the official site for the tournament at www.frenchopen.org.

Paris Air Show, Salon du Bourget. Third week of June. The Paris Air Show, held at Le Bourget Airport north of Paris, is the world's largest aeronautic show and it coincides with the end of the business travel year, class trips, and the height of spring travel, making it one of the busiest travel periods of the year. Le Bourget Airport, between Charles-de-Gaulle Airport and Paris, is where Charles Lindberg arrived in 1927 after his 33-hour solo flight from New York. For show dates and information visit www.salon-du-bourget.com.

June 21. Fête de la Musique. The music festival celebrating the summer solstice is one of the most joyous days in Paris as musicians, both amateur and profession, take to the streets, squares and public building, where they're joined by nearly everyone else in the city. Planned and unplanned concerts are held throughout the city, including major pop, classical and jazz concerts.

***July 14. French national holiday**, what we (not they) call Bastille Day. See The Marais: The Bastille for more.

Tour de France. Three weeks in July. The Tour de France bike race, also known as the Great Loop, is one of the world's major sporting events. It ends on the Champs-Elysées on the third or fourth Sunday in July. For dates and information visit the official site: www.letour.fr.

Summer sales. Mid-July to mid-August.

***August 15, Assumption Day.**

Paris Auto Show, Mondial de l'Automobile. Two weeks beginning late September. Among the world's major motor shows, a biannual event (2004, 2006) attracting more than 1.4 million visitors. Paris held the first international exhibition of automobiles in the Tuileries Garden in 1898. For dates and information visit the official site: www.mondial-automobile.com.

Fashion Week, proceeded by Fabric Trade Show. Early-mid October.

October 31. Halloween. Not a traditional French holiday yet, though it began to find its place on the French calendar around 1999. Halloween in Paris takes the form of nightclub parties and mild store-window decorations that stay up through November.

***November 1. All Saints' Day.** The traditional day for visiting the tombs of deceased relatives.

***November 11. Armistice Day.** While the holiday specifically marks the Armistice of 1918, it more generally honors all veterans. Ceremony at the Tomb of the Unknown Soldier beneath the Arc de Triomphe.

American Thanksgiving. Fourth Thursday in November. Not a French holiday, of course, but homesick Americans will find a number of American restaurants offering turkey and some of the trimmings. And you're sure to find plenty of good fowl and winged game in French restaurants at this time of year.

***Christmas. December 25.**

GOOD SCIENCE

Electricity requirements

Electricity in France runs on 220-volt, 50-cycle current, whereas the United States uses 110-volt, 60-cycle current. Furthermore, the plug itself is different in France. Electrical appliances, including computers, purchased in the United States and brought into France therefore require both voltage transformers and plug adapters. When possible, avoid bringing electrical appliances that need to be plugged in, such as hairdryers (most of the hotels in this book have them in the room) and shavers. Many portable computers now have a built-in adapter that may or may not require that you turn a switch. Verify that your computer has one before bringing it, otherwise, without a transformer, you may damage it when plugging it in. In any case, you will still need a plug adapter. So-called "universal adapters" may be available in your local hardware store. If you are a frequently returning traveler, you may wish to purchase a simple France-U.S. plug adapter at a hardware store in Paris, such as in the basement of the BHV department store at 52 rue de Rivoli, 4th arrondissement, across the street from City Hall (Metro Hôtel de Ville).

Weights and measures

France uses the metric system, as does the rest of continental Europe. Having a sense of it will come in handy if you go to an outdoor food market.

For most situations it's enough to know that:

- a kilogram weighs a little more than two pounds,
- a meter is a little longer than a yard, and
- a liter fills a little more than a quart.

More accurately:

1 U.S. pint = 0.47 liter
1 U.S. quart = 0.94 liter
1 liter = 1.06 quarts
1 U.S. gallon = 3.78 liters

100 grams = 3.52 ounces
1000 grams = 1 kilogram = 2.2 pounds
1 ounce = 28.25 grams
1 pound = 450 grams

1 yard = 0.91 meter
1000 meters = 1 kilometer = 0.62 miles
1 inch = 2.54 centimeters
1 centimeter = 0.39 inch
1 foot = 30.4 centimeters
1 meter = 3.28 feet = 39.4 inches
1 mile = 1.6 kilometers

1 acre = 0.40 hectare
1 hectare = 2.47 acres

Miscellaneous

In France, the ground floor (*rez-de-chaussée*) is not considered the first floor; rather it is the next story up that is designated as *1er étage*, or first floor. I try to avoid confusion in this book by speaking of the ground floor or of one floor up, but for higher floors I have used the number on the buttons visitors would push on the French elevator, where the ground floor is indicated as 0 or RdC.

Water spigots are marked F (*froid*) for cold and C (*chaud*) for hot.

Dates throughout Europe are noted day/month/year, e.g. Oct. 13, 2004 would be 13/10/04.

Time is generally given in France according to a 24-hour cycle. Midnight is 0:00 or 0h, noon is 12:00 or 12h, 8:30pm is 20:30 or 20h30.

In France, streets—*rues, avenues, boulevards*—proceed the name and are written in lower case letters, as are *places* and *squares*. While I have kept streets in lower case, squares are more like monuments and are therefore capitalized here, giving an inconsistency between rue de la Paix or avenue des Champs-Elysées on the one hand and Place Vendôme or Square du Temple on the other. Apologies to the purists.

SAFETY, FEAR AND THE FOREIGN TRAVELER

"Is it safe to drink the tap water in Paris?, to take the metro in the evening?, to eat French beef?"

In less anxious times those were the kinds of questions I would get. I would keep my answer brief: Yes, though the water may taste a bit chlorinated; Yes, but avoid walking alone through tunnels; Yes, according to European officials, furthermore the beef is hormone-free.

But travelers' concerns about travel to France now sound like **the 10 Plagues of the Road**:

1. thromboembolism from sitting still too long on the plane,
2. second-hand smoke from sitting in too many cafés,
3. surly waiters from hesitating when ordering,
4. sullen salespeople from requesting assistance,
5. pickpockets in the metro,
6. road accidents, the #1 cause of violent death in Paris,
7. anti-Semitism,
8. anti-Americanism,
9. the face of fascism and far right-wing ideals,
10. terrorism.

Travel to and within Paris is as safe as ever—and that means pretty safe. But faced with unsettling events in the world, many travelers see foreign travel as an unnecessary risk. Foreignness itself is often associated with danger. Furthermore, as Americans there is the concern that any danger will be particularly aimed at us.

Certain countries, populations and individuals are indeed anti-American, but don't confuse warnings about travel to Syria, Columbia, Sudan, etc. with warnings about travel in France. France and the United States certainly have cultural, historical, geographical and religious differences (isn't that why you've come?), but France remains an important ally.

The most common forms of anti-Americanism in France are far too subtle, too ambiguous or too political for most travelers to get a whiff (at most) of anything but its intellectual variety. You should actually consider yourself lucky to encounter anyone who will discuss critical views of the United States, given that few travelers manage to speak with the French outside of service situations. Poor or cool service should not be seen as a commentary on your nationality but rather on theirs.

American Jews may sense a further personal danger. Anti-Semitism has deep roots in French history and is a staple of far-right European politics, and there have been incidents of Arab youth, not indifferent to conflicts in the Middle East, acting violently or delinquently toward Jews or Jewish property. Yet such events are too isolated or linked with the general rise in delinquency to color the view of Paris as a generally safe and tolerant travel destination. Furthermore, Paris is an excellent place for Americans, Jewish or not, to become familiar with French first or second generation immigrants from North Africa, both Jewish and Muslim.

No one knows better than the U.S. State Department that anything can happen anywhere. But even the State Department has a sense of perspective. State's most recent consular information sheet on France available at press time recognizes that the major concern of American travelers in Paris should be to guard against pickpockets and thieves.

Paris is a relatively wealthy city as well as the nation's capital and cultural, business and tourist center. That makes it a target for criminal elements. A significant police and national security presence therefore exists, often quite visibly. Yet while rates of violent crimes have risen in France over the past two year, they remain lower in Paris than in major American cities and fall in the middle range compared with other European capitals.

Take a look at the State Department's information sheet on France (http://travel.state.gov/france.html) as you plan your trip, then again before flying overseas to see if there's been an update. Other international advisories and warnings are posted at http://travel.state.gov.

If you're in a complete panic about going overseas, professional help may be sought. But if you go to your psychiatrist and say "Doctor, I get anxious whenever I turn on the news," – well, you know the punch line.

It isn't easy to be a bold traveler these days, but visiting

Paris doesn't demand boldness—it demands a sense of cultural adventure, one that is closer to low-impact aerobics than mountain climbing. Travel in unsettling times can actually teach you a thing or two about culture, history, art and people in the way that news channels and their insatiable appetite for dramatic images, personality debates, political snippets and air-brushed fluff cannot.

You've told your loved ones where you're staying, you've looked into traveler insurance before leaving, you know to be aware of where your valuables are at all times, you have your passport and credit card, you have this book. The rest you can improvise.

Pickpockets and Thieves

These must be banner times for pickpockets. With the arrival of the millennium their number suddenly increased as though their natural predator had died and they descended upon the center city like emboldened pigeons looking for food. After 9/11, France, which has long been familiar with terrorism on its territory, immediately reinforced its "Vigipirate" anti-terrorism measures. This included an increased security presence in the metro and in heavy tourist areas. One affect was a decrease in pickpocket activity in the center of Paris.

But by fall 2002 they had been emboldened again and on certain lines they operate quite obviously—obviously, that is, until you're a victim. Pickpockets are often adolescent boys and girls in a group of 2 to 6, of an age and statelessness that leave them nearly immune to trouble from the police. Another type of pickpocket is young men, typically working in pairs and with jackets or raincoats over their arms. Indeed, pickpockets can come in any shape, size, sex, color and age.

On the metro: The metro system is generally safe, but do be vigilant. Know where your valuables are at all times and use common sense and you should have no problem. **Wallets, purses and backpacks should never be held behind your back when in a crowd, especially on the metro.** Don't let yourself be unduly distracted by a stranger asking questions, for his partner(s) may be stealing your belongings.

In particular, the #1 line, Château de Vincennes–La Défense, which runs by many major tourist attractions and is frequently crowded, is especially attractive to pickpockets. Lines passing by the Eiffel Tower and approaching

Montmartre also require particular vigilance. Announcements in the metro in French, English and other languages broadcast frequent warnings to pay attention to your personal belongings.

Tourists milling around the Eiffel Tower, Notre-Dame, Sacré Coeur, the Orsay Museum, on crowded sidewalks outside major department stores and by other major tourist sites are also targeted.

On the RER from the airport: The RER rail link from Charles de Gaulle Airport to downtown Paris is a practical way to enter the city, particularly if you're already familiar with the public transportation system in Paris. It is also relatively safe, but you should take caution, especially if arriving jetlagged and disoriented.

The U.S. State Department information on safety in Paris notes that "Gangs of thieves operate on the rail link from Charles de Gaulle Airport to downtown Paris by preying on jet-lagged, luggage-burdened tourists. Often, one thief distracts the tourist with a question about directions while an accomplice takes a momentarily unguarded backpack, briefcase or purse. Thieves also time their thefts to coincide with train stops so that they may quickly exit the car."

When taking the train, the best safety measure is to choose a wagon with other travelers and to keep your luggage within sight and on the window side rather than to the aisle side of your seat.

The train's first Paris stop (after a number of suburban stations) is at the Gare du Nord train station, which, for tourists changing from there to the metro system, "is a high-risk area for pickpocketing and theft," according to State's report. The next stop, Châtelet, has an extensive array of connecting tunnels which can be confusing for first-time visitors and tiring for anyone carrying luggage. In fact, Châtelet is said to be the largest metro station in the world, which isn't anything to brag about. The State Department suggests that "Travelers may wish to consider traveling from the airport to the city by bus or taxi."

These are points well taken, nevertheless, the train from the airport is very practical for those who have a sense of where they're going, especially when headed to a hotel near the Saint-Michel or Luxembourg Garden stops. Both of those stops are direct from the airport and therefore do not require changes at the Gare du Nord or Châtelet stops. Vigilance is generally an effective arm.

Travelers on Paris Revisited tours or using Paris Revisited business travel services may wish to inquire about airport pick-up services.

Other areas of vigilance: In cafés, restaurants, and hotel lobbies and breakfast rooms, purses and backpacks should be placed somewhere secure, not merely hanging off the back of the chair or placed on the floor. The flea markets, particular at Clignancourt, are also favorable pickpocket territory.

Useful Websites

Websites are mentioned throughout this book, particularly in the hotel and restaurant sections. Here are some other sites useful in planning your trip:

U.S. State Department information sheet on France www.travel.state.gov/france.html

U.S. State Department's other international advisories and warnings www.travel.state.gov

U.S. Customs information www.customs.gov

French Embassy in the U.S. www.info-france-usa.org

Consular Section of the French Embassy in the U.S. www.france-consulat.org

French customs information www.info-france-usa.org/customs Provides information for businesses and individual travelers entering France

City of Paris www.paris-france.org

Paris Convention & Visitors Bureau www.paris-touristoffice.com

French Ministry of Culture www.culture.fr Provides information in French on major cultural events.

French Yellow Pages www.pagesjaunes.fr

Paris airports www.adp.fr

French National Railroad (SNCF) www.sncf.com

Paris metro and bus system (RATP) www.ratp.fr

Paris Revisited www.parisrevisited.com Updates and travel articles to complement this book as well as information for customized tours and business travel.

INDEX

A

B

C

D

E

F

G

H

I

J

L

R

S

T

U

V

W

THE RETURN TRAVELER TELLS ALL

The following pages have been reserved for your own personal critiques and reviews of hotels, restaurants, bars, gardens, museums... whatever you would or would not recommend to other travelers.

Share them with your friends or
feel free to send them to reviews@parisrevisited.com
or to

Gary Lee Kraut
c/o Words Travel International, Inc.
740 River Road
Trenton, New Jersey 08628, U.S.A.

Your Hotel Review

Name of hotel ______________________________

Dates ________________ Price ______________

Type of room ____________________ Room # ____

Comments ______________________________

Your Hotel Review

Name of hotel ______________________________

Dates ____________________ Price ______________

Type of room ______________________ Room # ____

Comments ______________________________

Your Restaurant Review

Name of restaurant____________________________________

Date________________ Reserved? ☐ yes ☐ no Time_______

Dining companion(s)____________________________________

☐ A la carte and/or ☐ Fixed-price menu

Total price ______________ Wine/Drinks________________________

Comments:____

YOUR RESTAURANT REVIEW

Name of restaurant ______________________________

Date ____________ Reserved? ☐ yes ☐ no Time ______

Dining companion(s) ______________________________

____

☐ A la carte and/or ☐ Fixed-price menu

Total price ____________ Wine/Drinks ______________

____

Comments: _____________________________________

Your Restaurant Review

Name of restaurant______________________________
Date____________ Reserved? ☐ yes ☐ no Time______
Dining companion(s)____________________________

☐ A la carte and/or ☐ Fixed-price menu

Total price ____________ Wine/Drinks__________________

Comments:____________________________________

Your Restaurant Review

Name of restaurant______________________________

Date____________ Reserved? ☐ yes ☐ no Time______

Dining companion(s)____________________________

☐ A la carte and/or ☐ Fixed-price menu

Total price __________ Wine/Drinks__________________

Comments:______________________________________

Additional Comments

Use this space for any other noteworthy Paris adventures that you would like to share with other travelers. (For example, highly recommended experiences, sights, walks, sits, etc...)